MacLean's
MISCELLANY *of*
Whisky

MacLean's
MISCELLANY *of*
Whisky

Charles MacLean

With a foreword by
Alexander McCall Smith

Little Books by Big Names™

Special thanks to Ian Hughes for the hours
he has spent designing this book

First published in the United Kingdom in 2004 by Little Books Ltd,
48 Catherine Place, London SW1E 6HL

10 9 8 7 6 5 4

A CIP catalogue record for this book is available from the British Library.

ISBN: 1 904435 23 8

Many thanks to: Jamie Ambrose for editorial production and management,
Mousemat Design for jacket and text design,
Ann Barrett for indexing.
Printed by Scotprint in Scotland.

CONTENTS

FOREWORD

What does one need to know about whisky? That it is a heady drink; that the best variety comes from Scotland; that it is the colour of a peaty burn tumbling down a hillside in some Highland glen? Yes: most people know all that. Yet there is far more to this subject, and the more one finds out, the more romantic and intriguing does the story become.

Charles MacLean is a man who knows whisky. I have sat with him in his study in Edinburgh on warm evenings and cold, and tasted with him a small glass of amber liquid. While most of us would be inclined to raise the glass and allow the contents to slip down the throat, he instead noses the dram, thinks, and then noses it again. Then comes a well-chosen description of the olfactory response, sometimes surprising in the metaphor chosen. 'Wet straw,' he might say. Or 'like the interior of an old car: cracked leather and burned rubber'. These surprises are followed by comments on taste and on the provenance of the whisky. One learns how it is made; what its history is; how it fits into the whole colourful story of whisky production.

This miscellany brings together a broad taster of the encyclopaedic knowledge of this towering figure of the whisky world. My own scant knowledge of the subject, almost all learned (imbibed, perhaps) at the feet of Charles MacLean, has been much enhanced by reading it. Of particular interest, I feel, is the picture he develops of how whisky production has changed over the past hundred years, and how these small changes might have altered the character of today's Scotch. So far as I am aware, this aspect of the subject has not been explored before, but far from having a demythologizing effect, the mystery – even romance – of why whisky tastes as it does remains intact.

In the past, whisky has been associated with a certain defiance in the face of the excisemen. Things are different now, in an age of large distilleries and big business, but the essential romance of the subject is still there. There is no better guide to this whole story than Charles MacLean, a man of great conviviality and humour, a man whom I, like so many, am proud to call my friend. This is a very personal book. It is Charlie's book, and his generous voice can be heard in every anecdote within it. Listen.

Alexander McCall Smith

PREFACE

Strictly speaking, a miscellany is a mixture of writings on different subjects, or by different authors. I have interpreted the word more broadly as a mix of topics relating to the single subject of Scotch whisky, mingled with some favourite quotations about the same subject. I have tried to mine territories that haven't been delved before, and I have used the opportunity to chase down, fill out or follow up a number of topics that have interested me over the years. I should explain that I have been writing about whisky for twenty-five years, and was first introduced to the subject ten years before that, in the late 1960s.

Looking at the way the book has come together (for I did not start with a plan), I suppose the over-arching question the book sets out to elucidate (not answer) is: 'How has whisky changed over the past hundred years, and why?' This is rather a grand and serious subject for a small volume, and this Little Book means neither to be grand nor over-serious. It is a conversation piece, not a pedagogic exposition. If you like, it is a book to dip into from time to time.

In keeping with the general theme, early entries look at how the definition of whisky has evolved, and might continue to evolve; how distilleries have come and gone, and why; who owns what today. Then there is a clutch of essays relating to changes in production which may have affected the flavour of whisky: raw materials, maltings, how pot stills are fired, how the spirit is condensed, how it is matured. Next, I consider some aspects of packaging and marketing, and how they have changed over the years. Finally, there are some thoughts (not always serious), about the enjoyment of whisky. Each entry stands alone, and the book does not have to be read from cover to cover.

The archival photographs which embellish the book have been supplied by my friend George Gainsborough. George probably has the largest archive of whisky-related pictures in the world; he is also a distinguished natural-history photographer, with nineteen books to his credit under his nom-de-photo George Bernard – and one South American butterfly to his name!

In summary, *MacLean's Whisky Miscellany* is a rag-bag – as a miscellany should be. But I hope that, as well as being entertaining, it will also be useful to those interested in drinking or collecting Scotch whisky: the world's finest spirit, and Scotland's most generous gift to the world.

Charles MacLean,
Edinburgh

WHAT'S IN A NAME?

*'Usquebaugh': a compound distilled spirit, being
drawn on aromaticks; and the Irish sort is particularly
distinguished for its pleasant, mild flavour.
The Highland sort is somewhat hotter, and by
corruption in Scottish they call it 'whisky'.*

SAMUEL JOHNSON, *DICTIONARY* (LONDON, 1755)

Far be it from me to dispute with 'The Prince of Dogmatists', but I am afraid Dr Johnson is confusing his *uisge beathas* with his *usquebaughs*.

Uisge beatha, from which the word 'whisky' derives, is the Gaelic equivalent of *aqua vitae*: 'the water of life'. In the eighteenth century, official documents still referred to spirits by the Latin term, and the Gin Act of 1736 lists *Aqua Vitae* and *Usquebaugh* as different spirits. Two years previously, Lord George Murray had complained to the Duke of Atholl that 'I have not one drop of either *usquba* or *acquavitae* in the house'.

Twenty years after he had complied his famous dictionary, Dr Johnson had firsthand experience of whisky with his Scottish friend James Boswell, and was able to expand upon his definition in *Journey to the Western Isles of Scotland*:

> *The word whisky signifies water, and is applied by way of eminence to strong water, or distilled liquor. The Spirit drunk in the north is drawn from barley; I never tasted it except once for experiment, at the inn in Inveraray, when I had thought it preferable to any English malt Brandy. It was strong, but not pungent, and was free from empyreumatic [burnt, acrid] taste or smell; what was the process I had no opportunity of enquiring, nor do I wish to improve the art of making poison pleasant.*

WHAT IS WHISKY?

Uisge beatha and *aqua vitae*

'Whisky' derives from the Gaelic *uisge beatha*, 'water of life' (pronounced *Ooshky-bay*), progressively anglicized from *uiskie* (c. 1618) to *whiskie* (1715) to *usky* (1736) and 'whisky' in 1746. Until the late eighteenth century, the term was colloquial; official and unofficial documents referred to it as *aqua vitae* or *aquavite*: Latin for 'water of life' or the Gaelic *uisge beatha*. Even Robert Burns referred to Scotch spirit as *aqua vitae* in *The Author's Earnest Cry and Prayer* (1785):

> *Tell them wha hae the chief direction,*
> *Scotland an' me's in great affliction,*
> *E'er sin' they laid that curst restriction*
>   *ON AQUA-VITAE*

The first written reference to *aqua vitae* is in the instruction given by King James IV in 1494 to Friar John Cor 'to make *aqua vitae* VIII bolls of malt'. Earlier that year, and the year before, the king had been campaigning against the Lord of the Isles on the west coast of Scotland, and it is generally accepted that he encountered *aqua vitae* there, where it will have been known as *uisge beatha*.

So maybe *uisge beatha* is the earlier term? Certainly, the words *uisce* 'water' and *beothu* 'life' are both Old Irish, and thus date from AD 800-1000. The term *aqua vitae* was first applied to whisky in the thirteenth century by the great alchemist Roger Bacon.

> With songs and dance we celebrate the day,
> And with due honours *usher* in the May. *Dryden.*
> The Examiner was *ushered* into the world by a letter, setting forth the great genius of the author. *Addison.*
> Oh name for ever sad, for ever dear!
> Still breath'd in sighs, still *usher'd* with a tear. *Pope.*
>
> USQUEBA'UGH. *n. f.* [An Irish and Erse word, which signifies the water of life.] It is a compounded distilled spirit, being drawn on aromaticks; and the Irish sort is particularly distinguished for its pleasant and mild flavour. The Highland sort is somewhat hotter; and, by corruption, in Scottish they call it *whisky.*
>
> U'STION. *n. f.* [*ustion*; Fr. *ustus*, Lat.] The act of burning; the state of being burned.
>
> USTO'RIOUS. *adj.* [*ustum*, Lat.] Having the quality

Samuel Johnson's definition of 'whisky' – here 'Usquebaugh' – as recorded in his famous Dictionary *of 1755*

A problem arises with the common and early use of *usquebaugh* as a phonetic rendering of *uisge beatha*. It has been claimed that the spirits made in Ireland were the former, and those made in Scotland the latter. Would that it were as simple as this! Martin Martin, himself a Gael and Macleod of Dunvegan's factor (i.e. a land agent), made a tour of the Western Isles in the 1690s. He began his journey in Lewis, where he noted:

> *Their plenty of Corn was such, as disposed the Natives to brew several sorts of Liquors, as common Usquebaugh, another call'd Trestarig,* id est, Aqua-vitae, *three times distilled, which is strong and hot; a third sort is four-times distill'd, and this by the Natives is call'd* Usqubaugh-baul, id est Usquebaugh, *which at first taste affects all the members of the Body: two spoonfuls of this Last Liquor is a sufficient dose; and if any Man exceed this, it would presently stop his breath, and endanger his Life.*

In *The Compleat Body of Distilling*, published in London in 1725, George Smith gives various recipes for *Usquebaugh*, all of which describe it as a 'compounded liquor'. A typical example adds mace, cloves, cinnamon, nuts, coriander, cubebs [berries of the *Piper cubeba* plant], raisins, dates, liquorice, saffron and sugar to a mix of 'rectify'd Malt spirits and Molossus [molasses] spirits'. But when, in 1755, Dr Johnson published his famous *Dictionary*, he defined *usquebaugh* as being 'a compound distilled spirit, being drawn on aromaticks; and the Irish sort is particularly distinguished for its pleasant, mild flavour. The Highland sort is somewhat hotter, and by corruption in Scottish they call it *whisky*'.

So *uisge beatha* = *usquebaugh* (a compounded spirit, i.e. with herbs and spices added) = whisky? I tremble to contradict the good Doctor, but I do not think so. There is plenty of evidence for herbs and spices, and also berries and other fruits, being added to *aqua vitae* in the fifteenth, sixteenth and seventeenth centuries, for medicinal purposes, or simply to make a coarse spirit palatable. But it seems to me that, at least by the 1750s, the term 'whisky' meant the pure spirit (*uisge beatha* or *aqua vitae*) and *usquebaugh* a compounded liquor.

The final problem is the spelling of 'whisky' and 'whiskey'. As we all know, the latter spelling is now reserved for Irish and American whiskey (although the American brands Maker's Mark and Dickel perversely uses the Scotch spelling), while the former applies to Scotch, Canadian and Japanese. But this is a modern convention. There are many advertisements from the 1900s for both 'Scotch whiskey' and 'Irish whisky', and the Royal Commission on Whiskey 1908-09 includes the 'e' throughout its definitions.

A late seventeenth-century whisky still

THE FIRST LEGAL DEFINITION OF SCOTCH

The Royal Commission supplied the first legal definition of whisky as 'a spirit obtained from a mash of cereal grains saccharified by the diastase of malt' (meaning that starch in the grains had been converted to sugar), and Scotch whisky as 'whiskey so defined, distilled in Scotland, and Irish whiskey, as so defined, distilled in Ireland'. This meant that any kind of grain could be used (wheat, maize, rye, etc – not just malted barley) and that whisky could legitimately be made in any kind of still, not just pot stills.

This did not please the malt-whisky distillers, who used pot stills and argued that the definition should be limited to their product, excluding grain spirit and thus also blended whisky (a mix of malt and grain whiskies). But it was in keeping with popular feeling. As *The Times* put it two years before the Royal Commission sat:

> *If the public want mild whisky [patent-still spirit flavoured with 'high-flavoured whisky from a pot still'] they will get it, even if they should have to relinquish the romantic notion that it is descended from* usque-baugh. *It is rather a droll notion that a liquor which pleases the public is to be put under a ban because it is not made exactly as liquor was made by our rude fore-fathers in an apparatus of unknown antiquity.*

LATER LEGAL DEFINITIONS

Scotch whisky is the most tightly defined of all spirits. This prevents whisk(e)y made outside Scotland, or made with any additives (including artificial enzymes to achieve saccharification), from being sold as 'Scotch'.

The 1909 definition was tightened only six years later by the Immature Spirits Act of 1915, which required that whisky must be bonded for two years prior to bottling. This was increased to three years in 1916, and has remained part of the definition ever since. One of the reasons for the legislation was that it was believed that drinking young whisky made you 'fighting *fu*' ('full' or slightly drunk in Scots dialect), while mature spirits made you mellow!

The original definition did not cover a blend of Irish and Scotch whiskies, and this was tested in the Scottish courts in 1938, when a Glasgow firm was charged under the Merchandise Marks Acts with wrongly describing 300 bottles of blended whisky as 'Scotch', when they contained one-third Scotch malt and two-thirds Irish grain whiskey. The court of appeal maintained that both malt and grain components must be made in Scotland for the bottle to be labelled 'Scotch whisky'.

Until 1988, amendments to the definition of Scotch whisky – including the provision that all components of blended Scotch whisky must themselves be 'entitled to the description Scotch whisky' – were enshrined in the Finance Acts. The British government saw Scotch merely as a means of raising revenue. That year, Bill Walker, the teetotal MP for East Fife, introduced a private member's bill which became the Scotch Whisky Act of 1988.

The current definition is supplied by this important act (and the orders made under it, which came into effect in June 1990). 'Scotch Whisky' means whisky:

a) *which has been produced at a distillery in Scotland from water and malted barley (to which only the whole grains of other cereals may be added) all of which have been:*

i) *processed at that distillery into a mash;*

ii) *converted to a fermentable substrate only by endogenous [not artificial] enzyme systems;*

iii) *fermented only by the addition of yeast;*

b) *which has been distilled at an alcoholic strength by volume of less than 94.8 percent [96.4 percent is pure alcohol] so that the distillate has an aroma and taste derived from the raw materials used in, and the method of, its production;*

c) which has been matured in an excise warehouse in oak casks of a capacity not exceeding 700 litres, the period of that maturation being not less than three years;

d) which retains the colour, aroma and taste derived from the raw materials used in, and the method of, its production and maturation;

e) to which no substance other than water and spirit caramel has been added.

The act also prohibits the production in Scotland of whisky other than Scotch whisky, as defined.

A later order made under the act in 1990 adds the requirement that, to be sold as 'Scotch', the whisky must not be bottled at less than forty percent alcohol by volume (ABV). The reason for this is that there is a sharp falling off of aroma and flavour if it is bottled below forty percent.

RECENT DEVELOPMENTS

The provisions of the 1988 act were incorporated into European Economic Community legislation in 1989, and the Order of 1990, already referred to, tightened this definition. There is still room for further definition.

In 2003, there was a row within the Scotch whisky industry about Cardhu being changed from a single malt (the product of Cardhu Distillery) to a 'pure' malt (the vatted products of two or more distilleries). It was generally agreed that this move was confusing for consumers, especially since the packaging of the pure malt was very similar to that of the single malt.

Such a move is not unprecedented. Tobermory, long labelled 'The Malt Scotch Whisky', was a vatted malt from 1973 to 1993 – not the single product of Tobermory Distillery. During the 1970s, Mill Burn was a 'pure malt', not the product of Millburn Distillery. Longrow, Lochindaal, Glenfyne, Kincaple, Ferintosh, Adelphi, Octomore and many others are or were single-malt whiskies, but they are not the product of the distilleries named on the label, all of which are extinct.

When it comes to blended whiskies, the labelling is even less defined. 'Fine Old', 'Rare Old', 'Choice Old',

'Extra Special', 'Special Reserve', 'Aged', 'Finest', 'Oldest Matured' and so on are terms that need not necessarily bear any relation to the quality or age of the whiskies which make up the blend, although the description 'Liqueur', once common, has now been abandoned by general agreement within the whisky industry (and I believe by EC regulation), except for true 'whisky liqueurs' such as Drambuie, Glayva and Atholl Brose.

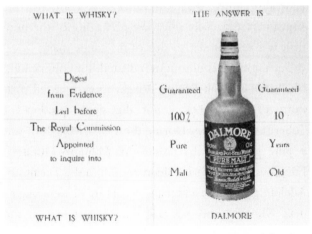

This early twentieth-century Dalmore advertisement responded to the question: 'What is whisky?', thereby capitalizing on the declared official status of Scotch by the British Royal Commission on Whisky, 1909

UNDERSTANDING THE LABEL

Scotch Whisky – defined by law (see above); the term implies a blended whisky.

Scotch Malt Whisky – defined by law (see above); the term implies a malt whisky.

Scotch Grain Whisky – defined by law (see above); the term implies a grain whisky.

Blended Scotch Whisky – defined by law (see above); the term implies a blended whisky: a mix of Scotch malt and grain whiskies.

Single-Malt Whisky – the product of a single distillery, usually but not necessarily from the distillery named on the label (it may be a brand name).

Single-Grain Whisky – the product of a single distillery, usually but not necessarily from the distillery named on the label (it may be a brand name).

Pure Malt Whisky – a mix of malt whiskies.

Vatted Malt Whisky – the same as a pure malt whisky.

Single Cask Malt/Grain – bottled from an individual cask.

Non-Chill-Filtered Whisky – (may be malt, grain or blended) where the whisky has not been 'polished' on the bottling line by reducing its temperature to close to 0°C and pushing it through a bed of filters in order to maintain its brightness and clarity.

Natural Strength/Cask Strength – not defined by law, but implies that the whisky is bottled 'straight from the cask', without its strength being reduced to the usual 'bottling strength' of 40 percent or 43 percent ABV. The strength varies from cask to cask, and is usually associated with 'single-cask' bottlings.

Wood-Finished/Double-Matured – where the whisky, usually malt, has been matured in one cask and then re-racked for the final months of maturation into another cask.

Age – if a whisky label bears an age statement, this is the age of the youngest whisky in the vatting or blend.

Glenturret Distillery, Crieff, circa 1887

THE DEIL'S AWA
WI' THE EXCISEMAN

The deil cam fiddlin thro' the town,
And danc'd awa wi' the Exciseman,
And ilka wife cries, 'Auld Mahoun,
I wish you luck o' the prize, man.'

Chorus:
The deil's awa, the deil's awa,
The deil's awa wi' the Exciseman,
He's danced awa, he's danced awa,
He's danced awa wi' the Exciseman.

We'll mak our maut, and we'll brew our drink,
We'll laugh, sing, and rejoice, man,
And mony braw thanks to the meikle black deil,
That danc'd awa wi' the Exciseman.

ROBERT BURNS, 1792

By 1792, Robert Burns had served four years as an exciseman, but his attitude to the service remained ambiguous. Indeed, even while his petition to join the service was being considered, in 1787, he nearly blew his chances by inscribing an anti-Hanoverian poem on a window in Stirling. He was visiting Stirling Castle, and was so dismayed by the condition of James IV's great renaissance palace (recently restored) that he wrote:

> ... Stewarts once in glory reign'd,
> And laws for Scotland's weal ordained...
> A race outlandish fills their throne:
> An idiot race, to honour lost –
> Who know them best despise them most.

Too late he realized that such lines were hardly flattering to a king whose service he hoped to enter. Indeed, excise officers had to swear an oath to defend the king personally against all 'traitorous conspiracies and attempts'. When he returned to Stirling two months later, Burns knocked out the window. But the verse had already been copied and publicly circulated. He felt humiliated and was admonished, but his petition was not barred.

WHISKY AND WHISKEY

As stated earlier (see page 16), it has become customary for 'whisky' without an 'e' to refer to Scotch, Canadian and Japanese whiskies, while 'whiskey' is reserved for the products of Ireland and America. But this is convention, not law; Maker's Mark (a Bourbon from Kentucky) and George Dickel (a Tennessee whisky) drop the 'e'; Paddy (from Cork) only adopted the 'e' in 1966. So-called whiskies (or whiskeys) – some good, some nasty – are made in dozens of countries around the world, and their makers use one spelling or the other. It matters not.

What does matter is the difference between them. The various kinds of Scotch – malt, grain, blended, vatted, liqueur – have been defined in the previous chapter. Here I want to look at what distinguishes the makes of Ireland, the United States, Canada and Japan: the leading whisk(e)y producers.

Broadly, the definition of Scotch is the same for Irish: i.e. distilled in Ireland from a mash of cereals, matured there in oak casks for at least three years, and bottled at no less than forty percent ABV. Additionally, Irish whiskey comes in five styles.

Irish pot-still whiskey

This is the key difference between Irish and Scotch. Pot-still (usually called 'pure pot-still') whiskey is made from a mix of malted and unmalted barley in pot stills. In the past, other grains (particularly rye, wheat and oats) were also added, making for a heavy, oily style. Typically it was also triple-distilled, which lightened it. There are only three distilleries in Ireland: Midleton (County Cork), Cooley (County Louth) and Bushmills (County Antrim). The first two produce pot-still whisky; the best-known brands such as Redbreast and Midleton are made at Midleton Distillery.

Irish malt whiskey

Like Scotch malt, this is distilled from a mash of malted barley in pot stills. By the 1880s, it had become customary to dry the malt in closed kilns, so it was not exposed to peat smoke. Traditionally, the whisky was triple-distilled. All bottled Irish malt whisky comes from Bushmills and Cooley Distilleries; Midleton has pot stills, but its malt goes for blending. Bushmills Malt was introduced in 1988, Cooley's Tyrconnell Single Malt in 1993 and its Connemara Peated Single Malt in 1996.

Irish grain whiskey
Like Scotch grain whisky, this comes from a mash of maize or wheat, saccharified with a small amount of green malt and is made in a continuous or patent still. None is bottled as a single grain.

Irish whiskey
A blend of Irish malt, grain and pot-still whiskies. The large Midleton Distillery produces around a dozen different styles of single whisky under one roof. Blended, these dozen styles make upwards of thirty blended whiskies, including the market leaders Jameson's, Powers and Paddy.

Irish liqueur whiskey
A mix of Irish spirit and cream, pioneered by Bailey's Irish Cream Liqueur, which was inspired by Irish coffee (itself invented at Shannon Airport in 1952), launched in 1974. Bailey's is the world's best-selling liqueur.

The secrets of distilling, and the fondness for spirits, were introduced to the Americas by the first European settlers: German and Dutch, as well as English, Irish and Scots. The earliest 'whiskey states' were Pennsylvania and Maryland. After the 'Whiskey Rebellion' of 1794, which was a rebellion against excise tax on distilled liquor, many distillers headed south and west through Virginia to Kentucky and Tennessee.

Most American whiskey is made in hybrid continuous stills,[1] comprising a columnar 'beer still and a pot-still 'doubler': copper stills that increase the strength of the spirit. Like Scotch grain whisky, it must be distilled at less than ninety-five percent ABV (190° US proof) to have 'the taste, aroma and characteristics generally attributed to whiskey'. If distilled at higher strength it becomes 'neutral spirit'. There are three classic styles of American whiskey.

Bourbon

Although Bourbon County, Kentucky, is considered the birthplace of America's most famous whiskey, Bourbon can be made anywhere in the US. Corn

---

1) All except one: Woodford Reserve, from the recently revived Labrot & Graham Distillery, where three pot stills have been installed.

(maize) is its principal ingredient (at least fifty-one percent), with between twenty percent and thirty percent of rye or wheat and some malted barley added. The difference between one Bourbon and another is largely down to the 'mash bill' (the proportion of corn to 'small grains') and what small grains are used. If the corn content is more than eighty percent, it becomes 'corn whiskey'. Another element that Bourbon-makers believe makes a difference (unlike Scotch distillers) is the yeast strain. These are carefully guarded and passed down from generation to generation of distillers.

An additional factor that differentiates the process from that of Scotch is the addition of 'backset' or 'sour mash' to the fermenting vessel, and in some cases to the mash tun as well. Backset is a slurry of liquid yeast and spent grains collected from the foot of the first still (called the 'beer still'). It comprises at least twenty-five percent of the volume of the mash – in some cases more – and performs the necessary function of lowering its alkalinity, since Kentucky water is very high in calcium.

Bourbon must be distilled at less than eighty percent ABV (160° US proof) and it must be matured in new, charred, white-oak barrels. There is no minimum period for aging, but it may not be called 'straight' rye unless it has been matured for at least two years, and it must bear an age statement on the label unless it has been in wood for at least four years. The term 'straight' also indicates that the whiskey has not had any neutral spirit added to it (see below), although it may contain Bourbon from more than one distillery.

Leading straight Bourbons include brands such as Jim Beam, Maker's Mark, Wild Turkey, Heaven Hill, Ancient Age, Woodford Reserve, Old Crow and Old Grandad.

Rye whiskey

This was the original American whiskey, but very little is now produced exclusively from rye. It is made and matured in a similar way to Bourbon, except that at least fifty-one percent rye is substituted for corn, the rest of the mash being made up of malted barley and corn. Notable straight ryes are Van Winkle Family Reserve, Old Overholt, Sazerac and Rittenhouse.

Tennessee sour mash

Although 'sour-mashing' is employed in making rye and Bourbon whiskey, the whiskeys of Tennessee use the term as part of their appellation. They are made in the same way as the other two, but the spirit is filtered through a ten-foot-deep bed of charcoal prior to filling into cask, a system known as the 'Lincoln County Process'. The leading brand of Tennessee whiskey (and the best-selling American whiskey) is Jack Daniel's. George Dickel Tennessee whiskeys also sell around the world.

In addition to the three main styles described above, there are two blended styles of American whiskey.

Blended rye or Bourbon
This is a mix of either rye or Bourbon with neutral spirit, in proportions of no less than fifty-one percent to forty-nine percent.

Blended American whiskeys
These are permitted to contain a minimum of only twenty percent straight whiskey, the rest being neutral spirit. They are cheaper to make, and tend to be smoother, blander and lighter-bodied than straight whiskies. Typical blends are Seagram's 7 Crown, Kessler, Kalvert Extra and Imperial.

*As governor of Virginia, Thomas Jefferson offered
pioneers sixty acres of land in Kentucky if they
would raise 'native corn' (maize). Because no family
could eat sixty acres worth of corn a year and it was
too perishable to transport for sale, much was turned
into whiskey, which solved the problem and paved
the way for the American whiskey industry.
As US president, Jefferson overturned the excise
tax that caused The Whiskey Rebellion of 1794*

Canadian whisky is almost all blended,[2] and the key to the blend is invariably rye whisky. Its definition (including that of 'Canadian rye whisky' and 'rye whisky') is not as tight as that for Scotch and American, although it includes the Scottish three-years maturation rule. It states simply that the product must be 'whisky distilled in Canada and possessing the aroma, taste and character generally attributed to Canadian whisky'.

This allows Canadian distillers to use a high propor-tion of neutral spirit: as much as ninety-seven percent in cheaper blends. It also allows them to produce a baffling range of blending whiskies from their nine distilleries, and typically around twenty will go into a blend. Mash may contain rye, malted rye, barley, malted barley, corn and wheat; fermentation is achieved with different yeasts; distillation takes place in a range of different continuous stills, including both patent, Coffey stills, and American-style hybrid stills, at

---

2) A very small amount of single-malt whisky is offered by Glenora Distillery on Cape Breton Island, Nova Scotia. The distillery, modelled on a Scottish malt distillery, went into production in 1990. Much of its make goes into a blend called Breton's Hand & Seal.

different strengths; and maturation is done in new or refill casks, ex-brandy as well as ex-Bourbon. Within the definition it is even permissible to add flavourings such as sherry, wine (particularly prune wine) or fruit juices.

For example, Canadian Club uses a triple-distilled corn spirit, fermented with a specific yeast strain, a double-distilled flavouring spirit and a single-distilled spirit made from rye, malted rye and barley. Seagram's Crown Royal is made mainly from corn whisky matured for three years in new wood before being blended with aged rye whisky. Black Velvet combines young rye whisky and blends this with other base spirits prior to four years of maturation.

JAPANESE WHISKY

Japanese whisky is similar in composition to Scotch. The country has a clutch of traditional malt and grain distilleries, of which the most important are Yamazaki, Yoichi, Hakushu, Sendai and Sanraku. The first two are owned by Suntory, which makes around seventy percent of Japan's whisky; the second two by Nikka; the last by Sanraku Ocean. As well as making their own whisky, these companies also import Scotch malt whisky in bulk and blend it with their own malt and grains to produce a large number of blended brands.

Whisky distilling was introduced to Japan by a single individual: Masataka Taketsuru. Taketsuru came to Scotland in December, 1918, expressly to find out how Scotch was made. He was twenty-five years old and had been trained as a chemist. He served brief apprenticeships at Longmorn, Bo'ness (a grain distillery) and Hazelburn Distillery in Campbeltown, and attended a Glasgow University summer school in chemistry. In 1920, he returned to Japan with a Scottish wife, and was recruited by Shinjiro Torii, the founder of Suntory, who was interested in building a malt whisky distillery at Oh-Yamazaki, near Kyoto.

In the mid-1930s, Taketsuru left Suntory, founded Nikka and established his own malt-whisky distillery at Yoichi on Japan's mountainous northern island of Hokkaido, which has a landscape and climate similar to the Highlands of Scotland. Indeed, he was drawn to the spot by the availability of cold melt-water and an abundance of peat. Until the early 1970s, Yoichi malted its own barley, drying it over peat fires; today, malt is imported from various countries.

Nikka built another malt-whisky distillery in 1969 at Sendai, in the north of the principal island of Honshu, and a grain distillery with Coffey stills at Nishinomiya, near Osaka. The company produces a range of blends, and has recently started to offer Yoichi as a single malt to compete with Yamazaki single malt, which was introduced in the mid-1980s.

SCOTCH DRINK

O Whisky! Soul o' plays and pranks!
Accept a bardie's gratefu' thanks!
When wanting thee, what tuneless cranks
Are my poor verses!
Thou comes — they rattle in their ranks,
At ither's arses!

Thee, Ferintosh! O sadly lost!
Scotland lament frae coast to coast!
Now colic grips, an' barkin hoast
May kill us a';
For loyal Forbes' chartered boast
Is ta'en awa?

Thae curst horse-leeches o' th' Excise,
Wha mak the whisky stells their prize!
Haud up thy han', Deil! Ance, twice, thrice!
There seize the blinkers!
An' bake them up in brunstane pies
For poor damn'd drinkers.

Fortune! If thou'll but gie me still
Hale breeks, a scone, an' whisky gill,
An' rowth o' rhyme to rave at will,
Tak a' the rest,
An' deal't about as thy blind skill
Directs thee best.

ROBERT BURNS, 1785

stells = stills
blinkers = spies
brunstane = brimstone
Hale breeks = whole breeches
rowth = store

Burns had a fondness for drink, but his reputation as a drunkard is unjust. His brother Gilbert noted that he never saw Robert drunk until he was 'thrown into society by his fame', and Burns himself mentioned to Dugald Stewart that 'his habitual sobriety was not from virtuous choice'; it was just that too much to drink did not agree with his stomach.

The mention of 'Ferintosh' is interesting. This was the first large-scale distillery recorded in Scotland. We know about it because it was sacked by Jacobite sympathizers in 1689. Its owners, the Forbes of Culloden, were ardent Whigs. When the Whig cause triumphed and 'Dutch' William sat comfortably on the throne of Britain with Queen Mary, Duncan Forbes petitioned the Scottish Parliament for compensation and was granted the right to distil and sell whisky from grain grown on his own lands without paying duty.

Needless to say, he and his successors set about buying up as many adjacent farms as possible, and building more distilleries. By the middle of the eighteenth century, Ferintosh was supplying sixty percent of the legally made whisky in Scotland, earning the Forbeses the equivalent of £3 million per annum. The dispensation was withdrawn by Act of Parliament in 1784, the year Burns wrote 'Scotch Drink'.

> *Gie him strong drink until he wink,*
> *That's sinking in despair;*
> *An' liquor guid to fire his bluid,*
> *That's prest wi' grief an' care:*
> *There let him bowse, and deep carouse,*
> *Wi' bumpers flowing o'er,*
> *Till he forgets his loves or debts*
> *An' minds his griefs no more.*

SOLOMON'S PROVERBS, XXXI 6, 7

THE PROBLEM OF PROOF

The problem of determining the strength of an alcoholic liquid, or estimating the percentage of alcohol in a liquid, is, according to Sir Walter Gilbey (founder of the wine and spirit merchant W & A Gilbey), 'so complex and so beset with difficulties that its complete solution appears well-nigh hopeless'. But it is a problem of great importance to the taxman, since it provides the basis for duty, 'and the accurate measurement of [alcoholic strength] has always been an obsession of the exciseman'.[1]

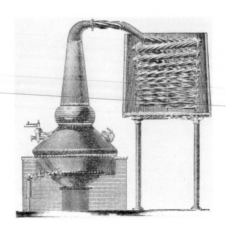

Engraving of a pot still, 1873

THE GUNPOWDER TEST

As with metals and other materials, the traditional method of measuring the quality of a spirit was by subjecting it to a trial, assay or 'proof'. Several crude methods were adopted. The liquid was vigorously shaken in a bottle and a note was taken of the time it took for the bubbles thus created (known as the 'bead') to disperse. Or the liquor was ignited and the amount which burnt away was measured.[2]

The commonest method of 'proving' spirits was by mixing them with gunpowder and setting fire to the mixture. The spirit was deemed to be proved when the mixture ignited; if it did not flash, it was termed 'under-proof'. This was a very unreliable test, since if too much liquid was added (even if the liquid was overproof) it would fail to ignite. In truth, it was an arbitrary measurement that really meant nothing more than a standard by which other strengths could be determined.

Nevertheless, proof was the measure for spirit strength until January 1, 1980, when it was replaced throughout the European Union by the simpler

1) Philip Morrice, *The Schweppes Guide to Scotch*, (Sherborne, 1983)

2) J Marshall Robb, *Scotch Whisky: A Guide* (Edinburgh, 1950)

measurement of the percentage of alcohol present in a mixture. This measurement was recommended by the Organisation Internationale de Metrologie Legale (OILM: an intergovernmental body established in 1955 to facilitate international trade by harmonization of measurement units) and was based on the European system devised by Joseph Louis Gay-Lussac (1778-1850).

Since then, the strength of spirits throughout most of the world has been measured in percentage of alcohol by volume, or ABV. Thus, the traditional strengths at which whisky was bottled – seventy or seventy-five degrees proof – became forty percent or forty-five percent ABV. At the same time (January 1, 1980), bottle sizes were changed from twenty-six and two-thirds fluid ounces to seventy-five centilitres (cl). In 1992, the standard bottle size was reduced to 70cl.

The United States retains its own proof system, where 100° US proof equals fifty percent ABV at 60°F. Bottles are still 75cl in the US.

The Chemistry of Proof Spirit

Ethyl alcohol weighs less than water, so the chemist can measure the amount of alcohol present in a mixture by comparing its weight to that of the same quantity of water at the same temperature and pressure. This is the 'specific gravity' of the solution.

In 1818, proof was defined by an act of Parliament as 'that which, at a temperature of fifty-one by Fahrenheit's thermometer, weighs exactly twelve-thirteenths of an equal measure of distilled water'.

So the specific gravity of proof spirit at 51°F is .9238 when compared to water; at 60°F, the mixture will contain 49.28 percent alcohol by weight or 57.1 percent alcohol by volume. One hundred percent alcohol, or pure alcohol, is 175° proof spirit (usually termed 75° overproof, although, to further confuse the issue, it was sometimes referred to as a hundred percent proof).

HYDROMETERS

Given the unreliability of the gunpowder test, and the knowledge that alcohol is less dense than water, scientists devised instruments called hydrometers to measure the amount of alcohol in a solution more accurately.

Archimedes

It is said that the earliest hydrometer was invented by Archimedes (c. 287-212 BC), when he jumped in and out of his bath, realizing that he could test whether gold was pure or impure in the same way. If the displacement of a known weight of pure gold in a tank of water was compared with the same weight of alloy, the latter, being bulkier, would displace more water.

Robert Boyle

It seems that Archimedes' discovery was lost, allowing the English chemist, Robert Boyle to 'reinvent' the hydrometer, which he called a 'New Essay Instrument', in 1675. Like Archimedes' instrument, Boyle's 'common hydrometer' was devised to detect counterfeit coin. It consists of a glass bubble partially filled with mercury or lead shot, with a stem marked with equal graduations. The coin to be tested was attached below the bubble, and immersed in a liquid of known specific gravity (e.g. water); the reading thus obtained was compared with that obtained by a true coin. Boyle's hydrometer was also capable of measuring the specific gravities of liquids, including a solution of alcohol and water, but the instrument was fragile and inaccurate, so was not widely used for this.

John Clarke

The first hydrometer to be designed specifically to determine the density of liquids was invented in 1730 by John Clarke, a Scottish instrument-maker. The bulb was made of copper, with a brass spindle running through it; above the bulb, the spoke was filed flat and marked 'Proof', 'one-tenth over-Proof' and 'one-tenth under-Proof'. Below the bulb, the spindle was cut into a screw, onto which weights of various sizes could be attached, the weight being varied according to the proof of the liquids being examined.

Clarke's hydrometer was adopted by the Excise Board in 1787, equipped with thirty-two main weights and eleven smaller weights (called 'weather weights') to correct variations in temperature. The instrument was not completely accurate, and by adding other constituents (especially sweeteners like molasses) distillers or importers could reduce the reading and thus evade tax. But it was used until the arrival of Sikes' hydrometer.

Bartholomew Sikes

Sikes was secretary of the Excise Board from 1774–83, and at one time collector of excise for Herefordshire. In 1802 (the year before his death), the British government held a competition to find a better hydrometer than Clarke's. A legal decision was only reached on January 17, 1817, and Sikes's widow was paid £2,000 for the rights.

Sikes's instrument simplified Clarke's by allowing weights to be slid onto the base spindle. It had nine weights, and the upper spindle was graduated into ten equal parts, each subdivided into five. To take a reading, the top measurement was added to the number of the weight, then the reading converted into density and proof by consulting the instrument's accompanying tables.

Sikes's hydrometer was adopted in 1817 by an act of Parliament, and The Spirits (Strength Amendment) Act of 1818 established it permanently. It remained the legal standard measurement until January 1980, when OILM measurements were introduced, but Sikes's hydrometers are still commonly used, notably in spirit safes.

An allusion to the medicinal benefits of whisky, circa 1880

RECENT DEVELOPMENTS

During the 1980s, electronic instruments were developed for measuring the density of a solution and its alcoholic strength. Called densitometers, these instruments base their measurements on the resonant frequency oscillation of a sample in an oscillation cell. More recently, near-infrared spectroscopy and gas chromatography are also being used in laboratories and larger distilleries. The former is especially useful for measuring the alcoholic strength of whisky-based liqueurs and low-strength 'alcopops': ready-to-drink concoctions.

Transporting whisky from the Glenlivet Distillery to the railway station with a traction engine, August 1890

PROOF AND ALCOHOL

A table of US proof and British proof compared with alcohol by volume, as measured by the European system.

US proof	British proof	% ABV
200° *Absolute alcohol*	175°	100
189.6° *Legal max. whisky strength*	166°	94.8
188° *Av. strength: patent-still spirit*	165°	94
184.8° *Flash-point of spirit (15°C)*	162°	92.4
140° *Av. receiver strength: malt whisky*	122°	70
136° *Av. maturation strength: grain whisky*	119°	68
128°–132° *Av. blending strength*	112°–116°	64–66
126° *Av. maturation strength: malt whisky*	111°	63.4
86° *Av. bottling strength (export)*	75°	43
80° *Legal min. whisky strength;* *usual bottling strength (home market)*	70°	40

The still house at Ben Nevis Distillery, circa 1887

GOOD HEALTH

*The ancient association between alcohol
(particularly spirits) and health is recollected in many
languages when we drink a person's 'health'.
For example:*

Afrikaans *Gesondheid*

Arabic *Sakh-tain*

Catalan *Salut*

Chinese *Ganbei*

Danish *Skål*

Dutch *Proost*

French *Santé*

Gaelic *Sláinte*

German *Prost*

Italian *Saluté* or *cin-cin*

Japanese *Kampai*

Norwegian *Skøl*

Polish *Na Zdrowie*

Portuguese *Saúde*

Russian *Na Zdrovye*

Spanish *Salud*

Welsh *Iechyd dda*

THE RISE AND FALL
OF DISTILLERIES

This section should be read in conjunction with Appendix II on pages 248 to 252.

In 1900, there were 142 operational malt-whisky distilleries and nineteen grain distilleries.

In 2004, there are six operational grain-whisky distilleries and ninety-eight malt distilleries, which are either in production (eighty-six), 'mothballed' and capable to returning to production (nine), or planned (three).

Closures generally follow overproduction and broader political, fiscal and economic factors. The table in Appendix II (see page numbers above), when read alongside the following summary of what was happening within the Scotch whisky industry and the wider economy, amply demonstrates this.

We may mourn the passing of distilleries – as do the local communities they support – but when all the facts are considered, a degree of inevitability becomes apparent.

1900 – 1920

The 1890s were the greatest boom era for the Scotch whisky industry. To meet demand, thirty-three new distilleries were built during the decade (twenty-one of them on Speyside). Then came a general economic downturn following the end of the Boer War, and investors' confidence in the industry evaporated.

Many distillers sold out to the Distillers Company Limited (DCL), which emerged as the industry leader; it remains so to this day (as Diageo). In order to prevent overproduction, the DCL followed a policy of 'buying up and closing down'. In 1909, Lloyd George's 'People's Budget' exacerbated the problem by raising duty substantially.

With the outbreak of the First World War in 1914, the government effectively took control of distilling, and in 1916, closed all malt distilleries and any grain distilleries that were not producing materials like acetone for the war effort.

Only one new distillery opened in the period, in 1908: the tiny Malt Mill within the Lagavulin Distillery on Islay, and that was a *jeu d'esprit*.

1920 – 1930

In the aftermath of the Great War, the world went into recession. The British government began to load extra duty on spirits; between 1919 and 1920, duty was increased almost fivefold from seventy-six pence to £3.62 per gallon. Whisky consumption in the UK dropped by one-third.

To make matters worse, the US had ratified the Eighteenth Amendment in 1919, which banned the manufacture and sale of liquor, while Canada, Australia (the biggest export market for Scotch until 1939), New Zealand and South Africa imposed tariffs and trade restrictions.

Over the course of the decade, three grain distilleries as well as just under forty malt distilleries ceased operation, and three-quarters of the latter never resumed production. Campbeltown was particularly badly hit; of the twenty distilleries which operated here in 1920, only three survived the decade, and one of these, Reichlachan, for only four years.

No new distilleries were built.

In the late twenties, the fortunes of the whisky trade began to recover. Prohibition in the States turned out to be a good thing, as demand for Scotch increased massively, and was met by bootleggers, who were well-supplied with good whisky from neighbouring countries like Canada and the Bahamas. By the time repeal came in 1933, the leading whisky companies had their distribution networks in place and were ready to meet the demand.

The depression that had gripped Europe in the early 1930s was passing; sixty-four distilleries went back into production in 1934, and ninety-two by 1939. Five older distilleries closed.

Then came the Second World War. Again, duty was hiked (by £1.25 per gallon immediately, then by a further £3.00 in 1943, which doubled the price of a bottle). In 1940, production was cut by one-third; the following year, grain distilling ceased for the duration of the war, and by October 1943, no grain was available for distilling. The malt distilleries closed as well.

Yet demand for whisky remained high, both at home and abroad, particularly in America. The government allocated a fifth of pre-war amounts of grain to distilling in 1944, allowing thirteen grain and thirty-four malt distilleries to open, with the proviso that the export markets must be kept supplied. At the end of the war, it was decreed that three-quarters of the whisky sold should go abroad.

Stocks of mature whisky had never been lower, and demand never higher; Scotch was now the symbol of the free world. Duty continued to rise. However, in spite of homegrown grain being taken off ration in 1953, and export regulations relaxed the next year, there was an acute shortage of aged whisky. Standard blends were rationed in the home market until 1959, and de luxe blends until the early 1960s.

As the economy recovered from the war, many distilleries that had been silent for decades were re-commissioned; others doubled in size. Two new grain distilleries opened, and the first new malt distilleries since 1900 were built.

1960 – 1980

The boom of the 1960s and early 1970s approached that of the 1890s in scale. Dozens of distilleries were refurbished and expanded; sixteen new malt distilleries were commissioned, as well as two grain distilleries; the output of malt whisky tripled (to 80 million gallons) and that of grain whisky doubled (to 101 million gallons). This was largely taken up by export markets, which tripled in volume between 1960 and 1970.

But then came the oil crisis and the end of the Vietnam War, which had stimulated the American economy. The seemingly inexorable rise in prosperity was abruptly reversed, and recession made a major impact on sales of Scotch, both at home and abroad, leaving the industry massively overstocked.

Towards the end of the 1970s, distilleries began to close once again.

By 1980, production had far outstripped demand. To compound the problem, the world economy began to slip into serious recession in 1981, and the strength of sterling made export prices uncompetitive. Furthermore, there was a shift in fashion away from Scotch towards white spirits and wine in both the US and the UK, where duty on wine was cut by twenty percent in 1984 while that on spirits was raised by nearly a third. Between 1979 and 1992, wine sales in the UK rose by forty percent, while sales of Scotch declined by twenty-one percent.

Blenders cut their orders for new-make (un-aged) spirit, and distillery closures were inevitable. It began with Ardbeg in 1981 (reopened under new ownership in 1989), which was soon followed in by the closure of twenty-one distilleries by the industry leader, the Distillers Company Limited (only six of which have resumed operation). Independent companies followed suit, closing fourteen distilleries, seven of which have re-opened. In 1993, the DCL closed four more distilleries, two of which were eventually sold and have resumed production.

One way of getting round the problem of the decline in orders from blenders was to bottle and sell your malt whiskies as single malts. Until the early 1970s, the few single malts available were not promoted; then brands like Glenfiddich, Glen Grant (in the Italian market), The Macallan and Glenmorangie began to be advertised and made more generally available. This move rapidly found favour with consumers; during the early eighties, the trickle of single malts became a flow, and by 1990, it had become a torrent.

In the last decade, the global market for malt whisky has increased steadily, and the interest and enthusiasm of consumers by leaps and bounds. The whisky industry has responded by releasing long-aged malts, single malts from closed distilleries, and a wide range of 'double-matured' or 'wood-finished' malts (where the whisky has spent the final months of its maturation in a wine cask to give it an extra dimension). The arrival of the first new malt-whisky distilleries for nearly a decade is significant. Four are under construction as this book goes to press, all of them small and planning to bottle their makes as single malts.

Malt-whisky distilling still depends upon the demand for blends; around ninety-five percent of whisky made goes for blending, yet the prospects for both are good.

Glen Grant Distillery, circa 1887

THE AUTHOR'S EARNEST CRY
AND PRAYER

TO THE RIGHT HONOURABLE AND HONOURABLE
SCOTCH REPRESENTATIVES IN THE
HOUSE OF COMMONS

Tell them wha hae the chief direction,
Scotland an' me's in great affliction,
E'er sin' they laid that curst restriction
On aqua-vitae;
An' rouse them up to strong conviction,
An' move their pity.

Paint Scotland greetin owre her thrissle;
Her mutchkin stowp as toom's a whissle;
An' damn'd excisemen in a bussle,
Seizin a stell,
Triumphant crushin' like a mussel,
Or limpet shell!

Then, on tither hand present her –
A blackguard smuggler right behint her,
An' check-for-chow, a chuffie vintner
Colleaguing join,
Picking her pouch as bare as winter
Of a' kind coin.

Is there, that bears the name o' Scot,
But feels his heart's bluid rising hot
To see his puir auld mither's pot
Thus dung in staves,
An' plunder'd o' her hindmost groat
By gallows knaves?

ROBERT BURNS, 1786

toom = empty; *chuffie* = fat-faced

Poet and hopeful exciseman Robert Burns

Until 1781, anybody could distil whisky so long as they did not sell it. That year, however, domestic distilling – which most Scots considered to be a human right – was banned by an act of Parliament.

Inevitably, this led to an increase in illicit distilling and smuggling, which was met by further legislation in 1784 and 1786 (the year Burns wrote the poem opposite), enforced by the Board of Excise.

Given the sentiments expressed here and elsewhere in his work, it seems paradoxical that Burns was seeking appointment as an excise officer, even at the very time he wrote his 'Earnest Cry and Prayer'. The truth is that, cheated by his publisher and crushed by debt and a failing farm, government service was one of the very few avenues that offered financial security.

THE 'NOBLE EXPERIMENT'

A visit to America during Prohibition

The prohibition of making, selling, transporting, importing or exporting intoxicating liquors in the United States was enacted by the Eighteenth Amendment to the Constitution, which was ratified in 1919, and came into force in January 1920. The measure was presented to Congress by an obscure Minnesota congressman named Andrew J Volstead, and became known as the 'Volstead Act', although in fact Volstead himself was not a hard-core prohibitionist. Prohibition remained in place until December 1933.

As might be imagined, the Scotch whisky industry was dismayed by the news, especially since, at precisely the same time, the British government raised duty to nearly five times the pre-war level. In fact, Prohibition turned out to be a huge boon. Demand for Scotch increased, and it was perfectly legal for whisky to be exported to countries adjacent to the US, such as Canada and the Bahamas. The whisky companies did not ask what happened to it after that, although they knew very well that it was smuggled into the States in huge quantities. By the time Prohibition was repealed, the foundations of what would become the world's largest market for Scotch had been laid.

The extent to which the Eighteenth Amendment was ignored or circumvented was reported to employees of the Distillers Company Limited in their trade magazine, the *DCL Gazette* (April 1929) by Francis Redfern, who had recently returned from a three-month tour of the States on behalf of John Walker & Sons. His observations were astute and accurate, and his conclusion was rather like that of the Prince of Wales (later King Edward VIII), who, when visiting New York in 1925 and asked what he thought of Prohibition, replied: 'Great! When does it begin?'

On arrival at his hotel in New York, Redfern noticed '…quite a number of quietly dressed and sad-looking individuals arriving and departing, all carrying suitcases'. 'On inquiry,' he continued, 'I was told that they were bringing in supplies of liquor to the guests. Nobody appeared to take any notice of them… The chambermaid in attendance on my room informed me that practically all the guests in the hotel had liquor in their bedrooms. I found during my stay in the States that this was general.'

Jean Boyer, a French film director en route to Hollywood, had a similar experience. No sooner had he checked into his room than a hand-bill was pushed under his door, reading 'Why come to us? We come to you', and listing drinks from Bacardi (Carta de Oro) at $1.75 a quart to Mumm Champagne at $7.50. When he arrived in Los Angeles, his experience was similar, and here he ordered some good French wine and Cognac. They were delivered in fifteen minutes by a man driving a black Cadillac limousine.

'Whilst staying in Washington, my hotel was invaded by hundreds of men attending a great trade conference,' Redfern reported. 'Most of these men had their private sitting rooms, where they dispensed "Scotch" to friend and foe alike. These congresses are very popular. Some people call them "souses".'

Many of the hotel rooms he stayed in displayed notices which read: 'The proprietors of this hotel have given an undertaking to cooperate with the Authorities charged with the enforcement of the National Prohibition Law' – yet Redfern could still order bottles of Scotch or rye from the 'Captain of the Bell Boys' in these establishments. Another familiar sign was: 'Gentlemen are requested to open their medicine in the bathroom', where there was inevitably a bottle-opener and a corkscrew, both chained to the wall. 'Hotel keepers soon found themselves compelled to defend themselves in this way after the "dry" law was enacted, as guests were known to wreck whole suites of bedroom furniture in desperate efforts to remove a closure,' Redfern observed dryly.

> *Everywhere I went, people sang the praises of the honest bootlegger. It was clear that no one enjoyed more respect than he, or stood higher in the social hierarchy. I visited many restaurants in New York where whisky is openly served. In private houses where I dined with friends not even remotely connected with our Trade, it was the custom to consume cocktails innumerable before the meal... I travelled hundreds of miles by motor. Every chauffeur I engaged had bootlegged liquor at some time or other and undertook to procure me anything I wanted.'*

In some places, the law was not rigorously enforced: 'I consumed beer with my lunch, along with hundreds of other good citizens, including policemen… These things are done openly in some towns.'

But in others, the story was different.

An American friend with two quarts of Scotch in his motorcar was held up by two Prohibition officers, who pushed automatics into his stomach whilst they secured his 'hooch'. These officers sat up carousing far into the night, whilst my friend languished in his cell. Next morning, in court, the officers were challenged by my friend to produce the bottles. Alas! They could not, since, as my friend wittily remarked, 'They had drunk the evidence'… In one town I visited, they had just sent the principal Prohibition officer to gaol for five years for making "moonshine" in the mountains. In another state I went to, a poor wretch was lying in prison serving a sentence for life for his third offence under the 'dry' law – the offence of "being in possession of one pint of whisky… Each town I visited boasted it was 'the wettest town in the States'.

In cities like New York, drinking was copious, but all 'underground'. As Groucho Marx quipped, 'I was teetotal until Prohibition!' As Redfern explained:

> In New York I visited a large number of 'speakeasies' [1] where you could get all the liquor you wanted. There are upwards of ten thousand of these in New York, all paying their "rake-off" to the police and the authorities charged with the enforcement of the law. These speakeasies vary in character from mere drinking dens to palatially appointed private houses, where you find whole families, including children, dining together with utmost decorum, the elders taking wine. Now and again these places are raided by the authorities just to advertise in the newspapers their determination to vindicate the majesty of the law. When the fuss is over, the same place re-opens and everything goes on as before… It rejoices the heart of a bootlegger to be fined. His name and address are then broadcasted [sic] in the newspapers, and he is engulfed in a new wave of prosperity.

---

[1] The first reference to 'a shop, bar or club where alcohol is sold illegally' as a 'speakeasy' was in 1889, in a New York newspaper, referring to such places in Pennsylvania.

As a matter of fact, Mr Redfern underestimated the number of speakeasies in New York. By the mid-1920s, the city's police commissioner reckoned there were around 32,000 illegal drinking houses – more than twice the number of licensed premises before Prohibition was introduced; a local Congressman put the total closer to 100,000. As Redfern says, some were lavishly appointed and attracted the *beau monde* of flappers, socialites and journalists, like Sherman Billingsley's 'Stork Club', Belle Livingstone's 'Country Club' and 'Texas' Guinan's 'El Fay Club'. Some survived numerous closures to become fashionable, post-Prohibition bars and restaurants; the 'Stork Club' was one, the '21 Club' another. Very many more were squalid dens, selling very poor-quality liquor.

All paid protection money, either to the local gangster boss or to the police. As Charlie Berns, part owner of the successful '21 Club', recollected in an interview:

> *Every speakeasy had to make some arrangements*
> *with the cops to survive. In our case it wasn't exactly*
> *a shakedown – nothing on a regular basis – more*
> *like an act of friendship. We would slip the captain a*
> *$50 bill from time to time and a box of cigars to the cops*

on the beat. They could always count on us for free meals
and drinks, and at Christmas-time, of course, we had a
gift for everybody.

The old saloons had been male preserves; the speakeasies welcomed women, and the recently enfranchised, 'liberated women' of the 1920s exercised their new freedom wholeheartedly: as much a manifestation of personal liberty as a fondness for alcohol. As one writer observed: '[Before Prohibition] women seldom drank Whisky – at least not in public. But Prohibition changed this… in the speakeasies a generation of college girls learned to drink hard liquor, not because it was available, but because it had become the thing to do.'[2]

Much of the liquor on offer was of poor quality, leading to an explosion in cocktail-mixing. Cocktails were an American invention, and had been around since at least the eighteenth century, but it was Prohibition which was the 'Cocktail Era'. The Eighteenth Amendment gave rise to hundreds of new concoctions, many designed to cover the foul taste of poorly made spirits. 'Everybody with a bottle of bathtub gin, a basket

---

[2] Ed Pearce, *Nothing Better in the Market* [London, 1970]

of fruit, and some ice-box leftovers invented a new cocktail. Almost any liquid, short of gasoline, added to the liquor of that era would help conceal its raw alcohol taste and would therefore improve it.'[3]

Redfern concluded his article by saying:

> *On my last day in New York I walked into the principal book store and said I was prepared to buy all the books dealing with Prohibition they had to sell. They had none. 'Prohibition!' said the salesman to me, 'Prohibition! Why there ain't no sech thing.' Next day I got on board the largest ship in the world, owned by the USA Government. It was bone-dry, not merely until the Statue of Liberty was passed but, after much fuss, scandal and debate in Congress, throughout the voyage… I had no need to worry. You could have filled the swimming bath of that ship with the Champagne and other liquors which were supplied openly to the passengers by the 'wine steward'.*

---

[3] David A Embury, *The Fine Art of Mixing Drinks* (New York, 1948; London, 1953)

The Whiskey Rebellion reached a climax in 1794 when President George Washington sent in troops to quell those opposed to the excise tax. Yet when Washington completed his second term as president, he tried his own hand at whiskey-making, establishing the George Washington Distillery in 1797. The distillery was one of the largest in colonial America at the time

How Times Have Changed

Today pure malt whisky is rare. To those who can still obtain it, a little water is permissible with the whisky, but preferably after it. Soda water is an abomination and degrades both the spirit and the soul. By and large the connoisseur still abides by the old Highland saying: 'There are two things a Highlander likes naked, and one is malt whisky.'

Personally, I regret the passing of single pot-still malt whisky. I drink it whenever I can find it. But I realize that it is the nectar of the young and the strong, that it goes best with Highland air and with long tramps over hill and moor, and that it is ill-suited to the man who sits all day on an office stool.

SIR ROBERT BRUCE LOCKHART, SCOTCH (1951)

Sir Robert Bruce Lockhart (1887–1970) was descended from the McGregors of Balmenach Distillery, and maintained his connections with Speyside all his life. He was a career diplomat, entering the consular service in 1911, and being sent to Moscow, where he became acting consul-general and, in 1918, the head of special mission to the (newly created) Soviet government. In truth, he was working for the British Secret Service, and assisting an attempted assassination of Lenin, and when this was discovered he was sentenced to be shot. He was imprisoned in the Kremlin for six months before being exchanged for Litvinov, who later became foreign minister of the USSR.

During the 1920s and '30s, Lockhart involved himself in banking and journalism, mostly in central Europe, and published five books, including *Memoirs of a British Agent* (1932) – a clue as to what he was really up to – and *My Scottish Youth* (1937). The Second World War found him as British representative to the provisional Czechoslovak government, and later as a deputy under-secretary of state at the Foreign Office (for which services he was knighted in 1943). He retired in 1945. His book *Scotch: The Whisky of Scotland in Fact and Story* (1951) is still in print.

WHISKY AND WATER

There has long been a keen debate about the role that water plays in the manufacture of whisky, the traditional wisdom being that the nature of the water (hard or soft) makes an essential difference to the flavour of the final product.

In the past, production water (usually called 'process water' to distinguish it from 'cooling water': the water which passed through the condensers) was granted semi-magical properties, and even today many distillery owners will proudly mention the source of their water in their promotional materials, as if it made *the* crucial difference to the quality of their brand – far more important than, say, the shape and style of their stills, and how they are operated, or the provenance of the wood in which their spirit matures.

Books about Scotch whisky tend to follow the distillers' lead. To mention three recent publications, Lamont and Tucek consider water to be important enough to warrant a heading in each distillery entry in their *The Malt Whisky File* (1995). Helen Arthur (*Whisky: The Water of Life* [2000]) states categorically 'the water source, whether it is acid or alkaline, hard or soft, plays an important part in the taste and smell of the final single malt'. Consultant geologist Stephen Cribb and his wife Julie open their excellent little book *Whisky on the Rocks* (1998) with the intriguing statement 'Nine hundred billion litres of rain fall on Scotland each year. From this, nine hundred million litres of whisky are made… Of all the ingredients that are combined to produce whisky, the effect of different types of water on the final product is the most mysterious and least-understood factor.'

Even that towering earlier authority, J A Nettleton, in *The Manufacture of Spirits as Conducted at the Various Distilleries of the United Kingdom* (1898) remarks 'As might be expected, mysterious influences are ascribed by these experienced operatives [i.e. Highland distillers] to the use of moss water [peaty water]'. Elsewhere he makes an intriguing suggestion as to why this might be so:

> *Whilst some distillers can safely risk the collection of spirits as low as 10° or 15° underproof [i.e. 48%–51% ABV], many others dare not do so at a lower strength*

than 40° or 45° overproof [around 80%–83% ABV]. Operative distillers in Scotland usually ascribe this to the action of the moss water used by Highland and Western distilleries for malting and mashing. Their evidence tends to support the view that, where presumably identical materials are used, and where the mashing, fermenting and distilling routine is the same, and nothing differs except the quality of the water used, this great difference of 50° or 60°… is compulsory.

The 'wrong' kind of water can apparently make a huge difference. Another leading authority, Aeneas MacDonald (*Whisky*, 1930) writes:

There was once a distillery built at considerable expense in a west Highland seaport to make use of the waters of a burn flowing from a most august mountainside [Ben Nevis Distillery, Fort William]. The water was all that could be wished for. It was clear and sparkling to the eye, pleasant to the palate, triumphant in the laboratory. But alas! It had one fault. Good whisky could not be made from it. Chemists, maltsters, and stillmen could try as they might: it was of no avail… But a mile away was another burn, this time a mere trickle of water and not particularly tempting to look at. Despair suggested an experiment with this water, which came from the same slopes as the deceiving burn. The result was astonishing – a whisky of high quality.

Furthermore, the importance of the water source seems to be amply proved by the fact that so many Highland distilleries were built on sites formerly favoured by illicit distillers – notwithstanding the fact that many of these sites were remote. From Highland Park in Orkney to Lagavulin, Laphroaig and Ardbeg in

An 1887 engraving of Lagavulin Distillery, Islay

Islay; Royal Lochnagar on Deeside to Oban in Argyll; Glenmorangie and Teaninich in Ross-shire to Aberfeldy and Tullibardine in Perthshire. And on Speyside: Mortlach, Glenlivet, Cardow, Balmenach, Aberlour and Tomatin, to name but a few.

Notwithstanding all this, contemporary scientists have grave doubts about whether the nature of the water makes more than a trifling contribution to the flavour of mature Scotch whisky. Let us consider where water impinges upon the production process. First, it is used in steeping, during the malting process; second, in mashing (the process water); third, to cool the condensers or worm tubs (the cooling water, which comes from a different source in some distilleries). Fourth, it is used to reduce the strength of the spirit prior to filling into cask (the reducing water, which is the same as the process water); fifth, in lowering the strength prior to bottling (de-mineralized water is usually used, and the process done at the bottling hall, which is almost invariably on a different site from the distillery). Sixth – should we choose to – water is used in reducing the strength yet again for drinking.

Steeping water is there merely to swell the grains, and is driven off again during kilning. It leaves no residues which might influence flavour, even if the water itself is heavily peated (as at Port Ellen Maltings in Islay).

Process water comes from springs (mainly), lochs, rivers or reservoirs (sometimes private, sometimes providing the public supply). The important factor is purity – the lack of any contamination; distillers go to some lengths to ensure the purity of their supply, although the water is not treated prior to use (beyond filtering out solid matter). It was always said that soft water was best for making whisky. In truth, this is simply because hard water tends to fur up the pipes and scale the stills with calcium deposits, just as happens in a domestic kettle. Some excellent whiskies are made with hard water, not least Highland Park and Glenmorangie.

Distillation, itself a purification process, removes any characteristics in the water, although it may just be possible that scaly mineral deposits from hard water might make a very small contribution to the flavour of the spirit.

Cooling water does not come into contact with the spirit, but, interestingly, its temperature does make a contribution to the style of the spirit: winter-cold water, especially in worm-tubs, reduces the effect of copper and makes for a heavier spirit. Experienced operators can tell whether their spirit was made during summer or winter.

The purity of reducing water is always checked carefully, but since only a relatively small amount is added to bring the strength down from around seventy percent to sixty-five percent (typically, 63.4 percent ABV – the magic distillers' figure of 111° proof), it contributes nothing to flavour. It has been noted, however, again by Nettleton,[1] although in a different book, that 'The quality of the reducing water affects the appearance and even the flavour of the reduced spirits. A hard water produces a temporary turbidity, especially when added to spirits of high strength.'

He goes on to remark that some distillers, in 1913, softened their reducing water by adding carbonate of soda, which precipitates the lime. Others boiled the water and allowed time for precipitation, or even distilled it prior to using it for reduction.

---

[1] J A Nettleton, *The Manufacture of Whisky and Plain Spirit* (Aberdeen, 1913)

The water used on the bottling line to reduce to 'bottling strength' (i.e. forty to forty-three percent ABV) is de-mineralized, so adds nothing to flavour.

In the 'water debate', it should be born in mind that, from mashing to filling takes a matter of days, to be followed by five or ten or twenty years of maturation. This is the time during which the chemistry of the whisky changes dramatically, overwhelming any flavour contributions that might have been made by the water with which the whisky was made.

So the biggest impact that water can make is when you add it to the whisky in your glass. If this water is tainted or chlorinated or over-mineralized, then you will surely taste it; if it is very cold, it will reduce the aroma of the whisky and may affect the taste or 'mouth-feel effect'. Bottled water (the still variety) is safe, and if you use Scottish bottled water, like Highland Spring, it will be soft as well – although I find it somewhat flat compared to good tap water. By 'good' I simply mean tap water that has no aroma or flavour.

A version of this article appeared in the newsletter of the Scotch Malt Whisky Society

WE, whofe Hands are hereunto fet, being the
Britain called *Scotland*, by virtue and in purfuanc
Year of the Reign of His Majefty King GEORG
James Armour junr refiding a
to erect, keep, and work, at *Campbellto*
County of *Argyle* ——————— but ne
of *Forty* ————————————————Gallons I
Beer, or Big, of the Growth of the Counties of
Aberdeen, Forfar, Kincardine, Banff, Nairn, and *E*
Clackmannan, and *Perth,* as are to the North and W
runs into the River *Leven,* and proceeding along
of *Stirling,* and from thence, along the great Roa
it meets with the great Road from *Kinrofs* to *Per*
along *the Water of Earn,* till its Junction with the
during the Term of One Year, and for no longer
and to ufe, fell, and difpofe of the Spirits fo diftill
above-mentioned Act of Parliament; he the fa
down the Sum of *ten pounds Sterli*
at the Rate of TWENTY SHILLINGS Sterling year
and having alfo found fufficient Security for the
of fuch Penalties as he may incur, in Terms of
GIVEN under our Hands, at the Chief Office of E
in the Year One thoufand feven hundred and nine

A Di

A distillery licence of 1791

art of the Commissioners of Excise in that Part of *Great*
Act of Parliament, made and passed in the Twenty-fifth
hird, do hereby LICENSE, AUTHORIZE, and EMPOWER
ampbelltown in the County of *Argyle*
in the Parish of *Campbelltown* in the
re, a STILL of the cubical Contents, including the Head,
easure, and to distil and draw off Spirits from the Barley,
aithness, Sutherland, Ross, Cromarty, Inverness, Argyle, Bute,
d of such Parts of the Counties of *Dumbarton, Stirling,*
Line, beginning at the Boat of *Balloch*, where *Loch Lomond*
Military Road from thence, by *Bucklivie*, to the Town
Hillfoot Road, on the South Side of the *Ochell Hills*, till
along the same, till it comes to *the Bridge of Earn*, and
y, and along that RIVER till it joins the *German* Ocean ;
Space, from the Date of this Commission, or Licence ;
ct to the Restrictions and Regulations contained in the
mes Armour Jun having paid
being One Quarter of the Composition or Licence Duty,
h *English* Gallon of the Content of the aforesaid Still ;
m of FIFTY POUNDS STERLING to answer the Payment
Act of Parliament in that Case lately made and provided.
Edinburgh, this *First* Day of *December*
e Years

A Whinton

John Grieve

Ja. Stodart

icence of 1791.

THE DISCOVERY OF WHISKY

*Down round the southern corner of the dun there was a field of barley
all ripened by the sun. In a small wind it echoed faintly the sound of
the ocean; at night it sighed and rustled as the earth mother thought
over things, not without a little anxiety. It was cut and harvested and
a sheaf offered in thanksgiving, flailed and winnowed, until the ears
of grain remained in a heap of pale gold: the bread of life.*

*In simple ways the grain was prepared and ground and set to ferment;
the fermented liquor was then boiled, and as the steam came off, it was
by happy chance condensed against some cold surface.*

*And lo! this condensation of the steam from the greenish-yellow
fermented gruel is clear as crystal. It is purer than any water from
any well. When cold, it is colder to the fingers than ice.*

*A marvellous transformation. A perfect water. But in the mouth – what
is this? The gums tingle, the throat burns, down into the belly
fire passes, and thence outwards to the finger-tips, to the feet,
and finally to the head.*

NEIL M GUNN, 1935

Neil Gunn (1891-1973) was raised in Wick, Caithness, and joined the Excise Service in 1910, working mostly at Glen Mhor Distillery, Inverness. He was friendly with Maurice Walsh (see page 219), who encouraged him to write, and following the publication of *Highland River* (1937), still considered to be a classic, he resigned his job to write full-time. He followed it with another classic, *The Silver Darlings* (1941).

The extract opposite is from an earlier book, *Whisky & Scotland: A Practical and Spiritual Survey* (London, 1935; pages 3-4), in which he also makes the telling comment: 'Indeed, it may be said that until a man has had the luck to chance upon a perfectly matured, well-mannered whisky, he does not really know what whisky is.'

BARLEY VARIETIES

John Barleycorn was a hero bold,
Of noble enterprise;
For if you do but taste his blood,
'Twill make your courage rise.

ROBERT BURNS

I have been told that there are around 300,000 varieties of barley in the world, but that only a few are suitable for making malt whisky. What's more, malting barley is graded on a scale of one to nine by distillers, and only the top three grades are acceptable.

The given wisdom of the whisky industry is that the variety of barley used contributes little or nothing to the flavour of the mature product.[1] It does, however, influence the yield; the amount of alcohol which can be obtained per tonne is based on the barley's capacity to germinate and on its starch content. The variety of barley also influences its 'processability': how well it mashes.

---

1) The leading exception to this view is Macallan Distillery, which makes a virtue of an old-fashioned variety called Golden Promise. Although GP only accounts for a proportion of the malt used by Macallan nowadays, the company maintains that it contributes an 'oiliness', a 'texture', that is an essential part of The Macallan's profile.

YIELD

The earliest kinds of barley grown in the British Isles are termed 'landraces' or 'heritage crops'. In Scotland, it was predominantly a variety called bere: low-yielding but resilient and capable of withstanding the cold, wet climate of the Highlands. Now it is only grown in Orkney and made into bere bannocks, and also a bere beer, or rather, ale.

Bere has four or six rows of seeds in each ear. As early as 1678, agriculturalists recognized that two-rowed barley was better that the coarser four-rowed bere, and in the early nineteenth century, landraces were selectively improved to perform better in specific regions. These were mainly two-row spring barleys; most were weak-strawed and low-yielding, but they did have the useful malting qualities of low dormancy and rapid germination. An example was a variety called Scotch Common.

By the middle of the century, these landraces had been replaced by other selections such as the higher-yielding Chevallier. This, in turn, was superseded at the turn of the century by the dense, narrow-eared Archer and the broad-eared Goldthorpe.

HYBRIDS

Variety improvement really began at the turn of the twentieth century, with the discovery of hybridization (landrace varieties are by definition improved by traditional methods, not by modern breeding practices). Archer was crossed with Spratt (an old Fenland variety), or Plumage (a Scandinavian variety) to produce Spratt-Archer and Plumage-Archer. By 1940, these were grown in eighty percent of the UK malting barley area.

Improvements in malting barley have been most marked in the last fifty years, when yields have risen by around twenty percent. The leading post-war varieties were Maris Otter and Proctor, but these did not thrive in the harsher climate of Scotland, so the barley was brought up from England (principally Yorkshire and Lincolnshire) and also from Australia, the US, Canada and Denmark. It came by rail, and the same trains took whisky back down south.

Increasing transport costs and the huge demand for Scotch whisky made it imperative to develop a variety which could be grown in Scotland, and the result was Golden Promise: a semi-dwarf variety introduced in 1966 which matured early and so could stand the colder, windier conditions of the north. It grew particularly well in the fertile Laich o'Moray, close to Speyside.

Notwithstanding the development of Golden Promise, Maris Otter and Proctor still accounted for slightly over three-quarters of the barley used during the 1970s, and this all came from England. Today, over eighty percent of malting barley is grown in Scotland.

Golden Promise was capable of producing 385 to 395 litres of alcohol per tonne of malt; in 1980, the variety Triumph was approved, producing 295 to 405 litres of alcohol per tonne. This was followed by exotic names such as Camargue (1985), Derkado (1992), Chariot (1992), Optic (1995) and Decanter (2000). Optic accounted for nearly three-quarters of the malting barley grown in 2002, the other leading current variety being Decanter.

AFTERTHOUGHT

It is interesting to note that, in the 1820s, a typical Highland distillery produced around 6,500 litres of pure alcohol per annum, requiring about twenty tonnes of malt, which could be grown on approximately twenty-five acres of arable land. Today, even a medium-sized distillery, such as Lagavulin or Cardhu, produces this amount of alcohol in a day!

Fields overlooking Dunblane, 1693

This 1909 advertisement for Usher's depicts Demeter, Greek goddess of the harvest, showing the importance of purity in all stages of production, starting with the barley itself

MILD AS MILK

*Lord Conyngham, the Lord Chamberlain, was
looking everywhere for pure Glenlivet whisky; the
King drank nothing else. It was not to be had out
of the Highlands. My father sent word to me – I
was the cellarer – to empty my pet bin, where there
was whisky long in wood, long in uncorked bottles,
mild as milk, and the true contraband goût in it.
Much as I grudged this treasure, it made our
fortunes afterwards, showing on what trifles great
events depend. The whisky, and fifty brace of
ptarmigan all shot by one man, went up to
Holyrood House, and were graciously received
and made much of, and a reminder of this attention
at a proper moment by the gentlemanly
Chamberlain ensured to my father the
Indian Judgeship.*

ELIZABETH GRANT OF ROTHIEMURCHAS,
MEMOIRS OF A HIGHLAND LADY, 1898

It is a charming thought that George IV drank nothing but illicit moonshine during his visit to Edinburgh in August 1822!

More interesting from a whisky historian's perspective is Miss Grant's mention of maturation improving the quality of the whisky – the first such reference I know of. Her mention of the benefit of being 'long in uncorked bottles' is, however, most mysterious.

The intimate and matter-of-fact style of Elizabeth Grant's (1797–1886) memoirs, begun in the 1850s and not written for publication, has been compared with that of Jane Austen. Her book has remained in print ever since it was first published, a dozen years after her death.

Elizabeth's father was in fact a lawyer in Edinburgh, and he experienced 'considerable professional and financial difficulties until he became a successful judge in India' – thanks to his daughter's good offices.

PEAT

In recent years, the smoky malts from the island of Islay have taken the world by storm. Laphroaig's sales have increased six-fold in seven years; Lagavulin now has to be rationed, such is the demand, and Bowmore won two gold medals and 'Distiller of the Year' at the International Spirits Challenge in September 2002. All three are ranked in the top-ten globally best-selling malts. Ardbeg has tripled its sales in three years, while the last two smoky Islays, Caol Ila and Port Ellen, are less often encountered (although sought after by connoisseurs), the first because almost all its product goes for blending, the second because the distillery closed in 1983.

Not long ago, it was thought that these pungent whiskies were very much an acquired taste. The familiar pattern was to graduate from blended whisky to a gentle malt – a Speyside, perhaps – and only after years of experience to move on to the Islays. An eminent Scottish judge, now deceased, once remarked to a friend of mine that his father would 'never have Islay whisky in the house'; when she raised an eyebrow, he explained that 'it was for outdoor consumption only, powerful and elemental, not for douce [sedate] dining rooms, let alone the drawing room'.

Today, an increasing number of younger drinkers are acquiring a taste for whisky via the big Islays. A recent straw poll I conducted around the bars of Edinburgh showed conclusively that the best-selling malts were Laphroaig and Lagavulin. How do you account for this? Does the contemporary palate, familiar with barbecued spare-ribs and smoked salmon, crave smoky flavours? I think not. I believe it has to do with both the 'obvious' style of these whiskies and their pronounced character.

They are unlike any other drink, including other whiskies, and their character is positive. Whether you like them or not, they are definitely not bland. Their success mirrors that of other 'not bland', full-flavoured products that have become popular in recent years: real coffee and virgin olive oil, farm cheeses and ethnic foods, cigars and cocktails. They are also perceived by younger drinkers as being challenging and aspirational: like jumping out of a helicopter wearing skis or riding a mountain bike over a cliff.

Where does this smoky character come from? It comes from the peat that is burned in the kiln while the malt is being dried. Most distilleries on Islay buy their malt from the maltings at Port Ellen, the island's main harbour, although both Laphroaig and Bowmore have their own small maltings and make around twenty percent of their requirement. Each distillery specifies the degree of peating/smokiness it requires, as we shall see.

Peat is decayed vegetation, decomposed over thousands of years by water, and partially carbonized by chemical change. The word itself is Celtic, reflecting the importance of the material as fuel in these windswept lands. My 1911 edition of *The Encyclopaedia Britannica* informs me that there were then 212,700 square miles of peat bog in Europe. This has been drastically reduced over the last forty years by draining for forestry (particularly in Finland) and (in central Europe) by demand from gardeners.

The vegetation from which peat is made varies slightly from place to place but usually includes mosses, heather, sedges and rushes; for it to develop, the climate must be cool and wet, the drainage must be poor and the ground ill-aerated. As decomposition proceeds, the vegetable matter becomes waterlogged and sinks to the bottom, piling up and being compressed and carbonized. In some places, the peat layer is as deep as nine metres; some peat bogs are 10,000 years old. Once the bog has formed, the peats are 'won' (to use the correct term) by removing the turf, then digging a trench as deep as the peat layer allows (usually about two metres) and slicing out the peats with a peat spade (a *fal*, in Scots Gaelic; a *slane* in Irish) as from a vast, black pat of butter. The individual peats are then spread out to dry. Peat stacks are still a familiar sight in the west of Ireland and Highland Scotland.

The peats close to the surface are crumbly, rooty and smoky; this is what maltsters want. The deeper peats are darker and burn hotter, and the deepest of all are dry, hard and black – almost like coal. These are the best domestic peats. In Orkney, the various levels are called 'fog', 'yarphie' and 'moss'; in Islay, they refer to 'top', 'second' and 'third' peats, and only use the 'top' peats for kilning.

The smoke produced by peat is highly aromatic and tarry, and if malt is dried over it, these compounds – 'phenols' is the chemical group – coat the grains and imbue the whisky made from them. Laying and tending a peat-fire in a kiln requires considerable skill, and the maltmen at Port Ellen vie with each other to make the most effective fire: one that will pile on the phenols. It must burn slow and cool, since the phenols only attach themselves to the grains during the early stages of kilning, when the malt is still moist; if the fire is too hot, the phenols will themselves be consumed. So there is a limit to the phenolic level achievable, and this is not simply a matter of the length of time the malt is exposed to the peat smoke (although this is clearly an important factor); the big, smoky Islay malts require between four and six tons of peat, burned for between fourteen and twenty hours. In truth, much depends upon the way the wind is blowing and how strongly, and upon the age and nature of the peat.

Degrees of peating are measured in 'parts per million phenols', or ppm. The peating specification for Ardbeg, Laphroaig, Lagavulin, Caol Ila and Bowmore is between thirty and fifty ppm. Bruichladdich Distillery at Port Charlotte, which traditionally makes an unpeated malt, is now producing a stablemate, Octomore, peated to sixty ppm, (with difficulty). The highest level of peating ever achieved at Port Ellen maltings, experimentally, was just over 100ppm phenols.

The Lowland Scots for smoke is 'reek' – Edinburgh, with its smoking tenements, was once known as 'Auld Reekie' – and after 1824 'peatreek' came to be used to describe illicit homemade hooch, no doubt a reference to the smoky aroma and flavour of such whisky. In the remote Highlands, where peat was the main (in some places, only) source of domestic fuel, the kilning of malt was done entirely over a peat fire. But bearing in mind that phenols will only adhere during the early stages of kilning, before the malt dries out, it is possible to speculate that some homemade whisky was probably not much more smoky than the Islay malts we have been considering.

When defining 'peatreek', *The Oxford English Dictionary* notes: 'The peatreek flavour is really that of amyl alcohol, due to imperfect rectification'. This is nonsense; amyls are part of that other leading group of chemicals found in whisky called 'esters', with characteristics of peardrops, nail-varnish remover and acetone. More commonly (though tasting notes for illicit whisky of the eighteenth and nineteenth centuries are rare) peatreek was described as being 'empyreumatic', which my *Chambers Dictionary* defines as having 'the burned smell and acrid taste that comes when vegetable or animal substances are burned'.

Empyreumatic off-notes can arise in several ways. The most likely cause is driving the still too hard, heating it too fiercely and scorching solid matter in the wash that might stick to its base. After about 1790, large stills were fitted with rummagers – lengths of copper chain-mail, dragged mechanically around the base of the still to prevent solids adhering – but these contraptions were not available to home distillers, and it must have been difficult for them to prevent scorching. Nevertheless, one should not underestimate the skills handed down through generations: Elizabeth Grant of Rothiemurchus, it must be remembered, describes the peatreek she sent up to Edinburgh for the delectation of King George IV in 1822 as being 'mild as milk… and the real contraband *goût* in it' (see page 98). The King drank nothing else, and rewarded Elizabeth's father with an ' Indian Judgeship'.

So perhaps the big Islays, the smokiest of all malt whiskies, recollect the whisky of the past. And perhaps one of the reasons for their current popularity is their 'authenticity', their 'heritage'. An atavistic folk memory, like candles and open fires, Christmas trees and stormy nights.

This article first appeared in Decanter *magazine*

NOTED FOR ITS GREAT AGE AND PURITY

"HIGHLAND NECTAR"

A BLEND OF THE VERY FINEST
SCOTCH WHISKIES.

The Distillers Company Ltd.

EDINBURGH

REGISTERED.

CERTIFICATE OF ANALYSIS.

From Dr CLARK, Public Analyst for the City of Glasgow and the
Counties of Lanark and Renfrew, &c.

I have made a minute and careful analysis of a fair Sample of The Distillers Company's
"Highland Nectar" Blend of Scotch Whisky, taken by myself from a considerable Stock
lying in bond, and the results which I have obtained indicate that it is a pure Whisky
which has been well matured in Sherry Wood, and I am of opinion that it is a high-class
Whisky of very fine flavour and excellent quality.

CITY ANALYST'S LABORATORY,
GLASGOW, 30TH DECEMBER 1895.

John Clark

---

*An 1895 label for 'Highland Nectar', one of the brands
created by the Distillers Company Limited. The brand name reflects
the heritage and esteem with which whisky became associated – whether
it was 'mild as milk' or the strong, peaty type*

THE SELKIRK GRACE

Some hae meat and canna eat
And some wad eat that want it;
But we hae meat and we can eat,
And sae the Lord be thankit.

ROBERT BURNS, 1794

Robert Burns was often asked to pronounce grace before the meal, and expected to extemporize and come up with something new. One might assume that this, his most famous grace, would have been composed in the Border town of Selkirk – but this is not the case.

Burns visited the town only once, on Sunday, May 13, 1787. He was touring with a companion and it was raining hard, so they took shelter in Veitch's Inn, where the local doctor and two friends were sitting by the fire. The innkeeper asked the doctor if the strangers could join them, but he refused, on the grounds that 'they did not look like gentlemen'. Three days later, Dr Clarkson learned who the stranger was. A contemporary, James Hogg ('The Ettrick Shepherd') wrote that 'his refusal [to allow them to join him] hangs about the doctor's heart like a dead weight to this day, and will do till the day of his death, for the bard had no more enthusiastic an admirer'. Such are the rewards of snobbery!

The grace itself was probably first delivered at the Heid Inn in Kirkcudbright High Street, in the presence of Dunbar Douglas, 4th Earl of Selkirk, in July 1794 (the inn is now named the Selkirk Arms). It is also possible that the grace, was traditional, and not in fact composed by Burns at all. He certainly never wrote it down. And while Burns himself never drank much whisky, the Selkirk Grace has nonetheless become a grace that is traditionally drunk with Scotch.

MALTINGS

Barleycorns are mainly starch. To make alcohol, this must be turned into sugar and fermented with yeast. Malting does not effect the conversion into sugar, but it prepares the starch for conversion by breaking down the tough cell walls and proteins which bind the starch cells, and by activating enzymes in the grains which will do the job of conversion when hot water is added to the ground malt in the mash tun. I have heard it compared to unwrapping a sweetie prior to eating it.

In nature, the cell walls break down when the plant begins to grow. The maltster tricks the barleycorns into believing that spring is here and it is time to germinate. He does this by steeping the grains in water, resting them (moist) so they begin to sprout and then stopping the germination by drying them (now called 'green malt') after the cell walls have gone, but before the new plant has consumed any of the starch.

FLOOR MALTINGS

Until the twentieth century, this process was carried out in so-called 'floor maltings', and every distillery made its own malt. In floor maltings, the damp grain is spread out on a cool (cement or slate) floor to the depth of between one and two feet. Germination generates heat, so the grain has to be regularly turned with wooden shovels and rakes to keep the temperature even, and to prevent the little rootlets becoming entangled and matting. This was a laborious task, and tended to develop a repetitive strain injury called 'monkey shoulder' among maltmen. After about nine days (depending on the ambient temperature; it will be less in warm weather, more when it is cold) the cell walls will have broken down and the green malt is ready for kilning.

In the Lowlands, malt kilns were fuelled by anthracite and coke; in the Highlands and Islands, where peat was the universal fuel, this fired the kilns and the fragrant peat smoke made an important contribution to the flavour of the whisky (see 'Peat', pages 100–106).

DRUM MALTINGS

As early as 1885, engineers turned their attention to inventing a method of mechanical malting which would do away with the manual handling of the grain and better control temperatures, so as to produce more even germination, and thus better malt.

The key to such methods was aeration, and the systems are generally referred to as 'pneumatic'. A pneumatic system employing cast-iron cylinders or 'drums' was invented by a Monsieur Galland, and perfected in London during the 1890s by the Scottish engineer R Blair Robertson. Early drums held only from 2.5 to 10.5 tons of grain (today, they typically hold 100 to 300 tons). They were mounted longitudinally, and within each was another, perforated drum which was capable of being rotated. This was half-filled with barley.

In the first stage, the grain was cleaned and steeped by being revolved through a shallow trough of water, while being simultaneously aerated. Next, the water was drained off and the grain 'rested' and encouraged to germinate: aerated by a fan at one end of the drum, sprayed occasionally with fresh water and turned automatically from time to time to ensure even 'modification'. Once conversion was complete, the green malt – 'sweet and fresh, without mould or any damaged corns'[1] – was transferred to the kiln for drying. Later, the drums were adapted to dry the malt as well. Called SGKVs (Steeping, Germination and Kilning Vessels), these are now the most common method of malting

A Galland pneumatic drum was installed at Glen Grant Distillery in the 1890s and at Speyburn in 1905. The latter was described as a 'very compact unit with a central belt-drive mechanism to turn the drums and the ventilation fans, with a double-deck kiln for fuel efficiency'. It was successfully operated for sixty years by the Distillers Company. Drums were also introduced at St Magdalene Distillery, Linlithgow, in the 1920s and operated successfully until the 1950s. But it was in the manufacture of grain whisky that they were mainly used; even by 1913, J A Nettleton was able to remark that 'such methods were in general use at distillery maltings, especially at patent-still distilleries'. Most malt distillers stuck with floor maltings, however.

---

1) Sleeman, quoted by J A Nettleton (*The Manufacture of Whisky and Plain Spirit* (1913)

SALADIN MALTINGS

Around the same time as drum malting was being perfected (i.e. the 1890s), another form of mechanical malting was invented by Charles Saladin, called the 'Saladin box'. This was simply a concrete trough equipped with revolving rakes; in it, the barley was steeped, turned by the rakes and mechanically aerated. The method was quickly taken up by the brewing industry in Europe, but, as with so much else, the whisky industry held back for fifty years.

The first distillery to install Saladin boxes was North British, in 1948 – not without teething problems (the works manager was sent to Copenhagen to 'ascertain the best methods of overcoming the difficulties of condensation'). Further boxes were installed at North British in 1963. Glen Mhor Distillery, Inverness, followed in 1949, and Tamdhu in 1950 (where they are still in use). Dalmore Distillery, Alness, installed them in 1956, where the mechanical turners were of a different design, and Glen Moray, at Elgin, in 1957. Around ten malt distilleries installed Saladin boxes in the 1950s and early 1960s, including Dailuaine (1959–60), Glen Albyn (1961), Ord (1961) and Imperial (1967).

CENTRALIZED MALTING

But even by the early sixties, on-site distillery maltings were doomed, whether floor, Saladin or drum. The phenomenal growth in demand for Scotch after the Second World War created such a demand for malt that they could not cope, and in a short period most distillery maltings closed, malt being bought in from dedicated, centralized maltings.

In 1968, Scottish Malt Distillers (or SMD, the malt-whisky production division of the Distillers Company Limited) ceased floor malting at twenty-nine distilleries. Two years before, the company had built a huge drum malting at Burghead, on the Moray Firth, and the same year the maltings at Muir of Ord were substantially expanded, with six drums added to the existing Saladin boxes (Ord Distillery itself used malt from the boxes; the drums met the requirement of SMD's seven distilleries in the north of Scotland).

SMD followed this by building a seven-drum malting adjacent to its Port Ellen Distillery, Islay, in 1973, and at Roseisle in 1979-80. Both these plants have the ability to produce peated malt – a capacity which most of the new maltings did (and do) not have. Roseisle was the first fully automated malting to be used in the UK.

Other distillers also centralized their maltings. For example, Hiram Walker's subsidiary, Robert Kilgour, built a large drum malting at Kirkaldy in 1968, and the same year Inver House Distillers opened 'the largest commercial malting plant in Europe' at its Moffat distillery, Aidrie. Independent maltsters like ABM, Bairds, Moray Firth, Simpsons and Pauls followed suit to supply the independent whisky companies.

AFTERTHOUGHT

There is no doubt that centralized, pneumatic maltings produce a more reliable product than the old floor maltings, although those distilleries that retain their floor maltings believe they allow for greater control of the level of peating. Some years ago, Highland Park closed its maltings for a season and bought in all its malt requirement, peated to the specified level with Orkadian peat, but it did not produce the character of spirit desired and the company resumed in-house malting.

Let Neil Gunn have the last word:

In all this malting process, skilled judgement is needed, for the goodness of the malt determines not only the quantity of alcohol that may result from its fermentation but the quality of the ultimate distillate itself.

MALTINGS CURRENTLY OPERATING IN SCOTLAND

Bairds — Arbroath, Angus; Moray Firth, Inverness; Pencaitland, East Lothian

Bass — Alloa, Kincardineshire

Crisp — Portgordon, Banffshire

Diageo — Burghead, Morayshire; Glen Ord, Inverness-shire; Port Ellen, Islay; Roseisle, Morayshire

Kilgour — Dunnikier, Fife

Pauls — Buckie, Banffshire; Carnoustie, Angus; Glenesk, Angus

Scotmalt — Kirkliston, West Lothian

Simpsons — Berwick on Tweed

DISTILLERIES WITH MALTINGS

Balvenie — floor malting; supplies 10% of requirement

Bowmore — floor malting; supplies 20% of requirement

Glen Ord — Saladin and drum maltings; supplies 100% of requirement and the requirements of six other distilleries

Highland Park — floor malting; supplies 20% of requirement

Laphroaig — floor malting; supplies 20% of requirement

Springbank — floor malting; supplies 100% of requirement, and the requirement of Longrow and Glengyle

Tamdhu — Saladin malting; supplies 100% requirement, and most of the requirement of Glen Rothes

Glendronach still has its floor maltings, but they have not been used since 1998

MEMORIAL

𝕸𝖆𝖑𝖙=𝕿𝖆𝖝.

Printed in the Year M. DCC. XXVI.

[Price Three Pence.]

A pamphlet from 1726, 'mourning' the demise of the malt tax which had been proposed by Chancellor of the Exchequer Robert Walpole

MORE THAN JUST A DRAM

Take clear water from the hill
and barley from the Lowlands,
take a master craftsman's skill
and something harder to define,
like secrets in the shape of coppered still
or the slow, silent, magic work of time.

Chorus
Whisky, you're the Devil in disguise,
at least to some that's the way it seems,
but you're more like an angel in my eyes,
catch the heady vapours as they rise
and turn them into dreams.

Bring home sherry casks from Spain,
Sanlúcar de Barrameda,
and fill them up again
with the spirit of the land.
Then let the wood work to the spirit's gain
in a process no one fully understands.

Repeat Chorus

Now, the spirit starts out clear
but see the transformation
after many patient year
when at last the tale unfolds,
for the colours of the seasons will appear,
from palest yellow to the deepest gold.

Repeat Chorus

When you hold it in your hand
it's the pulse of one small nation;
so much more than just a dram,
you can see it if you will –
the people and the weather and the land,
the past into the present is distilled.

Whisky, you're the Devil in disguise,
at least to some that's the way it seems,
but you're more like an angel in my eyes,
catch the heady vapours as they rise,
and turn them into peaceful, pleasant dreams.

ROBIN LAING (1995)

Robin Laing is one of Scotland's leading singer-songwriters. He has also recorded two CDs of whisky-related songs and poems, *The Angel's Share* (1997) and *The Water of Life* (2003), and has published a seminal collection of poems and songs about whisky, *The Whisky Muse* (2002). The author tells me that *More Than Just a Dram* was begun on the island of Eigg and finished on the island of Islay.

THE FIRING OF STILLS

Stills may be heated in two ways: directly (with a naked flame beneath) or indirectly (by steam-heated pans and coils within the body of the still itself, not unlike an electric kettle). A form of indirect heating by steam is employed by patent stills, and as early at 1888-89, the Glenmorangie Distillery installed steam coils: the first malt distillery to do so, and possibly the only one for many years,[1] for indirect firing was not generally adopted by the whisky industry until the early 1960s. Indeed, direct firing was considered to be one of the key factors in distinguishing malt whisky from patent-still grain whisky, and one malt from another. Thus, Sir Walter Gilbey was able to write in 1904:

> It is a curious fact that the heat of the fire [in pot-still distillation] also imparts a Flavour to the vapourized matter. The fire heat gives the spirit a character which distinguishes it from Spirits distilled by the Patent Still. It imparts to the Spirit the character known as empyreumatic, which is easily recognized in the product of the Pot Still and which is quite absent in Spirit produced by the Patent Still.

---

1) An early 20th-century steam-jacketed still survived at Auchentoshan until 1975

Nearly half a century later, in 1951, the inaugural lecture of the Wine and Spirit Association of Great Britain expanded upon this view:

> *The Still is heated by a naked fire, and it follows inevitably that the heat applied is not constant at all times or at all portions of the Still in contact with the fire. It is this unequal heating in parts which is believed to cause changes in the Whiskies which distinguish one from the other, and it is generally considered that the process of slow heating of the Still bottom and of the wash contained in the Still is a vital factor in developing the character and quality of Scotch Whisky, and bringing out its special peculiarities... Brandy is also distilled over a naked fire, and I understand that many brewers prefer a naked fire to other, and perhaps more scientific, methods of heating, so probably there is something in the use of a naked fire which has a good effect, even though we don't know why.*

Distillers who have worked with both direct and indirect-fired stills are agreed that the spirit produced by the former was heavier. Ian Henderson, for example, whose first job in the whisky industry was at Strathisla Distillery, recalled that there were two pairs of stills, one pair coal-fired and the other steam-fired. 'The two spirits were completely different,' he explained. 'Direct-firing produced much more body in the spirit.' It was the company's policy to vat the two makes together to create Strathisla single malt.

Engraving of a whisky still from 1729

The Rise of Indirect Firings

Direct-fired stills were dirty, difficult to run and extremely labour-intensive, however. The fire had to be controlled physically by raking out the furnace or damping down with a hose when the boiling point was reached. Soap was often used in the wash stills as a surfactant, but in spite of this, it was not uncommon for the wash or low wines to rise up into the neck of the still and carry over into the 'worm' or condenser.

In the late 1950s and early 1960s, many distilleries installed mechanical stoking systems, and some even experimented with oil-firing (notably Ord and Tomatin Distilleries), but this was later abandoned, since it caused the base of the stills to become brittle. Gas-firing, by North Sea gas, both natural and petroleum by-product, proved more successful and remains in use at Macallan Distillery.

As part of the general refurbishment and expansion that took place during the boom years of the 1960s, all but a handful of malt distilleries went over to indirect firing. In wash stills, the usual method of heating is via thin-walled cylinders, called 'kettles', while in spirit stills, coils are more generally used. Some, like

Glenfarclas Distillery (which remains direct-fired to this day), experimented, then retained the traditional method. In Glenfarclas's case, one spirit still was converted to steam coils for a week in 1980, but, in the words of John Grant, the distillery's owner, 'The spirit it produced was not Glenfarclas – it had no guts.'

Conversion is not done lightly. Certainly in more recently converted distilleries, months of tests are done to adjust the production regime and cut points so as to make sure the liquor made from indirect-fired stills has the same characteristics as that from the old, direct-fired plant. Nevertheless: 'There is general agreement that steam heating and the installation of tubular condensers both tend to result in the production of a more lightly flavoured spirit.' [2]

---

2) Professor R K Martin, Dr E B Duncan and John R Hume, *The Development of Scotch Whisky Plant and Associated Processes* (in *The Scotch Whisky Industry Record,* Dumbarton, 1994), p. 370

Remaining Direct-Fired Stills in the UK

Glenfiddich
Gas-fired (coal-fired until 2002–03);
ten wash stills, eighteen spirit stills

Macallan
Gas-fired

Glendronach
Coal-fired; two wash stills, two spirit stills

Glenfarclas
Gas-fired since 1972; three wash and three spirit stills

Springbank
Oil-fired, wash still (which also has steam coils);
two low-wines stills indirect-fired)

Glen Grant and *Longmorn Distilleries* were converted
to indirect firing in the late 1990s, *Ardmore* in 2002.

LIVING FOREVER

If a body could just find oot the exac' proper proportion
and quantity that ought to be drunk every day, and
keep to that, I verily trow that he might leev for ever,
without dyin' at a', and that doctors and kirkyairds
would go oot o' fashion.

THE ETTRICK SHEPHERD
– QUOTED BY CHRISTOPHER NORTH (1826)

'Christopher North' was the pseudonym of John Wilson (1785-1854), who was editor of *Blackwood's Magazine* and, after 1820, professor of moral philosophy in the University of Edinburgh. 'The Ettrick Shepherd' was the poet James Hogg, author of *The Confessions of a Justified Sinner*.

Under Wilson's editorship, *Blackwood's* became famous for its fearless polemics, savage reviews, literary jokes and wide-ranging conversations. The latter – from which the above quotation is taken – were set in Ambrose's Tavern (which stood on the site of what is now Edinburgh's Café Royal), and were reported in the long-running column, *Noctes Ambrosianae*.

James Hogg (1770-1835) was born in the Ettrick Valley and spent his youth working as a cowherd and shepherd, before educating himself and publishing a number of celebrated poems. He came to Edinburgh about 1818 and published a series of notable supernatural novels (all still in print), including the famous *Confessions of a Justified Sinner* (1824).

WORMS

In the early days of distilling, alcohol vapour was condensed simply by the surrounding air: the solution of water and alcohol was heated in an alembic, the alcohol vapour (since it boils off first, at 78.3°C) came over the neck of the still and passed down a beak-like tube called a cucurbit (today we would call it a 'lyne arm' or 'lye pipe'), where it condensed back into liquid. Sometimes there was a water bath around the head of the still, but it was only in the mid-1500s (1540–50) that the lower end of the lye pipe was placed in a tub of water: first straight across, then diagonally and finally in a coil, which increased the cooling surface available and allowed the distiller to produce more spirit.

This is the 'worm'. The earliest written reference to it in English is in *The Art of Distillation* by John French (1651): 'Put it into a Copper Still with a worme'. Yet around a hundred years earlier, Adam Lonicer's *Naturalis Historiae Opus Novum*, published in Frankfurt, included an illustration of a worm and worm-tub.

Until the late nineteenth century, worms were the only form of condenser available to distillers: a coiled pipe in a tub of cold water. In whisky distillation, the pipe was (and is) made of copper, not only because copper is more malleable, but, more importantly, because the chemical reaction which takes place between the distillate and the copper purifies the former and lightens the spirit.

In the 1880s, variations on the traditional worm-tub were invented, forerunners of the 'shell-and-tube' condenser that would later become the most common condensing method. The shell-and-tube condenser is a bundle of narrow-bore copper pipes, arranged in parallel within a copper canister. Alcohol vapour fills the canister and condenses on the copper pipes, through which cold water is passed. This requires less water than worm tubs, the plant is easier to clean and replace, and as condensers permit greater contact with the copper, the spirit produced is purer and lighter in character than that produced by worms.

Yet the whisky industry was slow to adopt this new method. Alfred Barnard, later editor of the trade journal *Harper's Weekly Gazette*, who toured all the distilleries in Britain and Ireland during the mid-1880s,[1] mentions only eight that were equipped with condensers. Glenugie, Bowmore, Milton (i.e. Strathisla) and Strathdee used their condensers in parallel with traditional worm-tubs; the wash still at Glenugie Distillery, Peterhead (built in 1875), had 'a Horizontal Condenser of a very modern design, having 200 tubes in it, the one for the Spirit Still being of the ordinary upright kind, with 50 tubes', while Bowmore had two condensers and three worm-tubs. At Kirkliston Distillery, near Edinburgh (est. 1795), 'six sets of Willison's Upright Condensers, and a Worm Tub of a most primitive pattern' provided for six pot stills. Condensers were also noted in passing at Dean, Edinburgh (built 1881), and Ardbeg, Islay (est. 1815). Barnard's book also contains advertisements from two companies listing condensers among the other distilling and brewing equipment they manufacture.

During the boom of the 1890s, when forty new distilleries were built, one might have thought that shell-and-tube condensers would have been the norm. This was not the case. In 1913, J A Nettleton could still remark:[2]

1) Alfred Barnard, *The Whisky Distilleries of the United Kingdom* (London, 1887)
2) J A Nettleton, *The Manufacture of Whisky and Plain Spirit* (Aberdeen, 1913) p. 493

It is abundantly evident that the old-fashioned worms and worm-tubs are doomed to disappear, and that far more convenient apparatus will take their place. Upright condensing cylinders or boxes, 6 to 10 feet in height and 1.5 to 2 feet in diameter, afford, in many cases, sufficient condensing and cooling power for the various vapours and liquids from a large still.

It was not until after World War II that shell-and-tube condensers became common, and even then they were not adopted wholesale. The pioneering distillery architect Delmé Evans incorporated them into his designs for Tullibardine (1949), and later Macduff (1960), Jura (1960–63) and Glenallachie (1968), as did Sir Albert Richardson in his designs for Tormore (1958–60), but worm-tubs were installed at the strikingly modern Glen Keith Distillery (1957–60).

However, when building regulations were relaxed in 1960, many whisky companies embarked on large-scale refurbishment and expansion to meet the rapidly growing demand for Scotch. Engineers and accountants at Scottish Malt Distillers, the production division of the mighty Distillers Company Limited, embraced shell-and-tube condensers enthusiastically and installed them whenever they were expanding or replacing plants in their forty-five distilleries. The independent malt-whisky producers pursued a similar policy during the same period and expanded their distilleries, some to double their capacity, and all with condensers.

By the late 1970s, only a dozen or so distilleries had their original worm-tubs, although in at least one case – at Dalwhinnie, in 1996 – worm-tubs were reinstated, at considerable expense. The relevance of this to the consumer is that the spirit produced by worm-tubs is heavier than that produced by condensers, for the simple reason that the spirit vapour has greater contact with copper (a purifier) in condensers than in worms. During the winter months, when the water in the tub is colder, there is even less copper uptake in the worm, so the spirit is even heavier.

In the days of 'dramming', when distillery workers were issued with approximately a gill of new-make spirit at the end of their shifts (two or even three times a day, with extra rations on the completion of 'dirty' jobs), they could tell whether the spirit had been made during summer or winter. Dramming was stopped by health and safety regulations during the 1970s.

So whisky made by distilleries with worm-tubs is likely to be heavier in texture, and some would say, more characterful, although much depends upon other features (such as purification devices) and the distilling regime. If the stills are run hot and fast, there will be greater copper contact.

DISTILLERIES THAT STILL USE WORM-TUBS

Balmenach

Benrinnes

Cragganmore

Dallas Dhu
*Now preserved at a museum
by Scottish Heritage*

Dalwhinnie
*Worm-tubs removed
1985; reinstated 1996*

Edradour
*Still operates a worm
installed in 1825*

Glen Elgin

Glenkinchie

Mortlach

Oban

Rosebank
Wash-still only; closed 1993

Royal Lochnagar

Speyburn

Springbank
Wash-still only

Talisker

Glendarroch Distillery, circa 1887

I used to endeavour to supply my cask with, and to keep independent jars of, the following: Clyne Lish, Smith's Glenlivet, Glen Grant, Talisker, and one of the Islay brands – Lagavulin, Ardbeg, Caol Isla, etc. The picturesquely named 'Long John', otherwise Ben Nevis, is less definite in flavour than any of these, but blends very well. Glendronach, an Aberdeenshire whisky, of which I did not think much forty years ago, improved greatly later; and I used to try both these in my cask. But I always kept separate supplies of all, and amused myself with these, alone or variously blended, at intervals. A friend of mine from Oxford days, now dead, held some mixed Clyne Lish and Glenlivet of mine to be the best whisky he had ever drunk.

GEORGE SAINTSBURY, 1920

George Saintsbury (1845–1933) is often described as 'the first oenophile', although he considered his seminal and delightful *Notes to a Cellar Book* (published in his seventy-fifth year) as 'very personal… so very little a book'.

This is not surprising from the author of the monumental *History of Criticism*, *History of English Prosody* and *History of the French Novel*; a man described in his *Times* obituary as 'cast in a mightier mould than most professors and students of literature… who had read and remembered everything worth reading'.

His study of whisky began in 1875, and was deepened when was appointed regius professor of rhetoric in the University of Edinburgh in 1895, a position he held until 1915. Malt whisky was his passion; grain whisky he described as 'only good for blending, and for mere drinkers for drunkee'. Elsewhere, he remarks on how whiskies had changed over forty-five years, one of the very few descriptions of taste that has survived: 'The older whiskies were darker in colour, from being kept in golden sherry or Madeira casks, rather sweeter in taste, and rather heavier in texture; the newer are "lighter" in both the first and the last respect, and much drier in taste.'

'THE WOOD MAKES THE WHISKY'

*The transformation of new spirit into mature whisky is
as miraculous as the change from caterpillar to butterfly.
The chrysalis is the oak cask.*

Dr Jim Swan

Of all the factors that influence the flavour of Scotch
whisky, the cask in which the whisky matures is
probably the most potent. While the cask cannot make
good a badly made whisky, it can certainly make a
good whisky great. On the other hand, defective or
exhausted casks can also make good whisky pretty
nasty. As the 'good old boys' in the whisky trade used
to say: 'The wood makes the whisky.'

If you think of it, this makes perfect sense. It takes
less than a week to produce a batch of (malt) spirit,
from milling the malt to filling the cask; the spirit then
lies in its cask for three or five or ten or twenty years…

THE MYSTIC OAK

Once upon a time, new Scotch spirit could be filled into any kind of wood, but now only oak may be used: whisky cannot legally be called 'Scotch' unless it has been matured for a minimum of three years in 'oak casks of a capacity not exceeding 700 litres', and this in an excise warehouse in Scotland. (see 'What Is Whisky?' pages 12–23). Somewhat surprisingly, the requirement was only enshrined in law in 1988; previous definitions demanded only that the spirit be matured in 'wooden casks'. However, long before this time, oak was the wood of choice throughout the industry – although I am told that there may still be the occasional chestnut cask lurking in the murky depths of remote warehouses…

It is safe to suppose that, in the past, distillers would fill whatever wood came to hand, and the cheaper the better. Casks were merely containers in the days when whisky was drunk straight from the still. What's more, since wooden casks were the only vessels available for storing and transporting liquids of any kind, there were plenty of second-hand ones around. Wine barrels, rum puncheons, port pipes, beer barrels, brandy casks and sherry butts… all were cheerfully filled with whisky, whatever wood they were made from. However, most will have been made from oak grown in the great forests of central Europe, in Limousin or in Galicia (*Quercus robur*). English and Scottish oak, although also *Q. robur*, does not cooper well, so it was rarely used for making barrels. Today, ninety-five percent of the casks coming into the system arrive from the US and are made from American White Oak (*Q. alba*).

Some of the 6,000 casks of A Usher & Co, August 1890 – at the time, the largest bonded warehouse in the world

More Than Just a Tub

As soon as the benefits of maturation were discovered (in other words, as soon as it was realized that the cask is more than just a container) came the discovery, first, that oak does a better job than all other woods and second, that second-hand casks produce better Scotch than new casks.

WHY SHOULD THIS BE?

Scientific understanding of the chemistry of oak wood and of what is happening during maturation is relatively new, simply because, before the 1970s, the scientific techniques for exploring such matters were unavailable. Big advances were made in the late 1970s by Strathclyde University, Pentlands Scotch Whisky Research, and the Distillers Company Limited, and this knowledge began to be applied in the 1990s. Yet there are still areas which remain mysterious.

Chemists now talk about 'cask activity', and believe the wood performs three crucial functions, described as 'subtractive', 'additive', and 'interactive'.

HIGHLAND WHISKY.

THE SUBSCRIBERS have just received from the North a few casks REAL GLENLIVIT, bought at an Excise sale in Aberdeenshire.

They have also on hand an extensive Stock of FOREIGN SPIRITS, WINES, and TEAS, of finest quality and flavour, all of which will be sold genuine, and at reasonable prices.

ANDW. USHER & COMPANY,
44, Lothian Street.

A classified advertisement for A Usher & Co as featured in
The Edinburgh Star *on April 3, 1821*

SUBTRACTIVE MECHANISMS

In order to be bent into a barrel shape, the staves must be heated. Heat performs the vital function of altering the chemical structure of the inside surface of the cask. Without heating, the spirit will not mature; it will instead merely acquire a 'green', woody note. European casks are 'toasted' to bend them into shape; American casks are flamed once they have been raised, so their inside walls are charred to the depth of about a millimetre.

The carbon char itself acts as an important 'purifier', removing immature characteristics and extracting certain compounds (principally sulphur-based molecules) from the new spirit. The capacity of carbon to do this is exploited by vodka distillers, and also by some Bourbon distillers, both of whom filter their spirits through beds of charcoal to increase their purity. Since European casks do not have a heavily charred interior, their subtractive activity is not as pronounced as American casks, which may account for the fact that mature whisky from such casks often has a sulphury aroma.

ADDITIVE MECHANISMS

Oak is made from cellulose (which contributes nothing to maturation and no flavour), but it also contains hemicellulose (which caramelizes when heated, adding sweetness and colour), lignin (a long-chain polymer which, like hemicellulose, degrades when heated to produce vanillin and coconut flavours) and tannins (which produce astringency, fragrance, delicacy and colour).

As might be imagined, a brand-new cask is much more active than one that has been filled before, so much so that Scotch is never filled into fresh wood.[1] If it were, it would emerge after a few years tasting very like Bourbon (vanilla, oaky), and a very bitter Bourbon at that if the cask was European. So all casks used to mature Scotch whisky, both malt and grain, are 'second-hand': they have been used previously for maturing Bourbon (mainly) or other spirits, sherry or other wines. The first time they are filled with Scotch they are called 'first-fill casks', thereafter they are called 'refills'[2].

---

1) The only exception to this that I am aware of is Glenfiddich's Solera Reserve, where a tiny proportion of the casks which go into the '*solera* vat' are filled new.

2) Some companies refer to 'second-fill' or even 'third-fill'.

The first time they are filled, there will be residues of the previous incumbent (Bourbon, sherry, etc) lurking in the walls of the cask. These leach out into the maturing whisky, adding winey notes to the spirit. After three or four fills (depending on the length of time they matured the first and second fills, and upon the chemistry of the individual staves), they lose their 'activity': their ability to mature their contents. They become mere vessels, and are termed 'exhausted' or 'spent'.

They can be rejuvenated, however, by being reamed out and reburnt, a process called 'de-char/re-char' in American casks and 'de-tartrate/re-toast' in European casks. This re-activates the layer of wood immediately beneath the charred/toasted walls of the cask, but it does not make the cask as good as new. Ex-sherry casks will sometimes then be refilled with sherry for a period of weeks or months, to imitate the effect of a first-fill cask. However, a rejuvenated cask will not mature its contents in the same way as a first-fill cask.

The most obvious 'additive mechanisms' are in relation to colour: European oak, being more tannic, lends its contents a deeper hue than American wood. The degree of colour depends upon how often the cask has been filled (see 'The Amber Glass', page 200), but as a general guide, European wood hue runs from 'old polished oak' to 'young mahogany' (old oloroso to amontillado sherry, to put it another way; but beware of thinking the colour comes from the first incumbent), while American wood hue is all gold: 9ct through to 18ct (pale straw to deep amber).

INTERACTIVE MECHANISMS

Oak is semiporous, which allows the contents of an oak cask to 'breathe' and interact with the air outside. This leads to oxidation, which removes harshness, increases fruitiness and enhances complexity. The interaction between the wood and the atmosphere is the least understood of the mechanisms of maturation, – and, some would say, the most important.

It is this aspect of maturation that is most affected by the microclimate of the warehouse in which the cask rests during maturation. Heat, humidity and atmospheric pressure all play a part. Most warehouses are cool and damp, even in the summer months, and these conditions are ideal. In a hot, dry warehouse, the cask will lose water vapour, so the overall volume will go down, while the strength remains relatively high. In a damp, cold warehouse (especially where the cask is racked close to the ground), the opposite happens: volume remains high, but strength declines more quickly. H M Customs & Excise allow for two percent of the volume of the cask to evaporate every year. This is called 'The Angels' Share', and amounts to around fifty litres over ten years.

Attractive though the thought may be, it is unlikely that extraneous factors like salt-spray, seaweed smells or adjacent plant life (heather, bog myrtle) play any part in the favour of the mature spirit.

Most whisky firms produced an annual price list, such as this one by Chivas Brothers from 1891

How the Casks Have Changed

Until 1946, almost all the oak used by the Scotch whisky trade was European, and many of these casks had originally contained sherry, which was shipped in bulk (i.e. in cask) and bottled by the shipper in the UK. The desirability of sherry as a first incumbent is recorded as early as the 1860s, but as sherry's popularity declined, fewer such casks were available to the whisky industry. However, since all but a tiny amount of the whisky made went into blends until the 1980s, the crucial influence of individual casks upon the flavour of the mature whisky was ignored, and casks were filled time and again until the wood was thoroughly exhausted.

The availability of European oak ex-sherry casks was dealt a further blow in 1983, when the practice of shipping in bulk was prohibited by the European Economic Community, which made ex-sherry casks very expensive – around five times as expensive as ex-Bourbon casks. Whisky companies that want European casks now have to buy their wood 'on the tree', have it staved and coopered in Spain, and make special arrangements with Spanish *bodegas* (wineries) to have them 'seasoned' with sherry before they are shipped. Currently, only around five percent of the wood coming into the system is European oak.

The vast increase in production of Scotch whisky since the Second World War has been made possible by the availability of American oak: ex-Bourbon barrels. These were almost unknown pre-1946, and their availability in large numbers since that date is simply explained. Shortly before the outbreak of the war, (I think it was 1936) the American coopers' unions brokered a deal with the US distillers that whiskey must be filled into new wood if it was to be described as 'Bourbon', 'rye', etc.

The massive increase in international demand for Scotch was mirrored by a demand for American whiskey, so there were plenty of ex-Bourbon barrels available to the Scotch distillers. And they came cheap (although the price today is substantially greater).

Bourbon is matured in barrels holding around 200 litres. Some are shipped as such, and are termed 'American Standard Barrels' (ASBs). To save space on the ships transporting them, most are broken down into staves and labelled, and arrive in bundles called 'shooks'. In Scotland, they are reassembled in a slightly larger format (250 litres, by cannibalizing one barrel in three) as 're-made hogsheads'.

The first advertisement to add 'The Famous' to 'Grouse',
which appeared in 1897

The Influence on Flavour

As I have said, European oak casks add and subtract different flavours from American oak casks. The latter are higher in vanillin (sweet toffee, coconut notes) and lower in tannin (fruity, complex, astringent notes) than the former. Also, since American oak casks are charred, rather than toasted, they extract more sulphur compounds. And finally, since European casks are typically twice as big as American casks, they last longer and mature their contents more slowly: the smaller the cask, the greater the surface area exposed to the spirit, the more rapid the maturation.

In short, and notwithstanding the fact than most whisky matured before the war will have been filled into less active (i.e. refill casks), 'the whisky of the old days' was darker in colour, richer and drier to taste, more fragrant of scented wood (sandalwood, cedar), and often infused with sulphur notes. These deductions are confirmed by nosing and tasting old whiskies. Yet they are not necessarily better than the whiskies of our times. Many connoisseurs would argue that American white oak is the perfect vehicle for maturing Scotch whisky – fresher, sweeter, lighter – and I have tasted many examples which would support this argument.

CASK CAPACITIES

Cask Type	Gallons	Litres
Gorda *Also called 'bodega butt'; rare*	130	600
Butt	110	500
Puncheon	110–120	500–545
Hogshead *Also called 're-made hogshead' or 'dump hogshead'*	55	250
Barrel *Also called 'American Standard Barrel'*	40	200
Quarter *Also called 'firkin'*	9–10	45–80
Anker *Archaic*	8–10	c.40
Octave *Archaic*	5	22.5

THE BROKEN GLASS

*On receiving the poet on the quarter deck, His Majesty called
for a bottle of Highland whisky, and having drunk his health
in this national liquor, desired a glass to be filled for him.
Sir Walter, after draining his own bumper, made a request that
the King would condescend to bestow on him the glass out of
which he had just drunk his health; and this being granted,
the precious vessel was immediately wrapped up and carefully
deposited in what he conceived to be the safest part of his dress.*

*So he returned with it to Castle Street, but on reaching his
house he found a guest established there of a sort rather different
from the usual visitors of the time – the poet Crabbe. Scott
entering, wet and hurried, embraced the venerable man with
brotherly affection. The royal gift was forgotten – he sat down
beside Crabbe, and the glass was crushed to atoms. His scream
and gesture made his wife conclude that he had sat down on
a pair of scissors: but very little harm had been done except the
breaking of the glass of which he alone had been thinking.*

JOHN GIBSON LOCKHART,
MEMOIRS OF THE LIFE OF SIR WALTER SCOTT
(EDINBURGH, 1837–38)

Elsewhere in his Memoirs, J G Lockhart (1794–1854), who was Scott's son-in-law, makes the interesting observation that Sir Walter 'could never tell Madeira from Sherry' and considered Port to be a 'physic'. 'In truth, he liked no wines except sparkling Champagne and claret; but even as to this last he was no connoisseur; and sincerely preferred a tumbler of whisky-toddy to the most precious "liquid ruby" that ever flowed in the cup of a prince.'

Along with John Wilson (see page 129), Lockhart edited *Blackwood's Magazine* between 1817, when they took it over, and 1825, when he went to London to edit *The Quarterly Review*. He was the author of several novels and biographies of Napoleon and Burns, as well as Scott.

JARS AND PIGS

There's whiskey in the jar…

Whisky only began to be sold in bottles when blending became widespread, after 1860, and even in the heady days of the 'Whisky Boom' of the 1890s more was sold 'in bulk' – by the cask or stoneware jar – than as 'cased goods': i.e. by the bottle (or case of bottles). Right up until the Second World War, advertisements for well-known brands like *The Famous Grouse* still offered the whisky to private customers by the small cask, and you can still buy barrels (200 bulk litres) from Bruichladdich Distillery.

Early whisky casks had to be small enough to be transported on horseback or cart. They were generically called *ankers* – the word is Dutch, the term used throughout northern Europe – and held between eight and ten imperial gallons (thirty-six to forty-five litres). Larger casks were called hogsheads, a term first recorded in English in 1392, two years before the first written record of whisky-making in Scotland; these held around fifty gallons. The most common vessel for maturing whisky today is still the hogshead, now holding fifty-five gallons or 250 litres.

From the late eighteenth century, stoneware flagons or jars known as 'pigs' became a common method of purveying smaller quantities of whisky. Originally, these were imported from Germany and Holland, although pot-banks soon became established throughout Britain. Famous Scottish ones were Buchan of Portobello, near Edinburgh (which is still in business, and still makes whisky jars), Cochrane's, Govencraft, Port Dundas and Grosvenor Potteries, all in Glasgow.

Spirits merchants, publicans, hotels and wealthier private customers bought by the cask or jar and either bottled or decanted the contents themselves (this was the job of the butler or 'bottler'), or, in the case of pubs and taverns, filled the whisky into decorative ceramic casks and glass dispensers.

Spirits merchants, and many public houses kept supplies of smaller jars, jugs and bottles of quart, pint and half-pint capacities, which they filled and dispensed to customers. They were returnable, a charge being levied by the owner and paid back when they were returned.

Both pigs and small jars were branded by their owners – whether retailer, wholesaler, blending house or distillery – sometimes lavishly, using a process pioneered in the 1860s by Port Dundas Pottery called 'underglaze transfer printing'. About the same time 'liquid glazing' was discovered, whereby biscuit-ware was dipped into a vitreous solution prior to kilning, giving rise to the familiar cream body and dark-brown lining and upper parts of many pots. Previously, pots were glazed by simply throwing salt onto the kiln fire, a technique known as 'salt glazing', which gave rise to an overall brown glaze.

Stoneware whisky jars remained popular until well into the twentieth century, particularly for exporting whisky overseas. They were durable, especially when sheathed in wicker baskets, which larger jars usually were; the owner's name or trademark could be incorporated into the glaze, avoiding the need for paper labels, which were easily lost or damaged; and they were not subject to duty as cased goods were in some markets.

Whisky jars are much sought after by collectors, especially those which are attractively transfer-printed or embossed, or rare editions to commemorate events such as the Great Reform Act of 1830 (known as 'Reform Flasks') or Queen Victoria's Jubilee. There are thriving bottle-collectors clubs in the UK, the US, Canada, Australia, New Zealand and South Africa.

'The very essence of human bliss – a glass o' whisky'.
A portrait (1782) by John Kay of Thomas Fraser, an Edinburgh
street cleaner, whom he described as a 'natural' (i.e. simpleton)

A ROYAL PICNIC

*Further, this Earl gard make such provision for the
King, and his Mother, and the Embassador, that
they had all manner of meats, drinks, and delicates
that were to be gotten, at that time, in all Scotland,
either in burgh or land; that is to say, all kinds of
drink, as ale, beer, wine, both white and claret,
malvesy muskadel, Hippocras* aquavitae.

ROBERT LINDESAY OF PITSCOTTIE, 1528/29

This is from an account of a hunt on the Braes of Atholl in either 1528 or 1529, which appears in *The Historie and Chronicles of Scotland* by Robert Lindesay of Pitscottie (1530–1590). The king was James V (1513–1542), the father of Mary Queen of Scots; the queen was Mary of Guise; and the (English) 'Embassador' was Lord William Howard.

The reference to whisky (*aquavitae*) is one of only a few known from the sixteenth century, and indicates the transition from it being a medicine or tonic to being drunk for convivial purposes. 'Hippocras' was also used as a medicinal drink, usually made of wine mixed with spices such as ginger, cinnamon and sugar strained through a 'Hippocrates sleeve' or sieve. Hippocrates is, of course, the 'Father of Medicine' and the patron of physicians.

WHISKY BOTTLES

Glass bottles began to be used for holding wines and spirits in the mid-seventeenth century, but they were very expensive, so only the wealthy could afford them. They were used mainly as 'serving bottles' or decanters, rather than 'binning bottles' for storing wine in the cellar.

Glass pads, impressed with the owner's mark or coat of arms, were attached to each bottle, and the bottles themselves were taken to be filled by the wine merchant, or filled in their owners' cellar by the butler (i.e. 'bottler'). Within only a decade or so, the middle classes were also able to afford glass bottles; Samuel Pepys records in his diary of 1663 that he 'went to the Mitre' to see wine put into his 'crested bottles'.

The earliest glass bottles had spherical bodies and long, parallel necks, with a rim at the top to hold down the string that kept the stopper in place. They are known as 'shaft and globe' bottles. By 1700, the neck had begun to taper and the body to become compressed into what are now known as 'onion bottles'. They continued to be treasured, and in Scotland were commonly used as decanters for whisky in public houses. In the Highlands it was traditional to give them as marriage gifts, crudely engraved with the names of bride and groom, the date of the nuptials and even with an illustration of the event.

Between 1700 and 1720, the onion shape was sometimes exaggerated, so the body became wider than the height. Then, about 1720, the sides began to be flattened by rolling on a steel plate while the glass was cooling – a process called 'marvering' – in order to be able to rack them in the 'bins' of the cellar.

Early marvered bottles were 'mallet-shaped', where the straight sides tapered away from the base. Over the next twenty years, however, they became taller and more cylindrical, particularly after 1740, by which time the value of maturing wine in the bottle was becoming generally recognized. By mid-century, many wine and spirit merchants had created their own bottles, with their name or trademark pressed into the glass pad, which could be returned for refilling with whatever liquor was available.

The classic French wine-bottle shapes familiar to us today had evolved by about 1800. There was a huge growth in the number of glass factories in Bordeaux, particularly, which was producing around two million bottles a year by 1790. Bottles from this period can often be identified by a slight swelling around the base, caused by the glass sagging while the bottle cooled in an upright position.

Until 1821, bottles were free-blown, which meant that capacities and dimensions were not standardized. So when one reads of hearty drinkers of the late eighteenth century downing three or four or even six bottles of wine at a sitting (this seems to have been especially common among Scottish judges of the period, who habitually drank claret while sitting in judgement), it might be supposed that the bottles of their time were smaller than those of today. Not so. Research done in the Ashmolean Museum in Cambridge shows that the average bottle size was, if anything slightly larger than that of today.

In 1821, Henry Ricketts, a glass manufacturer in Bristol, patented a method of blowing bottles into three-piece moulds, which made it possible to standardize capacity and dimensions. Such moulds left seam marks (the way in which collectors identify them today), but during the 1850s, a process was developed to remove these by lining the mould with beeswax and sawdust, and turning the bottle as it was cooling.

Until about 1850, all wine and spirit bottles were made from so-called 'black' glass; in fact, it was very dark green or dark brown, owing to particles of iron in the sand used in the manufacturing process. Clear glass bottles and decanters were made, but they were taxed at eleven times the rate of black glass.

Indeed, owing to the Glass Tax, which was first introduced in England in 1699, then reimposed in 1746, bottles remained expensive, and continued to be hoarded and re-used until after 1847, when duty on glass was abolished. The earliest known 'whisky bottles', such as a Macallan bottled by the local grocer in Craigellachie in 1841 (and reproduced in facsimile in 2003), were re-used wine bottles. Even after the duty had been lifted and clear glass began to be used more, whisky-makers continued to favour green glass bottles, often with glass seals on their shoulders. VAT 69 continues this style of bottle.

Many whisky companies continued to fill their wares into small casks and stoneware jars and offered them for sale in bulk. It was not until 1887 that Josiah Arnall and Howard Ashley patented the first bottle-blowing machine, and this invention allowed bottled whisky really to take off. In the trade, bottled whisky was termed 'cased goods', since it was sold by the twelve-bottle lot packed into stout wooden cases – like top-quality wine today.

Bottled whisky, properly stoppered and sealed, was less liable to adulteration or dilution by unscrupulous publicans and spirits merchants than whisky sold in bulk. During the 1890s, cased goods became the commonest way for whisky to be sold, particularly in the off-trade.

The use of plastic (polyethylene) bottles, developed during the 1960s and adopted by soft-drinks manufacturers, has largely been eschewed by the whisky industry, except for miniatures supplied to airlines. These bottles are called PETs – not a reference to their diminutive size, but to the material they are made from: polyethylene terephthalate. Their clear advantage is weight, and they began to become commonplace in the 1990s. Concerns about shelf-life and contamination by oxygen or carbon dioxide have been addressed since 1999 by coating the outside of each bottle with an epoxy-amine-based inhibiting barrier.

BOTTLE CAPACITIES

As I have mentioned in relation to William Younger's examination of bottles from between 1660–1817 in the Ashmolean Museum, the capacity of wine (and therefore whisky) bottles remained relatively constant at around thirty fluid ounces during this period, in spite of bottles being free-blown. With the introduction of moulded bottles in the 1820s, however, it became much easier to standardize capacity, and this was soon fixed at 26⅔ fluid ounces (or one-sixteenth of a gallon, which is also equal to four-fifths of a US quart).

About 1900, this capacity was defined by law for a standard bottle, along with forty fluid ounces (equal to an imperial quart, or two pints), 13⅓ fluid ounces (half-bottle), 6⅔ fluid ounces (quarter bottle), 3⅓ fluid ounces (miniature). Brand-owners were not required to print the capacity on the label until after the Second World War, however, although some did. American capacities are slightly different. One US liquid pint = .832 imperial pint (twelve imperial fluid ounces). Whisky was commonly sold by the imperial quart (forty imperial fluid ounces) or by the 'reputed quart', four-fifths of a US quart or 26⅔ imperial fluid ounces.

Since January 1980 capacities have been expressed metrically on bottle labels, in line with the Système International d'Unités, when 26⅔ fluid ounces became 75cl, half bottles 37.5cl, quarter bottles 18.75cl and miniatures 5cl.

In 1992, the standard bottle size throughout the European Community was lowered to 70cl. The United States retains its (American) fluid ounces, with the 'reputed quart' remaining the standard bottle size (75cl). In Japan, both 75cl and 70cl bottles are acceptable.

GLASS: WHAT COLLECTORS ESTEEM

Age – free-blown and moulded (pre-1870) bottles have 'pontil marks' on their bases, created by the iron rod called a pontil, which was used to manipulate the molten glass.

Rarity – the fewer known examples, the more valuable the bottle will be.

Texture – variations in glass surface, number of bubbles in the glass, stretch marks, changes in colour.

Colour – unusual, dark or strong colours, or a colour which is rare for that kind of bottle.

Embossed – where bottles are embossed (uncommon in early whisky bottles), the clarity of the embossing, its heaviness (the heavier the better), its intricacy, and the interest of the design or words.

Shape – the aesthetic quality of some bottles.

Labels – any item with its original label, carton or box.

Contents – whisky collectors (as opposed to bottle collectors) are not interested in empty bottles!

It's a powerful solace for a man, the whisky...
Indeed it is a creature of infinite capacity...
There is nothing it cannot do. It warms the blood against
the chittering wind and refreshes you exhausted in the heat.
It can make you ill and yet it is a sovereign medicine in
sickness. It can exalt, so that a man sits with the so-called
immortals, careless of his kind, master for a time of his own
servile destiny. It can depress and humble him to crawl in
the excrement of his own miserable bowels of self-compassion.
It can sharpen a man's awareness of the world outside him
and of the specious prospects within him; and it can dull his
senses and his wits, equating him with the wormy clod
he is in fact. Without doubt it is an unpredictable,
multi-consequential intoxicant, imbuing its partakers with
manifold desires and proclivities: some to sleep and some to
bestir themselves; some to preach and some to blaspheme their
imagined creator; some to meditate and some to fornicate.
Much abused by its addicts and its traducers alike, it is a
complicated simple, the whisky, pure in essence but diverse in
effects; and against it none can prevail.

J P McCondach, 1983

The words opposite are spoken by the Reverend McAndrew, the sardonic central character of *The Channering Worm* (Canongate, 1983) by J P McCondach (1912-1997).

Jim McCondach was born and raised in Paisley, where he also spent his working life as a schoolteacher, latterly as principal of English at Paisley Grammar School. As well as the splendid *Channering Worm* – which must have shocked his friends and colleagues – he published *Reflections in a Clouded Mirror* (a collection of poems), and *The Unwilling Jacobite* (1996), a novel based upon broadcasts he had made for the BBC.

CORKS AND CAPS

The discovery of a fifth-century jug with a cork stopper in the Agora at Athens shows that the virtues of cork were known to the ancients, but this stopper was not tight-fitting, and the use of cork for long-term storage vessels was apparently unknown to the Greeks and Romans.

Cork is the bark of a species of oak, *Quercus suber*, which grows in southern Europe and North Africa (principally Spain and Portugal). It is stripped from the tree every eight or ten years for around 150 years, its quality improving each time.

It was not until the end of the seventeenth century that corks began to be widely used in northern Europe; prior to that time, bottles were stoppered with plugs of wood wrapped with paper or fabric 'bung cloths'. The development of the tight-fitting cork stopper was a major breakthrough, since it permitted wine to mature in the bottle. The wine writer Hugh Johnson says simply that it is 'the most important event in the history of fine wine'. By at least 1693, it was known that corked bottles must be stored on their sides, so that the cork was kept moist and did not shrink.

Driven Corks

Corks which fitted flush with the top of the bottle's neck were impossible until the invention of the corkscrew, which happened about the same time as the invention of the cork in question. In the 1690s, they were called 'bottle-screws', but became 'corkscrews' by the mid-eighteenth century.

Being able to seal a bottle securely was of great importance to the whisky industry as well as to the wine trade, not because the whisky could mature – it doesn't. Unlike wine, whisky remains relatively constant in a sealed bottle. But cork made it possible for the whisky maker or blender to guarantee the contents of the bottle.

When whisky was sold in bulk (see 'Jars & Pigs', page 158), it was easy for unscrupulous bar staff or spirits merchants to dilute or adulterate it; in truth, customers could never be certain they were receiving what they asked for. Furthermore, once the contents of the bottle could be guaranteed, it became possible to brand it and then to market it around the world.

STOPPER CORKS

The flush-fitting, driven cork, usually covered with a lead-foil capsule, was the only method of closing a bottle until the invention in 1913 of the replaceable 'stopper' cork by William Manera Bergius of William Teacher & Sons, the Glasgow whisky blender. Bergius was the eponymous William Teacher's grandson and became managing director of the firm when it incorporated in 1923. Highland Cream, the company's leading brand, was then advertised as the 'self-opening bottle' with the slogan: 'Bury the Corkscrew'. To allay fears that bottles sealed with replaceable corks were more easy to tamper with, the foil capsule used for driven corks was retained, often with a paper seal across it.

SCREW-CAPS

The next development was the screw-cap, originally made of aluminium, and sometimes of Bakelite, and pioneered by White Horse Distillers of Glasgow in 1926. The problem of tampering was addressed by fitting the usual foil capsule over the screw-cap, with a tape beneath it which tore open the capsule and revealed the cap. Such screw-caps were applied by hand, the bottle neck having a moulded glass thread.

A sales leaflet from White Horse announcing the invention summarizes its advantages as:

> *No corkscrew will be required. The Capsule tears off in a flash. The Cap is easy and quick to unscrew. Freedom from cork taint is assured, and no broken cork can enter the bottle. The lined Cap is absolutely airtight and therefore the Whisky remains in perfect condition.*

It is not surprising that White Horse was able to claim that sales of its whisky doubled in the six months following the screw-cap's introduction, although for a time the company continued to offer the blend with stopper corks as well, to satisfy more conservative customers.

LEVER CAPS AND JIGGER CAPS

The success of the screw-cap persuaded James Buchanan & Co, John Dewar & Sons and John Haig & Co to make a combined investigation into other available closures. The one they chose was the lever cap, made by the Kork-N-Seal Company, which was introduced for their brands by February 1928, and lasted for forty years. Barmaids called the lever-caps 'nail-breakers'!

In 1960, Whyte & Mackay of Glasgow introduced a larger plastic screw-cap called the 'jigger cap', which doubled as a measure or small cup. The company continued to use it for twenty-five years, and it was also adopted by Wm Teacher & Sons for its leading brand Highland Cream, between 1967–87.

Detail from an eighteenth-century engraving parodying
Johnson & Boswell's 1773 Tour of the Hebrides

Roll-on Pilfer-proof Caps

Also about 1960, a novel form of screw-cap was invented and quickly adopted by the whisky industry. It had the clumsy but self-explanatory name of 'Roll-On Pilfer-Proof' [ROPP], and remains the standard closure for blended whisky to this day. The manufacture of such caps was pioneered by United Closures and Plastics of Bridge of Allan, near Perth, which remains the primary supplier to the global spirits industry.[1]

The essential difference between the ROPP cap and the standard screw-cap is that the aluminium caps are issued to bottlers as blanks, their screw being created by machine on the bottling line. By doing this, it is possible to create a closure that has to be broken before the cap can be removed, the collar of the cap (an aluminium ring) being left around the neck of the bottle.

In spite of the obvious advantages of the ROPP, since the late 1980s the stopper cork has returned to favour, especially for malt whiskies and superior blends.

---

1) I am grateful to George Thomson and Ian McGregor of Crown UCP (the successor to United Closures and Plastics) for information about the ROPP cap.

BRANDING THE WATER OF LIFE

Until the late nineteenth century, there were few brands, and this was as true for whisky as for any other products. Retailers were supplied with goods in bulk; they weighed and measured them, packeted, poked, jarred and bottled, sometimes affixing their own labels, more often not. In some cases, retailers were supplied with labels by the producer of the goods, often with space for the retailer to overprint his own name.

Before 1847, glass was taxed (see 'Whisky Bottles', page 164), and clear glass was taxed at eleven times the rate of dark glass. Thus, bottles were precious and were hoarded. You took your own bottles to the wine merchant and had him fill them. Sometimes the bottles were embellished with your coat of arms or monogram in a glass seal on the shoulder.

Or you bought your wine or whisky by the small cask or earthenware jar and had your butler ('bottler') bottle it, or fill the decanters in the dining room. Whisky casks known as 'ankers' held eight to ten gallons; whisky jars, commonly called 'pigs', held from two pints to six gallons. You could still buy whisky like this in the 1950s.

QUALITY AND CONSISTENCY

In the days of bulk sales, quality and consistency were in the hands of the retailer, and this led to widespread adulteration in shops catering to the lower end of the market (as a select committee reported in 1855). Dried mashed potatoes, plaster of Paris or bone-dust was added to flour; horse-chestnut and sycamore leaves to tea; tallow and sheep's brains to butter, and so on. And with whisky, a pharmacopoeia of substances was used to disguise adulterated products, including 'sherry, shellac, tartaric and acetic acids, acetic ether, oil of wine, spirit of nitrous ether, glycerine and green tea', according to an investigation carried out in 1872 by the *North British Daily Mail*. Bottling, sealing and branding effectively took quality-control away from the retailer and gave it to the manufacturer – whether the product was whisky or soap powder, tea or jam.

Before you can 'brand', however, you must have a consistent and repeatable product. The brand-name acts in part as a guarantee that what you are buying has these qualities, wherever in the world you buy it. In relation to whisky, 'consistency' could only come about with the invention of vatted and blended whisky.

The reason for this is that every cask matures its contents in a slightly different way; each one is slightly different from the next, and even if it has been filled on the same day, the whisky each holds will be slightly (sometimes radically) different after three or five or ten years (see 'The Wood Makes the Whisky', page 140). In order for a single whisky to be the same, batch after batch, many casks must be vatted together to iron out any differences.

The bonded warehouses of Glenlivet Distillery, 1887

EARLY BLENDS

The first person to do this successfully on a large scale was Andrew Usher of Edinburgh, the agent for Glenlivet Highland malt whisky. An early notice in *The Edinburgh Star*, November 13, 1821, announces:

> *Andrew Usher & Co respectfully inform their customers and the public that their stock of spirits, wines, etc., is at present very extensive, and that they are daily receiving supplies of fine Highland whisky. They have just now on hand a few ankers of Glenlivit [sic] which in point of quality cannot be surpassed.*

By 1844, Ushers had developed its selling message and was advertising Glenlivet in London:

> *The Real Glenlivet Whisky. Matured in the bonded warehouses in Scotland. This whisky produced in the district of Glenlivet, upon the estate of His Grace the Duke of Richmond, in the Northern Highlands, and pronounced by all connoisseurs to be by far the purist and finest spirit made in any part of these dominions, is now, for the first time, publicly introduced into London, under the patronage of his Grace... By his Grace's permission, the Ducal arms, on the seal and label, will distinguish the Real Glenlivet from all others. Price 21s per gallon for cash.*

Ten years after this advertisement appeared (1853), Usher was vatting different casks and years of Glenlivet, in order to smooth out variations between one cask and the next, and to raise the quality of the whole by using some older whiskies. This was the first branded whisky: 'Usher's Old Vatted Glenlivet'. In 1860, following a change in the law which allowed the mixing of malt and grain whiskies before duty had to be paid, Usher (and others, such as Charles Mackinlay) began to produce 'blended whiskies'.

The mixing of whiskies from one distillery and another had long been practised by spirits dealers and publicans, but it had been done in a haphazard way, and mainly to 'cover' and add flavour to the fiery and comparatively bland – but cheap – Lowland grain whiskies (or vice versa: to reduce the impact of pungent malt whiskies). But before long it was realized that blends had a much broader appeal than malts, and this made it possible to achieve a consistent product batch after batch – a product which could be branded. This was a very significant development in the history of Scotch.

Most of the great whisky houses started as grocers. Or perhaps 'delicatessens' is closer – 'Italian Warehouses' was their contemporary name – selling exotic imported goods such as tea and coffee as well as wine and spirits. Many learned the skills of blending from mixing teas, cordials and wines. The foundations of most of these houses were laid during the early decades of the nineteenth century, although the whisky side did not take off until the 1870s, with the second generation.

For example, John Walker's Italian Warehouse was established in Kilmarnock in 1820, but it was his son Alexander who developed the whisky side in the 1860s, and his grandsons Alex and George who turned Johnnie Walker into a global brand.

John Dewar walked from the family croft near Aberfeldy in 1828 to work for a relative in the wine and spirit trade in Perth; his sons created and built Dewar's White Label in the 1880s.

William Teacher opened his first liquor shop in Glasgow in 1830, and by the 1850s, he owned a chain of respectable 'dram shops' and was producing his own blends of whisky. His sons, William II and Adam, developed Teacher's Highland Cream in the 1870s.

Arthur Bell became a salesman for a wine merchant in Perth in 1840, and was sole partner by 1865. His sons A K and Robert only began to use their father's name on their leading brand, Bell's Extra Special, around 1900.

The blending side of these whisky businesses was stimulated during the 1870s by the fashion for all things Scottish (led by Queen Victoria), by the dramatic improvement in communications (which allowed them to export their goods to England and abroad) and by the vine-louse *Phylloxera vastatrix* (aka 'the devastator') which arrived from America in 1863 and, over the next twenty-five years, exterminated most of the vineyards of Europe.

By the mid-1870s, phylloxera had reached the Cognac region, and Cognac became expensive and difficult to get. Yet Cognac (with soda) was the drink of the English middle classes. By this time, blended whisky (with soda) was ready to replace it. The key problems confronting the emerging Scotch whisky 'industry' by 1880 were thus 'acceptability' and 'respectability'.

ACCEPTABILITY

The opportunities presented by the new middle-class markets in England and overseas – starved of brandy or hankering for a taste of home – were immense. But the drink's historical association with rough Highland peasants, urban squalor, shebeens (unlicensed houses selling liquor) and drunkenness had to be overcome, as did its reputation for being 'hot and fiery', and having a 'bite' that was esteemed by aficionados but was not likely to appeal to those more used to brandy. In short, 'Whisky had hitherto been seen as a robust outdoor drink with perhaps some health-giving qualities, but it had an unfortunate association with the lower orders and therefore was quite unsuitable for the club or salon' (Colin McArthur).

The middle-class English sportsmen who had encountered whisky while on holiday in Scotland thought of it as an open-air drink, suitable for the hip-flask while stalking deer, shooting grouse or fishing for salmon, but certainly not to be admitted to the drawing room. As Winston Churchill, himself a great whisky enthusiast (Johnnie Walker Black Label was his brand), later recollected: 'My father would never have tasted Scotch, except on a moor or some other damp and dreary place. His generation drank brandy.'

Acceptability was closely linked to inconsistency. 'Londoners were often not sure what they were going to get when they ordered "Scotch", and when they got it they did not like it,' wrote James Buchanan, the pioneering whisky salesman and creator of Black & White.

'Scotch whisky of a drinkable sort was then a comparatively rare thing in England,' recollected the author Frank Boyd in 1920, 'and one still recalls the dreadful brass-cleaning concoctions which masqueraded under the style and name thereof.'

The solution, as these pioneering blenders recognized and acted upon, was to produce blends which were of higher quality and greater consistency, and more likely to appeal to the English palate: smoother, lighter, blander; the last, which would be deemed disparaging today, was considered to be a compliment and a selling point in the 1880s.

RESPECTABILITY AND BRANDING

The problem of respectability was addressed by branding, by advertising and by the tireless self-promotion of some of the leading figures in the whisky trade of the day, who loudly identified themselves (and their products) with 'High Society' and the mores of the English upper classes.

The most effective and most common way of achieving respectability by branding was simply for the blender to put his name on the label. Often this was writ large, so that the brand-owner's name was synonymous with the brand.

In other cases, brand names identified themselves with Scotland: either specific places (not necessary factual) – such as Dew of Ben Nevis, Dew of the Western Isles, Strathdon, Lorne Whisky, and the dozens of Glen This or Glen That – or with more general 'Scottishness' such as Johnnie Mac, Claymore, Roderick Dhu, Robbie Burns, Grand Old Ghillie, Spey Cast, Thistle, Scottish Arms, Highland Nectar, The Famous Grouse, and so on.

Such associations communicated on several levels. Grouse or Spey Cast, for example, made huntin'/shootin'/fishin' associations that would appeal to sportsmen. Highland Queen or Scottish Arms spoke of 'heritage'. And for an age fluent in the works of Sir Walter Scott, and in which Sir James Barrie could remark that 'a Scots accent is as good as a testimonial', the very fact of identifying a product with Scotland implied integrity.

Associating your brand with royalty was another way of bestowing distinction – Royal Arms, Royal Liqueur Whisky, King George IV, Queen Victoria, Queen Anne. Also, since the laws relating to claims such as 'As Drunk by Royalty and the Nobility' were looser than they are now, gullible consumers might be reassured. Further reassurance could be had from the testimonials of city and county analysts, attesting the purity and healthy properties of the blend. These were often attached as back labels to bottles of Scotch. Another popular and increasingly important way of achieving the same goal was to display medals and awards won at international exhibitions, either on the label or in the advertising or both. The supreme testimonial, of course, was the award of a royal warrant: from the monarch, the Prince of Wales, a royal duke, or even a foreign royal household. These were proudly displayed wherever possible.

The purity, wholesomeness and age of the contents of the bottle were often emphasized in the description on the label. In the early 1880s, many brands were content with 'Scotch Whisky', but by the late 1890s adjectives were piled up to reassure and add value: 'Extra Special', 'Fine Old', 'Finest Selected Old', 'Old Vatted Highland', 'Specially Selected Old Highland', 'Very Old Rare Liqueur'. Such descriptions did not necessarily bear any relation to the quality of the whisky, and even today there are no hard and fast rules about what entitles a whisky to call itself 'De Luxe' – a French term, unknown in the 1890s – or to attach to itself any other kind of superlative.

ADVERTISING

Early advertising capitalized on the association between Scotch and Scotland as much as branding did.

The prevailing idea was of Scotland as a mystic land of bens and glens, castles, clans and shaggy Highland cows – 'a delirious realm of the imagination in which the land itself, peopled by a noble race of bards, warriors and winsome lasses, exercised a magical, transformative sway over all who came there' (Murray Grigor).

Humour was often deployed, playing upon the popular stereotype of the Scot as a canny, parsimonious drunkard – albeit tough, brave and God-fearing. This image had been developed by *Punch* and other popular magazines since the 1860s and was enthusiastically adopted by the Scots themselves. Seventy-five percent of the jokes accepted from freelance contributors to *Punch* came from north of the Tweed.

King Edward's reign was also the age of Harry Lauder, the most popular comedian of the day, who built his act upon a grotesque parody of Scottishness. Although this might be an affront to contemporary Scots, we should bear in mind the millions of 'Jimmy hats' we produce each a year, not all of which are sold to tourists.

More commonly deployed – and key to the idea of gaining respectability with middle-class English and colonial drinkers – was to identify Scotch as an upper-crust choice. Increasingly in the 1890s (and continuing up to the Second World War), many advertisements depicted whisky being enjoyed by gentlemen in their clubs, or at the races, or on the shooting field. Military themes were common, especially during the Boer War and the First World War, and usually involving officers. A bizarre poster from 1900 promoting 'W S Philips & Co (of Carmarthen, Dundee and Glasgow), proprietors of 'My Own Glenlivet Scotch Whisky' and 'Prince's Own Highland Whisky', depicts six senior generals (Baden-Powell, Kitchener, Buller, Kekewich, White and Field Marshall Lord Roberts) enjoying the whisky at a table overlooked by a portrait of Queen Victoria, with the Home Fleet at anchor in the background.

The kilted Scottish soldier was highly respected by all levels of British and colonial society, from the Queen-Empress downwards, and an image of him, as well as being wonderfully colourful and universally recognizable, communicated glamour, heroism, honour, steadfastness and tradition: a perfect combination of male virtues, and a message which said to the male target audience 'If you drink this Scotch, you'll be just like him'.

A further theme was tradition and heritage, applied both to the product and the blending house; like any parvenu who has made good, blended Scotch was eager to show a long and distinguished pedigree. Haig's was able to claim to be 'the oldest distillers in the world', thanks to the family's forbear having been found distilling on the Sabbath in 1627. White Horse, or 'The Old Blended Whisky of the White Horse Cellar (Estab. 1742)' to give the full label description, claimed to be 'From the Original Recipe 1746'.

But the most successful of the lot was Dewar's. Its 'The Drink of Your Ancestors' campaign ran for years in magazines before it was turned into the first-ever film commercial for any product. In the print advertisements, an aristocratic gentleman in Highland evening dress (kilt, stiff shirt and white tie; the type has been splendidly described as 'that modern centaur who is a Scot from the waist down and an English gentleman from the waist up'!) is pouring a late-night

The Dewar's 'ancestors' campaign ran for years, capitalizing on the public's association between whisky and Scottish heritage. This ad dates from circa 1897

dram of Dewar's Whisky, unaware that the portraits of his 'ancestors' hanging behind him (a Highland warrior, a red-coated, kilted soldier and an early eighteenth century laird) have come to life and are eagerly reaching for the bottle in his hand. In the two-minute film, made in 1900, they climb out of their frames and dance crazily about in a parody of a reel, before climbing back into their pictures again.

In 1896, Dewar's acquired premises on the South Bank of the Thames, by Waterloo Bridge, which included a tall tower, formerly used for making lead shot (dropped molten from the tower to the river). By 1898, the tower had been embellished by the largest neon sign in the world: a Highlander, with his kilt blowing in the breeze, quaffing, day and night, glass after glass of Dewar's Whisky.

THE POWER OF BRANDING

By 1900, three companies had emerged as the leaders in the whisky trade: Walker's, Dewar's and Buchanan's. Johnnie Walker & Sons was the leader in both the home and export markets; then, after 1904, it began to lose the lead, so that by 1908 both Dewar's and Buchanan's had overtaken it at home and abroad.

What did the Walker brothers, Alex and George, do? In 1908, they registered the brand name 'Johnnie Walker' and the following year commissioned Tom Browne, a well-known artist of the day, to come up with an image depicting 'Johnnie', their grandfather. Browne personified him as a striding Regency buck, complete with cane and monocle – unlike any citizen of Kilmarnock in 1820, but, we are assured by Alex Walker, based on a portrait of the old boy. At the same time, one of the directors of the company came up with the line 'Born 1820. Still going strong', and the company began to use both the image and the line in its advertising.

Next came the packaging. Walker had been filling into quirky, rectangular bottles with slanting labels since the 1870s. By 1909, the range of brands had been rationalized as Extra Special Old Highland Whisky, Special Old Highland Whisky and Old Highland Whisky. Now these were 'colour-coded' with black, red and white labels, and people began to ask for the whisky by the colour of the label.

Johnnie Walker, 'The Striding Man', was the first globally recognized logotype, long before Coca-Cola, Shell or Mercedes Benz. Distinctive. Tasteful. Memorable. By 1910-11, Walker's sales showed 'an extraordinary increase', pushing the company back into the lead in both home and export markets.

This essay is based on a talk given to the Chartered Institute of Designers in September 2002

*A 1920 advertisement which advised Canadian drinkers
that 'You must not drown Johnnie Walker' – i.e., by pouring
on too much water*

THE AMBER GLASS
MEASURING COLOUR

The colour, hue or tint of whisky is measured by scientists with an instrument called a 'colourimeter'. The earliest colourimeter – and it remained in general use by the whisky industry until the late 1980s – was the 'Lovibond Tintometer'.

It is a simple affair. You load a test-tube sample of whisky into a light-box alongside a standard tint on a glass slide (or, more usually, a revolving disc of slides), look through a viewing tube and change the standard tint slides until you find one which matches the sample. Then you read off the number of the slide; they are traditionally calibrated on a scale of one to twenty (from light to dark).

The tintometer was invented in the 1860s by Joseph William Lovibond (1833–1918), but not manufactured by him until 1885, when he founded The Tintometer Company Limited, which still flourishes. He was born in Somerset and went to sea aged thirteen, took part briefly in the California gold rush, then returned to work in his father's brewery at Greenwich. His interest in colour began as a hobby; he was the first to realize that there were only three primary colours (red, yellow and blue) – not seven as was previously believed.

Lovibond developed his tintometer as a means of measuring quality in his father's brewery (which, in due course, he inherited), but he quickly adapted it to evaluating colour (and purity) in all kinds of other liquids and solids: oils, fats, tallow, dyes, blood, water… even leather, flour, fabrics, copper and steel. In a pamphlet he issued for the Royal Jubilee Exhibition, Manchester in 1887 he adds a charming footnote:

> *The measurement of colour is so novel, and is developing in such unexpected directions, that the Inventor is prepared to entertain any new application of its usefulness.*

Lovibond's tintometer has mostly been replaced by instruments termed photometers that measure the light absorption of the whisky. A light beam is shone through the sample liquid and then through a filter which limits the range of wavelengths that emerge beyond it. The beam is then collected by a photo-electric cell, which generates a signal and a reading.

COLOUR SCALES

Lovibond's scale was arbitrary. Tintometer Limited refers to a set of reference slides for the use of the whisky and beer industries as the Lovibond Series 52 (Brown) Scale. It has twenty-three glasses, running from pale gold to deep brown, calibrated one to twenty (three of the slides are fractions).

More recently, the Lovibond scale was replaced by the American Standard Beer Colour scale (ASBC), and this has now been partly replaced in Europe by the EBC colour scale, developed by the Institute of Brewing and the European Brewing Convention. This has a range of two to twenty-seven visual units (unit one is colourless, and if a sample falls beyond twenty-seven – e.g. concentrates or syrups – it can be diluted), and uses a photometric method based upon the light absorbence of beer.

Somewhat confusingly, but based upon light absorption, whisky companies use their own scales – typically one to twenty, one to fifty, or one to 100 (from pale to dark) – and these vary from company to company.

Classical viscimetrists (see 'Awakening the Serpent', page 210) discerned five 'cardinal hues' in whisky, termed 'Pellucid', 'Xanthic', 'Rubious', 'Ambrous' and 'Umbrous'. Straight from the still, whisky is gin-clear (i.e. 'pellucid'); its colour comes from chemical compounds in the oak casks in which it matures. American White Oak casks (in which around ninety percent of whisky is matured) lend a 'xanthic' hue (*xanthos* means 'yellow' in ancient Greek), while European oak casks tend to lend a deeper, 'ambrous' (i.e. amber-like) or 'umbrous' (i.e. brown) hue to their contents.

The casks are always 'second-hand', having first contained Bourbon or sherry, and sometimes rum or wine. The first time a cask is filled with whisky, the original incumbent may add a little of its own colour: for example, an oloroso sherry, port or red-wine cask may well add 'rubious' hues to the natural umbrous wood-tint. The more times a cask is filled with whisky, the less colour the wood will impart, even after many years.

So the degree of xanthic (or ambrous, rubious, etc) colour in a whisky tells you a great deal about the cask it has matured in: what kind of cask it has been drawn from (American/European), how often that cask has been used (first-fill/refill), the approximate age of the whisky, whether it was finished in a wine cask, etc. Through this observation, we can anticipate its flavour: a key component of the enjoyment of malt whisky.

Because the colour varies from cask to cask, it should vary from batch to batch when the whisky is bottled. Yet it doesn't. To standardize colour differences from batch to batch, the whisky industry has long been accustomed (and allowed by law) to adding small amounts of highly concentrated spirit caramel to the blending vat, typically around 1:2000 (.05 percent), although some cheaper blends may add considerably more.

The industry maintains that, at such low dilutions, it is odourless and tasteless. Much depends upon the character of the whisky to which the caramel colour has been added; pungent whiskies can take more, delicate whiskies less. But at higher concentrations, it is apparent, smelling of burnt sugar and bitter-sweet to taste. Yet some blenders maintain that it performs a key function in pulling together flavour in blends and improving smoothness and 'mouth-feel'.

Connoisseurs have long wondered about the addition of caramel. As long ago as 1969, Professor David Daiches, in his important book *Scotch Whisky*, wrote:

> *I have seen a skilled tintometer operator carefully working out the amount of caramel colouring that goes into an eight-year-old (a very light colour, this), a twelve-year-old (somewhat darker) and a twenty-year-old (darker still) blend, colouring the whisky according to its age to fool the consumer into believing that the darker is the older. They say that the sweet, gooey caramel stuff that goes into the whisky is in too insignificant proportions to affect the taste, but in the case of the darker-coloured whiskies I am not so sure.*

DESCRIBING COLOUR

The vocabulary used to describe the colour of whisky is imprecise and undefined – well beyond the accurate and objective remit of science. Since there are no rules, there is plenty of opportunity here to exercise the poetic imagination.

Metallic imagery is commonly used, for the simple reason that it communicates the lambent effulgence of whisky, often augmented by shades of amber. Unfortunately, we run out of appropriate metals about two-thirds of the way down the scale, Connoisseurs of wine will often draw comparisons with wines, or use the vocabulary of wine-tasting.

The descriptor is sometimes qualified by the addition of a secondary hue, usually referred to as 'lights' – as in 'pale gold with green lights'; 'polished copper with magenta lights' – and sometimes with other adjectives such as 'deep', 'mellow', 'dull', 'muted', 'lustrous', 'sparkling', 'brilliant', 'effulgent', etc.

A VOCABULARY OF WHISKY COLOURS

LOVIBOND	CARDINAL	TINTS	METALS	'WINES'
TINT SCALE	HUE			
00	**PELLUCID**	–	Silver	Gin-clear
01	**XANTHIC**	Oyster	Tarnished Silver	Vin Gris
02		Bisque	Electrum	Manzanilla
03		Ecru	Talmi Gold	Champagne
04		Flax	Pale Gold	Soave
05		Gamboge	9ct Gold	White Burgundy
06		Jonquil	Yellow Gold	Chardonnay
07		Deep straw	18ct Gold	Eiswein
08		Maize	Old Gold	Sauternes
09	**RUBIOUS**	Solferino	Rose-gold	Rosé
10	**AMBROUS**	Fulvous	Burnished Copper	Amontillado
11		Topaz	Pale Amber	Old Sauternes
12		Saffron	Amber	Australian Muscat
13		Ochre	Deep Amber	Old Madeira
14		Henna	Deep Copper	Old Bordeaux
15	**UMBROUS**	Auburn	Tarnished Copper	Old Burgundy
16		Chestnut	Bronze	Old Amontillado
17		Mahogany	–	Dry Oloroso
18		Old Oak-	–	Old Brown Sherry
19		Dusky	–	Stout
20		Fulginous	–	Porter

*Dewar's White Label Whisky destined for the White Star Line,
circa 1910. Dewar's White Label was served aboard the* Titanic
and the company's other great ships

AWAKENING THE SERPENT

The Science of Viscimetry, Now Lost

I suppose all of us who enjoy the contemplation of whisky in a glass might pompously be called viscimetrists, although few of us are aware of it. What was once as important for sages as considering the movement of the heavenly bodies or examining the spilled innards of goats is now all but forgotten. I have even heard one chemist refer to viscimetry as a 'lost science… as little understood at hepatoscopy or xylomancy', but, like the latter (dowsing or divination by the use of rods) it had (indeed has) its uses, and its influence upon the minds of our forbears cannot be denied.

First, some definitions. Viscimation is what happens when two liquids of different viscosity mix, creating eddies and visible threads or ribbons. These are referred to as viscimetric whorls. The capacity of a liquid to create such whorls is termed its viscimetric potential or index. The study of the phenomenon is called viscimetry.

The essential difference between viscosity and viscimetry is that in the former the flow is continuous – a steady fluid motion of particles, where the motion at a fixed point is always constant – while the latter is irregular and generally flows in spirals. Semantically, the difference is that 'viscous' derives from the Latin *viscosus*, sticky (also *viscum*: bird-lime), while 'viscimetry' derives from the Greek, *ixos*: mistletoe.

Viscimetric effects are not observable where the liquids involved are immiscible (e.g. oil and water), and although some such liquids may be made miscible by the addition of an emulsifier (e.g. soap), viscimation does not take place. This only happens when the liquids have synergy.

The most commonly observed instance of viscimetry is where water is added to spirituous alcohol, especially whisky, where the colour makes the effect more observable. Since time immemorial, whisky-drinkers have referred to the phenomenon as 'awakening the serpent', and it seems likely that the Japanese expression 'killing the snake' (i.e. getting drunk) derives from the same source. Although apparent in white spirits, the whorls are less obvious, and with grape-based spirits the effect is more 'cloudy', even to the degree of 'false viscimation' or 'pseudo-viscimation'.

The same happens when a whisky has been heavily tinted with spirit caramel, the only additive allowed within the legal definition of Scotch, and added for cosmetic reasons, so there are no colour variations between one bottling and the next. But the fact that heavy tinting leads to pseudo-viscimation encourages some enthusiasts to limit their use of viscimetry to judging how much caramel has been added. A valid use, but something of a party trick.

The higher the strength of the spirit, the longer viscimation will be observed, but a spirit's viscimetric potential is also governed by its 'texture' and viscosity. So the familiar tests of 'beading' and 'swirling', both crude measures of strength and viscosity, fall within the science of viscimetry.

If the stoppered bottle is vigorously shaken, and the froth thus created lingers and forms small, silver bubbles (the 'beads') on the surface of the liquid, the spirit will have a high viscimetric potential. No beading occurs below about fifty percent ABV, and for the beads to linger longer than a few seconds, the whisky must have good texture.

Likewise, if it is swirled in the glass (which should be a snifter or spirits nosing glass), and if the 'legs' which trickle down the sides of the glass (also called 'tears' or 'church windows') run slow and thick, the spirit has a high potential. If they run fast and skinny, it has a low potential. Brandy-drinkers are especially fond of swirling, perhaps because the glasses in which brandy is traditionally served lend themselves better to the practice. I have heard it said that the viscimetric whorls revolve clockwise in the Northern Hemisphere and anticlockwise south of the equator, but I have been unable to check this.

For the ancients, the science of viscimetry was a manifestation of the mystic spiral observable throughout nature and discovered in megalithic and neolithic monuments on every continent. In Scotland, the spiral is at the heart of Celtic decoration and architecture: from megalithic stone balls, via cup-and-ring marks to the flowering of Pictish stone- and metalwork in the middle of the first millennium, and later embracing the illuminated manuscripts of Iona and the sculptural and metalworking schools which flourished on Islay during the Lordship of the Isles.

The relationship between viscimetric whorls and Celtic spirals is made clear by two further links. First, the root of viscimetry in *ixos*, 'mistletoe', the mystic plant which grew upon the sacred oak-tree, called *drus* in P-Celtic and giving rise to *druid* 'the servant of the oak', who cut the mistletoe with a golden sickle. Second, the colloquial (but ancient) reference to 'awakening the serpent' makes a linguistic association with 'the Serpent Paths' or 'Dragon Currents' (more commonly called ley lines), which connected the sacred sites and tombs erected by druids and their shamanic antecedents in the British Isles, and by priests from Crete to China, Polynesia to Hawaii, Africa to Australia.

It seems likely that the Romans were introduced to spiral decoration during the conquest of Gaul and Britain. So far as I am aware, there is no evidence that they understood the mysticism that lay behind the patterns, although there is a suggestion that viscimetric whorls were ranked among the auspices by the College of Augurs during the Augustan era and used for purposes of divination.

These connections suggest that the discovery of distilling, and thus the possibility of observing viscimetric whorls, might have been many centuries earlier than is generally thought. The problem is the lack of evidence from classical authors, all of whom are silent on the subject. But there again, if distilling and viscimetry were ranked among the 'occult' sciences, a veil of silence will have been drawn over them, as with other forms of augury, other so-called 'occult' practices.

Before we drink, we peer at the viscimetric whorls – evanescent and timeless as the aurora borealis – and wonder. Perhaps it takes the mind of a mystic to comprehend their full implication, and nobody has expressed this vision better than William Blake, himself a leading viscimetrist, in his poem 'Milton', subtitled, significantly, 'Thro' a Glass Darkly':

> *The nature of infinity is this: That everything has its*
> *Own vortex, and when once a traveller thro' Eternity*
> *Has passed that Vortex, he perceives it roll backward behind*
> *His path, into a globe itself unfolding like a sun…*
> *Thus is the heaven a vortex pass'd already, and the earth*
> *A vortex not yet pass'd by the traveller through Eternity.*

Drinking the health of the Duke of Rothsay at the Festival of Highland Society, 1872

ROME WAS BUILT ON SEVEN HILLS, AND DUFFTOWN BUILT ON SEVEN STILLS

I knew one small town with seven distilleries and I knew an expert who could distinguish the seven by bouquet alone. These seven distilleries were in one mile of a Highland river; they used the same water, peat and malt, and the methods of brewing and distillation were identical, yet each spirit had its own individual bouquet. One, the best, mellowed perfectly in seven years; another, the least good, not a hundred yards away, was still liquid fire at the end of ten years.

MAURICE WALSH, 1950

Maurice Walsh (1891–1973) was an excise officer. He joined the service in 1901, and served all over Scotland, but particularly in distilleries on Speyside. Elsewhere in this memoir (which forms the introduction to J Marshall Robb's book *Scotch Whisky* (Edinburgh, 1950), he modestly writes that he cannot be called an expert, since he has only been acquainted with whisky for forty-nine years, 'and you need half a century at least to claim some knowledge'.

He was also a popular novelist, enjoying his first success with *The Key Above the Door* (1926), followed by many other romantic and humorous novels set in vividly described rural situations in Scotland and Ireland.

One of his short stories, *The Quiet Man*, became a cult movie (1950), starring John Wayne and Maureen O'Hara; another, *Trouble in the Glen* (1954), starred Orson Welles and Margaret Lockwood.

A ROSE BY ANY OTHER NAME...

Most of those who wrote about whisky in the past say that the proper way to drink it is straight, or with a dash of water, or with a glass of water on the side. They repeat the tired old saw: 'Whisky is the only other thing a Scotsman likes naked'.

This is nonsense. You should enjoy whisky however you like: straight, with ice, soda, lemonade, Coke, ginger ale. But for a full and proper *appreciation* of the drink, there are certain guidelines.

While enjoyment is principally to do with taste and effect, appreciation engages all our senses: sight, smell, taste, touch (i.e. texture), even, some would say, hearing.[1] This is why, in the trade, the procedure is termed 'sensory evaluation' or 'organoleptic assessment'. But of the five senses, far and away the most important for assessing whisky is smell.

---

1) I know a distillery manager who can tell the difference between whisky which has been chill-filtered and non-chill-filtered whisky by the sound it makes as it pours. There is also the undeniable sensory pleasure of cracking open or drawing the cork of a new bottle!

The Sense of Smell

Compared with sight and taste, our sense of smell is infinitely more sensitive.

- While there are only three primary colours (blue, red and yellow, from which we construct our entire visual universe) and four primary tastes (sweet, sour, salty and bitter; a fifth one, *umami*, a sweet/sour flavour associated with monosodium glutimate, is also sometimes accepted as a primary), it has been estimated that there are thirty-two primary aromas.

- While we are equipped with around 9,000 taste buds, we have between fifty and 100 million olfactory receptors.

- We can detect odours in minuscule amounts: commonly in parts per million, in some compounds in parts per billion, and in certain chemicals (some of them found in whisky) in parts per trillion. To grasp the enormity of this, it is useful to think in terms of time: one part per million is equal to 10.5 minutes in twenty years; one part per billion to 10.5 minutes in 20,000 years; and one part per trillion to 10.5 minutes in 20,000,000 years!

CONGENERS

The volatile, odour-bearing chemical compounds found in whisky (and other liquids) are called congeners (congenerics in America). Sensory scientists have identified over 300 in whisky, and they suspect there are as many again which have still to be isolated and described.[2]

It is these congeners that allow us to distinguish one whisky from another – and whisky from brandy or vodka or wine – yet they make up only .3 percent of the contents (the remainder being water and ethyl alcohol, both of which are odourless). This is equivalent to the depth of the meniscus in the neck of an unopened 70cl bottle. Vodka, a much purer (and therefore less aromatic) spirit than whisky, contains only .03 percent congeners, yet we can still distinguish one vodka from another by its smell.

2) Coincidentally, it is reckoned that there are around 300 volatile odour-bearing compounds in human scent – a personal olfactory signature, picked up by sniffer dogs.

EMOTION AND DESCRIPTION

Smell is collected by receptors in the olfactory epithelium, a mucous-covered patch above and behind the nose, which traps odour molecules and sends messages to the brain via the olfactory nerves. It is not known precisely how these receptors work, but the neural pathways from the olfactory epithelium connect directly to the lower brain without being mediated by other receptor cells (as with taste buds).

The lower brain was among the earliest parts of the brain to evolve, and includes the limbic system: the seat of our emotions. Perhaps this is why smell is the most evocative of our senses and the most closely related to memory.

Scents can bring feelings and images flooding back in vivid detail. The smells of childhood Christmases (the piney smell of the tree, raw and cooked Christmas cake, mince pies, spices, mulled wine, candles), the smells of school-days (floor polish, disinfectant, chalk, sweat, carbolic soap, sweets of all kinds), the smells of Guy Fawke's Night (fireworks, cordite, wood smoke), traditional household smells (cooking and baking, wax polish, cleaning products, coal or wood fires), smells associated with foreign holidays (markets and bazaars, foreign food, hot sand, tropical forests).

Barbecues and parties; flowers and perfumes; tobacco, car interiors, seaside smells, country smells, pleasant and unpleasant smells – even smells you have never smelled before. Among the many remarkable attributes of smell is that we can identify smells we have never encountered, although we may have difficulty in describing them.

Putting words to smells is often difficult and takes practice, but it is hugely rewarding, since the very attempt to isolate and identify an odour focuses the mind, raises awareness and stimulates appreciation. It is also an essential part of the fun of enjoying whisky (or wine) with friends.

There is no fixed whisky vocabulary – even less of one than there is for wine, which connoisseurs have been trying to describe for far longer. Yet the words used will tend to be dictated by the audience and the purpose of the communication, and arise from both objective and subjective analysis.

OBJECTIVE ANALYSIS

Objective analysis sets out to describe only 'what is there', limiting, as far as possible, the interpretive faculties of the person or panel doing the analysis. This is the kind of analysis done in the laboratories of whisky companies, and since the audience for such communications are colleagues, the vocabulary used is very limited and often derived from chemistry.

It is not necessarily descriptive; those with responsibility for assessing the quality and consistency of whisky need only to be certain that they are singing from the same hymn-sheet – not that their language means anything to outsiders. Thus, when they describe a sample as 'grassy' or 'smoky', they must be certain only that they all mean the same thing, even though these descriptors might not be the words that immediately spring to mind if outsiders are smelling the same samples. The vocabulary varies slightly from company to company. As an example, here is a list of the words used by Diageo's sensory experts to describe the character of new-make spirit:

Butyric, Clean, Grassy, Green, Fruity, Meaty, Metallic, Nutty, Oily, Perfumed, Peaty, Spicy, Sulphury, Sweet, Vegetable, Waxy.

Subjective Analysis

Subjective analysis gives free rein to the experience, imagination and recollection of the individual, limited only by the opinion of the rest of the panel.

The language is descriptive and figurative; it abounds in similes (which compare one aroma with another: 'smells like old socks', 'reminiscent of petrol') and metaphors (where an aroma is described in terms of what it resembles, not what it actually is: 'wood-smoke and lavender' or 'distant bonfire on a weed-strewn beach').

It also makes use of abstract terms, such as smooth, clean, fresh, coarse, heavy, light, rich, mellow, young, etc, and these, usefully, give rise to contrasting pairs: 'smooth/rough', 'clean/dirty', 'fresh/stale', etc. But often abstract terms are relative ('smooth compared with what?') and sometimes double meanings are possible ('young' = immature; 'young' = supple, lithe, well-shaped). In general, abstract terms are useful for overall impressions – the general style and character of a whisky, its 'construction' and quality – rather than for describing specific aromas.

The language of subjective analysis can also be rhetorical – used to persuade or sell – but the effectiveness of the rhetoric depends upon the audience's understanding of the allusion. There is no point in describing a whisky as 'minty as a box of After-Eights' to a customer who is unfamiliar with these chocolates.

CHEMICAL FOUNDATIONS

Smells have an objective existence as volatile aroma-bearing molecules; they are not figments of our imagination. We are all similarly equipped to identify them, although some of us are more sensitive to certain aromas than others, and some suffer from a degree of 'odour blindness', called 'specific anosmia' (total anosmia is rare).

Our noses are the ultimate arbiters of quality in whisky, and although there are expensive scientific instruments available to help quality-control departments with their objective analyses,[3] no device has yet been invented which is as sensitive as the human nose. Sensory chemists acknowledge the supremacy of the nose, and sometimes think of it as a 'human instrument' which can be trained and calibrated. But the calibrations are of our own making when it comes to purely subjective analysis. The fact that scents are founded in chemistry provides a scientific basis for objective descriptors, but is also validates subjective descriptions and figurative language.

At its best, the language used to describe the aroma and flavour of whisky is both colourful and objective; at worst, it is marketing hyperbole, bearing little relationship to the product described. Increasingly, the tasting notes addressed to connoisseurs (such as members of the Scotch Malt Whisky Society), or to customers buying from reputable specialist retailers and independent bottlers, are detailed, accurate and helpful, while also being entertaining and appetizing.

---

3) These instruments are called gas chromatographs. They register smells by measuring the amounts of volatile compounds present in a sample and communicate the information graphically.

Mortlach Distillery, Dufftown, Banffshire, circa 1887

GOOD TASTE

I pass on to another kind of enemy, the men who drink whisky. With pain, and not without a hope that they may yet be saved, let us number their sins. Foremost among these is that they drink not for the pleasure of drinking nor for any merits of flavour or bouquet which the whisky may possess, but simply in order to obtain a certain physical effect. They regard whisky not as a beverage, but as a drug. Not as an end, but as a means to an end. It is, indeed, a heresy of the darker sort, doubly to be condemned in that it lends a sad, superficial plausibility to the sneers of the precious. Whisky suffers its worst insults at the hands of the swillers, the drinkers-to-get-drunk who have not organs of taste and smell in them but only gauges of alcoholic content, the boozers, the 'let's-have-a-spot' and 'make-it-a-quick-one' gentry, and all the rest who dwell in a darkness where there are no whiskies but only whisky — and, of course, soda.

…As a result there has been a tendency to abolish whisky from the table of the connoisseur to the saloon bar and the golf-club smoke-room. The notion that we can possibly develop a palate for whisky is guaranteed to produce a smile of derision in any company except that of a few Scottish lairds, farmers, gamekeepers, and bailies, relics of a vanished age of gold when the vintages of the north had their students and lovers.

AENEAS MACDONALD, *WHISKY* (EDINBURGH 1930)

This interesting polemic reveals the state of popular appreciation of Scotch in 1930. Its author is mysterious. His contemporaries (Neil Gunn, Maurice Walsh, etc) had a very high regard for *Whisky* – his only book, so far as I am aware. It also influenced the next generation (Sir Robert Bruce-Lockhart, Professor Daiches, Professor McDowell), but nothing is known about MacDonald himself. His knowledge of the whisky industry is so accurate that he may well have been an excise man himself, or a distiller. I have it on good authority that 'Aeneas MacDonald' is a pseudonym.

THE THREE STAGES
OF INTOXICATION

Grades or measures of drunkenness are acknowledged and colourfully described in Scotland. Even our courts recognize the difference between one stage of intoxication and the next. Defences such as 'Ah, wiz fu, but no' that fu' or 'my client had taken only a slight refreshment' are familiar, and have succeeded. Indeed, in 1942, Lord Justice Clerk Cooper opined from the bench that 'the words "in a state of intoxication" *prima facie* suggest a condition graver and more extreme than that which is suggested by words such as "drunk" or "under the influence of drink", and it is desirable that that distinction should be kept clearly in view for the purposes of prosecutions based upon an alleged breach of [such] condition'.

The fullest and most colourful treatment of 'degrees of intoxication' I have come across is an unpublished memoir by one William Grant Stewart, who was brought up in a public house at Tomintoul on Speyside during the 1820s. Tomintoul is one of the highest villages in Scotland, and is well-known to listeners of BBC Radio 4 for invariably being the first to be cut off by snow drifts. I have been unable to find out anything about William Grant Stewart, but he supported his own recollections of life in the inn with the observations of one whom he describes as 'a late ingenious Highland physician', and this sage perceived three stages of drunkenness, which he described as 'Blythe', 'Bosky' and 'Borajo'.

Under the influence of the first bottle, the Blythe stage of excitement begins with an increase of heat, muscular strength and accelerated circulation, animated countenance; vivid powers of imagination, and an easy flow of wit and humour... Daily cares are left behind... And now and anon is heard a Gaelic song.

As the drinking continues [with bottle number two], the party verges on intoxication. Repetition of toasts; the vacant laugh and incoherent exclamation, mingled with emphatic oaths, perpetually burst upon the ear of the auditory. Noise and ribaldry usurp the place of mirth. It is at this stage that quarrelling and fighting generally take place. Construing some casual remark

> as an insult, a violent collie-shangie or altercation
> ensues. This is the 'Bosky' stage...
>
> [With bottle number three] all excessive excitement is
> followed by a corresponding collapse, the operators by
> degrees sink into a state of lethargy, or at best their
> exclamations are incoherent and confused, muttering
> unintelligible soliloquies; these subsiding efforts of the
> imagination soon subsiding into a state of profound
> somnolency, accompanied by snoring or stertorous
> sound. The drinker is now in the third or 'Borajo'
> state, or what is commonly called 'dead drunk'.

The words used by Mr Stewart's mentor to describe
the three stages are interesting. 'Blythe' is simply the
Old English 'blithe': joyful, cheerful, gay (in its original
usage). 'Bosky' derives from *boscus*, Latin for bush, via
the Middle English *busk* and *busch* (also meaning bush).
So in its usual meaning bosky is 'bushy – a thicket'.
It does, however appear in William Cope's *Glossary of
Hampshire Words and Phrases* (1883) as 'elated with
liquor', which leads me to conclude that the good
physician was a Hampshire man.

His use of *borajo*, Old Spanish for 'drunk' (the contemporary Spanish is *boracho*) to describe the extreme

stage of intoxication is inexplicable. In truth, polite Spanish has only a handful of words to describe intoxication. Italian and Greek have even fewer, and I read in a learned Canadian journal, the name of which escapes me, that Yiddish has only one. The article in question was in praise of Latin and Jewish moderation. The Scots tongue, by contrast, has dozens, and it is instructive to translate Mr Stewart's 'Three Stages' into demotic contemporary Scots.

In Scots, the 'Blythe' period would usually be referred to as 'fu', where the drinker is seen as a container of finite capacity beyond which the contents are likely to spill. This is similar to the English expression 'tanked up'. Equally widespread is 'bevvied', which is what happens when you consume lots of 'bevvy' (i.e. beverage), but also a corruption of the French *bouvoire* (to drink) and a recollection of *La Vieille Alliance*.

'Pished' is another familiar descriptive term for the first level of euphoria, perhaps describing the diuretic effect of alcohol. In spite of the enormous Scottish influence in the US, Americans look at you strangely if you use the word as a synonym for 'mildly drunk', since 'pissed' means irritated (i.e. 'pissed off') in America.

Some parts of Scotland vary 'pished' with 'bladdered', or 'pure bladdered', but this is not to be confused with the more common expression, 'blootered', its diminutive 'plootered', or its extreme 'a mental blooter', all of which come from football: to blooter is to 'kick hard', as in 'blooter yir windae in wi the baw'.[1] The words are applied to excess generally, however, and particularly in relation to the consumption of alcohol.

'Miraculous' (pronounced in Glasgow 'marockyoolus' and sometimes abbreviated to 'maroc' or 'pure maroc') is a joyful description of the blythe state of mind, as is 'puggled' or 'half-puggled', which is usually applied to a 'foolish, clumsy or giggly' condition. The latter descriptors derive from the colourful term 'fu as a puggie' – 'puggie' being Scots for a piggie bank, a jackpot or a pool in cards. It is also a monkey, though this begs the question why poor monkeys should be considered 'fu'.

Then there is 'steamin', also 'steamboats' (as in 'he wuz steamboats'), perhaps a reference to the increased body

---

1) Stephen Mulrine, *The Coming of the Wee Malkies* (1937), included in *Voices of Our Time*, Ed. Maurice Lindsay (Edinburgh, 1971)

heat referred to by Mr Stewart, although a recent article in *The Scotsman* made a connection between this usage and the immemorial custom of Clyde steamers opening their bars as soon as they put to sea. In turn, 'steamboats' gives rise to a 'steamer' (i.e. a drinking bout) and 'reekin', or the more oblique 'lummed up' ('lum' being a chimney or funnel, which 'reeks', steams or smokes).

'Fleein' (i.e. 'flying') is clearly within the happy or lively stage, as is 'hauf-scooped' (curiously, the term 'scooped', as in 'fully scooped', is unknown), while 'stottin' (pronounced *stoatin*: staggering; literally 'bouncing' or 'reeling') and its interesting derivative 'stotious' (pronounced *stoshus*) indicate a transition to the bosky condition.

Here we encounter a clutch of expressions which graphically depict the reveller as 'birlin' (spinning), 'wellied' (the reference here is to Wellington boots, now difficult to walk in, possibly owing to an accident connected to the aforementioned diuretic properties of alcohol) or 'skooshed'. The last seems to have joined the lexicon when lemonade or soda water became popular mixers; 'skoosh' is a Scots term for both. An earlier term is 'skelped' – a 'skelp' is a sharp blow to the side of the head ('just you shut yer mooth, or I'll gie yoos a skelp') and derives from the Gaelic *sgailc*, a morning dram. 'A man of the Hebrides,' wrote Dr Johnson, 'as soon as he appears in the morning swallows a glass of whisky; yet they are not a drunken race, at least I never was present at much intemperance; but no man is so abstemious as to refuse the morning dram, which they call a *skalk*.'

Then there is a clutch of words which graphically describe a condition of being out of control: 'destroyed', 'smashed', 'banjaxed' (this is Irish in origin; *Chambers Dictionary* suggests it is an elision of 'bang' and 'smashed'), 'bazooka'd', 'blitzed', 'numb', 'wastit' – or just plain 'ridiculous'.

'Guttered', a jocular reference to falling down in or having to crawl home via the gutter, may be seen as the transition to the final, borajo stage of drunkenness. Now the drinker is 'paralytic' (pronounced *paralettic* in Glasgow) or 'legless', an incapable, falling–down condition;[2]

---

2) On the west coast of Scotland it is maintained that the expression 'Legless in Glesga' inspired the title of Aldous Huxley's well-known book *Eyeless in Gaza* (193?), rather than John Milton's work of the same name. It is not known whether Milton ever visited Glasgow.

'mortal', as in 'mortally pished' (also 'mortalled'; surely a reference to 'mortally wounded'); 'gutted' (evacuated, like a gutted fish), 'oot the box' or simply 'oot o' it' (it is debated whether 'box' here is 'brain' or 'coffin' – a related synonym is 'cased'). He may even 'take a whitey' (go deathly pale, prior to vomiting... or worse).

We may smile at such colourful descriptions, but I need hardly remind you, Dear Reader, that the three stages of intoxication are in direct correlation to the three phases of hangover: firstly, 'Fragile'; secondly, 'Very ill' and thirdly, 'Half dead'.

As ye sew, so shall ye reap!

This essay was first delivered to the Speculative Society, March 1998

A drunken Tam O'Shanter, as portrayed in Robert Burns's poem of 1790, escapes the witches by crossing the Brig O'Doon on his horse Meg

APPENDIX I
THE CLASSIFICATION OF MALT WHISKIES

This blender's list from September 1974 demonstrates how malt and grain whiskies were considered from a blending perspective. The spellings have been left per the original list. All bear the names of the distillery which made them, except the following:

Glen Craig was made at Glenburgie Distillery (1958–81), Mosstowie at Miltonduff Distillery (1956–81) and Lomond at Dumbarton Distillery (1959–91), all on Lomond stills.

Inverleven was a malt distillery within Dumbarton (grain whisky) Distillery (1959–91). Killyloch was within Moffat (grain whisky) Distillery (1965–85) and Kinclaith within Strathclyde (grain whisky) Distillery (1958–77).

Dumbuck and Dunglass were short-lived (1967) experimental malts, the former heavily peated, the latter with no peating, from Littlemill Distillery.

Ledaig is still being made at Tobermory Distillery, Inchmurrin and Rosdhu at Loch Lomond Distillery.

Glenisla-Glenlivet was an old name for Strathmill Distillery.

OBSERVATIONS

* All the top-class malts are Speysides.
* All the second-class malts are Speysides, apart from Highland Park, Talisker and (Royal) Lochnagar.
* The only Speyside malt to have disappeared since 1974 is Parkmore (distillery closed 1988); the make from the three other Speyside distilleries which have closed since 1974 (Dallas Dhu, Coleburn and Pittyvaich) is still available, although rare in the case of the first two.
* Since 1974, the axe has fallen on distilleries producing second- and third-class Highland malts and in the Lowlands.
* Although their malts were still available in 1974, four of the latter closed in the 1920s, as did Glencawdor (Nairn) and Towiemore (Botriphnie, Banff). Glenfyne (Ardrishaig) closed in 1937 and Strathdee (Aberdeen) in 1938.
* Seventeen Campbeltown distilleries also closed between 1920 and 1934, yet the only whiskies available to blenders in 1974 were from the two distilleries operating today.
* See page 248 for a complete list of distillery openings and closures since 1900.

HIGHLANDS

Top Class	1st Class	2nd Class	3rd Class
Aultmore	Balmenach	Aberfeldy	Balblair
Benrinnes	Balvenie	Aberlour	Ben Nevis
Cragganmore	Cardow	Ardmore	Benromach
Glen Elgin	Craigellachie	Banff★	Brechin★
Glen Grant	Dailuaine	Blair Athol	Edradour
Glenlivet	Glenburgie	Brackla	Fettercairn
Glenlossie	Glendronach	Clynelish	Glen Albyn
Glenrothes	Glenfarclas	Coleburn★	Glencawdor★
Linkwood	Glenfiddich	Convalmore★	Glengarioch
Longmorn	Glen Keith	Dallas Dhu★	Glenlochy★
Macallan	Highland Park	Dalmore	Glen Mhor★
Mortlach	Lochnagar	Dalwhinnie	Glen Turret
	Milton Duff	Dufftown	Glen Ugie★
	Mosstowie	Glenallachie	Imperial★
	Talisker	Glencadam★	Inchgower
	Caperdonich	Glendullan	Lochside★
	Benriach	Glenfyne★	Lomond★
	Strathisla	Glenglassaugh★	North Port★
	Tomintoul	Glen Moray	Scapa
		Glenmorangie	Speyside
		Glenspey	Strathdee★
		Glentauchers	Strathmore★
		Glenury★	Tomatin
		Knockando	Towiemore★
		Knockdhu	Tullibardine
		Macduff★	Ben Wyvis★
		Millburn★	Killyloch★
		Oban	Tamnavulin
		Ord	Dunglass★
		Parkmore★	Dumbuck★
		Pulteney	Inchmurrin
		Speyburn	Ledaig
		Strathmill	Braes of Glenlivet
		Tamdhu	Allt a' Bhainne
		Teaninich	
		Glen Craig★	
		Deanston	
		Rosdhu	
		Tormore	★ = distillery closed

LOWLANDS

Auchentoshan
Auchtermuchty★
Auchtertool★
Bankier★
Bladnoch
Glengoyne
Glenkinchie
Inverleven★
Kinclaith★
Linlithgow★
Littlemill★
Provanmill★
Rosebank★
Ladyburn★

CAMPBELTOWNS

Glen Scotia
Springbank

ISLAYS

Ardbeg
Bowmore
Bruichladdich
Bunnahabhain
Caol Ila
Jura
Lagavulin
Laphroaig
Glenisla★
Port Ellen★

GRAIN WHISKIES

Ben Nevis★
Caledonian★
Cambus★
Cameronbridge
Carsebridge★
Dumbarton★
Girvan
Invergordon
Lochside★
Montrose★
North British
North of Scotland★
Port Dundas
Strathclyde
Garnheath★

APPENDIX II
DISTILLERY OPENINGS AND
CLOSURES SINCE 1900

GRAIN DISTILLERIES 1900 TO PRESENT

14 distilleries closed
10 distilleries opened (7 of them now closed)

CLOSURES

Adelphi (1851–1902)
Dundashill (1899–1903)
Saucel (1855–1903, but malt
  distilling continued until 1915)
Ardgowan (1896–1907)
Camlachie (1834–1920)
Gartloch (1897–1921)
Bo'ness (1876–1925)
Yoker (1845–1927)
Montrose★ (1934–1964)
Strathmore (1957–1982)
Carsebridge (1852–1983;
  founded 1799 as a
  malt distillery)
Caledonian (1855–1987)
Cambus (1806– 1993)

OPENINGS

Strathclyde (1927–)
Dumbarton (1938– 2003)
Strathmore (1957–1982)
Invergordon (1959–)
Girvan (1963–)
Moffat (1965–1985)
Montrose★ (1934–1964)

★Montrose, aka Hillside or Glenesk, was
founded 1897, converted to grain
whisky production in 1934, and
reverted to malt whisky production
1964–1985

GRAIN DISTILLERIES CURRENTLY IN OPERATION

★Cameronbridge, Fife
Girvan, Ayrshire
Invergordon, Ross & Cromarty
★North British, Edinburgh
★Port Dundas, Glasgow
Strathclyde, Glasgow

★ *These founded pre-1900*

MALT DISTILLERIES 1900 TO PRESENT

C = Campbeltown; S = Speyside

1900–1920

14 distilleries closed
1 distillery opened

CLOSURES

Drumcaldie (1896-1903)
Ardgowan (1896-1908)
Nevis (1878-1908)
Bon Accord (1855-1910)
Grandtully (1825-1910)
Tambowie (1825-1910)
Auchnagie (1833-1911)
Benachie (1824-1915)
Devanha (1825-1915)
Glenaden (1882-1915)
Glentarras (1852-1915)
Greenock (1795-1915)
Langholm (1765-1915)
Clydesdale (1825-1919)

OPENINGS

Malt Mill (1908-1960,
within Lagavulin Distillery)

1920–1930
38 distilleries closed; no new distilleries

Camlachie, (1834-1920)
Kirkliston (1795-1920)
Annandale (1830-1920/21)
Dalaruan (C) (1825-1922)
Dean (1881-1922)
Provanmill (1815-1922)
Ardlussa (C) (1879-1923)
Argyll (C) (1844-1923)
Kintyre (C) (1825-1923)
Glenfoyle (1826-1923)
Glen Nevis (C) (1877-1923)
Burnside (C) (1825-1924)
Campbeltown (C) (1817-1924)
Dalintober (1832-1925)
Edinburgh, Sciennes (1849-1925)
Glengyle (C) (1873-1925)
Grange, Burntisland (1786-1925)
Hazelburn (C) (1796-1925)
Lochruan (C) (1835-1925)

Auchinblae (1896-1926)
Auchtermuchty (1829-1926)
Ben Wyvis (1879-1926)
Glenside (C) (1830-1926)
Glenskiach (1896-1926)
Isla (1851-1926)
Kinloch (C)(1823-1926)
Springside (C) (1830-1926)
Albyn (C)(1830-1927)
Auchtertool (1845-1927)
Ballechin (1810-1927)
Benmore (C)(1868-1927)
Glencawdor (1898-1927)
Bankier (1828-1928)
Lochhead (C) (1824-1928)
Stromness (1817-1928)
Stronachie (1900-1928)
Lochindaal (1829-1929)
Glencoull (1897-1929)

1930–1960
5 distilleries closed, 7 new distilleries

CLOSURES

Towiemore (1896-1930)
Parkmore (S) (1894-1931)
Riechlachan (C) (1825-1934)
Glenfyne (1831-1937)
Strathdee (1821-1938)

OPENINGS

Inverleven (1938-1991,
  within Dumbarton Distillery)
Tullibardine (1949-)
Speyside (S) (1955-)
Glen Keith (S)(1957-)
Kinclaith (1957/58-1976, within
Strathclyde Distillery)
Lochside (1957-1984)
Tormore (S) (1958-)

1960–1980

3 distilleries closed, 16 new distilleries

CLOSURES

Ladyburn (1966-1975, within
  Girvan Distillery)
Kinclaith (1957/58-1976)
Ben Wyvis (1965-1977, within
  Invergordon Distillery

OPENINGS

Macduff (1962-)
Tomintoul (S) (1964-)
Ben Wyvis (1965-1977)
Deanston (1965-)
Glen Flagler (1965-1985, within
Moffat Distillery)

Killyloch (1965-1985, within
  Moffat Distillery)
Lochlomond (1965-)
Tamnavulin (1965-)
Ladyburn (1966-1975)
Clynelish II (1967-)
Glenallachie (S) (1967-)
Mannochmore (S) (1971-)
Braes of Glenlivet (S) (1973-)
Auchroisk (S)(1974-)
Allt a'Bhainne (S) (1975-)
Pittyvaich (S) (1975-1993)

1980–present

22 distilleries closed, 7 new distilleries

CLOSURES

Dallas Dhu (S) (1899-1983)
Glen Albyn (1846-1983)
Glenlochy (1898-1983)
Glen Mhor (1892-1983)
Glenugie (1831-1983)
North Port (1820-1983)
Port Ellen (1825-1983)
St Magdalene, Linlithgow
  (1798-1983)
Lochside, Montrose (1957-1984)
Coleburn (S) (1897-1985)
Convalmore (S) (1894-1985)
Killyloch (1965-1985)
Glenesk, Hillside (1897-1985)
Glen Flagler (1965-1985)
Glenury Royal (1825-1985)
Millburn (1807-1985)

Glenglassaugh (1875-1986)
Inverleven (1938-1991)
Lomond (1959-1991)
Pittyvaich (S) (1975-1993)
Rosebank (1840-1993)
Littlemill (1772-1994)

OPENINGS

Kininvie (S) (1990-,
  within Glenfiddich Distillery)
Isle of Arran (1995-)
Glengyle (2004)
Ladybank (proposed 2004)
Blackford (proposed 2004)
Kilchoman (2004, under
  construction)
Barra (proposed 2004)

INDEX

Numbers in *italics* refer to illustrations.

DAILY
DEVOTIONS
for Men

365 INSPIRING READINGS

DAILY DEVOTIONS
for Men

365 INSPIRING READINGS

BARBOUR BOOKS
An Imprint of Barbour Publishing, Inc.

Compiled by Tracy Sumner.

ISBN 978-1-64352-461-0

Text compiled from *Daily Wisdom for Men* collections, published by Barbour Publishing, Inc.

Published by Barbour Books, an imprint of Barbour Publishing, Inc., 1810 Barbour Drive, Uhrichsville, Ohio 44683, www.barbourbooks.com

Our mission is to inspire the world with the life-changing message of the Bible.

Member of the
Evangelical Christian
Publishers Association

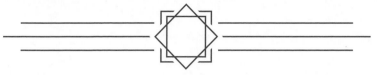

Thousands of years ago, a man of God wrote these words of praise for God and love for His written Word: "Your word is a lamp for my feet, a light on my path" (Psalm 119:105 NIV). Over several hundred years after that, God worked tirelessly to bring to us what we now call the Bible.

In many passages, the Bible tells us of the importance of reading, studying, and meditating on God's written Word. The writer of the epistle to the Hebrews wrote, "For the word of God is alive and active. Sharper than any double-edged sword, it penetrates even to dividing soul and spirit, joints and marrow; it judges the thoughts and attitudes of the heart" (4:12 NIV).

You probably already know how important it is to spend time reading the Bible. It's your source for everything you need to know to grow in your faith, to know God better, and to live in a way that pleases Him. But if you're like many men, it's not always easy to carve out time to read and study the Bible.

That's one of the purposes of this book, a collection of 365 scripture passages and writings (one for every day of the year) about how you can apply them. It is our hope that as you read the daily writings in this book, you'll feel encouraged, challenged, and comforted in the fact that God loves you so much that He gave you an amazing book called the Bible.

It's our prayer that as you take a few moments each day to meditate on the Lord and His Word, that you'll be drawn closer to Him and walk in His footsteps throughout the day. It's also our prayer that you'll be encouraged to spend even more time reading and learning from the Bible.

May the words in this book, and in the Bible itself, be a tremendous blessing to you—today and every day.

THE IMPORTANCE OF PREPARATION

Go to the ant, you sluggard; consider its ways and be wise!
It has no commander, no overseer or ruler, yet it stores its
provisions in summer and gathers its food at harvest.

PROVERBS 6:6–8 NIV

In the late 1980s and early 1990s, Mike Tyson was the most feared man in all of heavyweight professional boxing. But on February 11, 1990, a lightly regarded challenger named James "Buster" Douglas knocked out the then-undefeated (37–0) Tyson in the tenth round of a championship fight in Tokyo, Japan, to become world heavyweight champion.

Even the most casual sports enthusiasts still consider Douglas's win over Tyson one of the greatest upsets in sports history. But boxing insiders have since stated that Tyson lost, in large part, because he didn't take Douglas seriously and didn't train well for the fight. He didn't prepare properly.

The world is filled with supremely talented and gifted men who underachieved simply because they didn't put in the time and effort it took to accomplish big things. Among those men, sadly, are those God has called to do great things for His kingdom.

God has promised that He will give you everything you need to do the things He's called you to do. But that doesn't mean you shouldn't plan and prepare for what lies ahead. In fact, God calls you to do just that.

STRONG AND SILENT

*Don't make rash promises, and don't be hasty in
bringing matters before God. After all, God is in heaven,
and you are here on earth. So let your words be few.*
ECCLESIASTES 5:2 NLT

Many men need to be encouraged to speak up more—to communicate better and speak words of encouragement and endearment to their loved ones. But on other occasions there's a great deal to be said for being a man of few words.

You need to be especially careful when trying to resolve difficult problems. You're a limited mortal, and it's frequently impossible for you to be aware of all the bits of information that need to be factored into a decision. So tread carefully.

God "inhabits eternity" and says, "I dwell in the high and holy place" (Isaiah 57:15 NKJV). He is high above the earth and able to see all the pieces of the puzzle from His lofty vantage point, so cry out to Him to help you. Don't waste time trying to persuade God to go with *your* plan. Your plan might be doomed to failure from the onset.

When confused events swirl around you and deadlines loom, it will be very tempting to try to make a snap decision or to force a solution, but refrain from being impetuous. Don't commit yourself to a course of action until you're sure that *God* is in it.

A VALUABLE EMPLOYEE

*Be diligent to know the state of your flocks, and attend
to your herds; for riches are not forever, nor does
a crown endure to all generations.*
PROVERBS 27:23–24 NKJV

Shepherds need to be experts in the way their animals are bred, sheltered, fed, jugged (separated with their mother for a period after birth), mixed, weaned, dewormed, and even how they play if the shepherds want to make sure their animals thrive.

Just as shepherds need to be diligent about the state of their flocks, this scripture calls you to know the ins and outs of your occupation. You ought to know all of your industry terms and their nuances. As you grow and immerse yourself in your occupation, you should develop knowledge about what will work and what won't. This will make you a valuable asset to your employer, as well as give you some financial stability.

In so doing, you'll set yourself apart from other employees who are simply punching the clock to earn a living. A few of them might follow your example of diligence. Your boss will certainly take note at least. But most importantly, you'll be fulfilling your calling as set forth in Colossians 3:23–24 (NKJV): "And whatever you do, do it heartily, as to the Lord and not to men, knowing that from the Lord you will receive the reward of the inheritance; for you serve the Lord Christ."

THE RIGHT KIND OF PRIDE

I have spoken to you with great frankness; I take great pride in you.
I am greatly encouraged; in all our troubles my joy knows no bounds.
2 CORINTHIANS 7:4 NIV

Can you remember the last time you told a loved one or a friend or coworker "I'm proud of you!"? The word *pride* can make many Christians nervous because they know that God has stated repeatedly that He hates the sin of pride. But nowhere in the Bible are believers barred from speaking words of praise for a person who has done something well, and sometimes it's even fitting to use the word *proud* when you do so.

The apostle Paul gave voice to this expression of pride when he told the Christians in first-century Corinth, "I take great pride in you." The context of the apostle's kind words for the Corinthians was how they had handled an especially ugly incident of sexual immorality in their church.

There is absolutely nothing wrong with taking pride in a job well done or in the words or actions of our children or other loved ones. So when one of your children does something especially noteworthy (such as a great report card or an act of kindness toward another person) or when a coworker accomplishes something great at work, don't hesitate to let them know that you've noticed. You might even punctuate your recognition by telling them, "I'm proud of you!"

BEYOND THE BASICS

Let us stop going over the basic teachings about Christ again and
again. Let us go on instead and become mature in our understanding.
Surely we don't need to start again with the fundamental importance
of repenting from evil deeds and placing our faith in God.

HEBREWS 6:1 NLT

You don't expect a high school senior to act like a preschooler. Good fathers work to help their children grow up, demonstrate what age-appropriate behavior looks like, and help that child understand that adult maturity is the logical end result.

In the years following Jesus' time on earth, there were Christians who were satisfied to remain babies in their faith. There was much to learn, but they essentially said, "That's interesting, but tell us our favorite story again." Where there was history, psalms, law, and prophecy the people *could* have learned, they only wanted to hear their introduction to the faith over and over.

Christians can be guilty of the same thing today. Perhaps the struggle is that the more you know, the more responsibility you have for acting on that knowledge. The apostle Paul recalled his own struggle with this issue in 1 Corinthians 3:2 (NLT), writing, "I had to feed you with milk, not with solid food, because you weren't ready for anything stronger. And you still aren't ready."

God might need to nudge the complacent so they realize that growing up into a solid faith is a vital next step for every Christ follower.

EXCEED YOUR GRASP

But now they desire a better, that is, a heavenly country.
Therefore God is not ashamed to be called their God,
for He has prepared a city for them.
HEBREWS 11:16 NKJV

Some Christians have been accused of being so heavenly minded that they're no earthly good. While that may be so, without the promise of heaven's peace, justice, and reward to inspire you, putting all your hope in this world does you no eternal good. The poet Robert Browning was onto something when he wrote, "A man's reach should exceed his grasp, or what's a heaven for?"

When Joseph and Mary found their twelve-year-old son in the temple, He told them, "Why did you seek Me? Did you not know that I must be about My Father's business?" (Luke 2:49 NKJV). Through the parable of the minas, Jesus told His followers, "Do business till I come" (Luke 19:13 NKJV). The challenge is clear: do whatever you do with the ultimate goal of building God's kingdom.

The full impact of your work on earth is measured not in material wealth but spiritual. How have you used what God has given you to see souls saved? That effort starts at home, extends through the church, and goes out into the world, always with the objective of seeing as many as possible arrive at the wonderful home God has for them. If you look beyond the cares of this world, you can just see it.

ON THE BLEEDING EDGE

Have we not all one Father? Has not one God created us?
Why do we deal treacherously with one another. . .?
MALACHI 2:10 NKJV

On February 13, 1905, Teddy Roosevelt gave a stirring speech on race relations. The wounds of the Civil War and Reconstruction lingered between North and South, as did the question *When will every citizen be treated equally, regardless of color?* Though Roosevelt addressed primarily whites, exhorting compassion to all, his words did little to advance the conversation. To his credit, though, he nailed the issue at the end of his speech, quoting the wisdom of Solomon: "Righteousness exalts a nation, but sin condemns any people" (Proverbs 14:34 NIV).

Jesus died because God loved the whole world, and His blood unifies all believers in a family where no man-made distinctions apply (Galatians 3:28). When it comes to salvation, we all stand on the same ground: "For there is one God and one mediator between God and mankind, the man Christ Jesus, who gave himself as a ransom for all people" (1 Timothy 2:5–6 NIV).

Living that out, however, is much more complicated. That's the best reason for the church—and you as a Christian man—to take the lead in the discussion, modeling God's vision of equality, grace, and forgiveness. Start with prayer, and remember: the blood of Christ can unite us in ways that are beyond race and ethnicity.

HUMILITY'S FRIEND

True humility and fear of the Lord
lead to riches, honor, and long life.
Proverbs 22:4 NLT

Humility provides a correct view of who you are and the impressive power of God. Pride offends God, but humility brings unexpected benefits. There's wisdom in refusing pride, but humility doesn't seem logical when society promotes self-marketing. We often believe that if people don't know who we are, then we'll never get noticed and our talent will be wasted.

Humility promotes hard work with no demand for recognition, an advanced work ethic when no one's watching, and restful sleep because we've done our best. Humility doesn't refuse acknowledgment; it just doesn't chase it.

What Matthew 6:2, 4 (NLT) says runs parallel to humility: "When you give to someone in need, don't do as the hypocrites do—blowing trumpets in the synagogues and streets to call attention to their acts of charity! I tell you the truth, they have received all the reward they will ever get. . . . Give your gifts in private, and your Father, who sees everything, will reward you."

It's been said that humility isn't thinking less of yourself; it's not thinking of yourself at all. God knows what you do. He rewards you here or in heaven for acts of kindness and faithful service that don't seek a spotlight and don't demand applause. Humility refuses to do something positive in the name of God and then take all the credit for playing a supporting role.

FINISHING STRONG

*"I wholly followed the LORD my God. . . .
As yet I am as strong this day as on the day Moses sent me."*
JOSHUA 14:8, 11 NKJV

Following a five-decade career as a pitcher, Leroy "Satchel" Paige became the first Negro Leagues veteran to be nominated for the Hall of Fame on February 9, 1971. Paige broke into the majors in 1948 as a forty-two-year-old rookie and later pitched three innings at fifty-nine. Asked about his accomplishments at such an experienced age, Satchel famously quoted Mark Twain, "Age is a question of mind over matter. If you don't mind, it doesn't matter."

That's a statement Caleb, son of Jephunneh, would have fully embraced. As one of the advance spies Moses sent to scout the promised land, he brought back a report detailing the challenges but undergirded by his belief that God could handle whatever giants and walled cities awaited. Because of Israel's unbelief, he didn't get his chance to make good on God's promise until he was eighty-five years old.

But when the call to move into the land came, there he was, ready to take the battle to the enemy. Caleb knew that if God was with him, nothing could stop him, not fortified cities nor huge armies nor trick knees, cataracts, and high cholesterol. There are few things more inspiring than a godly man finishing strong, and it starts with the belief that God isn't done with you till He's done with you.

GOD IS THERE FOR YOU

*The righteous cry out, and the L*ORD
hears them; he delivers them from all their troubles.
PSALM 34:17 NIV

Those who have lived the Christian life for any length of time have likely had a good chance to learn an important lesson about a life of faith, namely, that God never promised that it would be easy or that there wouldn't be times of difficulty.

Indeed, any effort to find a scriptural promise telling us that the Christian life is a trouble-free life would end in frustration and failure. In fact, Jesus promised quite the opposite when He said, "In this world you will have trouble. But take heart! I have overcome the world" (John 16:33).

Yes, in this world, we're going to face times of trouble. But there is one promise God has made repeatedly in His written Word for believers facing times of difficulty. Time and time again, He tells us, "I'll be there for you."

God is our loving heavenly Father, and He's also a devoted Friend who is there for us in our times of greatest trouble. And not only that, He provides us all we need to emerge from the difficult times as overcomers.

With a Friend like Him, who needs . . . *anything else*?

REASON TO REJOICE

We can rejoice, too, when we run into problems and trials,
for we know that they help us develop endurance.
ROMANS 5:3 NLT

At various points in your life, you'll sit on the other side of the table from bad news. Sometimes, you'll see it coming, but more often than not, it'll ambush you, a single shot from a stun gun: *downsizing*, *accident*, *cancer*. Somehow, you press on, working through the immediate details as if from a distance, and it's only later, when you have a moment to breathe, that the grief comes on. You wrestle with the *whys* and the *what nexts* and begin to find out what you're made of.

Like a cup that's been filled to the brim with whatever you've poured into your heart over the course of your life, when a hard trial strikes, what's inside spills over. If you've habitually sown to the flesh, bitterness gushes out, blended with hopelessness. All your self-sufficiency comes to nothing, and you let God know how He has disappointed you.

But if you've habitually sown to the Spirit, it's different. Previous trials forced you to your knees, but that's where you found God waiting to comfort and strengthen you. You know that Paul wasn't just spouting some holy-sounding advice about tribulation, because you've seen the truth behind it: God uses trials to produce endurance, building character and producing hope. When hope spills over, you have reason to rejoice: God is with you.

ACTS OF KINDNESS

"If you lend money only to those who can repay you, why should you get credit? Even sinners will lend to other sinners for a full return."
Luke 6:34 NLT

Lending to relatives is generally considered a bad idea because hard feelings can develop when the loan isn't repaid. We're conditioned to believe good deeds *must* be repaid.

Jesus didn't seem to live by the phrase "You scratch my back and I'll scratch yours." While cooperation was important, His life, words, and deeds suggest a different phrase: "I'll scratch your back because it's itchy and I can reach it." To expect a return on your time investment suggests you believe in the *wages of deeds* instead of the *gift* of time, talent, and finances.

Certainly you're entitled to lend money and expect repayment, but the bank doesn't consider that same service a good deed. It's simply a loan. If you help a friend while expecting they'll help you in return, that's less a kindness than an agreement for mutually beneficial services.

In most cases, truly good deeds go unheralded and are rarely repaid. The idea of doing good without return means you'll do something for someone for a better reason. This concept is critical to understanding that Jesus paid the ultimate sacrifice to offer salvation. You can't pay for it, earn it, or return the favor. You simply have to accept the greatest intentional act of kindness mankind has ever known.

A GREATER VISION

*He made himself nothing by taking the very nature
of a servant, being made in human likeness.*
PHILIPPIANS 2:7 NIV

Though George Washington was elected America's first president in 1789, the most remarkable thing he ever did was *give up* his power. So potent were Washington's popularity and leadership that there was a public outcry that he remain president as long as he would.

His guidance of the nation in its infancy, however, was matched only by his desire to see it thrive beyond his life, and to do so, there needed to be a safe, stable transfer of power. It was unheard of to give up power—still true today!—especially when victory had been so hard fought for and won, but Washington had a bigger vision.

God had an even more impressive vision for all of mankind—a way to buy His people back from sin and its deprivations—and He had just the Man for the job. Where Washington gave up his office so that he could enjoy the fruits of his accomplishments (and justifiably so!), Jesus gave up His place in heaven at God's right hand to be bound by the frailty of flesh and blood, to have needs and urges, to face temptation and opposition and betrayal firsthand (unheard of!).

He fought your biggest foes—sin, death, and hell—to be able to adopt you as a son and brother.

OPEN YOUR HOME

God has given each of you a gift from his great variety
of spiritual gifts. Use them well to serve one another.
1 PETER 4:10 NLT

When Peter penned these words, the destruction of the Jewish temple and nation was at hand (1 Peter 4:7 NLT). With persecution imminent, Peter wanted believers to maintain their focus. He wanted them to be earnest and disciplined in their prayers while loving one another and opening their homes to one another (vv. 7–9). Finally, they were to serve one another by using the spiritual gifts that God had given them.

Are you concerned that the end of the American church and nation may be at hand? Are you angry about it—getting caught up in heated political exchanges, sometimes even with fellow believers? Is your bitterness poisoning your heart, affecting your attitude, and rendering you ineffective in your witness? Listen to Peter's advice. Open your home to fellow believers. Pray with them. Study with them. Laugh with them. Weep with them. Serve them using your spiritual gifts.

If you aren't sure about your spiritual gifting, talk to a leader at church to help you identify it. And then begin to exercise it. You'll notice a difference in your attitude as you minister to fellow saints. And you'll make a greater impact for the kingdom of God as unbelievers see your love for other believers in action.

A PLACE TO SIT

And seeing the multitudes, He went up on a mountain,
and when He was seated His disciples came to Him.
Then He opened His mouth and taught them.
MATTHEW 5:1–2 NKJV

When we think of the Sermon on the Mount, we picture Jesus (as Hollywood has coached us) perched on a high rock up in the hills, teaching the multitudes—or walking through tall grass on the mountainside, reciting the Beatitudes as he maneuvers among the masses congregated there. But scripture says he walked *away* from the crowd, headed into the hills, and found a place to sit. When his closest followers came to him, he taught them. This is a picture of intimate impartation to a few, not a scene with stage lights, microphones, and a megachurch multitude.

Evangelist Billy Graham spent a long life in the spotlight, and millions have responded to his presentation of the gospel. Yet, if he could live his life over, he'd do a few things differently. "For one thing," he said, "I would speak less and study more, and I would spend more time with my family."

Men too often long for the soap box and the spotlight. We want to hear the applause and the "amen." But Jesus looks for faithfulness in little things (Luke 16:10). He calls us to feed our own households and teach our own children first and foremost (Matthew 24:45; Ephesians 6:4; 1 Timothy 5:8). Whether or not we're called to speak to the many, we must often step away from the crowds and find a place to sit with the few in our lives who matter most.

HUMILITY'S ELEVATOR

Do nothing out of selfish ambition or vain conceit.
Rather, in humility value others above yourselves.
PHILIPPIANS 2:3 NIV

We can find a kernel of cynicism in some of the good news we read. Consider this story: A little girl takes the meal she's ordered at a restaurant and gives it to a homeless man on the street outside. It's a beautiful story that gets a little cloudy when her father follows her outside with his phone camera, capturing the moment and then uploading it to social media where it's shared repeatedly. Cynicism judges the motives of the father and the potential misuse of a child's good deed. It questions where the idea originated or whether this was a staged event.

Cynicism only sees what it wants to believe. However, cynicism can't get behind the outward gaze of the little girl who interacted with someone who had no ability to repay her. It doesn't take into account how this interaction may impact her life going forward.

If we reconstruct today's verse, it might read: "Motives associated with pride and selfish pursuits devalue others. Humility offers an opportunity for you to begin to see others with God's vision."

In God's playbook, personal ambition takes a backseat to helping others when they need help. Godly wisdom never steps on others to get to a place you want to claim, never overlooks someone because of perceived differences, and never elevates self while looking down on those with needs.

WHO ARE YOU ENCOURAGING?

"Martha, Martha," the Lord answered, "you are worried and upset about many things, but few things are needed—or indeed only one. Mary has chosen what is better, and it will not be taken away from her."

LUKE 10:41–42 NIV

When Martha asked Jesus to send her sister away from the disciples who were learning at His feet so that she could help prepare food for their guests, Jesus had to choose between the expectations of His culture and the gifts of Mary and Martha. Martha fully expected Jesus to take her side. Why else would she risk a public confrontation in front of their guests?

Surprisingly, the best thing for Martha wasn't necessarily what she wanted. While she wanted Jesus to remove Mary from an opportunity to learn with the disciples, she was actually trying to impose her gifts of hospitality on Mary. At the critical moment when Martha's frustration peaked, Jesus offered encouragement to both sisters, even if Martha received it as a rebuke. Jesus encouraged Mary to continue learning, to sit at His feet as a disciple, and to seek "what is better." At the same time, Jesus put Martha's many worries into perspective. She was concerned about a lot, but her gift of hospitality didn't have to leave her aggravated or resentful toward others. At a crucial moment, Jesus offered important insights that pointed both women toward fulfilling their callings. Who do you know who needs encouragement to take risks or to find contentment and peace in their present circumstances?

GOD NOTICES

*By faith Enoch was taken from this life, so that he did not experience
death: "He could not be found, because God had taken him away."
For before he was taken, he was commended as one who pleased God.*

HEBREWS 11:5 NIV

If you've ever read the Bible cover to cover, starting with the first verse of Genesis and ending with the last words of Revelation, and you still don't know much about a man named Enoch, don't feel bad.

Enoch is mentioned, seemingly in passing, in only four verses in Genesis 5 (vv. 21–24), in one verse in Hebrews 11, and from a quote in Jude 14–15. Nothing else is written of anything he did or said, and yet this man—whom we know little about other than that he "walked faithfully with God" (Genesis 5:24)—rated mention alongside some of the Bible's greatest people of faith.

Maybe Enoch never did anything of note other than walk faithfully with his God during his 365 years here on earth. Or maybe, just maybe, Enoch's short mention in scripture is there to teach you that your God is concerned first not with what you *do* but with the fact that your life is an example of choosing to walk faithfully with Him.

Either way, while you may read the Bible and barely notice Enoch, God most certainly noticed this man, and He counted him worthy to take him to heaven without experiencing physical death.

RECEIVING WISDOM

Listen to counsel and accept discipline,
that you may be wise the rest of your days.
PROVERBS 19:20 NASB

One of the many amazing things about God is that as long as you're committed to walking with Him, He never allows an experience to go to waste. That is especially true of the difficulties and suffering you're sure to encounter as you make your way through this journey called life.

The apostle James understood this well, so as he closed out a section of his epistle dealing with suffering, he wrote, "If any of you lacks wisdom, you should ask God, who gives generously to all without finding fault, and it will be given to you" (James 1:5 NIV).

James had no doubt observed what many Christian leaders since the first century have seen: that people don't always know how to respond wisely during difficult times. That is why he instructed the first-century believers, who lived during very perilous times, to seek God for wisdom—and to be assured that He would give them what they asked for.

God has promised to give wisdom to anyone who asks for it. And like many of His gifts, He uses many means to provide you with the wisdom you ask for—His written Word, His Holy Spirit, life experiences, and other people. So ask God for wisdom, but be open to the many different ways He can give you what you've asked for.

HOW MUCH IS "ENOUGH"?

*Whoever loves money never has enough; whoever loves wealth
is never satisfied with their income. This too is meaningless.*

ECCLESIASTES 5:10 NIV

The 1987 movie *Wall Street* contains an often-quoted line, spoken by the aptly named character Gordon Gecko, who said "Greed, for lack of a better word, is good."

But the Bible warns that greed is not good, that greed is a destructive force in the life of any man—especially a man of God.

The apostle Paul wrote that "the love of money is a root of all kinds of evil" and that some who have an insatiable desire have "wandered from the faith and pierced themselves with many griefs" (1 Timothy 6:10).

God is not against earning money—even against accruing wealth—as long as we do it through righteous means and with righteous motivation. In fact, the Bible repeatedly encourages His people to work hard so that they may prosper. What God is against—passionately against—is making money an idol, a life's focus ahead of family and, yes, ahead of God Himself.

So approach your work with passion. Work hard to provide well for yourself and your family. But never lose sight of the fact that your ultimate satisfaction, your ultimate source of all good things, is your heavenly Father.

LOVE THAT BREAKS THE RECORD BOOKS

Love is patient, love is kind. It does not envy, it does not boast,
it is not proud. It does not dishonor others, it is not self-seeking,
it is not easily angered, it keeps no record of wrongs.
1 CORINTHIANS 13:4–5 NIV

If we believe that God is love, as John assures us (1 John 4:8), and that love keeps no record of wrongs, then we have a staggering revelation on our hands. God's love isn't a conditional, record-keeping kind of love. Our wrongs have been forgiven AND forgotten. Perhaps our greatest barrier to loving others with this kind of generous abandon is our inability to receive God's love. We may believe that God can only love us if we pray more, live ashamed of our failures, or even hide our faults. This checklist approach to love alienates us from God and robs us from the experience of love that could revolutionize how we interact with our family, friends, and colleagues. Once we understand that God loves us and isn't keeping track of our wrongs, we'll begin to extend that generous love to others. That isn't to say others can't or won't hurt us. They will. But once we experience the depths of God's love and forgiveness for us, we'll have a solid foundation and assurance of our worth that doesn't require the approval of others. When we know that we are loved without condition, we become free to extend the same forgiveness to others—a forgiveness that keeps no record of wrongs.

TRUST HIM MORE

*When I get really afraid I come to you in trust. I'm proud to praise
God; fearless now, I trust in God. What can mere mortals do?*
PSALM 56:3–4 MSG

We survive in a world of broken promises. Products we buy struggle
to exist beyond their warranty. Promises made by family and friends
can be broken or forgotten. Something told in confidence becomes
the day's gossip.

We often respond to broken promises by putting up walls, keeping things to ourselves, and never really believing anyone who says,
"Trust me."

God encourages us to *trust* Him. He's never forgotten to supply
the air we breathe or the sunshine we enjoy. He keeps food sources
growing. In fact, He holds everything in His creation together (Colossians 1:17), even our very selves—" 'For in him we live and move
and have our being' " (Acts 17:28 NIV).

Some of us will still hesitate and say, "I'm not sure I can trust Him."

God is something more and different than humans. He cannot lie
or sin, and He always keeps His promises (Numbers 23:19).

The more we trust God, the more trustworthy we find Him.
The more we trust His ability, the less we question His authority. The
more we trust His love, the less fearful we find ourselves. The more
we trust in God, the less ominous life becomes.

When it's hard to trust others, it's the perfect time to trust God.

WHAT ARE YOUR CREDENTIALS?

Amos answered Amaziah, "I was neither a prophet nor the son
of a prophet, but I was a shepherd, and I also took
care of sycamore-fig trees."
AMOS 7:14 NIV

You may have felt challenged to get more involved in outreach or some other ministry at some point but thought, *I don't know how much help I can be. I don't have any kind of education or credentials.*

Men tend to put a lot of stock in credentials, don't they? They see those with high levels of education or impressive accomplishments as somehow more qualified or trustworthy. But God doesn't necessarily see it that way. As someone once wisely said, "God doesn't call the qualified; He qualifies the called."

God doesn't look first at your credentials, and He doesn't focus first on your training and natural abilities. He's concerned, first and foremost, with your willingness to obediently step out and be used of Him to influence your part of the world for His kingdom. When He finds you willing, He enables you to do what He's called you to do.

You don't need a doctorate in theology or a PhD in biblical studies for God to use you in your own sphere of influence. You need just one thing: willingness. So if you'd like to know what you can do to expand the kingdom of God, just ask Him! He'll never answer by first asking about your credentials.

A "HIDDEN" SIN

*"You have heard that it was said, 'You shall not commit adultery.'
But I tell you that anyone who looks at a woman lustfully has
already committed adultery with her in his heart."*

Matthew 5:27–28 niv

When we read God's seventh commandment—"You shall not commit adultery" (Exodus 20:14 niv)—it's easy to take comfort in knowing that we've never engaged in "the act" of sex with another man's wife.

But in today's verse, Jesus offered some tough teaching on the subject of adultery, namely, that it isn't just about where we take our bodies but (even more importantly) about the impure places our thoughts can so easily go.

Ouch!

So how do we keep those lust-inducing images from entering through our eyes and into our minds? Job, a godly man who lived thousands of years before Jesus came to earth, offers some practical advice.

Job was committed to keeping his mind from immoral, adulterous thoughts: "I made a covenant with my eyes not to look lustfully at a young woman" (Job 31:1 niv).

Job was on to something, wasn't he? What we allow to enter our brains through our eyes tends to stay there—as hard as we try to make it just go away. The key, he concluded, was to be very, very careful about what we look at.

That's no easy task, especially in today's world, where seemingly every other image that comes across our field of view can be problematic. But more than anything, it's a matter of commitment. . .to your spouse, your children, and your Father in heaven.

REPAYING DEBTS

Let no debt remain outstanding,
except the continuing debt to love one another.
ROMANS 13:8 NIV

Christians are to honor their debts and be faithful to pay them. When you don't have much cash, sometimes the last thing you want to think of is about repaying money you *owe*. You pray that they won't press you to repay immediately. In fact, truth be told, you probably wish that they'd simply forgive the debt.

Jesus said, "Love your enemies, do good, and lend, hoping for nothing in return" (Luke 6:35 NKJV), so you might think, *If they were a true Christian, they wouldn't expect me to repay them. They'd forgive my debt.* But that's missing Jesus' point. He was saying that if you lend money to an *unsaved enemy* because he needs it, do so with the full knowledge that he likely won't repay you. He *is* an unbeliever and an enemy, after all.

It's wonderful when someone is in a position to forgive a debt, but they may be unable to or may not feel that they should, so it's your responsibility to repay them—even if you have to do so little by little over an extended period of time. It will teach you discipline and faithfulness.

You can pray that God will supply the money to repay them. And yes, you *can* pray that, if they're in a position to do so, they'll have mercy and forgive the debt. But don't attempt to impose this desire upon them.

The only debt you should never finish paying off is your obligation to love others.

GRACE HAS A PRICE

*Should we keep on sinning so that God can show us more
and more of his wonderful grace? Of course not!*
Romans 6:1–2 nlt

God has freely offered grace to humanity to forgive sin and bring those who believe in Him into His family.

To demonstrate grace and forgiveness, Jesus paid a once and forever price—His life. He became the sacrifice for all who would accept it. Grace costs you nothing. Grace cost God the life of His Son.

While Jesus rose from the dead, the cost of forgiving grace was the most important payment in the history of mankind.

A man of integrity understands grace has a price. It isn't just a concept the mind agrees with. It changes decisions, actions, and motives.

A man of integrity brings God's command to love others into decisions, choosing to do the right thing rather than apologize after the fact. He knows he'll mess up and grace will be freely available, but he decides that sinning to *get* grace is something like abusing God's gift.

The price was high, so receiving the gift should have a life-altering impact. A man of integrity remembers what Jesus said of the sinful woman who anointed Him: that one who has been forgiven much, loves much (Luke 7:47). And this love and integrity sides with discipleship, discipline, and obedience. These are all hard things, but God's children are asked to trust Him and obey His commands. The man of integrity views this as an important, but not burdensome, directive because he understands the immense grace that has been given him.

THIRSTING FOR GOD

You, God, are my God, earnestly I seek you; I thirst for you, my whole being longs for you, in a dry and parched land where there is no water.
PSALM 63:1 NIV

Physical thirst is tangible. Your throat is dry. Your muscles begin to cramp. In extreme cases, confusion or hallucinations will set in. No matter how severe the case, nobody needs to tell you that you're thirsty. You instinctively know all the signs.

You also know all the signs of thirst for the good things of this world. You know the longing to finally watch a movie you've been waiting to see. You know how it feels to thirst for the presence of a spouse. You know the thirst you feel to hit a physical fitness goal when you're getting close.

But do you know the signs of spiritual thirst? David did. His whole being longed for God. Bible commentator John Gill suggests that spiritual longing will include a deep desire for the Bible, for worship, for church ordinances, for communion, for greater knowledge of Him, and for more grace from Him.

If you aren't thirsty for such things, something is lacking. When David penned the words of today's verse, he was in the wilderness of Judah. Even in such extreme circumstances, he knew and experienced all of the signs of spiritual thirst. If you don't experience this, engage with God and He will slake your thirst today.

THE END OF PAIN

And I heard a loud voice from the throne saying, "Look! God's dwelling place is now among the people, and he will dwell with them. They will be his people, and God himself will be with them and be their God. 'He will wipe every tear from their eyes. There will be no more death' or mourning or crying or pain, for the old order of things has passed away."

REVELATION 21:3–4 NIV

When we hear about tragedy in the news, experience a personal loss, or pass through a difficult season of life, it's tempting to think that our grief and sorrow have no end in sight. It may feel like life is an irredeemable mess that lacks direction or meaning. However, the final revelation of God will end all death, crying, and pain. As we consider the hope that God offers us, we can find peace in this assurance that our future is leading toward a day when God dwells among us and brings us the comfort we have longed for all our lives. The Bible points us consistently in this direction: God dwelling among us. From the days of the tabernacle among the Israelites in the wilderness, to the temple in Jerusalem, to the coming of the Spirit at Pentecost, God has consistently moved closer to us not farther away. While Revelation assures us that God's coming will bring justice, we do the story of scripture and the hope of the Gospel a great disservice if we overlook the comfort that God will bring to us. In the light of God's presence, darkness can't help but flee.

REPULSED BY PRIDE

Human pride will be brought down, and human arrogance will be humbled. Only the Lord will be exalted on that day of judgment.
Isaiah 2:11 nlt

Have you ever been forced, through a set of circumstances beyond your control, to spend time around a proud, boastful person? You know, the kind of person who never seems to have anything to say unless it's about himself and his accomplishments?

Being around that kind of man for any length of time can be draining, can't it? Pride is a sin each man struggles with in one way or another. But most men find those who seem ruled by pride and arrogance difficult to handle. In a very real way, most of us find excessive pride. . .well, kind of repulsive.

Think about it though. If you find pride repulsive, then how much more so is it for a God who lists humility as a high virtue and pride as a detestable sin? So much so that He tells you, "God opposes the proud but gives grace to the humble" (James 4:6 nlt).

James's use of the word *opposes* in this verse carries with it an ominous meaning. It connotes a God who doesn't just let the prideful man go about his way but who actually works against him in every way.

Pride is a serious sin that leads you nowhere good. On the other hand, God gives this promise to those who choose humility: "Humble yourselves, therefore, under God's mighty hand, that he may lift you up in due time" (1 Peter 5:6 niv).

PEACE AND STRENGTH THROUGH GOD'S WORD

*Great peace have those who love your law,
and nothing can make them stumble.*
PSALM 119:165 NIV

The writer of the epistle to the Hebrews once wrote of scripture, "For the word of God is alive and active. Sharper than any double-edged sword, it penetrates even to dividing soul and spirit, joints and marrow; it judges the thoughts and attitudes of the heart" (Hebrews 4:12 NIV).

That's a great summary of the role the Bible plays in the life of the believer. However, it doesn't mention one great benefit of spending time reading and studying the Word: it brings us peace and strength for our walk.

The writer of Psalm 119 points out that the words in the Bible (he refers to it as God's "law") have an amazing ability not just to bring us that inner peace God wants us to live in but also to keep us from stumbling and falling into sin.

Have you been lacking peace lately? Does it seem like your life in Christ lacks power? Do you find that you're not walking with Jesus as much as you are stumbling through life? It may be a matter of putting a daily time of reading and studying the Bible higher—maybe *much* higher—on your list of priorities.

Life in the twenty-first century is busy. Once we're finished with our daily work, our family, home projects, and friends all vie for our time. But if we want the peace and strength we need to live the life God calls us to live, we can't afford to miss out on time with Him and His Word.

BE STRONG: ASK FOR HELP

Oh, don't worry; we wouldn't dare say that we are as wonderful as these other men who tell you how important they are! But they are only comparing themselves with each other, using themselves as the standard of measurement. How ignorant!

2 CORINTHIANS 10:12 NLT

Guys are competitive. How do we reconcile being competitive and realizing we may not be the best? Whether it's football, video games, or trivia, there is a desire within guys to be the best.

At the end of the contest, there will be winners—and there will be losers.

Christian men can be guilty of wanting to wear a spiritual foam finger that suggests they're number one. God calls us ignorant if we think we're somehow better than those around us.

If we're looking for a standard of measurement, we need to look at Jesus—not ourselves or those around us. Jesus was perfect in following God's commands. How about you? Jesus gave His life to rescue humanity. Have you done the same, giving your time and talents to share the Gospel? Jesus loves everyone perfectly, no matter their background or how they act. Does your love come with conditions?

We can never compare favorably to Jesus, but that's exactly why we need to stay close to Him. He ensures that any man who humbly walks with Him measures up. Ask Him for the help you need to be more like Him in every way.

A LEGACY OF FAITH

All these people earned a good reputation because of their faith,
yet none of them received all that God had promised. For God
had something better in mind for us, so that they
would not reach perfection without us.
HEBREWS 11:39–40 NLT

The eleventh chapter of Hebrews is an amazing New Testament passage that gives you a pretty good idea of what kind of legacy God calls you to leave behind when your days on this earth are over.

As you read through this chapter, you may recall that the people listed by the writer of this epistle weren't perfect. Far from it! Noah got drunk, Abraham lied because he was afraid, Jacob was a deceiver, Moses doubted God, and David. . .well, his many failings as a man, as a king, and as a father are well chronicled in the Bible.

Yet the writer of Hebrews goes out of his way to tell you that all the people listed in this chapter played their own important parts in making God's plan of redemption a reality for men today—not because they were perfect, but simply because they believed God when He spoke.

As you read Hebrews 11, let it challenge you. Let it bring you to a place of asking yourself what kind of legacy you'll leave behind—for your friends, for your family, and for people whose lives you may touch without even knowing it.

NOT KNOWING WHERE YOU'RE GOING

*By an act of faith, Abraham said yes to God's call to travel
to an unknown place that would become his home.
When he left he had no idea where he was going.*
HEBREWS 11:8 MSG

On August 3, 1492, Christopher Columbus set sail from Spain with three ships. Unlike Abraham, Columbus knew—so he thought—where he was going: he intended to sail across the Atlantic Ocean and arrive at Japan by a westerly route. However, he ended up someplace completely different—the Americas.

As for Abraham, God said, " 'Leave your native country. . .and go to the land that I will show you.' . . . So Abram departed as the LORD had instructed. . . . When they arrived in Canaan. . .the LORD appeared to Abram and said, 'I will give this land to your descendants' " (Genesis 12:1, 4–5, 7 NLT). He didn't know till he got there that this was the place.

The Lord might also call you to uproot from a safe, familiar location and set sail for the unknown. You may have sensed God calling you, you may have been offered a better job elsewhere, or circumstances may have conspired to make the move obvious, so like it or not, you launch out. God has wonderful plans for you, but often in order for them to come to pass, you have to step out in faith.

Don't be afraid. God has promised, "I send an Angel before thee, to keep thee in the way, and to bring thee into the place which I have prepared" (Exodus 23:20 KJV).

OUR SHEPHERD GOD

*"As a shepherd looks after his scattered flock when he is with them,
so will I look after my sheep. I will rescue them from all the places
where they were scattered on a day of clouds and darkness."*

EZEKIEL 34:12 NIV

In the classic hymn "Come Thou Fount," Robert Robinson, the nineteenth-century hymnist, makes this very personal confession: "Prone to wander, Lord, I feel it. Prone to leave the God I love."

In these lyrics, Robinson, who was just twenty-two when he penned this hymn, demonstrated a keen understanding of human nature and how it is so often in conflict with the kind of relationship God desires to have with us as His most prized creation. At the time when Ezekiel recorded God's words in today's verse, people would have understood a few things about sheep that most people wouldn't today.

First of all, they would understand that domesticated sheep, not being the brightest of animals, tended to wander from their flock and from the safety of the watchful eye of the shepherd. Second, they would understand that sheep have notoriously poor eyesight and absolutely no way to defend themselves against predators looking for a quick, easy meal.

Though our human pride may tell us otherwise, God knows that we, like sheep, are prone to wandering away from the safety and security He has promised to provide us. He also knows that when we wander, we're defenseless against the temptations the world around us is sure to send our way.

There truly is no better place to be—and to stay—than under the watchful eye of our loving Shepherd Father.

ACTING ON WHAT YOU KNOW

But don't just listen to God's word. You must do what it says.
Otherwise, you are only fooling yourselves.
JAMES 1:22 NLT

You can't be a part of our modern-day culture without knowing a little something about what it takes to be physically healthy. Almost daily you see and hear messages encouraging you to eat right and get enough exercise to keep your mind and body operating at peak efficiency.

Sadly, too many people know about these physical truths but don't act on them. The results speak for themselves. Obesity and the physical problems that accompany inactivity are at all-time highs. As a whole, North Americans aren't very physically healthy.

Today's verse gives Christian men some very simple instructions for getting and staying *spiritually* healthy. It tells you that you're not just to read what the Bible tells you that you should do, but you are also to put what you know into action. Sadly, many Christians don't consistently put what they know the Bible says into practice. The result is that they're in a spiritually unhealthy condition.

God's written Word is filled cover to cover with all kinds of truths, wisdom, and commands. And while it's a good thing to read the Bible and learn what it has to teach you, that's only the first step. The second step—and this means everything—is to act on what you learn.

A TIME TO SIMPLIFY

"If God gives such attention to the appearance of wildflowers—most of which are never even seen—don't you think he'll attend to you, take pride in you, do his best for you? . . . Steep your life in God-reality, God-initiative, God-provisions. Don't worry about missing out. You'll find all your everyday human concerns will be met."

MATTHEW 6:30, 33 MSG

Some live off the grid. Others downsize into tiny homes. Whether you call them penny-pinchers, extreme cheapskates, or Luddites, these men and women have embraced simplicity in a time when most want *more*.

While some will downsize, others will cut their own hair, make their own butter, grow their own produce, and raise their own chickens. If you think that sounds radical, there are a growing number of individuals embracing a simpler lifestyle.

This isn't to suggest that you find a tiny house and move to an uninhabited corner of the smallest county in the least populous state. Perhaps on this National Simplicity Day it's just an acknowledgment that God never asks us to complicate our lives to the point where there is no room for Him.

Having nothing to do is one problem. Having too much to do invites other dangers.

In what ways could you simplify your life? How would that impact your ability to spend time with Jesus in prayer and in His Word?

WHEN IS GOD AT WORK AMONG US?

So he replied to the messengers, "Go back and report to John what
you have seen and heard: The blind receive sight, the lame walk,
those who have leprosy are cleansed, the deaf hear, the dead
are raised, and the good news is proclaimed to the poor.
Blessed is anyone who does not stumble on account of me."

LUKE 7:22–23 NIV

Perhaps we read the story of Jesus and John the Baptist, and we can't believe that John dared to harbor doubts about Jesus. How could John see the miracles of Jesus and His power over demons and doubt? What more could John have asked of God? If you know the backstory of John, he expected quite a lot more. John expected Jesus at least to destroy the Roman occupiers of Israel with His "winnowing fork." When Jesus preached a message of repentance for all people, even the Romans, and limited His power to healing the sick and demon-possessed, John was tempted to write Him off. John's story is a powerful reminder of the ways our own agendas can cloud our perspective. Perhaps God is working mightily in our lives or in the lives of those around us, but we've been missing out because we keep expecting God to show up in other ways, in other places, and among different people. Sometimes faith means learning to see where God is working right now in the moment rather than asking God to show up on our terms.

UNCONVENTIONAL TACTICS

So it was, when the Philistine arose and came. . .to meet David,
that David hurried and ran toward the army to meet the Philistine.
1 Samuel 17:48 nkjv

One day a huge Philistine army marched up the Valley of Elah, but the Israelite army learned they were coming and blocked their advance at the town of Socoh. Then an enormous man named Goliath, covered in heavy armor, stepped forward and challenged any Israelite soldier to face him in single combat. Only David accepted his challenge.

Saul offered David his armor and sword, but after trying them on, David realized that he didn't stand a chance using conventional methods. So, grasping his shepherd's staff, he walked down to the brook, picked five stones, and slipped them into his pouch. Then he headed up toward the giant. The only weapon Goliath could see was David's staff, so he roared, "Am I a dog, that you come to me with sticks?" (1 Samuel 17:43 nkjv).

Suddenly David rushed the giant. Startled, Goliath grinned. *He really is gonna try to hit me with that stick.* At the last moment, David dropped his staff, thrust a stone into his sling, began swinging it, then let it fly with punishing force. Goliath never realized what David was about to do until it was too late.

When you face impossible circumstances, God can inspire you with crazy, unconventional solutions. Be open to them! They can work when nothing else will.

A LIFE OF INTEGRITY

*The integrity of the upright guides them, but the
unfaithful are destroyed by their duplicity.*
PROVERBS 11:3 NIV

What would you do if your server brought your check at the end of a dinner at your favorite restaurant, and you noticed that your dessert was left off the bill? Or if you were overpaid for work you had just completed? Or if someone inadvertently gave you credit for a coworker's accomplishment?

Life is filled with all sorts of tests for that character quality called "integrity." Through big tests and small (relatively, that is) tests alike, you're constantly presented with opportunities to make sure you please God by doing what you know is right.

The Christian writer C. S. Lewis noted: "Integrity is doing the right thing, even when no one is watching." That's a great definition of integrity, isn't it? And it's also a great reminder to do everything you do, even in private, with an eye toward true integrity. Here's a question to test yourself and the level of integrity by which you live: Do you do what you know is right—even in the relatively "small" areas of life—even when you know no one is looking, even when you know there are no consequences?

When you walk in integrity in all areas of your life, you please your Father in heaven and also keep a clear conscience. That's a great way to live!

THE BLESSING OF AN ENDING

Teach us to number our days,
that we may gain a heart of wisdom.
PSALM 90:12 NIV

Aging sparks no end of troubling moments and crisis points. There's a quarter-life crisis that hits around twenty-five, the midlife crisis at forty, and then a crisis that typically hits around the sixties as many look into retirement. If anything, we may find less wisdom and more regret and recklessness as yet another year passes by. Each crisis of aging is rooted in the realization that death is a terrifying reality that we will all face one day. However, the writer of the Psalms assures us that numbering our days with the end in mind can actually lead us to greater wisdom. Perhaps this strikes some as impossible, but consider this—once we view our days as limited, aren't we compelled to consider how to use them best? Doesn't each day become all the more valuable once we see that our days aren't available in an endless supply? The wisdom that the psalmist talks about will help us ask hard questions about how we spend our time. We may be more driven to prioritize time spent in prayer. We may set aside more time to be with our family. We may change our professional goals or at least measure our success by different means. As we number our days with an awareness of their limited supply, we'll have greater clarity when discerning our priorities and will find greater peace in the knowledge of God's presence throughout each day.

OVERCOMING DESPAIR

He lifted me out of the pit of despair, out of the mud and the mire.
He set my feet on solid ground and steadied me as I walked along.
PSALM 40:2 NLT

The prophet Samuel had anointed David to be the future king of Israel. This was the clear will of God, so obviously God planned to keep David alive so this could happen. At first, David didn't doubt it. But after living like a fugitive in the wilderness for several years, constantly looking over his shoulder, his faith became worn down. "David kept thinking to himself, 'Someday Saul is going to get me. The best thing I can do is escape to the Philistines. Then Saul will stop hunting for me. . .and I will finally be safe' " (1 Samuel 27:1 NLT).

There's no indication that David prayed about this decision. He fled to the land of the Philistines due to his own discouraged reasoning, and this move ended up causing him serious problems.

Perhaps you're in a similar situation. You were convinced that something was God's will for your life, so you stood strong for quite some time, despite severe tests. But perhaps recently you've begun to grow weary and fray around the edges.

God knows this is a human tendency, so He encourages you in the words of Paul, which say, "Let us not grow weary while doing good, for in due season we shall reap if we do not lose heart" (Galatians 6:9 NKJV). The Word also says, "Fight the good fight of faith" (1 Timothy 6:12 KJV), so keep fighting and believing.

RADICAL LOVE

Husbands, love your wives, just as Christ loved
the church and gave himself up for her.
EPHESIANS 5:25 NIV

Sometimes when we're trying to fully understand what God is communicating through His written Word, it's helpful to look at the context in which it was first written.

The culture at the time when the apostle Paul wrote these words was radically different from ours today. In those days, men ran everything and had total legal and social authority over their wives and children, and women had no choice but to live—submissively and probably without asking a lot of questions—under their husbands' rule.

When Paul enjoined husbands to love their wives "as Christ loved the church," he was suggesting something greatly different from the norms of the day. This was a love that served in the most sacrificial kind of way, a love that looked out for the needs and desires of someone who likely wasn't used to being treated that way by a man.

Though things have changed greatly since the days of the apostle Paul, his instructions to husbands are in many ways still a radical departure for many married men. God calls us men today to love our wives and children—and others in our circle of influence—the same way Jesus loved His people. That's a radical, self-sacrificing kind of love, a kind of love that leads first with a heart toward serving without first being served.

ALL THE WORLD'S A STAGE

Let everyone see that you are considerate in all you do.
PHILIPPIANS 4:5 NLT

When Paul advises you to "let everyone *see* that you are considerate in all you do," he's saying to make a conscious decision to be kind and thoughtful since others are watching you. Not that you're supposed to do it simply for show, but be aware that others are observing you and judging the Gospel by how you live it out in your daily life.

Jesus said something similar: "Let your light so shine before men, that they may see your good works and glorify your Father in heaven" (Matthew 5:16 NKJV).

Shakespeare declared, "All the world's a stage," and explained that everyone acts out the part given them to play. The world *is* a stage for Christians as well. "We have been made a spectacle to the whole universe, to angels as well as to human beings" (1 Corinthians 4:9 NIV). And how are you to act? Considerate.

In common usage, to be considerate means to show kindness and awareness for another person's feelings; it literally means to ponder, to carefully consider others and their needs. In the most intimate of relationships—marriage—the Bible advises, "Husbands, in the same way be considerate as you live with your wives" (1 Peter 3:7 NIV).

To act in a considerate manner, you need to be motivated by love.

OVERCOMING YOUR SIN

I have hidden your word in my heart that
I might not sin against you.
PSALM 119:11 NIV

The great nineteenth-century American evangelist Dwight L. Moody is credited with many profound and inspiring quotations, one of them being: "The Bible will keep you from sin, or sin will keep you from the Bible."

The writer of Psalm 119 would heartily agree with this. In today's verse, he declared that he kept his heart and mind focused on the Word of God so that he could avoid falling into sin against his God. The same thing can be true for you today.

The writer of the epistle to the Hebrews wrote this of the Bible's power: "For the word of God is alive and active. Sharper than any double-edged sword, it penetrates even to dividing soul and spirit, joints and marrow; it judges the thoughts and attitudes of the heart" (Hebrews 4:12 NIV).

Sadly, too many Christians don't make sufficient use of what the apostle Paul called "the sword of the Spirit" (Ephesians 6:17)—and that results in weak, powerless lives. But if you can learn to walk in the tremendous power the Bible gives you to live an overcoming life, you find it possible to say yes to the things that please God and no to the things that displease Him.

Make it your goal to learn to wield this mighty sword by reading God's Word, memorizing it, and meditating on it.

TELLING YOUR OWN STORY

Give praise to the LORD, proclaim his name;
make known among the nations what he has done.
PSALM 105:1 NIV

Each Christian man has his own story about how he came to know Jesus. Not one of these stories may seem like a bona fide water-turned-to-wine miracle—at least not to the people hearing them—but they're all amazing in that they give an account of how Jesus came onto the scene, took what was once dead, and made it alive.

That's just the nature of salvation, isn't it?

The Bible tells you that you're to always be ready "to give an answer to everyone who asks you to give the reason for the hope that you have" (1 Peter 3:15 NIV). Among other things, that can mean being ready to tell others about how Jesus, through the Holy Spirit, brought you to a point of responding to God's love and receiving forgiveness and eternal life. It can also include your story of healing and deliverance from what you once were.

When you begin talking to a friend or family member who needs Jesus, very often the best place to start is not by talking about how that *person* needs Him but instead by telling your *own* story of what He has done for you and how He has impacted your life.

Always remember, your story of salvation is an amazing story people around you need to hear.

YOUR HELP

I look up to the mountains—does my help come from there?
My help comes from the Lord, who made heaven and earth!
PSALM 121:1–2 NLT

In the Old Testament, the Hebrews were accustomed to facing Jerusalem—which was built on a mountain—whenever they prayed (see Daniel 6:10). The temple had been built there on Mount Moriah. Judea itself was mountainous. The ark of the covenant once rested on the holy hill of Zion. So, it's understandable why the Israelites looked to the hills for spiritual help. Other nations believed, in fact, that "the Lord is God of the hills" (1 Kings 20:28 KJV).

But Jeremiah 3:23 (NLT) declared, "Our worship of idols on the hills and our religious orgies on the mountains are a delusion. Only in the Lord our God will Israel ever find salvation." Looking to the hills for help was useless.

Modern Christians turn to all sorts of things in search of spiritual help or deliverance: anointed artifacts, crucifixes, a word of knowledge, even statues. Some even elevate pastors, healers, and spiritual gurus. But your power and salvation don't come from any such activity. It comes from the Lord, who made heaven and earth.

Spend some time today taking spiritual inventory. Have you elevated anything or anyone above God? Maybe the better question to ask yourself is, if anything was removed from your life, would you lack spiritual power? If so, you're depending on that particular object or person too much.

A TIME OF FAILURE

"It's time to change your ways! Turn to face God so he can wipe away your sins [and] pour out showers of blessing to refresh you."
Acts 3:19 MSG

Men despise personal failure. We don't want to admit wrongdoing. We even hate asking for directions. Every difficulty becomes our own burden to bear.

Perhaps this is why men tend to spiral out of control when they are caught in sin. They've tried to correct things on their own, personally blamed others for their predicament, and then, when the secret is out, they decide it's no longer worth the effort, spiraling into behaviors they never dreamed possible.

Failure should bring us face to feet with Jesus. We come to Him and bow at His feet in the brokenness of a man finally willing to ask for help. There's no shame in this purifying act—it's exactly what God wants us to do. In fact, He makes a promise that He will heal us from our sin if we confess it: "If we admit our sins—make a clean breast of them—he won't let us down; he'll be true to himself. He'll forgive our sins and purge us of all wrongdoing" (1 John 1:9 MSG).

There is restoration after failure. There is hope after hurt. There is love after rebellion. It's only possible through the God who's all too aware of our failures and chooses to love us anyway.

If this describes the world you live in now, then stop wasting time. Admit your failings and ask God for the help you need.

KIND TO THE UNGRATEFUL

Love ye your enemies. . .and your reward shall be great,
and ye shall be the children of the Highest: for he
is kind unto the unthankful and to the evil.
LUKE 6:35 KJV

One thing that disturbs many Christians is Jesus' command to love their enemies. It just seems so far beyond what they're capable of or willing to do that they write it off as some unrealistic ideal that only the most super-spiritual, mature saints can ever attain to. But Jesus said that loving your enemies was sure proof that you were a child of the Highest God.

Why is this? Because God is loving and patient by nature. He loves the unthankful and is kind even to evil people. And as His child, you're to emulate your Father and show this same love and kindness.

You may have difficulty even showing kindness to those who don't express due thankfulness, let alone showing love and kindness to people who are evil and show no sign of repenting or changing. Yet Jesus, after explaining God's loving nature in Luke 6:35 above, added, "Be ye therefore merciful, as your Father also is merciful" (v. 36).

He doesn't expect you to be naive about where they're at or deny that they're evil, but He asks you to "overcome evil with good" (Romans 12:21 KJV). And yes, He knows that this is a difficult thing to ask. That's why He promises that "your reward shall be *great*" for obeying Him.

OUR DAILY BREAD VS. OUR ETERNAL BREAD

*"Do not work for food that spoils, but for food that endures to
eternal life, which the Son of Man will give you. For on him
God the Father has placed his seal of approval."*

JOHN 6:27 NIV

When Jesus taught His disciples how to pray, He told them to ask
God for the provision of their daily bread. Daily bread isn't something
that you can store up for the long term, especially back in Jesus'
day. He didn't instruct them to pray for storehouses of grain or
even reserves of coins that would give them the ability to manage
any crisis. They were welcome to ask God for provision, but only
daily provision. How often are we tempted to pray for a long-term
solution to our problems and needs? It's almost maddening to think
that a God with limitless resources would instruct us to ask for so
small a provision, but then perhaps Jesus knew something of human
ambition and our tendency to rely on our possessions and resources
rather than God. Ironically, even our best "long-term" solutions
are actually quite limited and fleeting. The presence of Christ in
our lives and a long-term faith in Him will never let us down, but
our strength, finances, and even relationships may well let us down
when we need them the most. The only sure "long-term" bet is the
eternal bread of Jesus Himself present in our lives, nourishing us
and providing for our needs day by day.

THE MIGHTY POWER OF GOD

*Finally, be strong in the Lord and in his mighty power. . .
so that you can take your stand against the devil's schemes.*
EPHESIANS 6:10–11 NIV

A scheme is a methodical, calculated plan for reaching a specific goal or putting a particular idea into effect. To *scheme* often describes plans done in a devious way or with intent to bring about an evil result. The devil schemes to bring your life to ruin, and he employs time-tested methods such as hatred, fear, lust, covetousness, addictions, and so on. C. S. Lewis gave insightful descriptions of his schemes in *The Screwtape Letters*.

What's the best way to combat the evil one's schemes? To submit yourself to God and pray, "May your will be done" (Matthew 26:42 NIV).

For example, it was God's will that Jesus be crucified for the sins of the world, but Peter argued against it. So Jesus told him, "Get behind Me, Satan! . . .for you are not setting your mind on God's interests, but man's" (Matthew 16:23 NASB). Man's interests and "the will of the flesh" (John 1:13 KJV) often parallel Satan's will because both are selfish.

How do you become "strong in the Lord. . .so that you can take your stand against the devil's schemes"? Simple. "Submit yourselves. . . to God." Then you will have spiritual strength. Then you can "resist the devil, and he will flee from you" (James 4:7 KJV).

DON'T LOSE YOUR NERVE

The children of Ephraim, being armed and carrying bows,
turned back in the day of battle.
PSALM 78:9 NKJV

The writer of Psalm 78 describes a situation where the men of Israel had been called to battle, so they assembled their armies and marched forth, armed with swords and shields and carrying bows and quivers full of arrows. But when the tribe of Ephraim saw the enemy, they turned back and headed home. Why was that? Although they had trained for war and were well armed, they lost their nerve. They didn't believe that God was with them.

This applies to challenges in modern life as well. You could be fully trained in your profession and have all the tools you need, but if a situation seems overwhelming, you may throw up your hands in defeat before you even start. It might be that you got out of the wrong side of bed that morning. But more often it's because of an attitude you've entertained for years.

One time when Moses doubted that he could do what God had commanded him, the Lord asked, "What is that in your hand?" Moses answered, "A rod" (Exodus 4:2 NKJV). It didn't seem like much, but God proceeded to do astounding miracles when Moses held it up. Even so, when large bills are looming and you have limited cash. . . you may simply need to get your eyes on your potential for earning the extra funds.

Never underestimate your ability to do what God asks you to do. When He is with you, you can do amazing things.

THE POVERTY OF PRIDE

"Blessed are the poor in spirit, for theirs is the kingdom of heaven."
MATTHEW 5:3 NKJV

The climb up the mountain with Jesus begins with a descent into the heart—and a commitment to humility. To be poor in spirit is to be humble. Only those who take themselves low will be lifted high enough to inherit heaven (Matthew 23:12). God opposes the proud but gives grace to the humble (James 4:6).

It's hard for men to humble themselves. We've been taught to stand tall, to take the lead, to pull ourselves up by our bootstraps, to never let anybody push us around. Even in the Church we are sometimes encouraged to "claim our rights" as sons of the King—as if God owes us something other than the mercy which Jesus bought for us by His blood. In a religious environment focused on winning the blessings of earth, humility gets stuffed in a closet. In a culture focused on worldly prosperity, spiritual poverty can seem almost heretical! But wait! Doesn't the Bible tell us that no man can muscle his way into heaven? Doesn't Jesus call us to admit that life is too heavy to carry on our own? Doesn't He tell us to link arms with Him and learn about Him? He said that He is "meek and lowly of heart," and only by embracing those qualities can we find rest for our souls (Matthew 11:29; Romans 8:29). No wonder we are called to be humble and poor in spirit, for this is who Christ Jesus is!

THE BIG DIFFERENCE

*"My thoughts are nothing like your thoughts," says the L*ORD*.
"And my ways are far beyond anything you could imagine. For just
as the heavens are higher than the earth, so my ways are higher
than your ways and my thoughts higher than your thoughts."*
ISAIAH 55:8–9 NLT

The biggest difference between God and man is that God is perfect—man is not.

We let people down—God can be trusted. We destroy—God makes things new. We tell lies—God speaks truth. We're selfish—God gave us everything. We want our way—God knows what's best.

These differences point to a God who's incredibly wise, but He is often thought of as foolish. For instance, His Word says we should lead by serving, find blessings by giving, and discover real life by losing what we thought was most important. In 1 Corinthians 1, the apostle Paul even states that the cross is "foolishness" to those who don't believe, but it is "the power of God" to those who are being saved (1 Corinthians 1:18 NKJV).

Sometimes we want to try to define who God is by what we experience, but God is beyond anything we can explain. He has no beginning or end. He created us and offers us restoration when we blow it. We don't have the credentials to be His children, but He welcomes us to be a part of His family through Jesus.

Thankfully, we don't have to understand everything about God to admit that He's right, trustworthy, and compassionate.

PROTECTED IN GOD'S SHADOW

He who dwells in the secret place of the Most High
shall abide under the shadow of the Almighty.

PSALM 91:1 NKJV

How do you find rest and calm when there's trouble and rumors all around you—when enemies seek your ruin and the winds of adversity are howling? You must stay close to God. You must dwell (consistently live) in the shelter of the Most High and abide (remain) under His mighty shadow. But what does it mean to remain under God's shadow?

Much of the Negev in southern Israel is one vast, barren, unforgiving desert baking under the heat of the sun and frequently blasted by high winds. Travelers took shelter behind great rocks during windstorms and rested in their shadow during the hottest part of the day. God is just like that to His people. He is "a shelter from the wind and a refuge from the storm. . .and the shadow of a great rock in a thirsty land" (Isaiah 32:2 NIV).

Because you're a Christian, Jesus lives in your heart. The Spirit of God's Son dwells in you. But there is more to the picture. He said, "Abide in Me, and I in you" (John 15:4 NKJV). Jesus lives in you, but you must also live continually in Him. This means seeking Him in prayer and staying close to Him by obeying Him.

God is a great rock in a hostile landscape, and He is more than able to protect you. So stay close to Him in His shadow.

WHEN YOU FALL, GET BACK UP

For though the righteous fall seven times, they rise again,
but the wicked stumble when calamity strikes.

PROVERBS 24:16 NIV

Jim Marshall was a key member of the Purple People Eaters, the imposing defensive front line for the Minnesota Vikings in the 1970s. At the time of his retirement in 1979, he owned NFL records for career starts (270) and games played (282). But Marshall's most memorable moment as an NFL player took place on October 25, 1964, when, in a game against the San Francisco 49ers, he scooped up a fumble and ran sixty-six yards *in the wrong direction*, leading to a safety for the 49ers.

The good news for Marshall and the Vikings is that he atoned for his embarrassing gaffe by forcing a fumble, which teammate Carl Eller returned for a game-winning touchdown.

Jim Marshall didn't give up after causing what many consider the most embarrassing moment in NFL history, and we shouldn't give up either when we make mistakes or stumble. Today's verse teaches us that a righteous man, a man who follows Jesus wholeheartedly, will stumble and fall but will always get up, dust himself off, and receive God's forgiveness.

How do you respond when you fall? Do you stay down and wallow in self-pity and self-condemnation? Or do you get back up and continue your journey with Jesus?

CARING FOR OTHERS

Don't look out only for your own interests,
but take an interest in others, too.
PHILIPPIANS 2:4 NLT

When the Bible says "take an interest in others," it's referring to *all* other people. This includes your wife, children, relatives, workmates, acquaintances, and total strangers—anyone who's not the person looking back at you in the mirror. God understands that you'll naturally look out for yourself and take care of business that's important to you. You have to. That's your responsibility. But this verse reminds you that you're also your brother's keeper.

Take your children, for example. Because they're children, they think as children and act like children (1 Corinthians 13:11). And they're also interested in the things that interest most children—things that long ago ceased to interest *you*. But since you love them, you make an effort to engage with them. This includes taking the time to listen to their jokes, as well as pausing to sympathize with their sorrows.

The Bible says, "Be willing to associate with people of low position" (Romans 12:16 NIV). This includes cousins who have made little of themselves and whose interests seem boring and mundane to you. It includes an elderly relative who seems to be a relic of a bygone century. To associate with them, you have to let go of the idea that your time is too valuable or that the rewards aren't worth the trouble.

Many people aren't willing to put forth the effort to care for others. But there are indeed great rewards for doing so.

OUR GREATEST NEED

*This is the kind of love we are talking about—not that we once upon
a time loved God, but that he loved us and sent his Son as
a sacrifice to clear away our sins and the damage
they've done to our relationship with God.*
1 John 4:10 msg

How do you remember your favorite days growing up? Some men remember crawling under a fixer-upper car as teenagers with big dreams, a utility light, and a wrench that could tighten bolts and remove knuckle skin in one single movement. Others remember spending time in the arcade with a fistful of quarters and an eye on the high score, lights flashing and machines beeping while other hopeful players cheer or groan around them. Some recall their cell phones that provided much-needed connection with friends, no less valuable though they rarely demanded skinned knuckles.

Every generation relates to our world differently and enjoys different pastimes, but one thing that never changes is the human need to love and be loved. That's why we get married and have kids. We hope that somehow the love we experience can be passed on to future generations.

God defined love. When we experience God's love, we can both love others and accept their love in a way that invites trust and inspires contentment. If we don't experience God's love, all we can reasonably expect is a less fulfilling imitation based on conditions and feelings. We will always question its legitimacy.

If you have more questions about true love, 1 Corinthians 13 can help you identify and demonstrate it in all your relationships.

PLANT, NURTURE, AND WATER

He that gathereth in summer is a wise son: but he that
sleepeth in harvest is a son that causeth shame.
PROVERBS 10:5 KJV

A farmer who doesn't put in the necessary work in the summer shouldn't expect to see a harvest in the fall. Nor should he expect to simply put in the work during the summer and then sleep during the harvest. Planting, nurturing, and gathering all have natural seasons and rhythms. They are not changed by human whims or bouts of laziness.

When you think of a farmer, do you think of someone who avoids work? No. Farmers understand that isn't an option. Often they don't even attend worship services during the fall because it's the time for harvesting and that window of time is very limited.

From the big-picture perspective, you're to be about the business of planting and nurturing during your prime income-earning years because a time is coming in the fall and winter of your life when you'll no longer be able to gather as much.

Today's verse is written with a family in mind. A son who gathers and harvests at the appropriate times is wise. He puts the needs of his family before his own wants. Does your work life resemble a farmer's? Are you consistent in your planting and nurturing, knowing that fall is on the way?

PHATTER THAN A PHARISEE

"For I say to you, that unless your righteousness exceeds the
righteousness of the scribes and the Pharisees, you will
by no means enter the kingdom of heaven."

MATTHEW 5:20 NKJV

Phatter than a Pharisee? Anyone could beat them to heaven! Didn't Jesus say so (Matthew 23)? He called them white-washed tombs. He said they were blind guides leading blind men, stumbling into a ditch together. Their lips spouted truths about God, but their hearts were light-years from heaven. Their evangelism turned converts into worse "sons of hell" than they were. Jesus called them snakes, vipers, hypocrites. He said they were blind, dirty, greedy, faithless, merciless. He called them fools and prophet-killers. He. . . But wait!

To think we are better than they are is to fall into the same pit with them. Yes, Jesus called them on their hypocrisy, but the shocking reality is that the Pharisees were 100 percent committed to righteousness as they understood it. They dedicated themselves to the honor of God's Word and the fame of God's name. The problem was they were so sure of themselves, they couldn't see that being sure of themselves was their biggest sin. They believed commitment to right made them right. They thought they had a patent on truth and were blind to their own falsehood—blind even to God in their midst (John 1:11).

Pride precedes a fall (Proverbs 16:18). Humility precedes wisdom (Proverbs 11:2). Wisdom says (as John Newton once declared), "I am a great sinner. Christ is a great savior."

Righteousness greater than the Pharisees' comes by grace, through faith in the only Righteous One who can save "a wretch like me."

WHOLEHEARTED OBEDIENCE

He did what was right in the eyes of the LORD,
but not wholeheartedly.
2 CHRONICLES 25:2 NIV

Amaziah, king of Judah, was *sort of* a good man. . .just like his dad. His father, Joash, had lived most of his life under the shadow of the high priest Jehoiada and had followed God as long as Jehoiada was alive. But after Jehoiada died, Joash quickly went astray. Amaziah too had been raised all his life to worship God but in his later years strayed into idol worship.

Many people raised in the church have a similar problem. They know all about God, know what is right, and even have a relationship with Him. But as they age, they gradually depend more and more on their own reasoning, follow their own inclinations, and eventually turn away from God. And their eventual backsliding largely stems from not following the Lord wholeheartedly to begin with.

It's wonderful to attend church faithfully, give to God, and read your Bible, but if you're mainly doing these things to put on a show, to please other people, and to be accepted as a "good Christian," eventually you'll run out of steam and come to a stop.

Don't let this be you. Remember the number-one commandment: "You shall love the LORD your God with *all* your heart and with *all* your soul and with *all* your might" (Deuteronomy 6:5 NASB, emphasis added).

LOVING THE UNLOVABLE

"But I say to you who hear, love your enemies, do good to those who hate you, bless those who curse you, pray for those who mistreat you."
LUKE 6:27–28 NASB

Have you ever thought about where humanity would be if God had looked down on sinful, lost people and just said, "Fine! They hate Me, they curse My Name, and they live lives that offend Me in every way. I'm through with them!"

The Bible teaches that you were once God's enemy (Romans 5:10), that you were alienated from Him and hostile toward Him (Colossians 1:21). But it also teaches that while you were still a sinner, Jesus, God's only Son, died for you so that you could be reconciled to Him.

God is the perfect example of Jesus' command to love your enemies and to do good to those who hate you. He tells you to love your enemies just like He did when He sent Jesus to die for you. And He tells you to do good for those who hate you and curse you, just like He did. But more than *telling* you to do those things, He *showed* you what that kind of love and blessing really looks like.

It's not easy to love and bless those who don't reciprocate. But when you do just that, you give those who dislike you and mistreat you a much-needed glimpse of what God's love is really all about.

SECURING THE INSECURE

[God said,] My grace is enough; it's all you need.
My strength comes into its own in your weakness.
2 Corinthians 12:9 msg

He was indecisive, but he wanted people to like him. He was shallow, but he had a lot to hide. He was miserable, but he wore a smile to mask the pain.

There was another man. He was demanding because it stopped any questions. He was aloof because he couldn't allow anyone to get close. He wore his pain proudly and never believed there was relief.

We've all resembled one of these men in their struggle with feelings of insignificance.

Many men believe they'll never live up to the expectations of others or are convinced they are failures.

These two men were attempting to keep others away from their secret place of pain and insecurity. Both were miserable. Both were unsure of their choices.

Only God can secure us from the outside influences and inner conflict in our lives. Our security isn't found in our own ability but in God's. We become sufficient or acceptable because of God's grace, mercy, and peace through Jesus. Though there will be hard days when our feelings sneak up on us, spending time in scripture will remind us of how Jesus loves us and came to rescue us when, in our sin, we couldn't offer Him anything in return, not even love (Romans 5:8).

Feeling insignificant is normal. Knowing we are accepted by God makes us secure, no matter what we are feeling at the moment.

THE COURAGE TO RUN AWAY
FROM TEMPTATION

One day he went into the house to attend to his duties,
and none of the household servants was inside. She caught him
by his cloak and said, "Come to bed with me!" But he left
his cloak in her hand and ran out of the house.

GENESIS 39:11–12 NIV

We often think of courage and strength in terms of taking a stand and never backing down. We imagine ourselves in situations where we must hold our ground at all costs. However, there are times when the most courageous thing we can do is run away. In a situation that offered no easy solution, Joseph recognized that his master's wife would continue to pursue him if he remained alone with her. Out of his love for God and loyalty to his master, he had the courage and strength to run away. There are some "battles" that cannot be won by staying put. When temptation threatens to trap us, there are times when our safest move is to retreat by changing our location, seeking help, or starting a new activity. Resisting temptation can be just as much a matter of where we choose to stay or not stay as it can be a mental battle. Whatever Joseph thought or felt in the moment, his resolve to run away made it possible for him to, in a sense, stand strong.

AN EXAMPLE TO OTHERS

*Be an example to all believers in what you say, in the way
you live, in your love, your faith, and your purity.*
1 TIMOTHY 4:12 NLT

This verse may seem like a tall order. You might be struggling with bitterness, question your faith at times, and have daily battles with lust. You don't feel like you're able to be an example to other believers. You're happy if you can hold your *own* act together enough to escape condemnation and self-doubt.

Don't give up on yourself. God hasn't thrown in the towel on you yet, and neither should you. Love and follow God today, and trust that He will continue working in your life and give you the victory in these areas as you cry out to Him to help you. Remember that when Jesus revealed God's power to Peter, the rough-hewn fisherman pleaded, "Depart from me; for I am a sinful man, O Lord" (Luke 5:8 KJV).

But Jesus *didn't* depart. He continued to work in Peter's life for the next three years. And even after all that time learning from the Master, Peter denied Him during a time of testing. But Jesus saw that coming too and said, "I have pleaded in prayer for you, Simon, that your faith should not fail. So when you have repented and turned to me again, strengthen your brothers" (Luke 22:32 NLT).

If there's hope for Peter, there's hope for you.

READ YOUR BIBLE!

Your word is a lamp for my feet, a light on my path.
PSALM 119:105 NIV

Life is busy, isn't it? We spend 8-plus hours a day, 5-plus days a week working, and then we have to make time for family, for friends, and for church and church-related activities. Sometimes we're squeezed for time, and one of the first casualties is time alone with God in prayer and Bible reading.

The psalmist who wrote today's scripture verse understood that the Word of God gives believers direction and lights the way as we follow its leading. But the apostle Paul had much more to say about what the Bible does for us: "All Scripture is God-breathed and is useful for teaching, rebuking, correcting and training in righteousness, so that the servant of God may be thoroughly equipped for every good work" (2 Timothy 3:16–17).

So the words recorded in scripture lead and guide us, teach us, rebuke and correct us, and teach us what it means to be righteous. Can there be any question as to how important it is that we spend time reading God's Word?

Reading books and other material about the Bible is a good thing, and attending group Bible studies is probably even better. But nothing should ever take the place of spending time alone with God, reading and meditating on His written Word.

CUSSIN' COUSINS

"But let your 'Yes' be 'Yes,' and your 'No' [be] 'No.' "
Matthew 5:37 nkjv

"Why, you dad-flustered, ding-dang, daisy-headed son of a drip-dried dervish!" Farmer Jones shouted over the fence at Farmer Smith.

Smith began to answer with his own string of original pejoratives then stopped himself in midsentence. The parson was coming down the road on his big black bay horse. Louder than before, Smith (a deacon at the local church) exclaimed, "Farmer Jones, our Lord said, 'Do not swear at all! Neither by heaven for it is God's throne, nor by earth for it is his footstool, nor by Jerusalem for. . .' "

Is that the kind of swearing Jesus was talking about in the Sermon on the Mount? No, doggone it! He was talking about swearing an *oath*, about making a promise, about giving our word. He meant: "Don't tie your promises to all kinds of crazy consequences. Don't cross your heart and hope to die. Don't swear on a stack of Bibles. Let your 'yes' be 'yes,' and your 'no' be 'no.' Put your money where your mouth is. Anything more than that comes from the evil one."

No need for oaths, because we can't implore heaven to make our pledges come true. We dare not ask the earth to assist us either. We must simply say what we mean and mean what we say.

The devil uses convincing words to assure us that his ways are better than God's ways. We don't need to use his tactics to sway others to our convictions or make them believe in our sincerity. We must be men of our word. Period.

PRAYING THROUGH THE PAIN

He touched the socket of his hip; and the socket of Jacob's hip was out of joint as He wrestled with him. And He said, "Let Me go, for the day breaks." But he said, "I will not let You go unless You bless me!"
GENESIS 32:25–26 NKJV

Today's passage is part of an account in which the patriarch Jacob became involved in an extended wrestling match with. . .God! It sounds odd to think of a mere man wrestling with the Almighty. Certainly, the Creator of the universe could have ended such an encounter in an instant with but a thought. But your Father in heaven had a lesson to teach Jacob—and you today too.

God wanted to bless Jacob, but He also wanted him to understand that prayer isn't always easy, that it means persistent, sometimes painful, times of pleading with God until he receives an answer.

If you've ever suffered through a dislocated joint, then you have some understanding of what Jacob went through in that hour before dawn. A dislocated toe or finger can be agonizing enough, but just think of the pain Jacob felt when God dislocated his *hip*!

When a nearly incapacitated Jacob still refused to let his God go that night, he set an example for believers to follow. Prayer hurts sometimes, but in the midst of your pain, you should keep praying and cling to your God with everything you have.

MERCY ME

"Blessed are the merciful, for they shall obtain mercy."
MATTHEW 5:7 NKJV

Second Corinthians 1:3 says that God is the "Father of mercies." Mercy is one of God's attributes, given to us in Christ so that we may extend it to others—even to our enemies. To be like our Father, we must be merciful (Luke 6:35–36).

A criminal is shown mercy when his sentence is shortened. A prisoner of war is shown mercy when he is treated humanely. The fallen gladiator in the Roman Colosseum was shown mercy when the dignitaries in the box seats gave a thumbs-up to let him live.

We extend mercy when we bless those who curse us, pray for those who persecute us, and do good to those who do us wrong (Matthew 5:44). We show our children mercy when we patiently give them another chance at something they've failed (or refused) to do. Mercy, like grace, is undeserved favor, something extended to others who may not merit it but need it.

Though we deserve judgment for our sin, God's great mercy has given us new birth instead and a living hope through the resurrection of Jesus Christ (1 Peter 1:3). Thus we show mercy and forgiveness to others (Ephesians 4:32).

Saint Augustine, an early church father who received the mercy of God through a dramatic conversion experience, wrote: "Two works of mercy set a man free: forgive and you will be forgiven. And give and you will receive." We could call this "the law of divine reciprocity." In other words, "You reap what you sow."

Do you need mercy? Give mercy.

SLOW, STEADY PROGRESS

The end of a matter is better than its beginning;
patience of spirit is better than haughtiness of spirit.
ECCLESIASTES 7:8 NASB

If you've ever been to a rally—spiritual, sports, or business-related—then you know how a great message can fire up a crowd. Everybody plans to go home and implement what they learned, but as soon as they walk through the door, reality hits them.

The sink is backed up, the car needs repairs, their son needs a ride to soccer practice, and the baby is crying. So, they dive into their responsibilities, and the end of the matter (their new goal) fades as quickly as the emotion that swept through the auditorium hours earlier. They're like "the man who hears the word and immediately receives it with joy; yet he has no firm root in himself, but is only temporary" (Matthew 13:20–21 NASB).

In today's verse, Solomon calls you to be patient of spirit as you set your mind on something. If your goal is to read God's Word every day without fail, then tend to your responsibilities, but try getting up a little earlier. If your goal is to walk five miles a day, start with one mile and work your way up. If your goal is to set a new sales record, then study the current leader and carefully implement his strategies.

Slow, steady progress beats quick, emotional commitment every time. The end is better than the beginning.

SEEING GOD IN HIS CREATION

*"But ask the animals, and they will teach you, or the birds in the sky,
and they will tell you; or speak to the earth, and it will teach
you, or let the fish in the sea inform you."*
JOB 12:7–8 NIV

The famous seventeenth-century English writer Izaak Walton, author of the famous fishing tome titled *The Compleat Angler: or, The Contemplative Man's Recreation*, once wrote, *"Rivers and the inhabitants of the watery elements are made for wise men to contemplate and for fools to pass by without consideration."*

Taking the time to get away and enjoy the outdoors is a pleasurable endeavor for just about anyone. But for a man of God, these activities offer something more, something of a truly "spiritual" nature.

One of the great things about fishing, hunting, hiking, camping, or any other activity that takes place in the context of the outdoors is just being in the places where we can enjoy those things. These are the settings where we see God's handiwork clear of manmade distractions.

No, the creation is not God Himself, but you can learn some great truths about His nature and character by looking at the wonder of what He has created.

So the next time you head out to enjoy a day—or a weekend, or a week—outdoors, don't forget to take your heavenly Father with you. It's in those settings where you can just enjoy His company, maybe even hear His voice, away from the world's noise.

THE EXAMPLE

[Jesus] withdrew from them about a stone's throw, and He knelt down and began to pray, saying, "Father, if You are willing, remove this cup from Me; yet not My will, but Yours be done."
Luke 22:41–42 nasb

Jesus was within hours of His death on the cross. This was God's plan from the beginning. Relationship with mankind would be restored and Jesus would defeat death, but in His human body there waged a war between the desire to live and the desire to honor His Father.

It can be a surprise to read that Jesus asked God for a second option. He prayed passionately. If Jesus' prayer ended with only a request for a way out, we might leave confused, but Jesus ended His prayer with what has become the best response of all mankind: "Not my will, but Yours be done."

No wonder we're told that Jesus understands humanity (Hebrews 4:15). If God had granted Jesus' request, salvation either wouldn't be available or God would have needed a new plan to rescue mankind. But Jesus believed in the rescue plan. He was at a critical point. Jesus chose to follow His Father's plan. . .and mankind was offered rescue.

You may not always see the wisdom of God's will. It may seem an unnecessary hardship, a burden too big to bear, or something that no longer applies. As hard as it may seem to follow God's will, it's always been perfect.

PRAYERS OF PROTECTION

*Because he hath set his love upon me. . .He shall call upon me,
and I will answer him: I will be with him in trouble; I will deliver him.*
PSALM 91:14–15 KJV

God tells the disobedient, "The LORD's arm is not too weak to save you,
nor is his ear too deaf to hear you call," but "because of your sins, he
has turned away and will not listen anymore" (Isaiah 59:1–2 NLT). When
people are far from God, they can't claim His blessing or protection.

However, the opposite is true when you draw *near* to God. Then,
you call upon Him and He *will* answer. He will be with you when you
face trouble and protect you. This doesn't mean that He will spare
you from *all* trouble, but it means that He will be *with* you.

Some people, however, question why God often *doesn't* seem
to be with believers who love and obey Him. Does that mean this
promise isn't true? No. What it means is that God is sovereign and
has His reasons for sometimes allowing suffering.

Notice in Hebrews 11:35–37 that He allowed His righteous followers to be tortured, whipped, to languish in prison, to die by stoning,
to be sawed in half, and to be killed with the sword. Many others were
destitute and oppressed and mistreated. Yet we remember these
people not as abandoned unfortunates, but as heroes of the faith.

HARDWIRED FOR SUCCESS?

*Earn a reputation for living well in God's
eyes and the eyes of the people.*
PROVERBS 3:4 MSG

Men seem to be hardwired to want to be considered a success. Go to most ten-year high school reunions and men will talk about how successful they are, or they may resort to reliving their high school successes.

Some men will fight for their marriage (and they should), but only to prove they're a success in marriage. They don't want to be viewed as a failure.

Men will do what they feel they have to in order to shore up the appearance of success. However, when failure comes, some men will shift directions completely. These men will embrace failure as an old friend and live as if success is no longer available. They rush to make bad choices, dismiss their wife and children because they view themselves as mistake prone, and move from job to job because they can't find a reason to be passionate about work.

God longs for men to be authentic, transparent fighters for what's right. He longs for us to stop wearing masks and believing that if we just try hard enough we can move all outside forces to be in our favor.

Our greatest success is to be *forgiven* men of God, to be in right relationship with Him. Let's focus our efforts on knowing and pleasing Him, and then, as we put our attention on what our loving heavenly Father thinks, what others think will not matter so much to us.

HELPING THOSE IN NEED

*As we have opportunity, let us do good to all,
especially to those who are of the household of faith.*
GALATIANS 6:10 NKJV

There are generally two ways God moves you to show kindness to fellow believers. One is when you're aware of their need, are thinking about it, and realize that you're in a position to help. So you talk it over with your wife and arrange to do it. It's really a logical conclusion, done out of love for others. Often you have time to think it over and get counsel about it.

The second way is when you first become aware of their need and right on the spot the Holy Spirit speaks, telling you exactly what to do to help.

However God works to get you to loosen your purse strings—and helping someone often involves finances—be obedient. Yes, God *may* call upon you to give to someone less fortunate than yourself, even if you're a manual laborer earning minimum wage. Paul said in Ephesians 4:28 (NKJV), "Let him. . .labor, working with his hands what is good, that he may have something to give him who has need."

James asked, "Suppose you see a brother or sister who has no food or clothing, and you say, 'Good-bye and have a good day; stay warm and eat well'—but then you don't give that person any food or clothing. What good does that do?" (James 2:15–16 NLT). The answer is obvious.

THE SOURCE OF OUR TEMPTATION

When tempted, no one should say, "God is tempting me."
For God cannot be tempted by evil, nor does he tempt anyone;
but each person is tempted when they are dragged
away by their own evil desire and enticed.

JAMES 1:13–14 NIV

Remember comedian Flip Wilson's famous phrase "The devil made me do it!"? While it was part of a funny routine, it was hardly sound theology. In truth, the devil can't *make* people do anything; he can only tempt us.

The Bible teaches that temptation comes from basically three sources: from the devil (remember, Adam and Eve sinned when they gave into the devil's temptation; also, the devil tempted Jesus Himself, though He did not sin), from the world, and from our own evil, fallen hearts (see today's verse).

Many young believers come into the faith believing that they will no longer be tempted to sin in ways they used to before they were saved. Some quickly become discouraged or disillusioned when they find that the temptation to sin doesn't just "go away."

Temptation will always be a part of our lives here on earth. It was in the beginning for humanity, and it still is today. But God can't and won't tempt us to sin. On the other hand, the Bible promises us that "God is faithful; he will not let you be tempted beyond what you can bear. But when you are tempted, he will also provide a way out so that you can endure it" (1 Corinthians 10:13 NIV).

INTIMIDATED BY GIANTS

*"There we saw the giants. . .and we were like grasshoppers
in our own sight, and so we were in their sight."*
NUMBERS 13:33 NKJV

When the Israelites arrived at the border of Canaan, Moses sent
twelve spies into the land. When they returned, ten of them said,
"The people who dwell in the land are strong; the cities are fortified
and very large. . . . And all the people whom we saw in it are men of
great stature" (Numbers 13:28, 32 NKJV).

They concluded, "We are not able to go up against the people,
for they are stronger than we" (v. 31). Their negative report so discouraged the Israelites that they were afraid to invade Canaan, even
though the Lord had promised He'd help them.

Does this ever happen to you? You're initially excited about a
project, and even though you're aware you'll face difficulties, you're
buoyed by feelings of optimism. God has promised to be with you, and
you know that He can do miracles. But when it actually comes time
to launch out, you allow yourself to get discouraged by naysayers,
get cold feet, and back out.

It's human nature to say, "There are giants in the land!" It's the
default setting of the natural mind to see problems as huge and to
feel grasshopper-sized compared to them. But have faith in God.
With His help you can overcome them no matter how big they are.

GAINING WEALTH GOD'S WAY

Dishonest money dwindles away, but whoever gathers money little by little makes it grow.
PROVERBS 13:11 NIV

According to many people, the way to get ahead financially is to make false claims on your income tax, to overcharge for goods or services, and to cut corners on quality whenever you can. But people find out after a while if you're dishonest, and your business will suffer as a result.

God's way to financial prosperity is to gather money honestly little by little and diligently set it aside in a savings account. If you start early enough, you'll eventually earn compound interest. There are no shortcuts, no maps leading to pirate treasure, and no leprechauns guiding you to a pot of gold. And if you're counting on winning the lottery, forget it.

If you gain enough money, you can earn even more by investing it. Jesus taught the importance of investments in the parable of the talents (Matthew 25:14–30). In His story, when a master entrusted each of his servants with a sum of money, the first two went out and invested it, earning double and even five times what they had started with.

And Solomon pointed out the best way to build your retirement savings, saying, "Take a lesson from the ants, you lazybones. Learn from their ways and become wise! Though they have no. . .ruler to make them work, they labor hard all summer, gathering food for the winter" (Proverbs 6:6–8 NLT).

As with most things in life, being faithful day after day is the best way to build a successful life, career, and savings account.

BROKEN CISTERNS

"For My people have. . .forsaken Me, the fountain of living waters,
to hew for themselves cisterns, broken cisterns that can hold no water."
JEREMIAH 2:13 NASB

Israel is dry most of the year, with rain falling predominantly in the winter, so water is a precious commodity. Then as now, the best sources were springs or fountains, as their supply was fresh and clean. Also, wells tapped into underground streams were another source of running water.

God referred to Himself as "the fountain of living waters," and Jesus called the Spirit of God "a well of water springing up to eternal life" (John 4:14 NASB).

When Israelite villages lacked sufficient water, they carved out underground reservoirs called *cisterns* to store water. They sealed the walls with plaster. Then they directed the winter rain into these cisterns. A great deal of mud ended up in the bottom of it (see Jeremiah 38:6). Also, Israel had many minor earthquakes, and the plaster was constantly cracking and the water draining away.

God pointed out how senseless His people were to choose broken cisterns with muddy, stale water over fresh spring water. Man's broken philosophies and stagnant religions are the same—far inferior to faith in the true God. Unfortunately, people today are still hewing out cisterns.

Ditch the stagnant water of man's philosophies and come drink of the water of life. "Let anyone who is thirsty come. Let anyone who desires drink freely from the water of life" (Revelation 22:17 NLT).

SERVING GOD BY SERVING OTHERS

"The King will reply, 'Truly I tell you, whatever you did for one of the least of these brothers and sisters of mine, you did for me.'"
MATTHEW 25:40 NIV

Today's verse—as well as some other passages, like James 2:14–26—seem to imply that serving others is a requirement for salvation. That's a real head-scratcher for some Christians, who know that the Bible is clear that salvation is based on faith in Christ alone and not on our good works.

When we step back and take a broader look at the entire biblical message of salvation, we see that Jesus'—as well as James's—words do not contradict or even confuse the message of salvation by faith in Christ alone. Instead, those who by faith have received salvation and therefore have God's Spirit living within them will be motivated to serve out of true love for God and others.

Doing good things for others doesn't make you a Christian, and it won't "earn" you God's eternal salvation. On the other hand, as a follower of Jesus Christ, you'll find yourself motivated to serve others, knowing that when you serve the "least of these," you're serving God Himself.

Do you believe God wants you to have a bigger heart for service? Have you been wondering what kind of service He has in mind for you? Ask Him to first give you the right motivation to serve, and then ask Him to show you ways you can serve others.

The opportunities are all around you, and you'll find them if you just ask and then keep your eyes open.

UNDERFOOT

"You are the salt of the earth; but if the salt loses its flavor. . .
[i]t is then good for nothing but to be thrown
out and trampled underfoot by men."
MATTHEW 5:13 NKJV

Peanut Butter was a lively, loud-barking golden retriever, always poised at her master's feet and ready to jump. Especially excitable when visitors came, her frenetic attentions were over-the-top. Mark gave her the nickname "Lady Underfoot."

Years later, with Lady Underfoot gone to her reward, Mark got another retriever, a male this time. The polar opposite of his predecessor, Bono hardly budged and never barked. He was salt that had lost its savor.

Christians are the salt of the earth. We give this tepid old planet the flavor of heaven, and we help slow its inevitable decay. But if we lose our saltiness, what good are we? Good for *nothing!*—except to be pitched on the sidewalk and "trampled underfoot."

In Christ's day, salt was sometimes contaminated by various minerals and therefore rendered worthless as a preservative. Such salt was thrown out, not in a field where it might kill the plants, but on the road where traffic would grind it into the dirt. Losing our "flavor" isn't the issue (real salt never loses its flavor). The concern is in nullifying our influence as a preservative, losing our civilizing ability to hold this world together by living like Jesus. A faith defiled by worldly philosophies and contemporary morality is good for nothing. An impure influence may kill rather than produce life. Only the truth can set men free. Everything else ends up underfoot, the dust of death on the broad road to destruction.

THE DUTY OF A WATCHMAN

"As for me, far be it from me that I should sin against the LORD
by ceasing to pray for you; but I will instruct you
in the good and right way."

1 SAMUEL 12:23 NASB

God told Ezekiel, "I have appointed you a watchman to the house of Israel; whenever you hear a word from My mouth, warn them from Me" (Ezekiel 3:17 NASB). Watchmen stood on city walls, keeping their eyes open for danger and sounding the alarm to rouse the people so the city wouldn't fall to the enemy. Men of God often watched over Israel. Samuel was one such man.

God declared, "I searched for a man among them who would build up the wall and stand in the gap before Me for the land, so that I would not destroy it" (Ezekiel 22:30 NASB). When the spiritual wall of a nation's defenses are weak, men of God are called to intercede for their people—to guard these gaps. You do this through intercessory prayer.

Samuel said that he'd be *sinning* if he ceased to pray for his people. Christian men today should also understand prayer as their duty. It's easy to just kick up your feet and relax after a day at work, and you *do* need rest, but it's *also* your duty to take matters to God in prayer. To do that, you must carve out some time in your schedule. Don't neglect this.

CAUTION TAPE CHRISTIANITY

Fix your attention on God. You'll be changed from the inside out. Readily recognize what he wants from you, and quickly respond to it. Unlike the culture around you, always dragging you down to its level of immaturity, God brings the best out of you, develops well-formed maturity in you.

ROMANS 12:2 MSG

What if there was the equivalent of yellow caution tape when it comes to places, circumstances, and events that we should avoid? Would we pay attention? Would we change direction?

If you go to the theater and the movie doesn't look like it matches God's heart, imagine yellow caution tape warning you to keep out. Imagine the same to be true for individuals the Bible describes as "bad company," or maybe it's arguments you need to stay away from. This visible reminder would solve all kinds of problems, wouldn't it?

God's Holy Spirit came to be that "caution tape." We don't see visible warning signs, but if we pay attention, we'll recognize those warning signs with as much personal impact as seeing bright yellow tape blocking the way to a dangerous area.

God has always provided the warning signs—we just need to recognize them. God gave us the help we need—we just need to stop rejecting it. If we humble ourselves and fix our attention on God and the help He provides in His Spirit, we will see Him "bring[ing] out the best in [us], developing[ing] well-formed maturity in [us]."

HONORED BY MEN

*"I know I have sinned. But please, at least honor me before
the elders of my people and before Israel by coming back
with me so that I may worship the LORD your God."*
1 SAMUEL 15:30 NLT

The prophet Samuel had just finished telling Saul, "Rebellion is as sinful as witchcraft, and stubbornness as bad as worshiping idols. So because you have rejected the command of the LORD, he has rejected you as king" (v. 23). Saul then admitted, "I have disobeyed. . . the LORD's command, for I was afraid of the people and did what they demanded" (v. 24).

Despite that, he *still* had the nerve to ask Samuel, "Honor me before the elders of my people."

Saul feared people, and being accepted and honored by them was all that mattered to him. He was not very concerned whether he pleased God. The religious leaders of Jesus' day were the same. "They loved human praise more than the praise of God" (John 12:43 NLT). As Jesus pointed out, "You gladly honor each other, but you don't care about the honor that comes from. . .God" (John 5:44 NLT).

The Lord understands the human need to save face and be respected. He *gets* it. Nevertheless, He insists that you seek to please Him above all. It can be difficult, but life would be so much simpler if people simply sought the praise of God first and foremost.

FORGIVENESS OF OTHERS: GOD REQUIRES IT

*"And when you stand praying, if you hold anything against anyone,
forgive them, so that your Father in heaven may forgive you your sins."*
MARK 11:25 NIV

If you've ever been around someone who harbors anger and bitterness toward another (for example, a man who hangs on to a wrong his wife committed against him years earlier), you know how uncomfortable it can be. You want to get as far away as possible as quickly as possible.

Anger and unforgiveness are like love and faith in that they always find outward expressions. You just can't be an angry, bitter person without those around you seeing it in you—or hearing it from you.

God, it turns out, takes our forgiveness of others very seriously, so seriously that Jesus instructed His followers to forgive one another from their hearts. Otherwise, He said, God would not hear their prayers.

Have you ever been in a place with your relationship with God where your prayers seem stale, where it seems like they aren't reaching God's ears? There could be a lot of reasons for that—hidden sin, a particular spiritual struggle, and even those "dry times" we all sometimes experience.

But what about unforgiveness? When you're in that place where you don't feel like God is hearing you, take the time to examine your personal relationships with others and ask yourself if it's possible you're harboring unforgiveness toward someone.

Then forgive. . .from your heart.

HOPE FOR HAPPINESS

Make me hear joy and gladness,
that the bones You have broken may rejoice.
PSALM 51:8 NKJV

In the ancient Middle East, a lamb that strayed from the shepherd and the flock put itself in great danger, since the surrounding wilderness was home to fierce animals. If a lamb continually strayed, a shepherd would break one of its legs. Until it healed, the lamb depended on the shepherd to carry it around and bring it grass. Once it healed, the lamb would usually stay nearer the shepherd than any other sheep.

Sometimes God allows accidents and misfortune to cause *you* to focus on Him and His doings. His desire is for your good and to draw you closer to Him, though it might not seem good at the time.

When he uttered the above verse, David was repenting for committing adultery with Bathsheba and for arranging for her husband to be slain. It almost seems inappropriate for him to pray, "Make me hear joy and gladness" and to ask that he might soon "rejoice." It seems he should have been pleading for God's mercy and forgiveness. That *is*, in fact, what he'd been doing in the rest of this psalm.

But David had tremendous faith in the Lord's loving-kindness. He knew that God was merciful, and he had the faith to look beyond his present distress to anticipate full restoration and the return of happiness. May you hope for the same.

GOD'S PURPOSE FOR LIFE'S TRIALS

Consider it pure joy, my brothers and sisters, whenever you face trials of many kinds, because you know that the testing of your faith produces perseverance. Let perseverance finish its work so that you may be mature and complete, not lacking anything.
JAMES 1:2–4 NIV

Albert Einstein once made an amazingly insightful observation about dealing with life's difficulties when he said, "Adversity introduces a man to himself."

When life brings difficulties our way (and it most certain will), we see where we're really at in our walk with our heavenly Father. The old analogy holds true: when you squeeze a sponge (you being the sponge) hard enough, you're sure to see what's inside.

God never promised His people an easy ride through life. In fact, the Bible is very clear—and in many passages—that trials, storms, and suffering will be part of every believer's life. If you don't believe that, just take a look at the lives of the apostles, the men Jesus chose to take His message of salvation to the world around them. We're talking imprisonment, beatings, even martyrdom for nearly all of them.

God also doesn't just automatically make you a patient person when you get saved, and He doesn't instantly make you a person of great perseverance, either. Instead, He uses a process whereby the trials and storms in your life strengthen you and make you the patient, persevering man He intends for you to be.

So when the going gets tough . . .rejoice!

DO-GOODERS

"Do good to those who hate you."
MATTHEW 5:44 NKJV

When wicked people lie on their beds and devise evil against us (as Micah 2:1 says they do), we are to lie on our beds thinking of ways to do them good.

"If your enemy is hungry, give him food to eat; if he is thirsty, give him water to drink" (Proverbs 25:21 NIV).

Why do that?

Because, "in doing this, you will heap burning coals on his head, and the LORD will reward you" (25:22 NIV).

Reward me for heaping coals on my enemies head?

Yes, because, your good will overcome his evil (Romans 12:20–21).

How so?

The goodness of God works on the heart to soften it (Romans 2:4). It works on the conscience to convict it. Right deeds done for those who do us wrong heap "hot coals" of conviction upon them. The Holy Spirit uses our good deeds to convict them of their own sin.

Chrystostom (fourth-century archbishop of Constantinople) wrote: "Heat makes all things expand. And the warmth of love will always expand a person's heart."

We are called to Christ in order to do good works which He has prepared for us long before we saw the light of our first day (Ephesians 2:10). Some of those good works are meant to be practiced on our enemies so that they "take the heat" of the Holy Spirit's conviction, their hearts expand to let Christ in, and their lips open in praise and glory to our Father who is in heaven (Matthew 5:16).

FEEBLE FOLK IN FORTRESSES

*The conies are but a feeble folk,
yet make they their houses in the rocks.*
PROVERBS 30:26 KJV

What, you may ask, are conies? The NIV translates this verse: "Hyraxes are creatures of little power, yet they make their home in the crags." The *Hyrax syriacus*, also known as a rock badger, is found in the Sinai Desert and cliffs along the Dead Sea. It's a small, shy, furry animal that resembles a guinea pig. It lives in rock crevices, safe from predators. Hyraxes feed in groups, watched over by sentries that sound an alarm when enemies approach.

They're reminiscent of the Ewoks, short furry bipeds in the *Star Wars* movies, who lived on the forest moon of Endor. They too were a "feeble folk" who proved to be mighty.

All believers are "feeble" in *some* area of their lives—weak, incapable, and lacking power. You may be ordinary, with no special talents, yet do things that compensate for your weakness. Maybe you're thrifty and good at saving, so despite a lack of good looks, strength, or other A-list abilities, you're able to provide a secure financial future.

"Remember. . .that few of you were wise in the world's eyes or powerful or wealthy when God called you. Instead, God chose things. . . that are powerless to shame those who are powerful" (1 Corinthians 1:26–27 NLT).

THE ONE NAME

What marvelous love the Father has extended to us! Just look at it—we're called children of God! That's who we really are.
1 JOHN 3:1 MSG

We are husbands, dads, employees, uncles, nephews, neighbors, plumbers, bakers, farmers, architects, writers, janitors, mechanics, truck drivers, accountants, comedians, gamers, athletes, actors, and a laundry list of other names that can define who we are and what we do.

We can also be called kind, gentle, loving, good, self-controlled, rude, rough, mean, or impulsive.

Of all the names men can be called, the one that should mean the most is *child of God*. This name defines who we are because it defines whom we follow. It indicates God has accepted us and we're part of a family of those accepted by Him. It suggests we're always in a position of learning because a child never knows it all. It holds within it the promise of being coheirs with Christ, inheriting both eternal life and God's blessing and help in this earthly life: "And we know we are going to get what's coming to us—an unbelievable inheritance! We go through exactly what Christ goes through. If we go through the hard times with him, then we're certainly going to go through the good times with him!" (Romans 8:17 MSG).

Knowing who we are as a child of God helps us put all the other names we may be called into perspective. It also helps us identify with names that describe how a child of God is different from those who aren't God's children.

What's in a name? Perhaps more than you may have thought?

ACCOMPLISHING ITS MISSION

*"As the rain and the snow come down from heaven, and do not return
to it without watering the earth and making it bud and flourish. . .
so is my word that goes out from my mouth: It will not return to
me empty, but will. . .achieve the purpose for which I sent it."*
ISAIAH 55:10–11 NIV

God's Word is eternal and is like buckets containing ever-fresh supplies of His Spirit. When you believe His promises and apply them to the different situations you face, it's as if you're pouring life-giving water on dry earth. This causes your situations to come to life like dormant seeds activated by water.

In the passage above, God promises that, just as water evaporates and returns as vapor to heaven, so His Word will return to Him—but not before it accomplishes the purpose He sent it to accomplish on earth.

You may sometimes wonder if the Word of God is truly effective, especially if you're claiming Bible promises for a very difficult situation. You can become discouraged if *years* go by without seeing promises fulfilled. But remember, explorers have found seeds in the deserts of Australia that have laid dormant, bone-dry, for hundreds of years, but after being watered, have miraculously and instantly sprung to life and bloomed.

If you're trusting God to do a miracle in your marriage, your finances, or your children, don't give up. God is powerful!

YOUR CONSCIENCE CAN BE YOUR GUIDE

*Holding on to faith and a good conscience, which some have
rejected and so have suffered shipwreck with regard to the faith.*
1 TIMOTHY 1:19 NIV

God has given human beings the wonderful gift of a conscience—a
sense of right and wrong. But the human conscience was exposed to
damage when sin entered into the human experience, when Adam and
Eve chose to disobey the one commandment God had given them
(see Genesis 3). Since that moment, sin has damaged the conscience
of every human being.

When you first received the free gift of salvation through Jesus
Christ, God placed His Holy Spirit within you. Part of the Holy Spirit's
role in your Christian life is to alert you when you're about to make
a choice that doesn't please God. That is partly what Jesus meant
when He told His followers that the Spirit would "guide you into all
the truth" (John 16:13).

When God's Holy Spirit is inside you, He allows you to better
understand the truths of scripture, which are the basis for every decision we make. And when we have the Spirit playing that role in our
lives, we can safely allow our conscience to be our guide.

THE LORD'S FAVOR

For the LORD God is a sun and shield: the LORD will give grace and glory: no good thing will he withhold from them that walk uprightly.
PSALM 84:11 KJV

This beautiful passage tells you that the Lord is like the brilliant sun, giving warmth and light as you make Him your center, orbiting your life around Him. As you do so, He will bestow His radiant qualities upon you, filling your life with grace and favor and causing you to reflect His glory. Furthermore, He's your strong defender, forming a protective shield about you.

Many people, however, fail to tune in to this overarching picture of God and His blessings and focus only on the last half of the verse: "no good thing will he withhold from them that walk uprightly." They view God as some kind of galactic candy machine and claim this truncated promise merely to get goodies.

Certainly God wants to bless you with your needs, but more than anything, He longs for you to walk close to Him, surrounded by and permeated by His presence. In turn, He wants you to shine His light upon the dark world. Only then, when you walk in the righteousness granted by His Spirit, will He be pleased to give you all good things.

JESUS, OUR ADVOCATE

*My dear children, I write this to you so that you will not sin.
But if anybody does sin, we have an advocate with the
Father—Jesus Christ, the Righteous One.*

1 JOHN 2:1 NIV

It might strike some of us as a bit odd that the apostle John would use the phrase "an advocate with the Father" to describe our Savior. In the context of today's verse, the word *advocate* implies someone who pleads our case before a legal court of justice; in other words, a lawyer.

In today's legal world, a lawyer pleads his client's case whether or not he believes that client is innocent. Our advocate before God in heaven is different from an earthly lawyer in that He pleads the case before the Father knowing that we're guilty as charged, that we've certainly committed the offense charged against us.

This goes far beyond today's legal standard of "guilty beyond a reasonable doubt."

Jesus knows of our guilt, and so does God the Father. But when Jesus pleads our case, He in effect says, "Father, I know this man is a sinner. But he has come to us and confessed and repented. He has been cleansed and forgiven."

But here's the best part of this arrangement: when Jesus pleads our case, it's not before a stern judge who begrudgingly offers absolution. On the contrary, Jesus pleads our case before a loving, holy God who promises us to "cleanse us from all unrighteousness" when we simply confess our sins (1 John 1:9 NIV).

A SURE SALVATION

But we are not like those who turn away from God to their own
destruction. We are the faithful ones, whose souls will be saved.
HEBREWS 10:39 NLT

You can't earn salvation by your own efforts. God gives eternal life to you as an undeserved gift. Also, once you're saved, it doesn't become *your* job to *keep* yourself saved; God keeps you saved (see John 10:28–29; Ephesians 2:8–9; Romans 10:9–10).

But some Christians suffer anxiety, worrying that they'll "lose" their salvation for some sin. After all, Jesus said in Matthew 24:13 (NKJV) that "he who endures to the end shall be saved." Some Christians also worry about 1 Corinthians 9:27 (KJV) where Paul speaks of disciplining himself to ensure that he didn't become "a castaway" (see also John 15:6).

However, Jesus said, "The one who comes to Me I will by *no means* cast out" (John 6:37 NKJV, emphasis added). Your salvation isn't like so much pocket change that you casually lose. Scripture indicates that people must knowingly, completely renounce their faith to be "fallen from grace" (Galatians 5:4 NKJV; see also Hebrews 6:4–6).

However, if you love God but constantly feel unworthy and worried about your salvation, be at peace. Remember that God has promised, "Being confident of this, that he who began a good work in you will carry it on to completion until the day of Christ Jesus" (Philippians 1:6 NIV).

THE ORIGIN OF STORIES

Come here and listen, let me tell you what God did for me.
PSALM 66:16 MSG

Each song you hear has a story attached to its creation. Some of those stories are as compelling as the song itself. Horatio Spafford wrote the hymn "It Is Well with My Soul" following the loss of his four daughters in a shipwreck at sea. Matthew West wrote the song "Day One" after reading the story of a man who had made many, many poor choices and was working hard to make each day a step toward positive personal change.

You have a story, and like the psalmist, you could gather people around to hear what God has done for you, whether over dinner at your house, at a conference, at a prayer group, on a blog, or in a book. Finding a way to share that story is important because your story shows evidence that the God who made you has always had a plan for you—even following your or others' poor decisions.

Depending on what you have to share, your story could provide a cautionary tale for others in their Christian lives, encouragement to the weary to continue standing strong, or an open door to welcome new stories told by those who've gained courage to speak after hearing *your* story.

At the core of your tale is the Author of your story. Whatever story you tell, give credit to God, who brings you through storms, knew your name before you were born, and prepares the way for your future.

WORDS LIKE MEDICINE

Gentle words are a tree of life; a deceitful tongue crushes the spirit.
PROVERBS 15:4 NLT

What is the most hurtful thing anybody has ever said to you? Can you recall the circumstances? How long ago was it? Did you embrace it as truth—even if it wasn't true—and allow it to affect your life for more years than you care to admit?

Have you ever said something hurtful to somebody that you wished you could take back a second after it left your lips? You saw the reaction on the other person's face, and it confirmed the devastation you realized it might bring. You can say you're sorry later, and that helps, but you can't unsay those words.

Gentle words are a tree of life. That doesn't mean you can't be truthful, but it does mean you should be gentle. Even tough love can be gentle. Some translations (NIV, NASB) use the word *soothing* in place of *gentle*, and the KJV has *wholesome*. The Hebrew word actually means "medicine, cure, deliverance, and remedy," among other things.

Are your words like medicine? Do they offer deliverance and a cure? Or are they sometimes deceitful or crushing? Consider how the negative words you recalled so easily at the beginning of this devotion affected you, and resolve to not weigh anybody down with such a tone going forward.

TRYING TO FEEL YOUR WAY

*"That they would seek God, if perhaps they might grope for Him
and find Him, though He is not far from each one of us."*
ACTS 17:27 NASB

In Isaiah 42:19 (KJV), somewhat in exasperation, God asks, "Who is blind, but my servant?" You may be faithfully serving God, like Elisha's servant, but still struggle to sense the Lord and know His will. You're unable to perceive exactly what He's doing. The mountains might be full of horses and chariots of fire all around you, but you can't see them (see 2 Kings 6:15–17).

Like many believers, you daily seek God and grope to discover His will, much like the people in Isaiah's statement: "We grope for the wall like the blind, and we grope as if we had no eyes: we stumble at noon day as in the night" (Isaiah 59:10 KJV).

You may wonder why God made it so difficult to sense Him and know what He's doing. But the most important thing to know is that He's never far from you and that He gently guides your hands as you struggle to feel the wall that marks the boundaries of His will.

Be encouraged! God promises, "I will bring the blind by a way that they knew not; I will lead them in paths that they have not known: I will make darkness light before them" (Isaiah 42:16 KJV).

WHAT GOD CAN'T DO

Why do you look the other way? Why do you ignore our suffering and oppression? We collapse in the dust, lying face down in the dirt. Rise up! Help us! Ransom us because of your unfailing love.

PSALM 44:24–26 NLT

Can God truly hide from you or turn away from His own people? Could God actually ignore what is happening in the world?

Your perceptions of God and reality can appear difficult to reconcile when life begins to fall apart. Whether you're going through a tragedy, a struggle, or a season of spiritual darkness, God isn't hiding, ignoring you, or looking away from you. But God's presence doesn't always mean your problems will be solved, life will go smoothly, or that all of your doubts and uncertainties will disappear.

This tension of suffering or doubt of God's presence goes back centuries, and there's no reason to expect that you'll be part of the generation that finally figures it out. The psalmist leads you to the only place where you can find rest. Even as you feel beaten down by life and struggle to rise up from where you have fallen, place your hope in God's unfailing love.

Even if you have your doubts and come to the end of your faith, because of His unfailing love, God can't turn away from you or ignore you. Even at your lowest point, you are always loved.

WHAT, ME WORRY?

"Do not worry about your life, what you will eat or what you will drink; nor about your body, what you will put on."
MATTHEW 6:25 NKJV

The hunting, trapping pioneer mountain men of America's West knew the privation of a wilderness where food and clothing were scarce. They knew the sure need of shelter in the bitter winter months. Most of them trusted their own hands for their needs, but Jedediah Strong Smith (as good with his hands as his fellow mountain men) put his faith in God.

Biographer Dale Morgan called Smith "an unlikely sort of hero for the brawling West of his time, that West about which it has been said that God took care to stay on his own side of the Missouri River." Jedediah, a modest man and true Christian, was also a man for the mountains who quickly emerged as leader among the most significant group of continental explorers ever assembled.

As he crisscrossed the wilderness with God as his provider, he in turn provided for his parents back east, sending money earned through the lucrative trapping trade. To his elder brother, Ralph, he wrote, "It is that I may be able to help those who stand in need that I face every danger—it is for this that I traverse the mountains covered with eternal snow. . .[and] pass over the sandy plains in the heat of summer, thirsty for water. . .[and] go for days without eating. . . . Let it be the greatest pleasure that we can enjoy. . .to smooth the pillow of [our parents'] age."

In that letter, Jed sent his family $2,200—no small sum in his day!

LOVE GIVES. . . IT HAS TO

"Do not be afraid, little flock, for your Father has been pleased to give you the kingdom."
LUKE 12:32 NIV

There's something about becoming a father that makes most men great givers. From the time a man first learns that he and his wife are going to be parents, he wants more than anything to give whatever he has to make sure his child has everything it needs—physically, emotionally, and spiritually—to grow and thrive.

In this way, earthly fathers become reflections—imperfect reflections, but reflections nonetheless—of our Father in heaven. The apostle John wrote that "God is love" (1 John 4:8 NIV), and Jesus Himself said that God loved sinful and fallen humankind so much that He gave His most precious gift: His one and only Son (John 3:16).

That's just the nature of love, isn't it? Love, by its very nature, has no choice but to give. Real love can't just be hidden away in the heart; it must find expression through gifts to its object. And the God who identifies Himself as the perfect embodiment of love doesn't just give. He gives *joyfully* and He gives *perfectly*.

This perfect, giving love is what the apostle James was pointing to when he wrote, "Every good and perfect gift is from above, coming down from the Father of the heavenly lights, who does not change like shifting shadows" (James 1:17 NIV).

Our God is perfect—perfect in His holiness and perfect in His giving love. He always has been, and He always will be.

LEARNING CONTENTMENT

I know what it is to be in need, and I know what it is to have plenty.
I have learned the secret of being content in any and every situation,
whether well fed or hungry, whether living in plenty or in want.

PHILIPPIANS 4:12 NIV

Modern advertisers and marketers have tapped into something about our fallen human nature that makes too many of us easy marks as customers who buy what we don't need and oftentimes can't afford.

The world around us does all it can to make us believe that we don't have everything we need, and if we're not careful, we can find ourselves falling into attitudes of discontent because we don't have the newest and best things.

The apostle Paul had learned that contentment has less to do with his setting in life (he was in a Roman prison when he wrote to the Philippian church), with his possessions (he had few), or with physical provision (he had apparently experienced real hunger) and everything to do with the fact that he was doing what God had called him to do.

Paul is an amazing example of what true contentment looks like. While we too often feel the pangs of discontent because we don't have the latest and best (fill in the blank), Paul knew how to feel content when he didn't even have a place to stay, enough to eat, or safe travels.

IN THE CAVE OF ADULLAM

David departed from there and escaped to the cave of Adullam.
1 SAMUEL 22:1 NASB

The title of Psalm 142 reads: "When he was in the cave. A Prayer." David and his men had moved to Adullam when the winter rains began, when life out in the open became miserable. For a couple months, they hunkered down in the damp cavern near the city. In Israel, it often rains heavily for three days nonstop, and to David it was like a prison (Psalm 142:7).

He had been a much-loved hero of Israel. Now he was vilified, and King Saul and his army were hunting David, seeking to kill him. David had been forced to flee, leaving his wife, Michal, behind. It was in this context that he poured out his complaint to God. "You are my refuge, my portion in the land of the living" (v. 5 NASB). God was about all David had left. So he looked to Him for help.

David was deeply discouraged, yet he prayed, "When my spirit grows faint within me, it is you who watch over my way" (Psalm 142:3 NIV). He knew that God was with him. You too can be assured of this (Hebrews 13:5).

Are you going through a similar experience? Do you feel hemmed in and trapped, abandoned by God? Look to Him for help. In your darkest moments, He will be right by your side.

THE INDWELLING WORD

Let the word of Christ dwell in you richly.
Colossians 3:16 NKJV

Jeremiah said, "When I discovered your words, I devoured them. They are my joy and my heart's delight" (Jeremiah 15:16 NLT). But what does this mean? How can you *eat* God's Word? You do this by taking His words into your mind and heart, meditating upon them and absorbing them, and allowing them to inspire you and give you life. Just as you must chew, swallow, and digest natural food, so you must take God's Word into your very being.

Paul wrote that you are to be "nourished in the words of faith and of the good doctrine which you have carefully followed" (1 Timothy 4:6 NKJV). You allow the word of Christ to nourish you and dwell in you richly when you make time every day to read it and learn from it. This can be difficult to do in today's busy world, especially if you have a high-demand job that taxes you mentally, physically, and emotionally every day. You may have so much to do that you feel you don't have time to take in God's Word.

But failing to read the Bible is like failing to eat regular meals: you may get away with it for a little while, but eventually this habit will catch up with you. You'll feel weak. And if you do without spiritual nourishment, you won't know right from wrong. So take in a meal of scripture today. "Your word I have hidden in my heart, that I might not sin against You" (Psalm 119:11 NKJV).

DISREPUTABLE DEALINGS

The buyer haggles over the price, saying, "It's worthless,"
then brags about getting a bargain!
PROVERBS 20:14 NLT

This proverb accurately describes events in an Eastern marketplace, but it also describes many dealings in the West. How many unsuspecting mothers have put their kids' entire comic-book collections in a garage sale, asking fifty dollars for the whole box, only to have some unscrupulous collector chisel it down even further, then cackle with glee as he carries off the loot, knowing he'll earn thousands in sales.

This same principle is at play when greedy companies pay mere pennies per garment to sweatshops in Third World countries where underage laborers work long hours for miserable wages, and when the manufacturers ask for more money, the companies moan, "You're cutting into my profit margin!"

Are there any areas of your life where *you're* living high on the hog, taking advantage of the poor or withholding from those in need? You might be surprised. For example, many waitresses in restaurants dislike the Sunday afterchurch crowds because Christians are often cheaper tippers than regular customers. (The Sunday crowds feel that, after giving to God, they've *already* given their limit.)

Jesus repeatedly encouraged generosity in giving—and in all your financial dealings. It seems at times He simply wouldn't let up on the subject. He had a good reason for repeating Himself. He didn't want His followers to be known as cheapskates.

ALL THINGS NEW

*Anyone who belongs to Christ has become a new person.
The old life is gone; a new life has begun!*
2 CORINTHIANS 5:17 NLT

A relationship with Jesus invites us to do things we never thought we could. Somehow impossible reactions become possible. Jesus helps us forgive when we would normally hold a grudge, love when it would be easier to hate, and share when we'd like to withhold. We become people who are generous in love, grace, and gentleness toward those who enter our path, and not because we are expecting anything in return.

God did this by making a new covenant with us. A covenant is a contract that God has bound Himself to fulfill. When we accept Jesus, there's nothing we can offer that would be considered valuable in God's sight—except ourselves.

God brings all the positive attributes, resources, forgiveness, grace, and love. It seems unfair. We get everything and He doesn't seem to get much, but this is exactly the contract (or covenant) God accepts.

Once we have access to all God offers, we find our perception, attitudes, and thoughts changed. We live life from the perspective of one who doesn't horde time or resources, but instead extends help to others. We remember what it's like to be outside a partnership with God and want to help others discover the new covenant for themselves.

We come to Jesus just as we are, but should never stay the way we came.

LITTLE EYES WATCHING

The righteous lead blameless lives; blessed are their children after them.
PROVERBS 20:7 NIV

Many if not most parents have found themselves red faced when their little one innocently shares something embarrassing Mom or Dad did or said when they believed it hadn't been seen or heard.

Dads should never assume that their little ones aren't watching and listening. They are, and the things they see and hear go a long way toward shaping the kind of adults they will become.

Make no mistake, your kids are watching and listening to. . .

- How you talk (Is it the same at home as it is in church?)
- How you treat your wife (Do you lead as a servant?)
- Your consumption of various entertainment media (Are you careful to watch movies and television that reflect a heart for godly standards?)
- Your behavior at home (Are you careful not to abuse or over-use alcohol? Is your speech the same everywhere you go?)
- Your walk with the Lord (Do your kids see you praying and reading your Bible?)

Fathers set examples their children are likely to follow in the short term and as adults. In other words, they are in the process of making little copies of themselves that grow to be big copies.

The Bible promises us blessing as God's children when we are careful in how we behave, talk, and think. One of those blessings is children who copy our words and deeds. The greatest gift a father can give his children is to be the kind of man God has called him to be.

FULL OF GOODNESS

And concerning you, my brethren, I myself also am convinced
that you yourselves are full of goodness, filled with all
knowledge and able also to admonish one another.
ROMANS 15:14 NASB

When a man is converted to Christ, a seismic shift takes place in his soul. He begins the process of being transformed into a new person as the Holy Spirit directs. The Christians in Rome eventually reached a point in which Paul said he was convinced that they were full of goodness, filled with all knowledge, and able to admonish one another. The three go hand in hand.

As your new nature becomes more concerned with pleasing God and helping others, you're filled with knowledge from on high to the point that you're able to teach new converts about putting off the old man. It's a lifelong pursuit, and you'll never arrive. You might even take one step forward and two steps back on occasion, but don't let that stop you.

If your pastor had to describe your level of spiritual maturity, could he say the same thing about you that Paul said about these believers in Rome? Would he be confident in your goodness? Has your pastor witnessed you being filled with godly knowledge? Has that led you to encourage fellow believers in your congregation? You shouldn't merely try to please your pastor, but he's bound to learn about your steady habits.

DOING GOOD . . . EVEN WHEN IT HURTS

Who is going to harm you if you are eager to do good?
But even if you should suffer for what is right, you are blessed.
"Do not fear their threats; do not be frightened."
1 PETER 3:13–14 NIV

Have you ever done everything you can to demonstrate godly love to someone, only to have that person repay your good with evil— evil words, evil attitudes, and evil actions? When faced with such situations—and they are a part of life here on earth—many Christians are tempted to turn to God and protest, *It's just not fair!*

No, it's not fair when a Christian suffers for doing what is good and right in God's eyes. But today's verse gives a twofold promise for the believer in such a situation. First, it promises that even if doing good is accompanied by persecution, the man of God needn't fear any lasting harm befalling him. Second, it promises that God sees his suffering and will find a way to bring him blessing in the midst of it.

Those are some amazing, comforting promises, aren't they? Your part in claiming them is to trust God enough to continue doing what you know is right in His eyes. It's to commit yourself to doing good for Him and leaving the results in His hands.

SHOWING KINDNESS

*And they [the men of Judah] told David, saying, "It was the men
of Jabesh-gilead who buried Saul." David sent messengers to the
men of Jabesh-gilead, and said to them, "May you be blessed
of the LORD because you have shown this kindness
to Saul your lord, and have buried him."*

2 SAMUEL 2:4–5 NASB

After David was anointed king of Israel in Hebron, he learned that the
men of Jabesh-gilead had buried King Saul. Very likely David inquired
about Saul's body because he wanted to honor him with a proper
burial, or maybe the men of Judah wanted to point the finger at the
men of Jabesh-gilead, thinking David might be displeased by their
actions. But either way, David sent a blessing back to them.

Regardless of how far Saul ended up going astray, he was the
Lord's anointed and was worthy of respect. David always had a firm
understanding of this concept, even when he was on the run from Saul,
fearing for his life. This is consistent with what the Bible says about
how God's people are to respect authority and treat their enemies.

Proverbs 24:17–18 (NASB) says, "Do not rejoice when your enemy
falls, and do not let your heart be glad when he stumbles; or the LORD
will see it and be displeased, and turn His anger away from him."

How do you respond when one of your enemies falls—either
literally or figuratively? How does that compare with today's verse?

WHERE DOES DESPERATION LEAD YOU?

As the deer longs for streams of water, so I long for you, O God.
I thirst for God, the living God. When can I go and stand before him?
PSALM 42:1–2 NLT

Streams can be few and far between in the land of Israel. That's why so many stories of the Old Testament include details about wells and major problems stemming from droughts that drained cisterns. A reliance on wells in the time of Jesus meant He had conversations with people around wells quite often.

With limited water sources, the deer of the land could be hard-pressed sometimes to find water. Perhaps in a season of drought it may have seemed nearly impossible to find a stream.

This intense thirst for a scarce water supply captures the spirit of desperation and longing that the writer of this psalm shares while waiting on God's deliverance. Although you have the assurance that God is alive and well, a season of doubt or isolation can leave you desperate.

Then again, you could just as well become distracted by something else, spending your days longing for things other than God. Perhaps the question you could ask yourself is: *What am I desperate for today?* Your seasons of searching and thirsting for God won't last forever, but that doesn't mean you won't have your times of trial, uncertainty, and longing for God's presence.

SPLINTER INSPECTION

"Why do you look at the speck in your brother's eye,
but do not consider the plank in your own eye?"
MATTHEW 7:3 NKJV

The tattoo on his arm read, "Only God can judge me." His lips spouted judgments about everything and everybody else around him. Jesus said, "Don't judge, and you won't be judged." But He also said, "Judge right judgment. Stop judging by mere appearances, but instead judge correctly" (John 7:24). So. . .we're allowed to judge if we do it right? Yeah, but we gotta do the *Judge-right Two-step* first: (1) take the log out of your own eye, and (2) then help your brother with the splinter in his eye.

Got dust (or an eyelash) in your eye? It hurts, you blink, a tear rolls. You want to rub it! Get a mirror, look close—lift the eyelid to see what you can see. Eyeball to eyeball, that little hair looks (and feels) like a Popsicle stick! It's a matter of perspective—and that's Jesus' point. The man who truly sees his own sin, knows it's no small thing and is far better able to help his brother with his troubles.

"If someone is caught in a sin. . .restore that person gently. But watch yourselves"—examine yourselves—"or you also may be tempted" (Galatians 6:1 NIV). The Message paraphrases it like this, "If someone falls into sin, forgivingly restore him, saving your critical comments for yourself. *You* might be needing forgiveness before the day's out."

"But if we judged ourselves rightly, we would not be judged" (1 Corinthians 11:31 NASB). Ouch! Where's the mirror?

LAUGHTER AND WELLNESS

A cheerful heart is good medicine,
but a crushed spirit dries up the bones.
PROVERBS 17:22 NIV

Many modern doctors affirm the truth of this scripture by embracing laughter therapy, which teaches that people who cut loose and laugh will begin to enjoy improved health.

Doctors know that laughter is a natural medicine. It benefits people's physical and emotional beings. It can aid in preventing heart disease by increasing blood flow and improving the way blood vessels work. Laughter has the ability to relax a person's entire body and relieve stress. It can also strengthen the body's immune system and release endorphins to alleviate pain.

Life is often serious business, but it's possible to be sober and serious to the detriment of your health. And definitely if you have a crushed spirit—a discouraged, depressed state of mind—your health is going to suffer. There are quite a number of psychosomatic illnesses caused by little more than negative mental attitudes.

It will do you a world of good to rent a comedy movie and spend a couple hours laughing. You can't live a life of unrelieved seriousness, stress, and worry without suffering for it. And besides the benefits to your physical and emotional health, laughter lightens your mood and causes you to have a more hopeful attitude. A happy, positive attitude will help you face life and rise above difficulties.

"For the happy heart, life is a continual feast" (Proverbs 15:15 NLT). So enjoy laughter as much as you can.

THE RIGHT CANDIDATE

Pride lands you flat on your face;
humility prepares you for honors.
PROVERBS 29:23 MSG

If you spend any amount of time in God's Word, you'll notice that the men God used never seemed quite ready for the job they were asked to do. They were fearful, impulsive misfits, oddballs, and sinners, and often the least ideal candidates to do something big for God. In other words, these men were entirely average, normal, and perhaps the last to be picked for a team.

Do you ever feel average or even below average? You just might be the right candidate God can use to do something incredible.

Maybe God never wanted men who *knew* they could do something big. Maybe He likes using men who *know* they need His help.

God seems to need a little more time when He's dealing with the prideful men who know it all and don't mind sharing it. He may set aside those who seem to believe God is fortunate to have them as part of His team. God sees pride as a barrier to usefulness.

So when you feel a little inadequate, a lot out of your element, or lacking in the skills God might need, you shouldn't be surprised when God gives you something only you can do—with His help.

FAITH WHEN IT REALLY COUNTS

"Do not rebel against the LORD. And do not be afraid of the people of the land, because we will devour them. Their protection is gone, but the LORD is with us. Do not be afraid of them."

NUMBERS 14:9 NIV

Joshua and Caleb were the only two men over forty years old who were allowed to enter the Promised Land. After forty years of wandering in the wilderness, these two men carried God's promise to their people as they faced the monumental task of taking the land that God had promised to them. Their courage is exemplified in today's passage as they urge their people to believe in God's presence, blessing, and encouragement.

Their faith in God was a gritty, all-encompassing, as-if-their-lives-depended-on-it kind of faith. Why? Because their lives actually *did* depend on God's promises. If Joshua was to lead Israel into God's promise, he would have to feel God's presence on a second-by-second basis and step out in faith, trusting that God would come through and stand true to His promises.

Understand this: Joshua's job as the leader of Israel was to encourage the people to attack fortified cities in the face of overwhelming odds. Through forty years, his confidence in God's strong arm had not wavered. And God rewarded Joshua's determined faith as He called him to bravery in the face of imminent battle.

Joshua's story of determined, consistent faith is strong encouragement for us today as well.

COVENANT–KEEPING GOD

"Obey what I command you today. I will drive out before you the Amorites, Canaanites, Hittites, Perizzites, Hivites and Jebusites."
Exodus 34:11 NIV

At this point in Israel's history, the Lord was establishing a covenant with His people, promising to "do wonders never before done in any nation in all the world" (Exodus 34:10 NIV). And He wasn't just promising to do such wonders in front of Moses, but rather before *all* the people. This was a foreshadowing of God drying up the Jordan River (Joshua 3), His destruction of the walls of Jericho (Joshua 6), and more.

As if that wasn't enough, commentators point out that God listed the six enemies that He would drive out before Israel if they would obey what He commanded them that day. He then went on to list His terms, what He expected of them: they were to cut down the Asherah poles (v. 13), not worship any other god (v. 14), not make idols (v. 17), faithfully celebrate His festivals (vv. 18, 22), honor the Sabbath (v. 21), and more. They could only expect to receive the promises of God if they were faithful to Him.

What sort of enemies are you facing today? If you haven't seen any progress against them, take inventory of your obedience to God. While you won't always be able to understand His ways, He's still a God who covenants with His people and therefore expects obedience.

TIME FOR SOME HONESTY. . .

*"Come now, let us settle the matter," says the L*ORD.
"Though your sins are like scarlet, they shall be as white as snow;
though they are red as crimson, they shall be like wool."
ISAIAH 1:18 NIV

The prophet Isaiah ministered in the kingdom of Judah at a time when the people had fallen into some very grievous sin. They had become both hedonistic in their behavior and complacent toward their God.

In short, they were very much like us today—lost in sin and without hope. . .at least had they been left on their own.

One of the great themes of Isaiah's prophecies—and of the entire Bible—is God's willingness to forgive and restore those who recognize their sin and turn from that sin back toward Him.

The words in today's verse are echoed hundreds of years later by the apostle John, who wrote: "If we claim to be without sin, we deceive ourselves and the truth is not in us. If we confess our sins, he is faithful and just and will forgive us our sins and purify us from all unrighteousness" (1 John 1:8–9 NIV).

We all need God's forgiveness and restoration. He has provided a way for that to happen by sending His Son, Jesus Christ, to die for our sins. Our part in that equation is to acknowledge that we are sinners and that we need to be washed "as white as snow."

GOD PROTECTS YOU

*The Lord is faithful, and he will strengthen
you and protect you from the evil one.*
2 THESSALONIANS 3:3 NIV

God can strengthen you so that you can resist the onslaughts of the devil. These can be dark, negative thoughts, sexual temptation, waves of paralyzing fear, accidents, inexplicable illnesses, and many other kinds of attacks. Fortunately, you don't need to depend on your *own* strength to withstand these calamities. God has promised to supply strength.

Jesus instructed believers to pray, " 'Our Father in heaven. . . deliver us from the evil one' " (Matthew 6:9, 13 NIV). Since Jesus commanded us to pray for this, we can certainly expect that this is a prayer that God will hear and answer. Jesus also told His Father, "My prayer is. . .that you protect them from the evil one" (John 17:15 NIV). It's reassuring to know that Jesus is backing up your prayers, praying along with you, entreating the Father to protect you.

And will God be faithful to respond? Yes, He will. As Paul stated, "The Lord is *faithful*, and he *will* strengthen you and protect you from the evil one" (2 Thessalonians 3:3 NIV, emphasis added).

Of course, you need to put forth some effort as well. As the famous description of our spiritual armor in Ephesians 6 says, you need to stand your ground, hold firmly to your shield of faith, and steadfastly resist the devil. This can be a difficult battle, but know that God is overshadowing you, infusing your spirit with strength, and—if you remain steadfast and continue believing—He will make you victorious.

DAY 118

THE GOLDEN RULE

"Whatever you want men to do to you, do also to them."
MATTHEW 7:12 NKJV

These words capture the essence of the Christian life—in every situation, treat others as we ourselves want to be treated. This is indeed the "Golden Rule" of civilized humanity.

Tragically, the human heart is anything but golden. It is, in fact, deceitful above all things (Jeremiah 17:9) and therefore incapable— apart from God—of living by this rule. It rewrites the rule to say: "Do to others *before* they do to you," anticipating the betrayal of other hearts. It says, "Do to others as they *have done* to you," to justify the age-old maxim of retribution: "An eye for an eye, a tooth for a tooth."

But Solomon wrote, "Whoever digs a pit will fall into it; if someone rolls a stone, it will roll back on them" (Proverbs 26:27 NIV). Any act against anyone will have its eventual payback, because "God cannot be mocked. A man reaps what he sows. Whoever sows to please their flesh, from the flesh will reap destruction; whoever sows to please the Spirit, from the Spirit will reap eternal life" (Galatians 6:7–8 NIV).

The Spirit enables us to obey the Golden Rule, so "Let us not become weary in doing good, for at the proper time we will reap a harvest if we do not give up. Therefore, as we have opportunity, let us do good to all people, especially to those who belong to the family of believers" (Galatians 6:9–10 NIV).

How do we define "good"? Apply the Golden Rule: what we think would be good for us, do the same for others.

WHAT IS A BLESSING?

All praise to God, the Father of our Lord Jesus Christ, who has blessed us with every spiritual blessing in the heavenly realms because we are united with Christ.

EPHESIANS 1:3 NLT

Blessings are prayers at mealtimes and gifts from God. There's another blessing we'll discover over the next four days.

This blessing is a personal gift a father shares with a child. A father's blessing can give a child permission to grow up, offer freedom, and invite the child to dream big dreams and follow God's unique plan.

We *pass* the blessing when we *speak* the blessing. We cannot assume our children understand they're loved and that we want the best for them. They need to hear it from our lips and see it in our actions. A blessing can change futures, strengthen relationships, and provide a vision for their journey.

When a child receives a blessing from her father, it proves he notices her, pays attention to her heart, and knows that by giving her wings, she will eventually fly.

Each child needs the blessing, but few receive it. Your children may be grown—it's never too late to bless them.

God has blessed mankind with a future and a hope. He offers a listening ear, a fully developed plan for your life, and forever companionship. He advises, comforts, and He *blesses*.

A LIVING SACRIFICE

I plead with you to give your bodies to God because of
all he has done for you. Let them be a living and holy
sacrifice. . . . This is truly the way to worship him.
ROMANS 12:1 NLT

You might sometimes think that being a disciple of Jesus is nothing but privation and suffering, since several verses talk about dying to self and killing your desires. Romans 12:1 describes laying yourself on God's altar as a "living sacrifice," and that might worry you since another verse says, "Those who are Christ's have crucified the flesh with its passions and desires" (Galatians 5:24 NKJV). You might begin to think that *truly* following Jesus is a life void of pleasure and fun.

Certainly you'll be called upon to make personal sacrifices out of love for God and others, and certainly you must not give in to the *sinful* passions and desires of your flesh—such as hatred, murder, adultery, and greed—but you will have many desires that are perfectly in line with the will of God. That's why He promises, "Delight yourself also in the LORD, and He shall give you the desires of your heart" (Psalm 37:4 NKJV).

So don't be afraid to yield your body as a "living sacrifice." Let His Holy Spirit have His way in your heart. Listen to Him when He tells you to say no to a selfish desire or urges you to crucify hatred, jealousy, and covetousness. He wants what's best for you, and though you'll die to sinful passions and desires, you'll be truly coming alive.

AN OFFENSIVE MESSAGE

Just as it is written, "Behold, I lay in Zion a stone of stumbling and a rock of offense, and he who believes in Him will not be disappointed."
ROMANS 9:33 NASB

We live in a time when many people in our culture seem to have made being offended not just a hobby but a pastime they pursue with passion. It's a time when speaking the truth about the Gospel of Christ and about godly life principles will get you labeled as "intolerant" and a "bigot."

People don't like being told that they need Jesus to save them and change them, and they detest being confronted with their own sins. Being told that there is only one way into the kingdom of God—through Jesus Christ—they probably like even less.

Of course, this shouldn't shock or even surprise those who follow Christ. It also isn't really anything new. In fact, on several occasions, Jesus Himself warned His followers that those who faithfully live and speak for Him would often pay a steep price for their obedience (see Matthew 5:11, 10:22; John 15:18–21).

When we share the Gospel message with others, we should be careful to do it with wisdom, gentleness, and respect (see 1 Peter 3:15). But at the same time, we also need to keep in mind that the truth won't always be well received. In fact, many will find it downright offensive.

FORTITUDE IN THE FACE OF BAD NEWS

*The LORD gave this command to Joshua son of Nun: "Be strong
and courageous, for you will bring the Israelites into the land
I promised them on oath, and I myself will be with you."*

DEUTERONOMY 31:23 NIV

In Deuteronomy 31, Moses and Joshua have been called to the tent of meeting to hear from God. God tells Moses that the time for Moses' death is near. God Himself predicts the failures of the people of Israel to follow Him once they take possession of the Promised Land:

> *"These people will soon prostitute themselves to the foreign
> gods of the land they are entering. They will forsake me and
> break the covenant I made with them. And in that day I will
> become angry with them and forsake them; I will hide my
> face from them, and they will be destroyed."*
> (Deuteronomy 31:16–17 NIV)

Imagine being Joshua in this situation: called to move ahead into battle, knowing that the people he will lead will eventually "be destroyed" because of their unfaithfulness. At that moment, many men might simply ask, "Well then, what's the point?" But there's no sign that Joshua was deterred.

So often in life we find that we can only control how we react in the face of opposition or bad news; there's not much we can do to control the reactions or responses of others to adversity. And we find, as did Joshua, that God rewards our personal faith in Him when the going gets tough.

HUSBANDS AND WIVES

*There is neither Jew nor Greek. . .there is neither
male nor female: for ye are all one in Christ Jesus.*
GALATIANS 3:28 KJV

The Declaration of Independence states "that all men are created equal, that they are endowed by their Creator with certain unalienable rights. . ." We understand that when it states "all men" that it means "mankind"; it is self-evident that women have unalienable rights before God as well.

These rights include, among other things, the right to vote. Yet it wasn't until January 10, 1878 that Senator Sargent introduced a bill in Congress to grant women this right. And it didn't become a reality for another 42 years; in 1920, the Nineteenth Amendment to the Constitution was ratified, granting women's suffrage.

The Bible shows the attitude that men should have toward women when it says, "You husbands must give honor to your wives. Treat your wife with understanding as you live together. She may be weaker than you are, but she is your equal partner in God's gift of new life. Treat her as you should so your prayers will not be hindered" (1 Peter 3:7 NLT).

If your prayers are frequently being hindered, you might want to check your heart and make sure that you're honoring your wife and treating her as you should. She isn't always right, any more than you are, but listen to her counsel, even as Manoah listened to his wife (Judges 13:21–23). Chances are good you'll be blessed and even learn something.

EXPECT HARDSHIP

*Can anything ever separate us from Christ's love? Does it mean he
no longer loves us if we have trouble or calamity, or are persecuted,
or hungry, or destitute, or in danger, or threatened with death?
(As the Scriptures say, "For your sake we are killed every
day; we are being slaughtered like sheep.")*

ROMANS 8:35–36 NLT

When hardship comes, and it will, you'll find out how strong your
faith is. But how can God allow His own children to be persecuted, or
starve, or be threatened with death? Doesn't He promise to protect
His followers?

After all, Job 5:11 (NLT) says, "He gives prosperity to the poor and
protects those who suffer." And Psalm 12:7 (NLT) tells you, "Therefore,
LORD, we know you will protect the oppressed, preserving them forever
from this lying generation." And Proverbs 19:23 (NLT) promises, "Fear
of the LORD leads to life, bringing security and protection from harm."

In some instances, God does intervene—offering physical protection to advance His kingdom. In other cases, He offers spiritual
protection against the advances of the enemy. And sometimes, He
allows hardship while preserving your soul.

Today's verse quotes Psalm 44:22, and one aspect of it that's
hard to miss is this: Christians face death every day for the sake of the
kingdom. But hardship never separates you from the love of Christ.

GUARDING YOUR REPUTATION

A good name is more desirable than great riches;
to be esteemed is better than silver or gold.
PROVERBS 22:1 NIV

The great Founding Father (and writer, scientist, philosopher, states-man. . . the list goes on) Benjamin Franklin once stated, "It takes many good deeds to build a good reputation, and only one bad one to lose it." "The First American," as Franklin is often still called, understood the value of a good name. So did the writer of today's scripture reading.

History—including some very recent history—is filled with examples of highly esteemed men who ruined their reputations (as well as their careers, their ministries, and their families) with just one misdeed. And a reputation once destroyed is exceedingly difficult, sometimes impossible, to reestablish.

You may not be a man who would make headlines with one big error in judgment, but your reputation is still important. The local or national news may not be watching, but others are—your wife, children, and the rest of your family, your coworkers, your business associates, your partners in ministry. . .those who know you follow Christ and may themselves be interested in following.

There are many things in life well worth guarding. Few if any of them are more important to protect than your personal reputation. So make sure your conduct in all areas accurately reflects who you are. . .and whose you are.

LETTING IT PASS

Overlook an offense and bond a friendship;
fasten on to a slight and—good-bye, friend!
PROVERBS 17:9 MSG

Everyone makes mistakes, but some men are definitely more prone to speak without thinking and cause offense. Other men are always scarfing up the last donut—their third one—without asking whether you've had one yet. Or they borrow a valuable tool and lose it. . .then inform you that they can't afford to replace it at this time. And you need it for work on Monday. Then the ball is in your court. How do you respond?

Hopefully, you'll be able to let the donut go without too many problems. It is, after all, a rather minor offense. But it may be more difficult to forgive hurtful words or larger losses, especially if this isn't the first time they've happened. But think carefully before you react. Is this really worth losing a friend? Probably not.

You can still express your disappointment and let him know how this makes you feel, calmly. And you probably should express your emotions. But it's not wise to hold a grudge. Leviticus 19:18 (MSG) says, "Don't. . .carry a grudge against any of your people." It then goes on to say, "Love your neighbor as yourself," which is the whole reason why you shouldn't nurse grudges.

God's commandments about love and forgiveness have practical applications in your everyday life and in the workplace. They may not be easy to implement, but they're guaranteed to work.

WHAT THEY NEED THE MOST

Lord Almighty, blessed is the one who trusts in you.
PSALM 84:12 NIV

If you're married, it's possible your family has been waiting for something only you can give. They may not know how to ask. They may not even know they need this, but you have the power to build up or crush your family.

You can change futures by offering your family a *blessing*.

Abraham offered Isaac a blessing. Isaac offered Jacob a blessing. Jacob gave Joseph a blessing.

A blessing speaks life into your family. It lets them know you recognize their importance to you. It indicates you believe they have the ability to make good decisions. It inspires confidence and encourages hope.

Your ability to clearly tell your family they're valued and that you believe in them can go a long way in giving them the courage to face life head-on. Too many families are waiting to be loved unconditionally by their husband or dad.

When we place conditions on our love, our families will still do everything they can to receive a blessing, but they will live with the knowledge that it probably will never happen. Give them a vision for their future that includes your backing.

You can be fifty years old and still be waiting for a father's blessing. Don't make your wife and children wait.

HOPE IN THE LORD

Unrelenting disappointment leaves you heartsick,
but a sudden good break can turn life around.
PROVERBS 13:12 MSG

Although difficulties are woven into the very fabric of life and many are designed by God to draw you close to Him, He also knows that a constant onslaught of problems can frustrate you and cause you to give up in despair. That's why He frequently sends relief in answer to your prayers.

Sometimes you can get by without the whole problem being solved immediately. But you desperately need a glimmer of hope to know that God is with you and that He will eventually work everything out. So you pray, "Send me a sign of your favor" (Psalm 86:17 NLT). This is very scriptural.

But how can you know that God even *desires* to do good to you? Because He promises this repeatedly in His Word—stating clearly that He will supply what you need, bring peace to troubled situations, and relieve intense pressure. When an unknown psalmist was downhearted and discouraged, he prayed, "I wait for the LORD, my soul waits, and in His word I do hope" (Psalm 130:5 NKJV). He put his faith in God's promises.

God knows that unrelenting problems and testing can dishearten you. And He loves you and thinks upon you even when He seems most distant. If you pray for it and look for it, He will not only send you a sign of His favor—to give you hope—but as dawn breaks after a long, dark night, He will send His full cavalry charging in to rescue you.

GOD'S JEALOUS LOVE FOR YOU

"Do not worship any other god, for the LORD,
whose name is Jealous, is a jealous God."
EXODUS 34:14 NIV

Perhaps the thought of a jealous God calls to mind images of a person in a relationship who is pushy or overprotective. However, the full picture of God presented throughout scripture, such as in Hosea, is a heartbroken lover who has been rejected time and time again by His beloved people. This is a jealousy that isn't pushy or overbearing.

When St. Francis of Assisi spoke of God's love, he noted that God has humbly made Himself vulnerable to the point that He allows us to break His heart. This jarring love means an all-powerful God cares deeply enough for us that He is willing to endure the pain of loss and disappointment when we turn away from Him.

God is jealous for our time and attention. When we fail to make God our top priority, He doesn't call us back with anger and obligation. He calls us back as a jealous lover who desires a relationship with us.

The costly love of God that suffered for our sake on the cross is the same jealous love of God that desires us with all of the passion tucked away in the simple message of John 3:16: "God so loved the world. . ."

Perhaps we need to believe that God loves us enough to be jealous, to allow Himself to be moved with grief when we turn away from Him. Perhaps we struggle to love and make space for God because we have yet to know and feel His jealous passion for us.

LOVE DOES NO HARM

Love does no harm to a neighbor;
therefore love is the fulfillment of the law.
ROMANS 13:10 NKJV

The five books of Moses contained the law of God, and the overwhelming majority of these laws were intended to promote the well-being of the Israelites' fellow men and to bring about justice and restitution for those who had been wronged. They boiled down to this simple precept: do no harm to your neighbor.

Since this was the whole point of the law, Paul explained that if you loved your neighbor, you'd automatically fulfill the law because you'd avoid harming him. Thus, you are to allow your life to be ruled by God's love. How do you do this? Simple. Yield to His Spirit because "God is love" and "the love of God has been poured out in our hearts by the Holy Spirit" (1 John 4:8; Romans 5:5 NKJV).

As a man, you may feel that you must be rough and tough; you can't let anyone push you around; you must be assertive in business dealings and never show weakness. Loving others and being gentle may seem soft and weak by comparison.

Not so. You can be gentle to the weak yet still be tough when you need to be. You can be assertive in business dealings, and adding love to the mix simply makes you honest and fair. You can act justly toward others without letting anyone push you around. Loving others takes courage and strength, and it proves you're a true man of God.

PROSPERITY AND SUCCESS—
GOD'S DEFINITION, NOT OURS

"Be strong and very courageous. Be careful to obey all the law my servant Moses gave you; do not turn from it to the right or to the left, that you may be successful wherever you go. Keep this Book of the Law always on your lips; meditate on it day and night, so that you may be careful to do everything written in it. Then you will be prosperous and successful."

JOSHUA 1:7–8 NIV

Every man longs to be prosperous and successful in life. We all want to be able to have a meaningful occupation, to provide for our families, and to lead the next generation to God. We want to live a faithful life in front of God and at the end hear the emphatic words, "Well done, good and faithful servant!" (Matthew 25:21 NIV).

Joshua's desire to be prosperous and successful was no different from ours. And the stakes were desperately high. In addition to leading a family, he was also leading a nation into hostile territory. And God gave him the surefire formula for success: an unwavering focus on God's revealed Word, leading to a resolute trust in God's promises.

Do not miss this word to you, *you personally,* today: The *only* sure way to prosperity and success, as God defines it, is by faithfully reading and following God's revealed Word. God has provided the path, with His promise of success, in His Word to you. Follow that template, and rest assured.

DOCTRINAL INTEGRITY

Likewise, exhort the young men to be sober-minded, in all things showing yourself to be a pattern of good works; in doctrine showing integrity, reverence, incorruptibility, sound speech that cannot be condemned, that one who is an opponent may be ashamed, having nothing evil to say of you.
TITUS 2:6–8 NKJV

In today's verses, Paul addressed Titus, his partner and fellow worker (2 Corinthians 8:23), telling him about the importance of the older generation teaching the younger one. But they were to go beyond teaching. They were to display a pattern of good works, showing integrity, reverence, and incorruptibility in their doctrine—so much so that even an opponent might not have anything to say against them.

Doctrinal integrity doesn't mean perfection. It simply means living out truth as best you understand it, without walking in contradiction. If you know anger to be a sin, and you teach it as such, but everybody knows you as a hothead, that's the type of inconsistency that signals to the next generation that you don't really believe what you're saying. It also shows that your doctrine lacks power.

If you're older, say forty-five years of age or more, are you teaching younger men in the faith? Do they see inconsistencies in your life, or do they see a repentant heart? If you're younger, how quick are you to accept the teaching of the older generation while acknowledging your own weaknesses?

WISE INVESTMENTS

Lay up for yourselves treasures in heaven.
MATTHEW 6:20 KJV

On January 3, 1959, Alaska was admitted as the forty-ninth state. When Secretary of State William Seward bought this vast northern territory from the Russians back in 1867, many Americans considered it a waste of money, calling it "Seward's Icebox." In hindsight, however, it was an extremely wise investment. For a mere $7.2 million ($121 million in today's dollars), 586,412 square miles were added to the nation.

Investing in the future always costs money, and it often seems at the time that you can ill afford it. And frankly, some things you *don't* need. Not yet, at least. For example, if you can get by with your present tools and business machines, you should. "If it ain't broke, don't fix it"—and don't squander your money on a new one.

But when it comes to vital things like health insurance, if you think you can get by without it and save yourself a few dollars, you usually find your wallet smarting you in the end. Similarly, it's unwise to neglect investing in your eternal future. Jesus advises all Christians to invest in heavenly treasure. You do that by having faith in Him, living a godly life, giving generously, and doing good to all men.

Typically, when you invest in your future eternal life in heaven, worldly people will speak disparagingly and insist that you're wasting your time. That's because they have no vision for the future. Like Seward's critics, they don't recognize a truly wise investment when they see one.

RESTORATION AFTER GOD'S REBUKE

*"The Lord your God is with you, the Mighty Warrior who saves.
He will take great delight in you; in his love he will no longer
rebuke you, but will rejoice over you with singing."*

Zephaniah 3:17 niv

When we fail, and we surely will all fail, we may go through a season of the Lord's discipline or rebuke. Perhaps we dread such seasons. Perhaps we even fear being cut off or losing the Lord's favor forever. Could we ever sin so grievously or repeatedly that God would ever turn us away?

Understandable as these fears may be, a season of discipline is always intended to lead us to restoration with God. In fact, if God merely let us go our own way or spared us the consequences of our disobedience, we could argue that He isn't all that concerned about us. What parent would not reach out in discipline to a beloved child with any other goal than complete restoration? Isn't God's rebuke the ultimate sign that He is truly for us, even if He isn't primarily concerned with our comfort?

And even if we pass through a season of discipline or distance from God, it is never destined to last forever. God longs to rejoice over us with singing and joy. We are His beloved people, the source of His joy and the focus of His song. How surprising it is to pass through a season of failure and discipline only to discover that God remains with us and has never let us go.

WORK, REST, AND PRAY

*Be still in the presence of the LORD, and wait patiently for him
to act. Don't worry about evil people who prosper or
fret about their wicked schemes.*

PSALM 37:7 NLT

Bible commentators point out that being *still* in the Lord's presence is about more than simply not moving. They say it's about silencing the tongue from all murmuring and complaint. It means to be resigned, content in Him. That doesn't mean you can't ask Him to act, but it *does* mean there should be times when you meet with Him without making requests.

The real test comes when evil people appear to prosper. Shouldn't a Christian fret then? Doesn't God call Christians to speak for the voiceless? Indeed, He does. But not always. Solomon said this in Ecclesiastes 3:1 and 7 (NLT), "For everything there is a season. . .a time to be quiet and a time to speak." If you're always speaking or if you're always quiet, you haven't found the proper balance.

Either way, today's verse says don't worry about evil people. Instead, wait patiently for the Lord to act. That looks different in every circumstance, but isn't it nice to know that the success of His kingdom doesn't rest in your hands? Neither does toppling evil. You're called to work, rest, and pray—always trusting in Him.

BUILDING WITH GOD

Commit your actions to the Lord, and your plans will succeed.
Proverbs 16:3 NLT

You may be involved in a complex project that has many unsettled issues surrounding it, and you might not know how to resolve them. Or its chances of succeeding might be slim. You're wracking your brain, and your thoughts are all over the place. But have you committed the project—lock, stock, and barrel—to God? That's the way to gain peace and clarity. If you commit what you're involved in to God, He will see to it that your plans succeed.

The devil often fights what men of God are doing, so you need divine assistance to bring your works to completion. A solid Bible promise states, "Commit everything you do to the Lord. Trust him, and he will help you" (Psalm 37:5 NLT). He'll help you, that is, if the project was His will to begin with.

On the other end of the spectrum, however, the Bible warns, "Except the Lord build the house, they labour in vain that build it" (Psalm 127:1 KJV). Too many men are spinning their wheels trying to accomplish something, but they didn't check it out with God first to get His stamp of approval. So their labor is potentially in vain. Whether they're building a house or whatever they're trying to accomplish, it won't succeed, or it won't last.

Before you embark on a project, big or small, humbly lay it before God's feet and be sure to get His blessing and authorization before you sink time and energy into it.

STAY ALERT

*Watch out that you do not lose what we have worked so hard to
achieve. Be diligent so that you receive your full reward.*

2 JOHN 8 NLT

Deception has been an issue in every church age. At the heart of one
deception was the denial that Jesus came in an actual physical body
(2 John 7); this was, ultimately, a rejection of Christ. Jesus is always
the sticking point with those who come in the spirit of antichrist.

In this epistle, the apostle John warned the church to be on
guard—to be diligent against such people. Otherwise, the Christian
is in danger of losing his heavenly reward. John went on to say that
anyone who wanders from this teaching has no relationship with
God (v. 9). With such consequences, it's no wonder that he called
the church to be so diligent.

If you knew your car might veer off the road and cause you to
plummet off a mountainside at any moment, leading to your certain
death, you'd be on heightened alert. Your radio would be off. Your
hands would have a firm grip on the steering wheel. And your eyes
would be giving the road their full attention.

Spiritual diligence works in a similar fashion. It includes keeping
an eye out for deceivers, praying for discernment, and staying close
to the Body of Christ so you can experience the process of iron
sharpening iron (Proverbs 27:17).

DON'T LOSE YOUR CROWN

Hold on to what you have, so that no
one will take away your crown.
REVELATION 3:11 NLT

James said, "Blessed is the man who endures temptation; for. . .he will receive the crown of life which the Lord has promised to those who love Him" (James 1:12 NKJV). This crown symbolizes your salvation and is a gift—free and undeserved—to those who believe in and love Jesus.

Elsewhere, Peter speaks of another crown: "When the Chief Shepherd appears, you will receive the crown of glory that will never fade away" (1 Peter 5:4 NIV). Many Bible scholars believe that when Peter speaks about the "crown of glory," it's *separate* from the crown of life. Can someone have more than one crown in heaven? Jesus does. "On his head were many crowns" (Revelation 19:12 KJV).

When promising "the crown of glory," Peter was talking to older, mature Christians who watched over the church and set an example for other believers. The crown of life is given to *all* believers and cannot be taken from you by any man, but the crown of glory is an award for exceptional service.

Unlike the crown of life, however, it appears that people *can* lose this crown by not fulfilling what God has called them to do, as Revelation 3:11 warns. If God has given you a task to do and you neglect it, He will have to find someone else to do it. . .and they will receive the reward originally intended for you. So be faithful to obey God and fulfill your calling.

HOW TO WAIT ON GOD

Let all that I am wait quietly before God, for my hope is in him.
He alone is my rock and my salvation, my fortress
where I will not be shaken.
PSALM 62:5–6 NLT

We are told repeatedly to wait on the Lord throughout the Psalms. However, this particular psalm adds a jarring addition to our waiting: wait *quietly*. The manner in which we wait is very much the test of our faith. When I wait on God, I'm tempted to make requests, to complain, to suggest solutions, and even to pray for specific outcomes, as if I know the best way for God to act in my life. Most of us can be persuaded into waiting on God, but waiting quietly is a whole other matter. Those who wait quietly have truly surrendered themselves to the direction and provision of God, for they have no other hope than the action of God.

And for the times when we stop waiting and seek our solutions or build our own safety nets and fortresses, it often takes a tragedy, crisis, or difficult situation to shake us loose. Perhaps the quiet waiting leaves us restless and fearful. However, anything that we trust more than God will not last, especially in a time of trouble that shakes our foundations.

Placing our trust completely in God does not guarantee smooth sailing. In fact, the need for God to act as a fortress suggests that we should expect conflict. Trouble is surely coming, and the question is whether we are truly waiting in expectant quiet before God.

ANSWER THE CALL

*He saw a large crowd, and He felt compassion for them
because they were like sheep without a shepherd;
and He began to teach them many things.*

MARK 6:34 NASB

When Colonel William Travis sent out a desperate plea for help to defend the Alamo on February 24, 1836, he knew things were headed south in a hurry. Only thirty-two men from a nearby town responded to his call, and while it's likely that even a turnout of hundreds wouldn't have been enough to hold off the Mexican army, no one will ever know because so few came to the aid of their brothers-in-arms.

When Jesus told us to pray for God to send workers out into the ripe harvest fields, the next thing He said was, "Go! I am sending you out like lambs among wolves" (Luke 10:3 NIV). Even if you leave the work of conviction to its rightful handler, the Holy Spirit, it still takes courage to go out and share about Jesus.

If you don't feel equipped, get equipped. Seek an experienced, trustworthy believer to guide you through walking with God. If you already know how, equip others. The battle is right there, not just in the world, but in your home, at work, and in the church. Keep your knees bent and your eyes peeled; ask God to break your heart with what breaks His. The call has been sent to get involved. How will you answer Him today?

LOOKING BACK AT GOD'S FAITHFULNESS

*"Do not be afraid. Stand firm and you will see the deliverance the
Lord will bring you today. The Egyptians you see today you will never
see again. The Lord will fight for you; you need only to be still."*

Exodus 14:13–14 niv

As we watch Joshua prepare to lead the people of Israel into the Promised Land, let's look back for a moment at God's work in Joshua's past.

Moses and the Israelites, including Joshua, stood at the edge of the Red Sea. God had delivered them from slavery in Egypt, but Pharaoh, true to form, had changed his mind—he wanted his free slave labor back. So the Egyptian army pursued the nation of Israel as they left Egypt.

Panicked, the nation of Israel despaired at their impending slaughter. But God's reassurance to Moses was, in a word, astounding: "Moses, you don't have to lift a finger. I've got this."

Those of us who know the story know what happened:

> *But the Israelites went through the sea on dry ground, with
> a wall of water on their right and on their left. That day the
> Lord saved Israel from the hands of the Egyptians, and Israel
> saw the Egyptians lying dead on the shore. And when the
> Israelites saw the mighty hand of the Lord displayed against
> the Egyptians, the people feared the Lord and put their trust
> in him and in Moses his servant.* (Exodus 14:29–31 niv)

Keep this story in mind today as you face your own adversity.

SPIRITUAL EYES

"The LORD will repay each man for his righteousness and his faithfulness; for the LORD delivered you into my hand today, but I refused to stretch out my hand against the LORD's anointed."

1 SAMUEL 26:23 NASB

Sometimes, faithfulness means inaction.

That was the case in today's verse when Saul got wind of the fact that David was hiding from him in the wilderness of Ziph (1 Samuel 26:2–3). Saul took three thousand men in search of him, but David outfoxed him. Then he showed up at Saul's camp early one morning while everybody was sleeping. His cousin Abishai wanted to kill Saul on the spot, but David recognized that Saul was God's anointed and restrained Abishai.

David's faithfulness to the Lord outweighed an opportunity to kill his oppressor. The Hebrew word for *faithfulness* in this verse means "moral fidelity." To kill Saul would have been the equivalent of being unfaithful to God, and David wouldn't do that. He had other moral failings over the course of his life, but here he saw his situation through spiritual eyes and it made all the difference.

Are you on the cusp of making a decision you'd feel justified in making, yet you know deep down inside that it would mean being unfaithful to God? Put off the flesh and look at the situation through spiritual eyes.

WHEN YOU MISSED THE BLESSING

*"GOD bless you and keep you, GOD smile on you and gift you,
GOD look you full in the face and make you prosper."*
NUMBERS 6:24–26 MSG

What you believed about yourself when you were a small child is likely what you believe today. We were, in many ways, children who believed what we were told by our parents, friends, or schoolhouse bullies. We each carry invisible tattoos reading *last to be picked*, *slow*, *stupid*, or *worthless.*

On bad days, you'll believe what someone said when you were five. It doesn't matter if it's true or not, you'll accept it as true even when the evidence suggests otherwise.

Our future isn't defined by our five-year-old selves, but we'll act the part.

If no one's ever spoken a blessing into your life, consider this. Before you were born, God knew your name, fit you together in your mother's womb, and called you a masterpiece (Psalm 139:13–16). He wants you on His team. He created you for something only you can do. He loved you enough to send His Son, Jesus, to make it possible for you to be a part of His family.

You'll sin, but God can forgive you, and He wants to. He's never abandoned you. He's always loved you. He wants to partner with you on His plan for you.

Don't pay attention to what others called you; pay attention to His call.

AVOID DRIFTING AWAY

*We must pay the most careful attention. . .
to what we have heard, so that we do not drift away.*
HEBREWS 2:1 NIV

Most people who leave their faith in God behind don't make a sudden, deliberate decision to do so. Rather, they slowly drift away, little by little, day by day. They gradually become colder to the Lord, lose interest in prayer, reading the Word, and fellowshipping with other Christians, and, over time, value their relationship with God less and less.

Hebrews 2:3 (NIV) asks, "How shall we escape if we ignore so great a salvation?" But that's what many people do. They don't dramatically revolt against God. They simply ignore Him for prolonged periods of time. Eventually such people become "nearsighted and blind, forgetting that they have been cleansed from their past sins" (2 Peter 1:9 NIV). First, they become nearsighted, their eyes out of focus. Eventually they completely lose all spiritual sight.

They often still go through the outward motions of being a Christian, but their heart has departed. They question the basic beliefs of the faith and believe it's irrelevant to their life in this modern world.

What is the solution? How can you avoid this happening to you? You must pay careful attention to what you have heard from the Bible. When you hear the Word, ponder it and allow it to change you. "Today, if you hear his voice, do not harden your hearts" (Hebrews 3:7–8 NIV). Pray and ask God to renew your relationship with Him. And determine to truly *live* your faith.

FREED TO SERVE

"I, the Lord, have called you in righteousness; I will take hold of your hand. I will keep you and will make you to be a covenant for the people and a light for the Gentiles, to open eyes that are blind, to free captives from prison and to release from the dungeon those who sit in darkness."

Isaiah 42:6–7 niv

Perhaps we all know quite well that God has made us righteous and freed us from sin's power, but perhaps it's harder to consider what's next. Are we freed from sin only for our own benefit? Today's passage from Isaiah says that we have been freed in order to liberate others from bondage, both spiritual and physical. If this calling strikes you as intimidating, or if you simply don't know where to start, there's good news for you.

God holds you and shapes you. The life of God is taking hold in your life and reshaping your heart, desires, and thoughts. As God brings liberation into your life, you'll start to long to share it with others. You'll even begin to recognize the opportunities to share that light with those who are blind or to bring freedom to those who are trapped.

As God renews our minds, He also says He will take us by the hand, guiding us forward in our calling. Perhaps the thing holding most of us back is doubt that God is reaching out to us. Are you open to God's renewal and guidance? Are you too distracted? Do you need to set aside time today to allow God's renewal to begin taking hold in your life?

AUTHENTIC GRATITUDE

*In everything give thanks; for this is the will
of God in Christ Jesus for you.*
1 THESSALONIANS 5:18 NKJV

Sometimes knowing God's will for your life is as simple as reading His Word. For example, it's always His will for you to express gratitude. Wisdom proclaims thankfulness as a daily exercise matching actions with God's will, but at the end of the day you might discover some gratitude you still need to express.

You might be standing in the way of God's will. Every time you choose self-pity over gratitude, God's plans are set aside and delayed. The same is true whenever you entertain greed, envy, lust, covetousness, hatred, bitterness, selfishness, and cynicism.

The list is longer, but the common reason for setting aside God's will is. . .*self.* When you pay too much attention to what you don't have, what you want, and how others have hurt you, then there's no room for authentic gratitude.

God is good, and He supplies everything you need to live. He sends bonus moments like beautiful sunsets, impressive scenery, and the love of family and friends. Yet it's possible to develop a blindness to the good things because difficulties frequently demand your attention. . .and God's will is set aside for another day.

You can't be thankful when you think you deserve more than you have. When you're grateful for what you have, you not only position yourself to follow God's will, but you also give yourself the greatest chance to enjoy contentment.

NOTHING ESCAPES HIS ATTENTION

*"For all that is secret will eventually be brought into the open,
and everything that is concealed will be brought
to light and made known to all."*

Luke 8:17 NLT

One of the first things you'll notice if you ever have the opportunity to take a hot air balloon ride is how quiet it can be. Because you're blowing with the wind, you don't typically hear it. Because there's no engine, the only noise is the occasional blast of the propane burner to heat the air. Because you're floating on air currents, there's little turbulence.

Equally remarkable are the clear sounds from the earth below. You can hear dogs barking, the excitement of children when they notice you, and the sounds of people calling to you thinking you can't hear them.

While not a perfect picture, this is a bit like God's relationship with us. Nothing escapes His attention—even when He's not recognized. He sees all. He hears all. He knows who we are.

We can't hide from God. Hiding is a lie our adversary asks us to believe is possible, and when we believe it, he comes back to accuse us of being unfaithful to God.

If you've never been in a hot air balloon, it can be hard to imagine what it is like. If you've never really trusted in God, it can be hard to imagine what it's like for God to know all about you while you continue to ignore His presence.

God knows we *will* break His law. He watches, not as a judge, but as one who can compassionately offer forgiveness.

FEAR GOD

"We have been rescued from our enemies so we can serve God without fear, in holiness and righteousness for as long as we live."
LUKE 1:74–75 NLT

You're in daily battles with three enemies: the world, the flesh, and the devil (Ephesians 2:1–3). All three are formidable, but in the eternal sense, you have already been rescued from all three. In the here and now, though, the battles will continue. And those battles can weigh you down, throw you off track, and cripple you with fear.

In today's verse, Luke mentions Zechariah's prophecy about the coming Messiah who descended from the royal line of David, just as God promised (Luke 1:69–70). He would be merciful and rescue God's people from their enemies. While Zechariah looked forward to the coming Messiah, you look backward, knowing He has already arrived. Your salvation has been secured. And even now, He's in the process of conquering your earthly enemies while preparing a heavenly place for you.

But for now, live out your salvation. Don't fear persecution or even death for Christ's sake. Instead, fear God. Serve Him faithfully in the spheres of influence where He has placed you, being confident that His work will continue no matter what His enemies do. Yes, they may prevail in some battles, but the war has already been won.

GOD BUILDS YOU UP FROM THE DUST

*The LORD is like a father to his children, tender and compassionate
to those who fear him. For he knows how weak we
are; he remembers we are only dust.*
PSALM 103:13–14 NLT

Do you feel pressure to appear capable, strong, or holy? Have you ever feared being "found out" as a fraud because you struggle either privately or publicly?

Your masks always fall off in God's presence, and while that may be devastating or humiliating for you, God knows full well that it is for your benefit. You will only find freedom from your weaknesses and the false sense of self that you fight to maintain when you see with clarity that although you're little more than dust, God still cares for you like a father cares for his children. You are His child. This is the only identity you have to claim.

When you wish to appear strong or capable, your admission of weakness and dependence opens you to God's strength. You will finally tap into God's greater compassion and mercy for you, and you will then be able to share the same with those around you. God is rebuilding you from the dust on the ground on up.

MEDITATE ON GOD

Be still, and know that I am God.
PSALM 46:10 KJV

There's a time to earnestly pray for what you need, and there's a time to praise God for providing all your needs. But there is *also* a time to meditate, to simply think deeply on who God is for an extended period. At times like that, focus entirely on Him and keep your mind from wandering. God will reward you with a deeper knowledge of His nature and His love.

Some Christians shy away from meditation, thinking that Eastern religions have a monopoly on it, but the Bible talked about meditation thousands of years ago, long before any modern fads. God commanded, "Be still, and know that I am God" (Psalm 46:10 KJV). You are to still your heart and focus on knowing Him—that He is almighty God, exalted above all else, supreme, holy, beautiful, and glorious in every way.

You should also meditate on the wonderful things God has done in your life and in the lives of others. Think of His miracles, both great and small. "I meditate on all Your works; I muse on the work of Your hands" (Psalm 143:5 NKJV).

Also, when you read the Bible, don't simply hurry through it. Pause at a verse and meditate deeply on its meaning. "Oh, how I love Your law! It is my meditation all the day" (Psalm 119:97 NKJV). Paul said, "Meditate on these things; give yourself entirely to them" (1 Timothy 4:15 NKJV). Meditate on God and the things of God today.

THE JOY OF RELYING ON GOD

But I trust in your unfailing love;
my heart rejoices in your salvation.
PSALM 13:5 NIV

We can only approach God because of His mercy, and once again it's His mercy that sustains us. I've found the greatest frustration and discouragement when I've tried to approach God based on my own merits and efforts, as if I could prove myself worthy of God's mercy and saving help.

In light of today's passage, begin by asking what you're trusting in or leaning on today. Are you joyful? Are you feeling fearful or frustrated? Our emotions and thoughts are helpful clues to what we think and practice about God. They provide the evidence of a life of faith or a life attempting to get by on its own.

While following Jesus never assures us of smooth sailing, we are assured of God's presence based on His mercy for us. If you aren't joyful today and even find yourself stuck in despair, it could be that you're trusting in yourself to earn God's mercy or simply relying on your own resources and wisdom to help yourself.

There is great joy and contentment in trusting in God's mercy and falling back on God's saving help. We don't lean on God because we've earned His help or favor. Rather, we start with His mercy that assures us of His saving help and presence whether we are going through good times or bad.

BOASTING COULD COST YOU

*Do not boast about tomorrow, for you do
not know what a day may bring.*
PROVERBS 27:1 NIV

In Luke 12:16–20, Jesus shared a parable about a rich man who had an abundant harvest. Presuming upon tomorrow, he decided to tear down his barns and build bigger ones to store his surplus grain. And he said to himself, "You have plenty of grain laid up for many years. Take life easy; eat, drink and be merry." Making such a presumption was a critical mistake because God said to him, "You fool! This very night your life will be demanded from you. Then who will get what you have prepared for yourself?"

The rich man's error wasn't in planning for the future or saving for a rainy day. It was in his boasting of having plenty of provisions and living a life of ease—but not caring about spiritual riches.

James 4:15–17 addressed the same problem. James instructed believers to say, "If it is the Lord's will, we will live and do this or that." He added, "As it is, you boast in your arrogant schemes. All such boasting is evil."

When you talk and plan for the future, do your words include anything that could be construed as boasting? If so, be careful. All your hard work and effort might be for naught.

START STRAIGHT

"Which one of you, when he wants to build a tower, does not first sit down and calculate the cost to see if he has enough to complete it?"
LUKE 14:28 NASB

On February 27, 1964, the Italian government decided to take suggestions for how to extend the life of the leaning tower of Pisa. The tower has been tilting almost since its construction began in 1173, because engineers either weren't aware of or didn't consider that it was being built over an ancient river estuary, which made the ground watery and silty.

Because of the grandiose efforts over the centuries to keep the tower from crumbling, it's been esteemed an architectural marvel. However, it also serves as an object lesson in the value of counting the cost before undertaking a project.

If something starts out off-center or crooked, it's harder to repair later. There are obvious parallels for raising kids here. As Frederick Douglass noted, "It is easier to build strong children than to repair broken men."

Don't worry about being a perfect husband, father, or son; you won't be. What matters more is that you let your Father in heaven, who is perfect, guide you as you follow Him. When you count the cost of being the man God wants you to be, you're deciding that the cost of trying to go it alone or in half measures isn't worth it. There's too much at stake.

REVERSE BLESSING

If you honor your father and mother,
"things will go well for you."
EPHESIANS 6:3 NLT

What if you had one or more parents who just weren't there for you? What if they didn't have what it took to show what love looked like? What if they seemed uncaring and spoke words that couldn't be considered blessings?

Maybe one or both parents were likely never serious candidates for Parent of the Year. They didn't seem to find any joy in *you*.

You may be waiting for a blessing you've never received, validation that never came, an encouraging parent that only seemed the stuff of fairy tales, and you're in conflict. Sure, sharing the blessing with your own children is something you want to do, but giving a blessing to a parent who never blessed you sounds like an awkward impossibility.

Some parents were likely broken by an unspoken blessing that should have come from *their* parents. Even parents may be waiting to be told they're loved.

As much as they may have hurt you, a rebuilt relationship may be possible when *you* give your *parents* a blessing. It may be hard, but it's entirely possible your blessing will put a noticeable crack in the walls they've built around their hearts. If this restored relationship is something you desire but you feel hesitant to try, ask God to increase your love for your parents and to guide you into the right words to say and actions to take.

ON FIRE IN THE WRONG WAY

When the disciples James and John saw this, they asked, "Lord,
do you want us to call fire down from heaven to destroy
them?" But Jesus turned and rebuked them.
Luke 9:54–55 niv

Zeal and passion can be tremendous assets for followers of Jesus, provided we point our zeal and passion in the right direction. When Jesus and His disciples met opposition from the Samaritans, James and John responded with zeal, asking Jesus if they should ask God to destroy them. Jesus had a different kind of zeal in mind.

Just as Jesus had responded to the Samaritan woman's controversial comments and questions with wisdom and an invitation, He had no desire to exact revenge when someone resisted Him and His message. His disciples had yet to realize that Jesus came as a doctor to heal the sick, not as a judge prepared to bring destruction. Jesus showed patience and mercy, demonstrating that God is far more concerned with changing lives than with condemnation.

We're going to meet people who are negative, insulting, and opposed to Christianity. Jesus challenges us to avoid dehumanizing them. Just as Jesus didn't come to bring judgment but to heal those who were willing, we have a similar calling to respond to criticism and opposition with patience and wisdom.

The "calling down fire" approach is too concerned with the short term. God takes a long-term, big picture view of our world, patiently waiting for people to come to Him. In fact, God's patience isn't just for His opponents. He's also patient with His people who keep trying to call down fire from heaven.

SAVED ONLY BY GRACE

*Christ Jesus came into the world to save
sinners, of whom I am chief.*
1 TIMOTHY 1:15 NKJV

Paul wasn't just acting humble when he declared that he was the worst of sinners. He never forgot that, in his blind zeal for Jewish religious traditions, he had arrested and tortured numerous Christians and urged that they be killed. Looking back on his crimes years later, he bluntly stated that any righteousness he once thought he'd had he now realized was "rubbish" (Philippians 3:8 NKJV).

Why did God choose such a violent sinner for one of His leading apostles? Paul explained that God wanted to show by *his* example that there was no person so vile or sinful that He couldn't redeem them (1 Timothy 1:16). You might also ask why God chose Peter as a leading apostle after Peter cursed and swore that he didn't even *know* Jesus (Matthew 26:69–74). Again, the Lord wanted someone presenting His Gospel who knew that he was unworthy, who was convinced that he, and others, could only be saved by God's grace.

However, sometimes after you've been serving the Lord for a few years, have cleaned up your life, and have overcome several bad habits, you can forget what a bad state you were once in. You can begin to think that you're quite righteous and can even start to believe that you're good enough to make it on your own.

But think for a moment about the life Jesus saved you from, and remind yourself that it was by grace you were saved, not by your own goodness (Ephesians 2:8–9).

TESTING GOD'S PROMISES

*Then Gideon said to God, "Do not be angry with me. Let me make
just one more request. Allow me one more test with the fleece,
but this time make the fleece dry and let the ground be covered
with dew." That night God did so. Only the fleece was
dry; all the ground was covered with dew.*

JUDGES 6:39–40 NIV

Gideon's weakness shows through in the face of God's call on his life.
Not once, but twice, he asks God for a visible sign that he will have
success in defeating the Midianite army.

Please take a few minutes to read the entire chapter in Judges 6.
You'll find God reassured Gideon time and time again that He would
do as He had said and work through Gideon to save His people Israel. Yet He also allows Gideon's questions and answers them without
showing anger or frustration.

When we're called to move into an unfamiliar or uncomfortable
situation where the outcome is in doubt, God allows our questioning.
He provides wise counsel from others when we ask; He leads us in
answer to our prayers.

Let's look at Gideon not as a doubter, but as a man convinced of
his own inability to do what God has asked him to do—utterly reliant
on God to be true to His word and act on His promises. Sometimes
God allows us to come to the end of our own strength so that He
can prove Himself stronger.

GOD FORGIVES YOU

LORD, if you kept a record of our sins, who, O Lord,
could ever survive? But you offer forgiveness.
PSALM 130:3–4 NLT

Many men find it very difficult to forgive themselves for past mistakes and moral failures—particularly if they're living with the ongoing consequences of past actions. Daily reminded of their sins, they trudge on in condemnation and defeat, feeling that God has turned His back on them.

Though they experience His care and provision, they conclude that God is just putting up with them, barely tolerating them, but doesn't really love them. They may believe that they're saved, but often feel that they'll barely squeak into heaven.

If this describes *you*, you need to read Psalm 103:8–13 (NLT), particularly verse 12, which says, "He has removed our sins as far from us as the east is from the west." In Isaiah, He says, "I. . .will blot out your sins for my own sake and will never think of them again" (Isaiah 43:25 NLT). And in the New Testament, John tells us, "If we confess our sins to him, he is faithful and just to forgive us our sins and to cleanse us from *all* wickedness" (1 John 1:9 NLT, emphasis added).

If you've confessed your sins to God and turned from them, He has forgiven you. Now you must trust in the depth and power of His forgiveness, forgive yourself, and rest daily in His love.

A GENTLE DEFENSE

*But sanctify Christ as Lord in your hearts, always being ready to make
a defense to everyone who asks you to give an account for the
hope that is in you, yet with gentleness and reverence.*

1 PETER 3:15 NASB

You probably live for instances when someone genuinely inquires about your faith, asking you to give an account for the hope they see in you. But even during genuine inquiries, conversations can sometimes become heated—or become focused on one-upping the other person. Has this ever happened to you?

Peter says to give an account but to do so with gentleness and reverence. This is much more difficult. But in Spurgeon's commentary, he explained why it's so important: "If they wish to know why you believe that you're saved, have your answer all ready in a few plain, simple sentences; and in the gentlest and most modest spirit make your confession of faith to the praise and glory of God. Who knows but what such good seed will bring forth an abundant harvest?"

A gentle, reverent response does a work that has the potential to bring forth great results. It's good seed because it isn't tainted by pride and arrogance. And it's good because the planter is seen as being in just as much need as the receiver. If this describes your evangelism, then carry on. If not, take Peter's words to heart.

WAIT FOR IT

Through patience a ruler can be persuaded,
and a gentle tongue can break a bone.
PROVERBS 25:15 NIV

Paul said, "Love is patient" (1 Corinthians 13:4 NIV). The Greek word for *patient* means "bearing offenses" or "persevering through troubles"—the idea being that if you're being patient, you're suffering bravely.

That implies intention; you have to *want* to be patient, you have to be willing to put up with slings and arrows of outrageous fortune because you see a greater goal beyond them. Otherwise, your patience does no good. It drives you nuts, and an unappreciative recipient will just carry on as usual once the danger of your wrath is past.

In a parable, Jesus told of the king who forgave his servant a huge debt after the man begged him, "Be patient with me" (Matthew 18:26 NIV). But then the guy demanded payment from another servant who owed him far less than he had owed the king. When his pal asked for patience, he had none and had the guy thrown in jail. The king was stunned. His patience came to an end because the servant hadn't taken it to heart—didn't appreciate the gravity of his debt or the extent of his mercy.

God requires you to be patient—slow to boil, waiting for understanding. Fortunately, God offers patience as a gift of the Spirit (Galatians 5:22 NASB). You can love someone who is unlovable because God loved you first: He was patient.

ROCK SOLID

"Whoever hears these sayings of Mine, and does them. . .
[is like] a wise man who built his house on the rock."
MATTHEW 7:24 NKJV

In 2011, Hurricane Irene poured out her tears on Lancaster County, raising the Conestoga River higher than most folks have ever seen it. In the city of Lancaster, a new biking trail ran along the river, separated from the water by a rugged rail fence. When Irene sent the river running down that trail, its waters carried away most of the rails and fence posts. Only a few hardy posts were still standing when the river receded at last. Those posts had been secured in a concrete section of the path where folks could park to access the trail. The other posts had been installed only in the soil beside the path.

When Jesus finished His Sermon on the Mount, He told a parable about two houses: one with a foundation on rock, the other with a foundation on sand. When Hurricane Irene (or one of her great-grandmothers, anyway) came whistling through, both those houses took a bad beating. The rains fell, the floods came, and the winds blew. When the storm was gone, only one house was still standing—the house built on rock.

"Anyone who listens to my teaching and follows it is wise," said Jesus, "like a person who builds a house on solid rock. . . . But anyone who hears my teaching and doesn't obey it is foolish, like a person who builds a house on sand."

There's always a storm coming, brothers. Build on rock.

PLUG INTO THE POWER

When I am afraid, I put my trust in you.
PSALM 56:3 NIV

The big choices you make—the woman you marry, the job you take, the place you live—should be guided by your trust in and understanding of God, but the main mark of a son of God is his battle against sin. "For if you live according to the flesh you will die; but if by the Spirit you put to death the deeds of the body, you will live" (Romans 8:13 NKJV).

Fear is a red flag that alerts you to oncoming danger. God's Spirit helps you move past that fear, giving you the strength and will to do what is right. "For as many as are led by the Spirit of God, these are sons of God" (Romans 8:14 NKJV). As an adopted son, you don't have God at your beck and call; rather, you're a tool in His hands. His role isn't limited to responding to your needs; you're being led and moved and shaped by Him.

If your sin doesn't scare you as much as those big decisions you face, you're poised on a precipice. But when you confess your sins to God, you're grabbing a live wire and plugging into hopeful expectation. The results will be initially painful but ultimately empowering. That ruthless approach to being more like Jesus is what conquers fear and confirms you as His son.

LOVE DRIVES OUT FEAR

*There is no fear in love; but perfect love casts out fear,
because fear involves torment. But he who fears
has not been made perfect in love.*
1 John 4:18 nkjv

This is a beautiful scripture, but what exactly does it mean? Well, in the verses leading up to this, John wrote: "We have known and *believed* the love that God has for us. God is love, and he who abides in love abides in God, and God in him. Love has been perfected among us in this: that we may have *boldness* in the day of *judgment*" (1 John 4:16–17 nkjv, emphasis added).

Elsewhere, Paul wrote: "I am convinced that neither death nor life. . .nor anything else in all creation, will be able to separate us from the love of God that is in Christ Jesus our Lord" (Romans 8:38–39 niv). If you've believed this amazing love God has for you and are convinced that *nothing* can separate you from it, then you know you have nothing to fear from God in the day of judgment.

These are basic Christian truths, but it's good to be reminded of them. Sometimes you may worry that you're not *good* enough to be saved. That's true, by the way. None of us are good enough to deserve salvation. We are all utterly dependent on the mercy of God. That's how you were saved in the first place, and nothing has changed there.

When you know that God loves you more than words can express and that nothing can separate you from His love, this drives out all worry and fear.

FEED THE SPIRIT

Therefore put to death your members which are on the earth:
fornication, uncleanness, passion, evil desire,
and covetousness, which is idolatry.

Colossians 3:5 nkjv

If you have been raised with Christ, then you are to seek the things that are above (Colossians 3:1). One of the primary ways you can seek the heavenly is by putting the earthly to death. Jesus called His disciples to a life of self-denial. Matthew 16:24 (nkjv) records one instance: "If anyone desires to come after Me, let him deny himself, and take up his cross, and follow Me."

Easier said than done though, right? What does self-denial and putting your earthly members to death actually entail? Romans 8:5 (nkjv) is the key: "For those who live according to the flesh set their minds on the things of the flesh, but those who live according to the Spirit, the things of the Spirit."

Your spiritual power will increase or decrease based on which aspect of yourself you feed the most. If you feed the flesh, you should expect your earthly appetites to get stronger. If you feed the spirit, your spiritual appetites will increase. Once your flesh's power source is cut off (or starved), it will decrease.

So, the obvious question is: Are you feeding the flesh or the spirit? What can you do to feed the spirit even more?

SEEING SCRIPTURE ANEW

Open my eyes that I may see wonderful things in your law.
PSALM 119:18 NIV

Have you ever sat down and watched your favorite movie, one you've watched several times before, and noticed something in that particular film you'd never noticed previously—maybe a line of dialogue or an action on the part of a key character that you somehow missed during past viewings?

The same thing can happen when you read your Bible. As you read, you can find yourself focused for the first time on a particular word or phrase that hadn't made much of an impression before. On that second or third (or fourth, fifth, or sixth) reading, it's as if God has opened your eyes to some truth or some piece of wisdom you'd never before picked up on.

This is why it's important to read your Bible daily even if you've already read it cover to cover. And this is also why it's important to devote your time of reading to the God who authored every word of it. When you sit down and read your Bible, even if you're rereading a familiar passage, first stop and ask God to reveal what He wants to reveal to you in His Word that day. You might be amazed at how He'll open your eyes to a new truth (new to *you*, that is!) you'd never seen before.

FINISHING WELL

*Then Samuel left for Ramah, but Saul went up to his home
in Gibeah of Saul. Until the day Samuel died, he did not go
to see Saul again, though Samuel mourned for him. And the
LORD regretted that he had made Saul king over Israel.*

1 SAMUEL 15:34–35 NIV

The prophet Samuel, leader of Israel after the time of the judges, also presided over the anointing of Saul, the first king over Israel. He anointed Saul at God's command, and King Saul ruled over Israel for forty-two years.

By all accounts, God chose and empowered Saul during his reign. Why then do we read about God's regret at the end of Saul's reign?

Late in his reign, Saul's disobedience dogged him. He relied on himself against God's specific commands. In Saul's life, we come to understand a powerful truth—that finishing well is critical to the legacy we leave in this life.

Pastor James MacDonald writes, "You could decide to destroy your life by 5:00 tonight. And would God forgive you? Yes. But would you bear the consequences of that decision for the rest of your life? Yes, you would! Don't ever mix up God's forgiveness and [real-life] consequences."

Samuel, who'd invested decades of his life into Saul, mourns Saul's failure. God even regrets His choice of Saul, despite the king's multiple decades of faithful leadership. And Saul, frustrated at his own failures, ends his own life ignobly (1 Samuel 31).

Make no mistake: finishing well matters.

STABILITY IN UNCERTAIN TIMES

But you, O LORD, will sit on your throne forever.
Your fame will endure to every generation.
PSALM 102:12 NLT

When everything else appears to be shaking around you, you can still deal rightly with fear, anger, and uncertainty about the future. You can't control what tomorrow brings, but you can return to the one certainty that will endure from one generation to another and has remained from the very beginning of time: God will be with you.

Whatever else you may lose, the Lord can't be taken away. As despair sets in during a time of suffering or loss, you have a powerful opportunity to consider what you have placed your trust in. Have you placed your confidence in your health, your finances, your career, or some other material thing?

God is merciful and compassionate, empathizing with you when you're at your lowest point. However, your circumstances don't change the presence of the Lord; rather, your despair and grief can become opportunities to discover His never-changing mercy. While you aren't guaranteed the desires of your heart, you're given something far better: a loving God who will not abandon you and can never be moved.

There surely have been worse times, and tragedies are certain to come in the future, but none of this can disrupt God's presence.

AFTER. . .

After you have suffered a little while, [God] will himself
restore you and make you strong, firm and steadfast.
1 PETER 5:10 NIV

Peter reminds us that when we are tested, we suffer for "a little while" (1 Peter 5:10 NIV). It doesn't feel that way. Pain stretches time. We feel like it's always been this way, and we fear it will always be this way. It won't.

But we need to understand "a little while" not in terms of this life but in terms of eternity. This life is a quickly evaporating vapor. For those who overcome, who pass the "midterm exam," joy everlasting awaits. We are "called to his eternal glory in Christ" (v. 10).

You and I can rely on God's grace to "restore [us] and make [us] strong, firm and steadfast." Tests purify us, temper us, and make us stronger. Testing won't destroy us. It solidifies those gains and prepares us for the next great step in our spiritual journey.

Perhaps the most comforting words in this passage are found in 1 Peter 5:11 (NIV): "To him be the power for ever and ever. Amen." There has never been and will never be a time when God is not sovereign. His dominion encompasses heaven and earth, spiritual and material, and includes everything that has happened to us or ever will happen!

In times of testing, life feels out of control. It may be out of our control. But it is not out of the control of God, who loved us from before time, who only seeks our good, and who has dominion over all things, including our suffering!

SITUATIONAL AWARENESS

I send you forth as sheep in the midst of wolves:
be ye therefore wise as serpents, and harmless as doves.
MATTHEW 10:16 KJV

On August 30, 1918, near the end of World War I, an American colonel discarded a false set of plans for a major Allied offensive, knowing that a German spy would find them. The misdirection, called the Belfort Ruse after the French town near where it occurred, was a last-ditch effort to capture key ground when all standard efforts had failed. The trick worked, the Germans pulled back, and the Allies were able to open crucial supply lines.

Sharing your beliefs sometimes requires similar cleverness—not deception but awareness of people and situations. The dove comparison sounds nice, with its associations with peace and problem-solving. The serpent, not so much. But Jesus would never tell you to emulate Satan's behavior, so He was clearly evoking a serpent's positive qualities, a shrewd sort of cunning that enables them to survive in hostile environments.

Jesus wasn't always gentle, and He used His wits to avoid being killed by His enemies for years. Paul followed His example. He stood up for himself, employing his legal rights as a Roman citizen to serve his ministry, and wisely considered his audience, whether it was Athenians or Pharisees. But he lived in good conscience before God and men and curbed his fleshly desires to protect his ministry.

Ask God to help you make the most of your Gospel-sharing opportunities, standing for truth with love and compassion.

WHEN GOD'S MERCY INCREASES

*Our ancestors in Egypt were not impressed by the Lord's miraculous
deeds. They soon forgot his many acts of kindness to them.
Instead, they rebelled against him at the Red Sea. Even so,
he saved them—to defend the honor of his name
and to demonstrate his mighty power.*

Psalm 106:7–8 nlt

Unfaithfulness toward God often begins when you forget how God
has acted in the past. As the people of Israel lost sight of God's miracles and kindness, they began to seek other gods and even openly
rebelled against God.

The stories in scripture about unfaithfulness, worshipping other
gods, or failing to trust God could just as easily be your own stories.
It's possible that the fantastic details of these historical accounts cause
you to forget that the daily worries of life, the threats of political
turmoil, and selfish desires or ambition caused God's own people to
forget even the wonder of seeing the sea split before them.

The sins of those who went before you are most likely part of your
story as well. If those who witnessed the greatest miracles could forget
them, how much more should you be aware of your own weaknesses?

Even during these repeated acts of unfaithfulness and forget-
fulness, God's mercy didn't cease. In fact, God's mercy increased in
order to save His people. God didn't stop revealing His power.

SO WHAT?

"Therefore go and make disciples of all nations."
MATTHEW 28:19 NIV

Heroes and adventurers come home. Those who take the journey to a greater, richer spiritual life come back to the reality of day-to-day life. But they are not the same men.

The disciples had completed an incredible journey. They saw Jesus crucified and raised from the dead, and they spent forty days with Him, twice (Matthew 28:16–20; Mark 16:14–20). Jesus called them into the future. He answered the "So what?" question. What difference does the journey make?

Their journey and ours fundamentally changes our relationship with Christ and should result in changes in our place in the world and in us.

"When they saw him, they worshiped him" (Matthew 28:17 NIV). Our spiritual journey should change what we worship, what is of supreme value in our lives. We may enjoy the things of this world, but we no longer worship and slavishly pursue them as the source of life.

"All authority in heaven and on earth has been given to me" (Matthew 28:18 NIV). Christ is the authority, not us. We submit to Him, obey His commands, and pursue His purposes.

"Surely I am with you always. . ." (Matthew 28:20 NIV). But the sweetest result is our connection to Christ and His abiding presence with us.

"But some doubted. . ." (Matthew 28:17 NIV). Seeing the resurrected Christ didn't convince all His disciples. We can expect some doubts and struggles to remain. They energize our pursuit for more of God. Doubts are not failures. They are proof of our hunger for another adventure in God!

DON'T BE COVETOUS

Don't set your heart on anything that is your neighbor's.
Exodus 20:17 MSG

In the New King James Version, Exodus 20:17 says, "You shall not covet. . .anything that is your neighbor's." But *covet* is a bit of an archaic word, not in common use today. You might have a vague idea that to be *covetous* means to be greedy or selfish, but what exactly does it mean? *The Message* translates *covet* well: "Don't set your heart on anything that is your neighbor's."

The dictionary defines it this way: "to desire wrongfully, inordinately, or without due regard for the rights of others." Thus, if you covet your neighbor's wife, you'll eventually seek to commit adultery with her—not caring about the pain this causes her, her husband, and their children.

If you covet your neighbor's wealth, you'll seek ways to get it from him—or coveting will cause you to be bitter that you don't have what he has. The Bible advises, "Keep your lives free from the love of money and be content with what you have" (Hebrews 13:5 NIV). In fact, you do well if you keep your life free from covetousness of *all* kinds. You spare yourself a lot of trouble if you're just content.

One good way to be content with what you have is to remind yourself of the tremendous rewards that you'll one day have in heaven. God will abundantly compensate you for your lack in the here and now. That's why Jesus said, "Blessed are you who are poor, for yours is the kingdom of God" (Luke 6:20 NIV).

WHAT'S YOUR SLING?

"The LORD who rescued me from the paw of the lion and the paw of the bear will rescue me from the hand of this Philistine."

1 SAMUEL 17:37 NIV

When we read of David's anointing, sometimes we wonder what the older brothers were thinking: *This scrawny kid, God's anointed?* Yet we have no indication that David inspired the hatred that an earlier upstart, Joseph, provoked in his older brothers (Genesis 37:5, 12–32).

David's father sent him to the front lines of Israel's battle with the Philistines to resupply his older brothers. There, David heard about Goliath's arrogance in the face of God's people. Evidently his brothers were only too happy to have him engage this giant, and even King Saul saw the fire in David's eyes and gave him his blessing (1 Samuel 17:37).

As this boy approached Goliath in battle, God's Spirit encouraged David's own spirit. As we've seen with other men in this month's readings, David was eager to prove God powerful in the face of God's enemies. He relied wholeheartedly on God to fight for him, trusting in God to engage—and to win.

This kind of practical faith is the hallmark of the man of God. David approached Goliath with what he had, using his God-given talent with the sling to fell the giant. How has God equipped you to face your own circumstances? What's the sling in your hand, and what are the stones in your pouch? God will use what He's given you to accomplish His purposes.

GENUINE REPENTANCE

That is why the Lord says, "Turn to me now, while there is time.
Give me your hearts. Come with fasting, weeping, and mourning.
Don't tear your clothing in your grief, but tear your hearts instead."
JOEL 2:12–13 NLT

In Joel 2:1–11, the prophet speaks about a coming day of judgment when everyone should tremble in fear. Nothing will escape. "Who can possibly survive?" asks Joel (v. 11 NLT). And then the Lord provides the answer above.

Anybody who turns to Him now while there is still time can escape judgment. But this is serious business. God calls those who wish to escape the judgment to come with fasting, weeping, and mourning. When is the last time you took your sin that seriously?

But God goes even further, saying that He's not interested in the kind of repentance that is expressed outwardly. Instead, He wants godly sorrow to seep inside, all the way to the heart. David spoke about this in Psalm 51:17 (NLT): "The sacrifice you desire is a broken spirit. You will not reject a broken and repentant heart, O God."

If your heart is broken over your sin, then you've fully grasped what Joel and David are saying. Rejoice in your salvation. If you have never experienced such a broken heart over your sin, ask God to help you repent and find forgiveness.

FREE AT LAST

And this is the plan: At the right time he will bring everything together under the authority of Christ—everything in heaven and on earth.
EPHESIANS 1:10 NLT

On August 28, 1963, in front of a quarter-million people gathered on the Washington Mall, Martin Luther King Jr., seized a crucial moment in American history and gave his stirring "I Have a Dream" speech. King hoped that, by hastening racial harmony, citizens would "be able to speed up that day when all of God's children. . .will be able to join hands" and sing a true song of praise to God for His freedom.

The day to which he referred will be the kingdom age, when Jesus reigns on earth, establishing true global peace for the first time ever. It was a theme King touched on throughout his speech, quoting Old Testament prophets who looked forward to that time too. "Let justice run down like water, and righteousness like a mighty stream" (Amos 5:24 NKJV).

God's plan from the foundation of the earth was to see His people gathered together and unified in worshipful living—a time King referenced: "The glory of the LORD shall be revealed, and all flesh shall see it together" (Isaiah 40:5 KJV). In the meantime, there is work to do, and God wants you to be a part of it—as a peacemaker and reconciler in the only name that puts all men on equal, valued footing: Jesus Christ.

GOD IS ALWAYS GENEROUS

" 'Is it against the law for me to do what I want with my money?
Should you be jealous because I am kind to others?' "
MATTHEW 20:15 NLT

It's tempting sometimes to imagine that God is holding Himself back from you. You go through spiritual darkness or dry seasons, and *generosity* may be the last word that comes to mind. In fact, you may become so preoccupied with your own needs that you forget just how badly others need God's generous provision as well.

In the parable of the vineyard workers, some labored all day, while others only worked a few hours. Both received what they needed. As your own needs grow, you may not even be able to imagine that anyone else could need God's provision more. Perhaps you may be in a season of waiting for what you need from God, and it's particularly hard to see His blessings go to others. But remember, God is always generous—but not *just* to you.

Envy will dismantle the patience that God is growing within you, robbing you of the joy of His blessings when they finally come to you. The Lord is generous, but everyone experiences that generosity in different ways and at different times.

God's generosity won't spare you seasons of darkness and doubt. It's possible, however, that waiting will help you view His generosity with greater clarity.

GLOWING IN THE DARK

All the Israelites saw Moses, his face was radiant.
EXODUS 34:30 NIV

It's one of the Bible's strangest moments. Moses returned from the presence of the Lord glowing! (Exodus 34:29–35). Others could observe the changes in his life.

In 2 Corinthians 3:7–18, Paul used this moment to illustrate the transformation believers experience in the presence of God. "And we all, who with unveiled faces contemplate the Lord's glory, are being transformed into his image with ever-increasing glory" (v. 18).

Great spiritual transformation isn't just possible—it's real! God does great work in us to transform us into Christ's image. That is our great and glorious hope!

Great spiritual transformation should be observable. Those around us should notice the difference not because of pious posturing but because we truly are different. It isn't something we put on display. It's something we can't hide!

Great spiritual vitality can fade. Paul is clear: "Moses. . .put a veil over his face to prevent the Israelites from seeing the end of what was passing away" (2 Corinthians 3:13 NIV). Moses put the veil on because his appearance frightened people. He kept the veil on to hide the fact that the glory was fading. Our religious lives can function like that veil and hide the truth that our true spiritual vitality is waning.

Finally, great spiritual vitality can only be renewed in the presence of God. When the glory faded, Moses took off the veil and returned to the source of true transformation (Exodus 34:33–35). When he needed more of God, God was there for him. He's there for us too.

EQUAL BUT NOT IDENTICAL

*God created man in His own image; in the image of God
He created him; male and female He created them.*
GENESIS 1:27 NKJV

Men and women have equal standing before God. Paul observed that
"there is neither male nor female; for you are all one in Christ Jesus"
(Galatians 3:28 NKJV). However, God also designed male and female
relationships to follow a pattern: God gave men the authority to
take bottom-line responsibility for the welfare of women (1 Corinthians 11:3).

Both can show leadership and initiative, and they are "heirs
together of the grace of life" (1 Peter 3:7 KJV), but there are certain
responsibilities that fall to a man. And this is where too many guys
have fallen short.

God meant for men and women to complement each other
through physical and emotional differences. Respective roles are best
defined and experienced in marriage, but they still play into everyday
relationships. Even if you're not married, you can still look out for a
woman's best interests and make her feel valuable, and she can still
encourage you and show you respect.

If you're married, when you both submit to God and follow His
design for your relationship (Ephesians 5:23–33), good things will
follow. If you're single, practice emotional purity. If the woman you're
friends with isn't going to be your wife, she may be another man's
wife in the future. So while you can enjoy Christian fellowship, be
sure to keep your relationship pure and in the proper perspective.

BETTER DAYS AHEAD

*"You will surely forget your trouble,
recalling it only as waters gone by."*
JOB 11:16 NIV

Sometimes you're made to pass through a valley of suffering, and more often than not, it has to do with family issues, financial crises, or health problems. At the time, you may not even be certain that you'll survive. It looks like you'll crash. Perhaps you disobeyed God or you acted rashly or inconsiderately to others, and now the consequences of your actions are rising like floodwaters around you. Or perhaps problems have come upon you through no fault of your own.

Yet, difficult as your circumstances may be and difficult as it might be to believe it, soon enough you'll be laughing again and will forget your troubles. They'll be as waters that have evaporated away. David said of God, "For his anger lasts only a moment, but his favor lasts a lifetime; weeping may stay for the night, but rejoicing comes in the morning" (Psalm 30:5 NIV). It's vital to remember when passing through tests that God's favor lasts your entire lifetime; His discipline, by contrast, is usually brief.

God doesn't get any pleasure out of causing His children to suffer, yet some Christians have been led to believe that God is primarily focused on holiness, indignation, and punishment. He does allow suffering, true, but it usually only lasts long enough to bring about good in your life. "The LORD comforts his people and will have compassion on his afflicted ones" (Isaiah 49:13 NIV).

HOW GOD TURNS FAILURE INTO DELIGHT

*Who is a God like you, who pardons sin and forgives the
transgression. . . . You do not stay angry forever
but delight to show mercy.*
MICAH 7:18 NIV

What do you imagine about God when you sin? Do you imagine an angry God, eager to turn you away or leave you alone? Do you imagine a disappointed God, incredulous that you've failed yet again?

Whether you are struggling with habitual sin or worry that your transgressions are beyond God's forgiveness, there is a promise for you: God is more merciful than we can imagine. Micah compares our Lord with the false gods of his day—deities that arose from human imagination and demanded offerings in order to be placated. He assures us that our living God is completely unlike these gods.

There is no doubt that sins and transgressions are serious and can alienate us from God, but if we confess our sins, He is all too eager to forgive and restore us. If we imagine God as angry or towering over us to strike us with judgment, the Word assures us that His anger passes quickly and that He delights in showing mercy. In fact, God takes no pleasure in judgment. God's delight is in showing mercy and restoring us. If you want to delight God, stop hiding your sin and failures. Bring them out before God in plain sight so that He can show mercy to you with His pardon and forgiveness.

WHAT THE HEART WANTS

*"But the things that proceed out of the mouth come from the heart,
and those defile the man. For out of the heart come evil thoughts,
murders, adulteries, fornications, thefts, false witness, slanders."*
MATTHEW 15:18–19 NASB

Many a man has gotten himself into trouble by embracing "the heart wants what the heart wants" mentality—as if Christians are to be slaves to their hearts' desires. The problem with this thinking is that out of the heart come evil thoughts, murders, adulteries, fornications, thefts, false witness, and slanders.

Genesis 6:5 says that every intent of the thoughts of a man's heart is only evil continually. And Jeremiah 17:9 says the heart is more deceitful than all else and is desperately sick. The heart does want what the heart wants, but that's the *problem*. You can't trust your heart. It only wants all sorts of evil. But that doesn't mean that all is lost.

In the parable of the sower (Luke 8:15 NASB), Jesus explains that "the seed in the good soil, these are the ones who have heard the word in an honest and good heart, and hold it fast, and bear fruit with perseverance." When your heart has the Word in it, it's honest and good. Have you fallen victim to obeying your heart without first bringing it under the authority of the Word?

WAIT NO MORE

*If anyone, then, knows the good they ought to
do and doesn't do it, it is sin for them.*
JAMES 4:17 NIV

In AD 79, around noon on August 24, the ancient Roman resort town of Pompeii came to a swift and sudden end when Mount Vesuvius erupted. Pompeii's citizens were instantly preserved in their final acts, a few thousand men, women, and children memorialized in hardened, muddy ash. Vesuvius is still active, and another eruption is expected.

Europe's only active volcano is a reminder that Jesus could come back any day. Scripture warns us to pay attention to the signs of the times so we can warn nonbelievers and encourage other believers that "God has not destined us for wrath, but for obtaining salvation through our Lord Jesus Christ" (1 Thessalonians 5:9 NASB). You should be living each day for God and every day like it might be your last.

But here's the problem: most people put things off. There's an ongoing battle between the part of you that knows how to make mature, responsible decisions and the part that wants to do that thing over there. Even the urgency of impending apocalypse pales before the tyranny of YouTube and Candy Crush.

In between "breaks" though, identify what it is that paralyzes you: indecisiveness, perfectionism, fear, or laziness. Once you've narrowed it down, then you know what to pray for. God will help you get focused and back on task.

FINDING GOD EACH DAY

Praise the LORD! I will thank the LORD with all my heart as I meet with his godly people. How amazing are the deeds of the LORD! All who delight in him should ponder them.
PSALM 111:1–2 NLT

Today's psalm should encourage you to pause and to ponder the works of God around you. How is He present with you today? Can you see how the good and perfect gifts around you are from the Lord? You can see this moment today as an invitation to draw near to God and to become aware of His presence.

It's easy to run from one task to another, and by evening you may wonder where God was throughout the day. Perhaps you even feel abandoned by Him at the end of a busy day. While scripture assures you that He's always with you, you can surely overlook His presence and gifts for you. Unless you take time to see the Lord's works around you, you'll miss out on the delight and joy that belong to you.

You'll also see more of God's works if you spend time with His people. As you see the ways that He has blessed your friends and family, you'll become more aware of Him.

It's also likely that just as you hit a place of stability, someone in your circle will need a reminder of God's care. Your enjoyment of God isn't just for your own benefit, after all.

PERFECT PEACE

Those who love Your law have great peace,
and nothing causes them to stumble.
PSALM 119:165 NASB

Darlene Rose, a missionary to Batavia, Java, arrived there in 1938 with her new husband, Russell. They ended up as prisoners of war during World War II and were taken to the mountains, where eventually all of the men were shoved into a truck. As Russell took his place, he spoke words of comfort to Darlene.

"Remember one thing, dear," Russell said, according to an article on the *Charisma Magazine* website. "God said He would never leave us or forsake us."

Darlene never saw him again. But she said that as the truck pulled away, she felt at peace because she believed Romans 8:28 (NASB): "And we know that God causes all things to work together for good to those who love God, to those who are called according to His purpose."

The article went on to say that over the next few years, Darlene and her fellow missionaries were forced to eat dogs and rats to stay alive. They were also in constant danger from pirates and savage murderers. Eventually, the missionaries were rescued by Allied soldiers. A few years later though, she returned, spending forty more years in the jungles of Indonesia. Both she and Russell had perfect peace because they knew and trusted God's Word.

As you face hardship today, you too can experience perfect peace.

THE LOVE OF MONEY

But those who desire to be rich fall into temptation and a snare,
and into many foolish and harmful lusts which drown
men in destruction and perdition.

1 TIMOTHY 6:9 NKJV

It's not difficult to see the proof of the destructiveness of greed in the world around you. The federal prison system is filled with men whose love of money led them to commit crimes so serious that they resulted in long—sometimes lifelong—imprisonments. Just do a quick internet search of the following names for some stark examples of the consequences of greed: Bernie Madoff, Jeff Skilling, Bernie Ebbers, Dennis Kozlowski, and John Rigas.

The Bible teaches that greed, or "the love of money," is the driving force for all sorts of evil and wickedness and sometimes the ruin of men's lives of faith: "For the love of money is a root of all kinds of evil. Some people, eager for money, have wandered from the faith and pierced themselves with many griefs" (1 Timothy 6:10 NIV).

Money, in and of itself, is not evil, and neither is the desire to better yourself financially. Money is just a tool, one you can use to care for your family, to build yourself a better life, or to bless others. But you put yourself at serious risk when you make the acquisition of material wealth your life's focus.

KEEP HIS COMMANDMENTS

"If you love Me, keep My commandments."
JOHN 14:15 NKJV

Jesus made it very clear what it meant to be His follower. It goes without saying that you have to believe in Him, and as a Christian you do that, but do you wonder at times whether your faith is genuine, if you truly *know* God? Many Christians ask themselves this from time to time. The Bible even advises, "Examine yourselves as to whether you are in the faith. Test yourselves" (2 Corinthians 13:5 NKJV).

And *how* do you test yourself? The apostle John gave a very simple litmus test. He wrote, "By this we know that we know Him, if we keep His commandments" (1 John 2:3 NKJV). It doesn't get much simpler than that.

But which commandments are most important? According to Matthew 22:36–39, the two greatest commands—the ones you must make *certain* to obey—are to love God with all your heart and to love others as you love yourself. John also gave a very simple answer, saying, "This is His commandment: that we should believe on the name of His Son Jesus Christ and love one another" (1 John 3:23 NKJV).

There are a number of other doctrines that you must believe to be sound in the faith, but it's absolutely foundational to love and believe in God and His Son and to genuinely love your neighbor. If you have this foundation in place, you cannot only be assured that your faith is genuine, but you'll be certain to *grow* as a Christian.

GOD'S ECONOMY

There is one who scatters, yet increases more; and there is one who withholds more than is right, but it leads to poverty.
PROVERBS 11:24 NKJV

Compared to worldly views of wealth, God's economy seems built on paradoxes: to get, you must first give, but you shouldn't give to get (Luke 6:35). Jesus' encounters with the rich—Matthew, Zacchaeus, the rich young ruler—make it clear that you can have every material advantage in the world and still lack the thing that matters most. In fact, the more you have, the more you will be held accountable for (Luke 12:48).

Consider the following financial concepts: you're not an owner but a steward; give and you will be blessed; live within your means; save so you can invest in things with no tangible value. From God's perspective, they all make sense. If they make you scratch your head, you're living in the world's economy, not God's.

Since everything belongs to God (Psalm 24:1), His business should guide your finances. Give back to Him first—don't ever give up tithing even if you're down to a widow's mite.

Remember, God's business is seeing as many as possible receive the gift of salvation. Christ purchased a gift for you that you can never earn or purchase; the only thing you can do is share it, with your words, deeds, and resources. No other religion has Christianity's track record of helping; your involvement carries on that great tradition.

TRANSFORMATION ISN'T UP TO YOU

*But I will come—and soon—if the Lord lets me, and then I'll find out
whether these arrogant people just give pretentious speeches or
whether they really have God's power. For the Kingdom of
God is not just a lot of talk; it is living by God's power.*
1 CORINTHIANS 4:19–20 NLT

Division and discord among Christians is nothing new, but perhaps
Paul's approach to resolving it may surprise you. When facing a divisive
and contentious church, Paul reminded them that their words held
very little power for spiritual transformation. Whether relying on
your own words or the teachings of others, the true power of God's
kingdom is in the way His power takes hold in you.

Even your best attempts at encouragement may well fall flat if
you aren't empowered by God. This puts the responsibility for your
spiritual transformation on Him, so the pressure is off you.

You can't make people change and you can't change yourself. You
can only submit to the power of God, and that process of surrender
and submission will feel like a lot of work at times! However, the end
result of seeking God's direction and influence is that you'll change
into the kind of person who has something worthwhile to share with
others.

GOD IS WITH YOU

*David also said to Solomon his son, "Be strong and courageous,
and do the work. Do not be afraid or discouraged, for the LORD God,
my God, is with you. He will not fail you or forsake you until all
the work for the service of the temple of the LORD is finished."*
1 CHRONICLES 28:20 NIV

While Solomon seemed to experience little external opposition while
carrying out his father's wishes to build the temple, he must have faced
some sort of opposition, otherwise David wouldn't have encouraged
him to be strong and courageous in doing the work. In fact, doing
God's work *always* requires strength and courage.

Have you been called to start a Bible study at work or maybe
among your friends? Are you sensing that God wants you to start
volunteering at your local homeless shelter or maybe even to start
one? Maybe He's calling you into full-time Christian work of some
sort. Whatever the case, your primary opposition is probably mostly
internal.

Who are you to start a Bible study, or work in a homeless shelter, or
join the mission field, or become a pastor? You are God's chosen—His
anointed for this very task. And if He's telling you to do something,
don't be afraid or discouraged. Do the work. God is with you.

ENTERING INTO GOD'S PRESENCE

Let us come before his presence with thanksgiving.
PSALM 95:2 KJV

The book of Psalms commands God's people to come before His presence with thankful hearts and even to "come before his presence with singing" (Psalm 100:2 KJV). In Old Testament times, the temple in Jerusalem was the place where God sometimes manifested Himself as the Shekinah glory in the innermost chamber, the Holy of Holies. Thus, when people entered the temple, they went with an attitude of reverence and awe, offering thanks to God for His goodness and singing songs of praise.

Likewise today, when you worship God, it brings you into His presence. As a Christian, you must remember that you're not praying to a distant deity who may or may not be listening, but you are entering into the very throne room of God. "Let us therefore come boldly unto the throne of grace, that we may obtain mercy, and find grace to help in time of need" (Hebrews 4:16 KJV). You have an audience with your Father, and He's attentive to what you're saying.

But have you ever prayed and, while you were praying, realized that although you were speaking words, you didn't really have faith that you were actually talking to God? You weren't quite sure that He was listening? The problem may have been that you failed to enter His presence *before* you began praying.

Before you begin asking God for things, make sure that you've entered into His presence. And one of the best ways to do that is with a thankful heart and praise.

YOU ARE GOD'S BELOVED CREATION

"What is the price of five sparrows—two copper coins? Yet God does not forget a single one of them. And the very hairs on your head are all numbered. So don't be afraid; you are more valuable to God than a whole flock of sparrows."

Luke 12:6–7 NLT

Do you fear that God sees you as expendable? Are you worried that you could be on the brink of being cast away by the Lord? Perhaps you've gone through some season of life where you've felt abandoned by God and you aren't able to pinpoint what has gone wrong.

God is intimately aware of you and your needs. Most importantly, this intimate knowledge of you doesn't turn Him away or result in your expulsion from His presence. In fact, this is a reason for you to have confidence that your Creator remains near to you and desires to be with you. The Lord is deeply invested in knowing you and in caring for you.

That isn't to say that you'll be spared hardships. Rather, you're assured of God's presence and comfort day after day. Just as the birds He created can never escape His notice, you can also take comfort in His ongoing awareness of you. If even the most common, seemingly inconsequential creature is known by God, how much more will He hold on to you?

SETTING AN EXAMPLE

Join together in following my example.
PHILIPPIANS 3:17 NIV

Paul realized that he was leading the way and others were following him.

Every man who seeks a great adventure in God is leading the way. The question is: What kind of example are we setting? Are we living up to the life of Christ in us, or are we slipping back into old habits and patterns?

First, Paul knew his life was being watched. His example mattered. Our children, our friends, and the unbelievers who surround us every day are watching us too. We may not think about it, but it's true. Paul took that responsibility seriously.

Second, we ought to follow the example of others who are ahead of us on the path of spiritual growth. Paul wrote, "Keep your eyes on those who live as we do" (Philippians 3:17 NIV). We set an example by following the example of others.

Third, the impact of our example has eternal consequence. In the rest of the paragraph, Paul contrasts those who follow his example and those who are enemies of the cross (Philippians 3:17–21). Setting the wrong example has disastrous consequences.

Finally, our example must have integrity. It isn't about putting our best foot forward or presenting a handsome veneer that hides the truth. How we handle our flaws and failures, how we deal with challenges and difficulties, and how we respond to temptation are part of that example.

The world has plenty of hypocrites. It's men of true integrity who are in short supply.

A MATTER OF INTEGRITY

If a house be divided against itself, that house cannot stand.
MARK 3:25 KJV

The Lincoln-Douglas debates began on August 21, 1858. Much of the ammunition used in this battle for a Senate seat was supplied by a speech Lincoln had made two months earlier, when he characterized the issue of slavery in America as "a house divided." The biblical reference put Lincoln's arguments on high moral ground: "I believe this government cannot endure, permanently half slave and half free. . . . It will become all one thing or all the other."

Lincoln lost the Senate race, but his integrity played a key role in his election as president. His words then proved prophetic, as the South seceded and the Civil War began, four years of bloody, heart-wrenching conflict that saw the nation reunited under a single slave-free banner.

Jesus' "divided house" remarks were a prelude to His claim that whoever was not for Him was against Him (Matthew 12:30). No neutral ground exists in the battle between good and evil. As Matthew Henry put it, "There are two great interests in the world"—God's and Satan's. The heart of every person on earth is the battleground.

No enduring good can come from compromising God's truth. His words have integrity and the man who stands by them will too. You'll avoid hypocrisy and know for sure that, though a battle may be lost, you'll be on the winning side in the war.

GOD–HONORING HUMILITY

*Humble yourselves, therefore, under God's mighty hand,
that he may lift you up in due time.*
1 PETER 5:6 NIV

It's probably fair to say that pride is at the heart of nearly every sin we can commit against God and against others. Pride causes people to boast about themselves and to tear others down. Pride causes people to believe they can do for themselves what God has promised to do for them, and that leads to a lack of prayer. Pride causes conflicts between people, and it keeps us from confessing our sins to one another and to God so that we can be reconciled.

This list of the terrible results of human pride could go on and on, but when you read it, it is no small wonder that God has said, "I hate pride" (Proverbs 8:13).

God hates human pride, but He loves humility, which can be defined as the acknowledgment that apart from Him, we are nothing and can do nothing of value. When we are humble, in effect we are confessing that we have nothing to offer God apart from what He has already done.

So build your life on the words of the apostle Peter. Humble yourself before God. Don't seek to be exalted on your own, but wait patiently for God to give you what you are due.

THE ONLY WAY TO DEFEAT SIN

So I say, let the Holy Spirit guide your lives. Then you won't
be doing what your sinful nature craves.

GALATIANS 5:16 NLT

Discipline, intentional action, and accountability are all good things that can help us overcome our sinful desires and shortcomings. We won't live as faithful disciples by accident. However, Paul shares the heart of the Gospel with us—the driving force in our lives that both unites us with God and empowers us to live in holiness. The only way we'll definitively and consistently overcome sin is to yield ourselves to the Holy Spirit. With the Holy Spirit as our guide, we'll begin to recognize the power of our own desires and, most importantly, our powerlessness in overcoming them.

The "self" will not fade away if we deny it. Our cravings are too powerful. Our senses of self-preservation and enjoyment are too appealing. We can only educate ourselves so much in the consequences of sin. At a certain point, we need a more powerful guide to show us the way forward and to redirect our desires toward the presence and power of God. Ironically, the only way to overcome sin is to stop fighting it. We won't be shaped into God's people by what we deny but rather by whom we yield to and who guides us. By yielding our wills to God, we will find new cravings for the presence of God and will discover along the way that we have been shaped into renewed people.

GETTING DISTRACTED

*"While your servant was busy here and
there, the man disappeared."*
1 KINGS 20:40 NIV

One day a prophet of God called out to King Ahab after a critical campaign and said, "Your servant went into the thick of the battle, and someone came to me with a captive and said, 'Guard this man. If he is missing, it will be your life for his life. . . .' While your servant was busy here and there, the man disappeared" (1 Kings 20:39–40 NIV).

This was a parable to show Ahab that he, king of Israel, was guilty for letting the wicked king of Aram go free after he had defeated him. However, let's focus here on *this* important thought:

Many men have, at times, become so busy with a little here and there that they failed to focus on what was truly important. They allowed themselves to get sidetracked in nonessentials, and before they knew it, they'd fiddled away their time. Either they get continually distracted from a task or else they simply keep procrastinating.

The Bible tells you that you must cultivate the virtue of self-control (2 Peter 1:6 NIV). Paul said that men of God must be "self-controlled. . . and disciplined" (Titus 1:8 NIV). Even if you're bored with a task, such as a project at work, you must put forth the effort to focus on it and finish it. Or even if you shy away from a responsibility because it's difficult or unpleasant, such as disciplining a child, roll up your sleeves and do it. You'll be glad you did.

LIFTED LOW

The cords of death encompassed me and the terrors of Sheol came upon me; I found distress and sorrow. Then I called upon the name of the LORD: "O LORD, I beseech You, save my life!" Gracious is the LORD, and righteous; yes, our God is compassionate. The LORD preserves the simple; I was brought low, and He saved me.

PSALM 116:3–6 NASB

How often we find that being brought low is the only road to rescue! Sometimes it's the only way to see what the psalmist saw: that God is gracious, righteous, and compassionate, that He stands ready to save. We are frequently distracted by our circumstances or by other people or by our own thinking. Sometimes we discover a beseeching heart only when God gets our full attention through difficulty. It's merciful to shake us to the foundations of our faith, to crush our expectations, to allow distress and sorrow to "win" for a while, and thus force from us an earnest cry for God's help. The humbling of hardship and suffering is a kindness. "No discipline is enjoyable while it is happening—it's painful! But afterward there will be a peaceful harvest of right living for those who are trained in this way" (Hebrews 12:11 NLT).

Humbling ourselves means we stop looking for solutions, for *How* or *What*, and start looking for *Who*. God gives grace to the humble and answers the earnest prayers of His children with the gift of Himself. Being brought to our knees is to be brought into closer communion with our Father.

PURSUING GODLY AMBITIONS

My ambition has always been to preach the Good News where the name of Christ has never been heard, rather than where a church has already been started by someone else.

ROMANS 15:20 NLT

You probably have several ambitions. Professionally, you have your eyes set on a prize—maybe a promotion or ownership of your own business. Personally, you're striving to become a better leader in your home and working on taking care of yourself. What about your spiritual ambitions? Where do your spiritual passions lie?

After his conversion, the apostle Paul had his sights set on preaching the Gospel in places where the name of Jesus had never been heard, and he spent the rest of his life doing so. He wasn't disrespecting the work done in churches started by others. He just left that work to someone else who had a godly zeal for it.

Do you have such clarity of thought? You don't need a "calling" to pursue most of your godly ambitions. You simply need to acknowledge that it exists deep inside your heart and then prayerfully seek ways to live it out.

Maybe your ambition is outside of the box—like starting an online Christian news site in your city, or giving away everything you own to the poor, or starting a ministry to mentally ill men who have fallen through the cracks of society. Whatever it is, jump into it.

LEARNING WISDOM AND SELF-CONTROL

*[The proverbs'] purpose is to teach people wisdom and discipline,
to help them understand the insights of the wise.*

PROVERBS 1:2 NLT

Do you struggle with self-control? If you have given up hope and given yourself over to one sin or another, Solomon has something to say to you. In the verse above, he says the book of Proverbs will teach you wisdom and self-control. Hope does exist. You just have to access it.

When is the last time you worked your way through the book of Proverbs? There are thirty-one Proverbs, one for each day of the month. Would you be willing to spend some serious time and contemplation in one chapter of Proverbs per day for the next month? Would you be willing to journal about your revelations? How about enlisting another man to go through them with you? Commit to not talking about anything temporal during the month, but instead speak only about the truths you are learning. It might be awkward at first, but awkward is okay. All it will take is one revelation to set you on a new course.

Solomon says that in addition to gaining wisdom and self-control, you will learn how to understand sayings with deep meanings. This doesn't come as a natural gift or even a developed skill. It comes from the Spirit of God as you ingest the wisdom of His Word.

If your soul has been dry during this season of sin, expect a change. Expect deep understanding. Expect deep revelation. Expect victory.

BARE-BONES FAITH

Walk worthy of the Lord, fully pleasing Him, being fruitful in every good work and increasing in the knowledge of God.
Colossians 1:10 NKJV

"One! Two! Three! Four!" With a count-off that heralded the punk-rock revolution, the Ramones hit the stage for the first time on August 16, 1974, at CBGB's in Queens, New York. Seeking an antidote both for Woodstock's hippie-dippie psychedelia and the bloated excesses of mid-70s corporate rock, the foursome—clad in black leather jackets—hit the stage with a fast, furious wall of sound that struck in two-minute bursts.

The band's DIY ethos inspired a generation to get in the garage and start playing—whether they knew their instruments or not. Skill set aside, the Ramones took a deliberate approach to their art. Drummer Tommy Ramone described their philosophy: "Eliminate the unnecessary and focus on the substance."

That's a useful motto for Christians too. Look past trends and movements and refocus on what following Jesus is about. Pray for a wise heart to know Him better. Then, as He leads, remove anything that muddies the living water—worldly relationships, churchy jargon, legalistic attitudes.

Stripped-down, bare-bones faith follows Jesus' lead: Jesus sought God's will first and always. He embraced society's outcasts, healed broken lives and hearts, taught God's Word, and prepared leaders. He didn't put up with hypocrisy but served rather than judged. Take a fresh look at Jesus' priorities, eliminating the unnecessary and focusing on the substance.

NO SECOND-HAND STORY

Do your best to present yourself to God as one approved,
a worker who does not need to be ashamed and
who correctly handles the word of truth.
2 TIMOTHY 2:15 NIV

Hold on. Dig deep. Work out.

Does the Christian life sometimes sound like that? You might even hear someone say, "Get sweaty for Jesus."

It's true that the apostle Paul refers to the Christian journey as a race, but that's only part of the picture. There are two steps every Christian man should take. The first is love God enough to serve those He loves. The second is to know enough of God's message that we don't have to be ashamed when someone asks us why we're helping out. It doesn't do much good to lend a hand but then be unable to tell them more about what a relationship with Jesus looks like.

God wants us to teach a true message, not one that's made up or may be a misunderstood hand-me-down secondhand story.

The Bible is where we learn, and we have to balance our walk between helping those who need help and learning more about why we offer help.

In an earlier version of the Bible, we are asked to "study to shew thyself approved of God" (KJV). We don't assume, guess, or even make something up when it comes to answering questions of our faith. We *hold on* to God's hand, we *dig deep* in His Word, and our *spiritual muscles* grow when we really *know* what God said in the Bible.

Study and serve. Learn and give. Memorize and share God's love. He will approve this plan—every time.

GOD'S LIGHT ERASES YOUR DARKNESS

*Remember, O LORD, your compassion and unfailing love, which you
have shown from long ages past. Do not remember the rebellious
sins of my youth. Remember me in the light of your
unfailing love, for you are merciful, O LORD.*
PSALM 25:6–7 NLT

God's character defines how He interacts with you, not the other way
around. If you had to be on your best behavior in order to receive
God's mercy, you'd have no hope in the face of His holiness.

You can't hide your sins from God, but you can still approach
Him with confidence because of His unfailing love and mercy. Today's
psalm notes that in light of God's mercy, you have access to Him.
You've never been able to be good enough, but He has always been
good enough to receive you.

When God remembers you, He doesn't look at your failures,
hypocrisies, and faults. He sees you with compassion as His beloved
child. It's this love that changes and transforms you, renewing you
and drawing you near to Him on the merits of His unfailing love.

You don't have to bring anything to God because He desires to
show mercy and compassion to you. In the warm glow of His light,
your darkness is gone and you're free to be loved by Him.

DOUBLE, DOUBLE TOIL AND TROUBLE

But to those who are selfishly ambitious and do not obey the truth,
but obey unrighteousness, wrath and indignation.

ROMANS 2:8 NASB

In August of 1054, Malcolm Canmore avenged his father, King Duncan I of Scotland, by slaying his killer, King Macbeth. (Yes, he was an actual historical dude!) Shakespeare's play dramatized the story, adding a sense of mystical destiny and downplaying the real Macbeth's promotion of Christianity, but the emotional heart of the account—unchecked ambition—didn't require much massaging.

So much of history is stories of kings building monuments to themselves and then being unseated or overthrown by other kings who do the same thing, over and over. For all their wealth and power, it's hard not to picture the broken head of the statue in the poem "Ozymandias," half-buried in drifting sands, carrying the ironic inscription of its futility: "Look on my Works, ye Mighty, and despair!"

How do you do something with your life that matters beyond your life? By focusing your ambition on God. Ambition isn't bad in and of itself; it depends on whom it's focused. That requires humility—the understanding that, no matter how much you accomplish, it's chump change compared to God's works.

When you overcome your self-oriented agenda with seeking God's greater glory, you'll find contentment. You can only do that by focusing your goals and energy on God's character and agenda, not yours. Anything less makes you a Macbeth.

STOP YOUR GRIPING!

*Do everything without grumbling or arguing, so that
you may become blameless and pure, "children of God
without fault in a warped and crooked generation."*
PHILIPPIANS 2:14–15 NIV

Let's face it—life can sometimes feel like one frustrating situation after another. Who among us, when circumstances put the squeeze on us, hasn't felt like just griping and complaining to anyone who will listen?

While the Bible contains some examples of godly men who complained to God (David and Job, for example), it also warns us against grumbling and complaining and also shows us that having a complaining attitude and mouth can have very negative consequences (see Numbers 14).

When we complain, we separate ourselves from God and His peace, and we also ruin our testimony for Christ to a lost and hurting world. After all, who wants to listen to someone offering answers when that person constantly gripes about his own life?

So in those times when you don't think life is being fair to you, remember to do as the apostle Paul instructed and "give thanks in all circumstances; for this is God's will for you in Christ Jesus" (1 Thessalonians 5:18). Also remember God's promise that "in all things God works for the good of those who love him, who have been called according to his purpose" (Romans 8:28).

CHOICE AND CONSEQUENCE

"From everyone who has been given much, much will be demanded."
LUKE 12:48 NIV

The more of God we experience, the more He expects of us. It's always been that way.

Moses had the glory of the burning bush and was expected to set his people free. Paul met Jesus on the Damascus road and was expected to bring the Gospel to the world. Peter had the joy of three years at Jesus' side and was expected to lead the church in the face of great persecution and in a period of incredible expansion.

There is no doubt that this is true. As a matter of fact, one of the barriers to greater spiritual life is knowing that God's call accompanies God's joy. But why? Why are we not free to just enjoy the glory of knowing God without the burden of service?

First, growing in God isn't only about us. It is also about God's glory in the world. It's not about us. It's about Him.

Second, growing in God prepares us to participate in His great work in the world. Surely our relationship with Him is precious. But God wants everyone to know that joy and has chosen us as His emissaries.

Third, growing in God strengthens us for the inevitable challenges we face. We know Him, and we know He will strengthen, sustain, and stay with us.

Finally, it's good for us. We were created to live on purpose for a great purpose. We cannot fulfill that destiny or know that satisfaction without a great mission.

What is God expecting of you?

CONFIDENT IN CHRIST

In him and through faith in him we may approach
God with freedom and confidence.
Ephesians 3:12 niv

So often when men pray to God for a pressing need, a sense of sinfulness rises up to discourage them. The thoughts frequently come in waves: *You're unworthy. God won't answer your prayers. You might as well stop praying.* This is the voice of the enemy. His name, Satan, means "accuser" in Hebrew, and he doesn't just accuse *you* of sin. The Bible calls him "the accuser of our brethren" (Revelation 12:10 nkjv). He accuses *all* believers.

If you've given your heart to Christ, God has forgiven you and made you an heir of His eternal kingdom. If there's current sin that you haven't repented of, however, it will hinder God from blessing you in this life (Isaiah 59:1–2). That's why His Holy Spirit convicts you to repent (John 16:7–8).

But know this also: God *will* forgive you as you confess your failings to Him (1 John 1:9). The devil may try to accuse and condemn you, telling you that God won't forgive you—but don't listen to that lie! God *does* forgive. "Let us therefore come boldly to the throne of grace, that we may obtain mercy and find grace to help in time of need" (Hebrews 4:16 nkjv).

Are you in a time of need? Are you desperate for mercy? Christ's death on the cross, His shed blood, has made the way to His Father's throne open. Your sins are forgiven in Christ. You can come to God's throne with your prayer requests, boldly and with confidence.

LOVING OTHER BELIEVERS

We [Paul and Timothy] always pray for you, and we give thanks to God, the Father of our Lord Jesus Christ. For we have heard of your faith in Christ Jesus and your love for all of God's people.

COLOSSIANS 1:3–4 NLT

As God's people, you are called to exhibit love for everyone, including your enemies, but you have a certain affinity for other believers—an instant bond, no matter how long you've known them. You're united in Christ, and that bond is thicker than blood.

Paul wrote to the Colossian church that he wanted them to know how thankful he was for their reputation of loving all of God's people. We can't be certain how Paul and Timothy heard this information, although some commentators speculate that it was passed on by Epaphras (v. 7). We also don't know how they expressed this love, but it undoubtedly involved acts of kindness and mercy because love includes action, and you build a reputation for things you do consistently.

How is your church viewed by other Christians who have never stepped foot inside one of your worship services? Do other believers see your church at local events, praying and serving alongside fellow believers? Does your church reach out to other churches in your city during their time of need? Does your church celebrate with other Christians? If not, what simple steps can you take to change that?

OVERCOMERS

"But you, be strong and do not lose courage,
for there is reward for your work."
2 CHRONICLES 15:7 NASB

St. Louis Cardinals ace and Hall of Famer Bob Gibson threw the only no-hitter of his storied career on August 14, 1971, and prevented an old nemesis, the Pittsburgh Pirates, from getting a single hit the entire game. The Pirates had hit him hard over the years, including one batted ball that broke his leg. But overcoming adversity was old hat for "Bullet" Bob.

Gibson overcame several childhood ailments—among them rickets, asthma, and a heart murmur—to become a top-level athlete. Known as a ferocious competitor, Gibson never took credit for his abilities, saying, "It is not something I earned. . . . It is a gift. It is something that was given to me." God has given you talents too, but they will be tested through trouble.

No one asks for trouble, but trouble comes anyway. When it does, as a Christian, don't be afraid to embrace it—not because you're glad for the problem but because God will be with you, strengthening your faith and endurance.

In fact, until you have overcome adversity, you can't truly appreciate God's gift of salvation. Tribulation reminds you of two important things: one, you need Jesus desperately; and two, His Spirit and power make you an overcomer—*more* than a conqueror (Romans 8:37). Nothing should faze you because nothing can stand between you and God.

WISDOM FROM ABOVE

But the wisdom from above is first of all pure. It is also peace loving, gentle at all times, and willing to yield to others. It is full of mercy and the fruit of good deeds. It shows no favoritism and is always sincere.

JAMES 3:17 NLT

In today's verse, the apostle James provides a filter for understanding whether the wisdom you follow is actually from God or not. Is the message pure? (Will it purify the heart?) Is it peace loving rather than contentious? Is it gentle at all times? Is it willing to yield to others? Is it full of mercy and the fruit of good deeds? Does it show favoritism or is it sincere?

Compare the characteristics of wisdom that's from above to earthly wisdom, which is at times helpful but often tainted. Earthly wisdom says to look out for number one, to stand up for yourself, to get what you have coming. That's not to say you shouldn't stand up for yourself, but don't do it because you're motivated by pride or anger.

Jesus spoke only on the Father's authority. He was in constant communication with Him. The two go hand in hand. God does offer us guidance sometimes without being prompted, but even then, it usually happens as a result of being in close relationship with Him.

BREAKING DOWN WALLS

The LORD is a shelter for the oppressed, a refuge in times of trouble.
PSALM 9:9 NLT

On August 13, 1961, East German soldiers laid down the first barbed wire and bricks that would become the Berlin Wall, dividing the city and providing a global symbol for the Cold War conflict. Would-be defectors were often shot as they attempted to escape, ratcheting up tensions between the forces of freedom and tyranny.

The Wall is a perfect microcosm of the barriers created by sin. When Adam and Eve ate the fruit, their sin made them guilty and ashamed, and people have been building walls to defend themselves from sin's consequences ever since.

It's human nature not to show all your cards; it's hard to trust someone when you don't know their motives or agenda. Fear of the unknown drives behavior, and only perfect love can cast it out (1 John 4:18–19). God's love in Christ did just that. God reaches through your defenses, offering peace, forgiveness, and reconciliation.

That requires transparency on your part: you must be honest about your sin to come to Jesus—on both a general and daily basis. Being known for who you really are and still loved by the only One who has the right to condemn you breaks down fear's walls. Once there's no wall between you and God, it becomes easier to open up to others and for them to be open with you.

LIVING AN EMPOWERED LIFE

*Put on the Lord Jesus Christ, and make no
provision for the flesh, to fulfill its lusts.*
ROMANS 13:14 NKJV

You're told to "put on" the Lord Jesus Christ, which sounds similar to putting on a change of clothing—and that's exactly what the scripture means. In Luke 24:49 (NIV), Jesus told His disciples, "I am going to send you what my Father has promised [the Holy Spirit]; but stay in the city until you have been clothed with power from on high."

The Spirit of Christ is like a force field that clothes you; you step into Him and He envelops and surrounds you. Paul explained, "You have taken off your old self with its practices and have put on the new self, which is being renewed in. . .the image of its Creator" (Colossians 3:9–10 NIV).

Your "new self" is empowered by God's Spirit, enabling you to live victoriously in this fallen world. That's why scripture warns not to look for ways to indulge your fleshly appetites. You're a new person, so yield to God's Spirit dwelling inside you, not your old sinful habits.

The Bible commands, "As you therefore have received Christ Jesus the Lord, so walk in Him" (Colossians 2:6 NKJV). When you first became a Christian, you knew that living as a believer would entail resisting old temptations and living according to Jesus' teachings. And this is still true.

GOD CARES ENOUGH TO ACT

*Anyone who wants to approach God must believe both that he exists
and that he cares enough to respond to those who seek him.*
HEBREWS 11:6 MSG

You can believe in God, yet lack faith that He cares enough to respond to your heartfelt prayers. Many men believe that God exists and sent His Son to die for their sins; they even concede that He answered prayers in Bible times, but they have little faith that He *still* does. They've been disappointed when past prayers weren't answered, and this has led them to believe that God doesn't involve Himself with people today except in truly unusual circumstances.

They basically believe that God has already done about as much as He is ever *going* to do, and that from here on, it's up to people to work hard, seize opportunities, and take care of themselves. Small wonder that they don't bother to spend much time in prayer! No surprise that they end up thinking that they can pretty much manage life without God's help. They believe that they *have* to.

It's true that God expects you to work hard to provide for yourself and your family and that He expects you to think hard to solve many of your problems, but God is still very active in the world. He still helps the helpless. And He still helps ordinary people who find themselves in unexpected difficulties.

Yes, He cares. And yes, He responds to those who earnestly seek Him. But you have to continually seek Him and not give up easily.

YOUR PLACE IN THE BIG PICTURE

What, after all, is Apollos? And what is Paul? Only servants,
through whom you came to believe—as the Lord has assigned
to each his task. I planted the seed, Apollos watered
it, but God has been making it grow.

1 CORINTHIANS 3:5–6 NIV

Read most every list of the most important/influential people in the history of Western civilization, and you're likely to find the name of the apostle Paul mentioned prominently. Of course, Paul was largely responsible for spreading Christianity throughout the known world, and we can't forget that he wrote most of the New Testament.

But you only need to read today's scripture passage to know that Paul's response to being held in such high esteem in such a list would be along the lines of "I'm nobody!" Paul understood that God had given him a big assignment, but he also understood that it was God, not him, who was worthy of the glory for the results.

God has given us, His servants, responsibilities that are but small parts in the bigger plan of salvation for others. Our job is to sow the seeds by telling others the truth about salvation through Jesus Christ and to water those seeds through prayer. God's part is to illuminate the message we present (to make the seed grow) and bring people to Him through the work of His Holy Spirit.

GODLY REBUKE

*And they came to Him and woke Him, saying, "Save us, Lord;
we are perishing!" He said to them, "Why are you afraid,
you men of little faith?" Then He got up and rebuked
the winds and the sea, and it became perfectly calm.*

MATTHEW 8:25–26 NASB

The disciples were an unlikely mix of educated and uneducated;
craftsmen and professionals; strong character and weak. But nothing
breaks down barriers like a life-threatening event. When the storm
threatened to swamp their boat, the disciples were all in agreement:
wake up Jesus!

Of course, Jesus comes through for His fearful men, but the
storm wasn't the only thing that got rebuked that day. He wasn't
grumpy for being awakened; He was disappointed in their lack of
faith. It's ironic to think that calling on Jesus for help could bring a
rebuke. In this case, it would have shown more faith for the disciples
not to cry out for Jesus' help. After all, He was right there with them.
Peter repeats this watery lesson later: "Peter got out of the boat, and
walked on the water and came toward Jesus. But seeing the wind, he
became frightened, and beginning to sink, he cried out, 'Lord, save
me!' Immediately Jesus stretched out His hand and took hold of him,
and said to him, 'You of little faith, why did you doubt?' " (Matthew
14:29–31 NASB).

The lesson they seem to keep reviewing is that fear is the most
potent form of doubt. Jesus wants us to be free from fear and live
like He is truly with us, even in the storm.

COMPASSION FOR THE LOST

Seeing the people, He felt compassion for them, because they were distressed and dispirited like sheep without a shepherd.
MATTHEW 9:36 NASB

As Jesus traveled, He encountered people in the synagogues who were sick, diseased, distressed (because of the yoke the Pharisees had placed on them), and helpless—wandering like sheep without a shepherd. The religious leaders of the day ought to have been guiding them properly, but instead, they were caught up in rules and regulations as a means for achieving righteousness. When Jesus saw that, He felt compassion for the people.

Does this describe the way you feel as you look around at work or in your personal life? Do you feel compassion for those who are trapped in religion rather than being in a relationship with Christ? Most of those people probably grew up in faith traditions that taught them that if their good deeds outweighed their bad deeds, then God would accept them.

In essence, they grew up without true Christian leadership, so they embraced the false doctrine, believing heaven could be earned. Have compassion on them. Unless you grew up in a Christian household, you were once just like them.

As you exhibit compassion toward them, you might earn an opportunity to present the true Gospel of mercy and grace—one that no man can earn.

HOW TO CAPTURE GOD'S ATTENTION

But the eyes of the LORD are on those who fear him, on those whose hope is in his unfailing love, to deliver them from death and keep them alive in famine.
PSALM 33:18–19 NIV

God's attention and provision don't hinge on how well we pray or how much we sacrifice. It's all too easy to turn God into a holy slot machine that demands certain practices in order to meet our needs. We run the risk of domesticating God, demanding that God meet our needs and serve our purposes. Who hasn't veered too far toward prayers heavily laden with requests and desires without honoring God's unique, all-powerful qualities?

Those who can expect provision set God apart as holy and powerful, worthy of our reverence and respect. We don't pray for God's presence and power in order to manipulate Him for our purposes. Rather, we yield to God's majestic power because we recognize our place under this awesome God who is rightly feared.

Following quickly on this statement about the reverent fear of God, the psalmist reminds us that God's love is unfailing. We don't fear a monstrous, angry God, but we are reverent before a holy, all-powerful God who loves us deeply and will not fail us even if we have been unfaithful. As we rest in God's love for us and set Him apart as fearsome in His power, we will find the hope of His provision. Those who hope in God will find a constant, unmoving love that is deeply committed to them.

MAKE THINGS RIGHT

*All things are of God, who has reconciled us to Himself through
Jesus Christ, and has given us the ministry of reconciliation.*
2 CORINTHIANS 5:18 NKJV

When New England Patriot receiver Darryl Stingley cut toward the
middle of the field on August 12, 1978, searching for the pass coming his way, he never saw Oakland Raider safety Jack Tatum coming.
Tatum, known for his vicious hits, jarred Stingley with his helmet and
forearm, breaking the twenty-six-year-old's neck and rendering him
a quadriplegic for life.

The hit was within league rules and considered tragic bad luck.
However, not once did Tatum seek Stingley out afterward to apologize. Stingley, however, forgave Tatum, calling his predicament a
test of faith. He asked himself, "In whom, and how much, do you
believe, Darryl?" In the end, he was the one who was liberated as
God released him from the burden of anger and grief. Apparently,
Tatum took his to the grave.

Grudges are self-imposed burdens; they're not God's best for
you. Once you consider the lengths God went to so you could be
reconciled with Him, your perspective toward others should shift.
You reflect well on Jesus when you make peace with those who have
wronged you (or whom you have wronged).

Another part of the reconciling work God has for you involves
letting people know how they can get right with God, and there's no
room for bad blood in your life or theirs—only Christ's.

HOW TO FOLLOW GOD'S WILL

[God has] already made it plain how to live, what to do. . . .
It's quite simple: Do what is fair and just to your neighbor,
be compassionate and loyal in your love, and don't
take yourself too seriously—take God seriously.

MICAH 6:8 MSG

Christians want to know God's will because He might have something big for us to do and we don't want to miss it.

We're confronted with an up-close glimpse at a single verse that tells us exactly what God wants from us, but we tend to dismiss this as nonessential because it doesn't seem to point to a *personalized* plan God might have for us.

Yet we learn God can only trust us with big things when He can trust us with small things. So, God starts small. It's like He's saying, "You want to know My will for you? Treat your neighbor right. Be compassionate to others and show them My love. Take My Word seriously and don't be easily offended."

If you think this is easy, try it sometime. In a world where we don't know our neighbors' names, it can be hard to treat them right. At a time when people don't trust each other, it's hard to show compassion. In a place where God's Word is mocked, it can be difficult to take it seriously. In a world where humans live, it's too easy to be offended.

Therein lies the difficulty of your starting place. God's will starts here. Get to a place of faithfulness with these issues, and God will make sure you know what to do next.

RECEIVING GOD'S MERCY

"I entered this world to render judgment—to give sight to the blind and to show those who think they see that they are blind."
JOHN 9:39 NLT

If you feel like you can't figure out how to draw near to God or if you struggle with particular sins, then you're right where Jesus can help you. In fact, the bigger problem is if you think you have your act together and have no need of His mercy.

Jesus came to reveal your true spiritual state. You can either resist His offer of mercy or you can fight it, claiming that you're good enough on your own and have no need for Him and His help. Ironically, the more you insist on your wisdom and holiness, the less hope you have!

Your only hope is to stop pretending that you can see spiritually and fully admit your need for God's mercy. Jesus knows fully well how blind and lost you are. He came to seek you out, to reveal that He's not interested in people putting on a brave face and acting as if they have things together.

If you come to Him with honesty and a complete dependence on His mercy, you're in the best position to receive His help and to experience true restoration.

TRANSFORMERS

And we all. . .are being transformed into his image.
2 Corinthians 3:18 NIV

Passing through a great challenge changes us. Peter, the coward of the courtyard, became the lion of Pentecost. Paul, the persecutor, became the great champion of the faith. David, the shepherd boy, became Israel's greatest king. Moses, who ran for his life, faced down Pharaoh and delivered his people.

Paul outlined a great transformation in 2 Corinthians 3:18.

First, we encounter God with "unveiled faces." All pretense, self-righteousness, and hubris are stripped away. We see ourselves clearly and know who and what we are—sinners in need of a savior, weaklings in need of great strength, and fools in need of great wisdom.

Second, we "contemplate the Lord's glory." Like Moses, we are transformed by confronting the glory of God. We grasp the true majesty and infinite wonder of our Savior and His love. We are humbled and overwhelmed in His presence.

Third, all this "comes from the Lord." We can't do any of it! No matter how hard we try, how disciplined, rule-keeping, or religious we are, we remain shameful sinners. We only wash the outside of the cup (Matthew 23:25–26). If God doesn't change us, we can't change.

Fourth, we are "transformed into his image." Our destiny is to be like Jesus!

Finally, we are transformed "with ever-increasing glory." Transformation is a process not an event. We keep changing and will never, even in eternity, experience all the transformation or glory we long for or He intends. Hallelujah!

DON'T WAIT

*Then Caleb quieted the people before Moses, and said, "Let us go up
at once and take possession, for we are well able to overcome it."
But the men who had gone up with him said, "We are not able
to go up against the people, for they are stronger than we."*
NUMBERS 13:30–31 NKJV

The land of Canaan belonged to Israel. God had already promised it
to them. But they still had to take possession of it. So, in obedience
to God, they sent twelve spies—one from each tribe—who saw that it
was indeed a land flowing with milk and honey (Numbers 13:27), just
as God had promised (Exodus 3:8). But they also saw descendants
of Anak there—people who were strong and tall—so they hesitated
and issued an unfavorable report.

Caleb, however, wanted to go up at once to take possession of
the land. His eyes weren't on the circumstances, but on the Lord and
His promises. The Lord was with the Israelites, but they only trusted
in their own might. Sadly, their fear led to disobedience, even though
they didn't see things that way. They believed they were being astute
and practical.

How often have you allowed fear to lead you astray? To procras-
tinate? To put off the very thing God leads you to do? Today is the
day to throw off excuses.

FEELING LIKE A FAILURE

God is not unjust; he will not forget your work and the love
you have shown him as you have helped his people.
HEBREWS 6:10 NIV

Sometimes you may feel like a failure, as if your whole life of attempting to serve God has amounted to nothing. . .or to precious little. What do you have to show for years of faithfulness? You haven't even managed to lead your neighbor to the Lord. And then there's that rebellious child who, despite your admonitions and prayers, seems determined to go his or her own willful way.

Isaiah expressed his frustration this way: "I said, 'I have labored in vain; I have spent my strength for nothing at all. Yet what is due me is in the LORD's hand, and my reward is with my God' " (Isaiah 49:4 NIV). Even though he was despondent, he still couldn't help but believe that God saw his heart and would reward him accordingly.

Hebrews 6:10 (NIV) says, "God is not unjust; he will not forget your work and the love you have shown him as you have helped his people." He sees everything you do, and because He's *not* unjust, He will surely reward you. After all, by helping His people, you were showing love for God Himself. The same principle is at play in the following verse: "Whoever is kind to the poor lends to the LORD, and he will reward them for what they have done" (Proverbs 19:17 NIV).

It's worth it to serve the Lord. You may feel like you've failed, but God sees your faithfulness.

THE LIFE-CHANGING PRACTICE OF HOSPITALITY

Dear friend, you are faithful in what you are doing for the brothers and sisters, even though they are strangers to you. They have told the church about your love.

3 JOHN 5–6 NIV

Opening our home to a missionary, minister, or fellow Christian is a simple but important way to demonstrate the love of God. John notes in his letter that Gaius, the elder he addresses in today's passage, has recognized these unknown ministers as brothers and sisters rather than treating them as strangers. It's likely that Gaius went to great lengths to host these traveling preachers in his home at a time when most people lacked significant resources. When we talk about the cost of discipleship, the ministry of hospitality may be one of the most demanding.

Inviting fellow Christians into our homes, whether for a small group meeting, a family dinner, or lodging for several days, prompts us to change our schedules, to share our resources, and to literally make space for others. More importantly, if we truly believe that we are "brothers and sisters" with fellow Christians, the proof will be in how generously we share our most sacred spaces in our homes with them. Will we invite others into our living rooms and kitchens for rest and refreshment?

Hospitality is a sacrifice, but it is a vital way to encourage and support our fellow believers. Along the way, we'll enjoy deeper relationships with our Christian family and even benefit from the blessings and prayers of those who share our homes.

HAPPY ENDINGS

*For I am confident of this very thing, that He who began a good
work in you will perfect it until the day of Christ Jesus.*
PHILIPPIANS 1:6 NASB

To "perfect" something means to work on it until it's right. Another
way to translate "perfect" is to "carry it on to completion" (Philippians 1:6 NIV). Christ does not start something in us only to leave it
all in our hands. God already tried that, in a manner of speaking. The
Old Testament Law was that very opportunity, but it could not make
us right with God (Romans 3:20), and it had no power to make us
different from the inside (Romans 8:3). It takes Christ to do those
two things. That's why Jesus is the "*author* and *finisher* of our faith"
(Hebrews 12:2 KJV, emphasis added). We begin a journey with Christ,
who not only promises to walk with us but assures us of a happy ending.

Our journey with Christ is part of a process called *sanctification*.
The part we experience in our daily lives is when we begin to think
and choose the way Jesus would, approving "the things that are excellent, in order to be sincere and blameless until the day of Christ"
(Philippians 1:10 NASB). This is in stark contrast to the Law that didn't
require an internal change but still required blamelessness. The Law
was a long and burdensome road, traveled alone. But it was meant
to be so we would welcome the help of a Savior (Galatians 3:24).
Now, since it's His work *in* us and not our work *for* Him, we can have
confidence for a lifetime.

A SAFE PLACE?

Even in laughter the heart may ache, and rejoicing may end in grief.
PROVERBS 14:13 NIV

When Robin Williams was found dead of suicide on August 11, 2014, people were shocked—both outside and inside the church. The man who made so many laugh and feel through his versatile performances finally succumbed to his struggles, including severe depression and the effects of his past drug addiction and alcoholism. And he hadn't been ready to share his health problems with the world.

One of the church's biggest failures is the need we feel to put on a perfect face. We're afraid we'll be judged when another believer finds out that we're struggling or hurting. By ignoring the fundamental truth of the Gospel—that we're all sinners in need of forgiveness and grace—we make the church feel unsafe.

Remember, Jesus was a man of sorrows, acquainted with grief (Isaiah 53:3). He wept over loss and the pain of sin's destructive path. He came to set captives free, but He knows none of us will be completely healed until He returns and completes the work He began in us at our salvation (Philippians 1:6).

Jesus is the best friend a depressed person could ever have, and we need to reflect that truth—that light, relief, and peace—both inside and outside the church. When the church is seen as the place of healing it's meant to be, people will flock to it, seeking the chance to begin to heal. Do your part to leave the doors open.

SEEK RECONCILIATION

Do not repay anyone evil for evil. Be careful to do what is
right in the eyes of everyone. If it is possible, as far as it
depends on you, live at peace with everyone.
ROMANS 12:17–18 NIV

Twenty-five years ago, Oshea Israel (who was sixteen at the time) killed Mary Johnson's only son (who was twenty) when they butted heads at a party in north Minneapolis. While Israel's case crept through the court system over the next couple of years, Johnson wanted to see him pay for what he'd done.

But, according to an article in the *Winona Post*, Johnson was a Christian, and after reading a poem she came across in a book, and after much prayer, and after attending many worship services, the Holy Spirit did a work in her heart that she didn't expect. Johnson and Israel were eventually reconciled, with Johnson offering him forgiveness. They went on to become neighbors and began traveling together, sharing their story with inmates, at schools, and on television.

Today's verse calls Christians to not repay anyone evil for evil, which is far easier said than done. But Johnson did it. Many others have as well. How about you? Are you at odds with somebody over an injustice they did to you or someone you love? Work through the process of forgiveness. Talk to a pastor or counselor. And seek reconciliation.

DON'T GIVE UP

*Let us not be weary in well doing: for in due
season we shall reap, if we faint not.*
GALATIANS 6:9 KJV

An old saying goes: "Well begun is half-done." But even in cases when this overly cheerful maxim is true, well begun is still only *half*-done. It's not finished. You don't win the prize until you actually cross the finish line.

You can be temporarily "weary in well doing" because you're going through a lazy spell or you're overwhelmed by a new task or responsibility. But it's more serious when you're weary and giving up on doing good because you're simply worn out by a hard life or discouraged from years of setbacks and disillusionments.

In both cases, however, Jesus offers hope and can breathe new life into you. "Anxiety in the heart of man causes depression, but a good word makes it glad" (Proverbs 12:25 NKJV). The difference is that when you're temporarily weary, you can be cheered up quickly by one well-timed piece of encouragement—but when you've been worn down over a period of years, getting a positive attitude back takes time.

You may have to deliberately *focus* on positive, uplifting things— and *stay* focused on them and refuse to fall back into a negative mental rut. This is what David did when he faced great discouragement. "David encouraged himself in the LORD his God" (1 Samuel 30:6 KJV).

WHO'S REALLY IN CHARGE?

*The king's heart is like channels of water in the hand
of the LORD; He turns it wherever He wishes.*

PROVERBS 21:1 NASB

When Richard Nixon resigned the office of the president on August 8, 1974, his successor, Gerald Ford, called it the end of a "long national nightmare." The Watergate scandal had eroded trust in both the president, specifically, and high-level government in general. In many ways, that trust has never quite been regained, and the public has a deeper mistrust of elected government officials than ever.

During times of political turmoil, remember that God is still in control. No ruler takes charge without His permission. God's orchestration of authority doesn't mean He approves of what people do with the power He allows them to exercise. As Daniel told Nebuchadnezzar, "He removes kings and establishes kings; He gives wisdom to wise men and knowledge to men of understanding" (Daniel 2:21 NASB).

Your political role as a believer is to stay involved, especially when it would be easier to check out and wait for Jesus to return. You submit to governing authorities because you're really submitting to God's sovereignty (Romans 13), but you need to know the issues and exercise the privilege of voting. Biblical values matter most, not a person or a party. And if God leads you to run for office, pray hard about it—you could be the man for such a season as this.

TAKE HOLD OF GOD'S PEACE

"You will keep him in perfect peace, whose mind is stayed on You, because he trusts in You."

Isaiah 26:3 nkjv

As the spiritual leader of your family, the buck stops with you. While you're wise to discuss issues with your wife and seek the counsel of mature, experienced Christians, in the end, you're responsible for the big decisions. In those situations, how can you have peace?

When Jesus told His disciples, "Peace I leave with you, My peace I give to you" (John 14:27 nkjv), His peace was an actual thing, not an absence of something like conflict or confusion. Isaiah tied peace to trust, deliberately turning your thoughts toward God instead of your problems. Paul described peace as a shield "which transcends all understanding [and] will guard your hearts and your minds in Christ Jesus" (Philippians 4:7 niv).

Furthermore, Paul detailed the types of thoughts you should be turning toward God—things that are true, noble, just, pure, lovely, of good report, virtuous and praiseworthy (Philippians 4:8).

When you figure all of those into your decisions—thinking about what the cost might be or what it means to follow God in your circumstances—He will *give* you His peace. And it won't be the peace the world gives, the sort that leaves you doubting, second-guessing, and feeling more alone than ever. Once you grasp God's peace, you'll make the best decision possible, entrusting your cares to Him.

HE NEVER GIVES UP

Finish what you started in me, GOD.
Your love is eternal—don't quit on me now.
PSALM 138:8 MSG

Do you ever feel panicked, watching the days of your life stretch out before you and not knowing how to use them in the best way to become more like Christ? Or that you see the work ahead and don't know if you're up to the task?

If you've felt anything like that, take comfort in these truths.

- God is the author of your faith; He's writing your story (Hebrews 12:2).
- God is not a God of chaos. He's putting your life in order (1 Corinthians 14:33).
- God began a good work, and He'll complete it in you (Philippians 1:6).
- God saves through His power, grace, and love. When we believe that Jesus was the perfect sacrifice needed to make forgiveness available to all who would ask, we start a new journey that ends with us being called new creations (2 Corinthians 5:17).

You always have access to the God who is reshaping your heart, reordering your direction, and giving purpose to your tomorrow.

There's another benefit. God is faithful, and He won't give up on you. There will be moments when you're stubborn, rebellious, and unwilling to listen. He will wait, encourage, and put detour signs in your path. He knows your story and will do His part.

While God does the work, life transformation will require your cooperation. Go forward ready to work with Him.

DETERMINED TO STAY OBEDIENT

*But Daniel purposed in his heart that he would not defile himself
with the portion of the king's meat, nor with the wine which
he drank: therefore he requested of the prince of
the eunuchs that he might not defile himself.*

DANIEL 1:8 KJV

As one of the gifted Jewish youth taken by Nebuchadnezzar from Jerusalem to Babylon, Daniel had certain privileges, including a daily supply of meat and wine from the king's provisions (Daniel 1:5). But Daniel objected, purposing in his heart that he wouldn't defile himself in such a manner.

Commentators point to three probable reasons why he objected. The Babylonians had no regard for the Law of God and therefore would have eaten ritually unclean animals, as well as animals that had been strangled, and animals that had been offered to Babylon's false gods. Even in captivity, Daniel wanted to be obedient to God's dietary laws, and he was determined to remain as pure as possible— even going so far as to request a dietary change while in captivity. This surely came with a risk.

How would you have responded if you had been in Daniel's position? How determined are you to obey God's Word and ultimately God? Is it your highest priority? What lengths will you go to in order to remain obedient?

PERSPECTIVE ON REJECTION

*I have become all things to all people so that by
all possible means I might save some.*
1 CORINTHIANS 9:22 NIV

Witnessing for Christ has always been a challenge. In the current climate of political correctness, where truth is often replaced by opinion and personal freedom is idolized, you face unique challenges. Sharing about Jesus requires letting go of preconceived notions while still clinging to God's truth. You have freedom in Christ to share His love and grace without the shackles of shifting expectations and demands.

At the same time, those things have shaped people's opinions of God, Jesus, the church, and Christians. Earning the right to tell people about Jesus is like solving a puzzle box—you have to watch, listen, probe, learn from failure, and keep trying.

Remember a few things as you go. First, everyone matters to Jesus. They may not ever receive His gift of salvation, but that's between them and God. Your job is to treat them as Jesus did. He met people where they were—amid pain, complacency, ignorance, busyness—and told them God's truth in a way that fit their circumstances.

Also, don't fear being an imperfect messenger. Listen first, trying to learn each person's story, situation, and experience with God. If it helps, share your story of salvation. Sharing your faith carries risk, but if you're rejected, take heart. Jesus was too. Ask God for a wise and compassionate heart and for perseverance in the face of resistance.

ADMIT YOUR DISAPPOINTMENT WITH GOD

Martha said to Jesus, "Lord, if only you had been here,
my brother would not have died. But even now I
know that God will give you whatever you ask."
JOHN 11:21–22 NLT

When have you felt hopeless or disappointed in God? Were you afraid to speak exactly what you were thinking? Perhaps you didn't feel God would ever listen to your prayers again if you really told Him what you were thinking.

At her lowest point, Martha spoke her mind to Jesus. She didn't hold back. Her faith held the tension of Jesus' power and her disappointment. She could still believe in His care for her and His healing power, even if He hadn't shown up when she had requested.

Of course, Martha's story ends with a greater display of Jesus' power as He raised her brother Lazarus, but you don't always experience God's deliverance in such dramatic ways. Regardless of the results, Martha's faith after experiencing tremendous loss and grief shows that you can surrender your circumstances to God in faith, hope, and, most importantly, honesty.

Your honesty doesn't have to undermine your faith. Martha's spirit of surrender placed her future in Jesus' hands even as she faced her disappointment about the past. What do you need to speak to God about with complete transparency today? Is it possible that speaking about your disappointment in God could be a greater act of faith than holding yourself back from saying what you really think?

PRACTICING HOSPITALITY

When God's people are in need, be ready to help them.
Always be eager to practice hospitality.
ROMANS 12:13 NLT

The ancient Hebrews were urged to show kindness to strangers, to show hospitality by taking them into their homes for the night (Job 31:32). They were expected to feed them and were responsible to protect guests under their roof. Examples of this are Lot taking in two strangers (who turned out to be angels) in Sodom, and the old man in Gibeah taking in the man from Ephraim and his concubine (Genesis 19:1–3; Judges 19:14–21).

These days, such hospitality is rare. With so much crime and users eager to take advantage of soft-hearted people, it's considered dangerous and unadvisable. Granted, you should use wisdom when inviting strangers into your home for the night.

But the Bible still says, "*Always* be *eager* to practice hospitality" (Romans 12:13 NLT, emphasis added). So let's look at other important ways of showing hospitality. What about when a new family comes to your church, doesn't know anyone, and needs friends? Are you eager to practice hospitality? Do you talk with your wife about inviting them over for lunch? Do you help them get settled into your town?

And what about when poor families in your church are struggling without warm clothes, food, or other necessities? Do you simply smile, wave, and say, "Depart in peace, be ye warmed and filled" (James 2:15–16 KJV), or do you reach out in practical ways to help them?

Keep your eyes open. There are many ways to be "a lover of hospitality" today (Titus 1:8 KJV).

PRESUMPTUOUS SINS

Keep back thy servant also from presumptuous sins; let them not have dominion over me: then shall I be upright, and I shall be innocent from the great transgression.

PSALM 19:13 KJV

In today's verse, David asked God to keep him from presumptuous sins—that is, deliberate, intentional sins, what the NIV calls "willful sins." He knew that when he indulged in disobedient acts willfully, they'd end up becoming habits that ruled over him. It's not that unintentional sins cause any less harm than intentional ones, but they don't flow as readily from a person's heart and mind.

The last thing David wanted was to be guilty of "the great transgression," which some believe meant pride or even apostasy.

David knew his wicked heart well. He was a murderer and adulterer, and he lied to cover up both. He might even have been considered slothful, given that he didn't go out to war at the time when kings go out to battle, choosing instead to stay behind in Jerusalem (2 Samuel 11:1). That's when he spiraled out of control.

How about you? How well do you know your own heart? What sort of gross, presumptuous sins is it capable of? Do you fear being guilty of the great transgression? Use David's prayer in today's verse and make it your own. Ask God to intervene, to rule your heart, and to keep you from stumbling.

FAITHFUL TO AN IMPOSSIBLE MISSION

*"The people to whom I am sending you are obstinate and stubborn.
Say to them, 'This is what the Sovereign Lord says.' And whether
they listen or fail to listen—for they are a rebellious people—
they will know that a prophet has been among them."*

EZEKIEL 2:4–5 NIV

If you serve in a particular ministry or you prayerfully reach out to neighbors or colleagues, there's a trap that is all too easy to fall into when it comes time to measure your success. The Lord warns Ezekiel of this trap: measuring his success based on the responses of others. Ezekiel's calling is only to share the message that God entrusted to him. Whether or not the obstinate and stubborn people respond is well beyond his control.

Ezekiel is responsible only so far as he ensures that he has heard correctly what God has said and then communicated it. He plays the role of a prophet. If people won't listen, he may rightfully wonder if he has shared the correct message. However, in this case he has already received the bracing message from the Lord that his mission is doomed to fail.

Perhaps you aren't facing the same demanding challenges as Ezekiel today in your ministry or relationships. However, much like Ezekiel, you cannot control the thoughts, words, and actions of others. You can only prayerfully consider how God is directing you to live and speak. Sometimes your own faithfulness is the only measure of "success" that you'll have.

MOMENTS OF CONNECTION

Love each other with genuine affection,
and take delight in honoring each other.
ROMANS 12:10 NLT

On August 4, 1936, Jesse Owens won the second of his four Olympic gold medals in the long jump. In the final, Owens outjumped a young German, Lutz Long, who then joined him, walking arm in arm around the track as the crowd roared in support. War later separated the men, each loyal to his homeland, but never their friendship. Owens later said that moment in Berlin was worth more to him than all the medals and trophies he had ever won.

How are you at celebrating others' successes? Think of everything that goes into a moment of success—the dreaming, hard work, failures, sleepless nights, and small breakthroughs—and the lack of any sort of guarantee that you'll achieve your goal. Then, picture sharing that moment. Most champions would say that, after the cheering dies down and the euphoria wears off, the best part of winning is sharing it with someone.

Jesus honored His Father by giving His all to lift you up—and angels rejoice whenever someone chooses to receive His gift (Luke 15:7–10). To truly celebrate with someone, you have to know what they've been through to get there. Invest your talents in someone else's success. Look past worldly goals to godly ones—lifting others up, encouraging and admonishing with their highest good in mind. Their victories will become yours, and yours, theirs.

HERE TO REPRESENT

God hates cheating in the marketplace;
he loves it when business is aboveboard.
PROVERBS 11:1 MSG

Today, if we want to weigh something, we usually put it on an electronic scale and get a digital readout providing the result. There's a more ancient method that's still in use. This method allows someone to put a weight on half of a two-sided scale. On the second half, they would place what they were either buying or selling. When the scale was balanced, there was an equal amount on both sides. That's how people used to figure a price when buying or selling.

Sometimes business owners altered the weights. If they were selling something, they wanted the weight to weigh less so they didn't have to give as much to the buyer. If they were buying something, they would use a heavier weight so they could get more from the seller.

God calls this cheating and so would a customer. God would be displeased and so would the person who discovered the fraud. God could forgive, but a customer might never forget.

As a Christian, we're asked to bring integrity with us to the workplace. God wants us to represent Him in the way we do business. We should be willing to go farther than we have to in order to make things right.

We're God's ambassadors. We're not selective servants. We're not undercover believers. We're God's representatives to people who are all too familiar with dishonesty. Our story of God's faithfulness will always bear a hint of tarnish when we can't remember where we left our integrity.

FIVE THINGS TO HATE

To fear the LORD is to hate evil; I hate pride and arrogance,
evil behavior and perverse speech.
PROVERBS 8:13 NIV

It might surprise you to learn that it's not only kosher to hate certain things, but that, if you love God, it's actually *required*.

First of all, if you fear God, you are to hate evil. No surprises there. The Bible clearly states, "You who love the LORD, hate evil!" (Psalm 97:10 NKJV). And in case you think *hating evil* is just an Old Testament concept, note that this command is repeated practically word for word in the New Testament, where Paul writes, "Hate what is evil" (Romans 12:9 NIV). You're not to hate people, but you should definitely hate evil whenever you see it.

You are also to hate proud and arrogant attitudes, evil behavior, and evil speech. Where this goes quickly sour, however, is if you make a point of hating these things in *others*, first and foremost. This can cause you to have a critical and smug attitude. The big question is: Do you hate these sins when you find them lurking in your *own* heart? Do you ruthlessly root them out?

A psalmist prayed, "Search *me*, O God, and know my heart: try *me*, and know *my* thoughts: and see if there be any wicked way in *me*" (Psalm 139:23–24 KJV, emphasis added).

TALKING TO YOURSELF

Why, my soul, are you downcast? Why so disturbed within me?
Put your hope in God, for I will yet praise him, my Savior and my God.
PSALM 42:5 NIV

Do you ever look at the difficulties and trials in your life and then start talking to yourself? If you don't, then you're probably in a very small minority. At some point, nearly every one of us has taken stock of our lives—or at least our current situation—and started thinking:

There's no way out of this.

Things aren't going to get better. . .at least not anytime soon.

This is just the way things are going to be for me. . . there's nothing I can do about it.

This just isn't fair!

There are all sorts of voices in our world vying for our attention, especially when life becomes difficult. Among those voices is our own.

Of course, we as believers know to be careful not to listen to the voices of the world and of the enemy of our souls, the devil. But it's also important that we don't allow our own voices to drown out that of our heavenly Father.

So when you find yourself muttering to yourself about the hopelessness or unfairness of your situation, turn your attention instead to the Lord, who is big enough and more than willing to take control of everything going on around you and in you.

As the apostle Peter put it, "Cast all your anxiety on him because he cares for you" (1 Peter 5:7 NIV).

UNUSUAL KINDNESS

Once safely on shore, we found out that the island was called Malta.
The islanders showed us unusual kindness. They built a fire and
welcomed us all because it was raining and cold.

Acts 28:1–2 NIV

Paul was a prisoner aboard a ship bound for Rome, and he was destined to stand trial before Caesar. But while they were sailing across the Mediterranean Sea, a storm arose with winds of hurricane force (Acts 27:14). The vessel was driven by the fierce winds for many days. After it ran aground and all the passengers made it safely to shore, they discovered that they had landed on an island called Malta.

Malta was inhabited by heathens. Some translations, such as the KJV, translate the word *islanders* as "barbarous people"—probably because they didn't embrace the Greek or Roman culture, though they were ruled by Rome. Either way, they were different than the shipload of people who had crashed on their island, but their first response was unusual kindness. They built a fire and welcomed everyone.

Your church may already exhibit this type of kindness to outsiders and strangers. If so, jump into the action. Find a way to help those in need. Maybe you could become an usher or start an English as a second language (ESL) program there. If your church is lacking in this type of kindness to outsiders and strangers, talk to the leadership about finding ways to change that.

"I'LL PRAY FOR YOU"

"My intercessor is my friend as my eyes pour out tears to God;
on behalf of a man he pleads with God as one pleads for a friend."
JOB 16:20–21 NIV

The Bible has a lot to teach us about how to pray, when to pray, and what to pray for. One type of prayer the Word tells us to engage in regularly is called "intercession," which is a type of prayer in which we "stand in the gap" before God on behalf of another person.

But just how important is it to God that His people intercede in prayer for others? So important that Jesus, His very own Son, spends His time in heaven interceding for us this very moment (see Hebrews 7:23–28).

When a friend, a family member, or a brother or sister in Christ is hurting and in need of a touch from the hand of God, it's always good to offer comfort by promising to pray for that person. But as you spend time with the Lord, please be sure to make good on that promise. God loves to answer His people's prayers, and He is absolutely delighted to answer prayers of loving concern when we offer them up to Him.

So don't forget to make intercession for others a regular part of your prayer life. Someone may very well be counting on you.

WHO IS GOD'S WILL?

*"I searched for a man among them who would build up the wall
and stand in the gap before Me for the land, so that I
would not destroy it; but I found no one."*

EZEKIEL 22:30 NASB

When God wanted to do something on the earth to make Himself known or to teach His people, He always started with a person. Think of the history of the Bible—it's the story of people who demonstrated faith. Hebrews 11 provides a type of Hall of Fame of such faithful people: Abel, Enoch, Noah, Abraham, Isaac, Jacob, Sarah, Joseph, Moses, Gideon, Barak, Samson, Jephthah, David, Samuel, and all the prophets. These are some of the *Who* of God's will—men and women who became the fulcrum for God to move the world.

God's approach to working His will among mankind hasn't changed. God is still looking for individuals who will stand with Him and answer the call the way Isaiah did: "Then I heard the voice of the Lord, saying, 'Whom shall I send, and who will go for Us?' Then I said, 'Here am I. Send me!' " (Isaiah 6:8 NASB)

Of course, the ultimate *Who* in God's will is His son, Jesus of Nazareth—"All things have been created through Him and for Him. He is before all things, and in Him all things hold together" (Colossians 1:16–17 NIV). And He came "to purify for Himself a *people* for His own possession, *zealous for good deeds*" (Titus 2:14 NASB, emphasis added). Through Christ, we have the privilege of becoming the *Who* God is seeking to "build up the wall and stand in the gap."

AVOID PRIDE OF ACCOMPLISHMENT

By the grace of God I am what I am, and His grace toward me
was not in vain; but I labored more abundantly than they all,
yet not I, but the grace of God which was with me.
1 CORINTHIANS 15:10 NKJV

After Jesus departed, His apostles began to proclaim the Gospel.
Jesus had told them, "You shall be witnesses to Me in Jerusalem,
and in all Judea and Samaria, and to the end of the earth" (Acts 1:8
NKJV), and He had commanded, "Go into all the world and preach
the gospel" (Mark 16:15 NKJV). However, for the next twenty years,
all twelve apostles remained in Jerusalem, content to preach mostly
in nearby Judea and Samaria.

Paul, meanwhile, was going "into all the world," to far-flung cities
of the Roman Empire. So he wasn't exaggerating when he said, "I
labored more abundantly than they all." But those accomplishments
didn't make Paul think that he was better than others. He had just
finished stating, "I am the least of the apostles. . .not worthy to be
called an apostle" (1 Corinthians 15:9 NKJV).

Paul was aware that God was using him to accomplish great things,
but he also knew that it was the power of God doing the healing
miracles, anointing him to speak, and changing lives—not him. And
he was also painfully aware of his own unworthiness.

When you accomplish something great, don't put on false humility
and say it's nothing. If it was praiseworthy, acknowledge the fact. Admit
that God used you. But be sure to give Him the praise for using you.

PEACE BEYOND CIRCUMSTANCES

*"But the Advocate, the Holy Spirit, whom the Father will send in my
name, will teach you all things and will remind you of everything
I have said to you. Peace I leave with you; my peace I give you.
I do not give to you as the world gives. Do not let your
hearts be troubled and do not be afraid."*

JOHN 14:26–27 NIV

Mere hours before His arrest and crucifixion, Jesus promised to send
His Holy Spirit to comfort and instruct His followers. Even with the
relief of Jesus' resurrection in a few days, they would have great need
of the Spirit's peace and direction once Jesus ascended into heaven.
Perhaps we may think they'd have all the more reason to be alarmed
once Jesus ascended to heaven! However, Jesus assures us and them
that it's the exact opposite: because Jesus has sent the Spirit, they
should not let fear take root in their hearts.

Jesus passes along the assurance that we can seek the direction,
wisdom, and peace of the Holy Spirit. We will surely face situations
where fear appears to be more than warranted. In Jesus, we can choose
to turn to the Holy Spirit. This is not a guarantee that our problems
will be resolved or we'll suddenly have incredible wisdom to make the
best choices. Rather, the Spirit will reassure us that we are not alone
and that whatever may happen today or tomorrow, God remains with
us. The Spirit guards our souls and keeps us close to Jesus, even when
every other measure of peace appears to be far away.

WALK IN A WORTHY MANNER

Therefore I, the prisoner of the Lord, implore you to walk in a manner
worthy of the calling with which you have been called, with all
humility and gentleness, with patience, showing tolerance
for one another in love, being diligent to preserve
the unity of the Spirit in the bond of peace.
EPHESIANS 4:1–3 NASB

The apostle Paul was a prisoner in Rome as he penned this epistle to the church in Ephesus. As such, he could have asked for any number of things—a visit, support, prayer—but, under the inspiration of the Holy Spirit, he had something else on his mind.

He wanted Christians in this church to walk in a manner that was worthy of their calling, and then he spelled that out for them. For what distinguishes the Christian from the world any more than humility, gentleness, patience, tolerance, love, and unity? And what better way to show the world what a redeemed life looks like?

Gentleness, humility, and patience are often viewed as being consistent with certain personality types; nevertheless, Paul said they were basic callings for every Christian.

How are you doing in these areas? If you've fallen short in your calling, confess that to the Lord and then rely on the sanctifying work of the Holy Spirit to change you.

HOMEWORK NEVER ENDS

Parents rejoice when their children turn out well;
wise children become proud parents.
PROVERBS 23:24 MSG

You probably have many labels: man, boss, employee, husband, dad, or coach. Many of the labels we wear involve teaching.

If you're a dad, homework never ends, although some may refuse to accept their assignments.

Being a dad is hard work. Your children look to you as a model. Your behavior can become their behavior. What you accept is what they accept. What you say is, well, you get the idea.

When you're at home, work at being intentional as a parent. When you ask your children to do, be, or say something different than what they see in your life, they can be confused.

Intentional dads understand their legacy comes at a price. Either they pay the price or their kids do. Dads are investors who never gain a return on their investment when they refuse to invest.

The time you spend doing homework is not just an investment in your children, but also in your grandchildren. Leaving our kids without our example and encouragement will ultimately yield a generation with little direction or respect for others.

It's never too late to ask God to be intentional about helping you help your children. They need you, you love them, and God supplies the action plan. Find what you need in His Word.

The good news is you don't have to be perfect to be intentional. Admit mistakes, ask your children for forgiveness, and then return to the plan.

USING GOD'S APP

*I am not ashamed of the gospel, because it is the power of
God that brings salvation to everyone who believes.*
ROMANS 1:16 NIV

Use your phone and order lunch, conduct research, take pictures,
receive directions, listen to music, or send a video.

There's more. You can download apps for games, radio stations,
educational pursuits, and amusement.

Our lives seem consumed with rectangular-shaped phones. They
buzz and blip to alert us to incoming messages, calendar events, and
phone calls.

Relationships are important to God; they should be to us.
That's why we love our phones. With these mobile devices we—
communicate—right?

Well, sort of. We click *like*. We decide to *share*. We post a picture
of our food. Somehow we believe we're communicating.

There are times in our online world we don't even act like we do
in real life. We *pretend* and think no one really pays attention.

God is the master of communication. What He has to say has to be
shared. God's life app allows you to use your voice, your life, and your
generosity to share His love with real people who live with real hurts.

Remove the electronic tether and discover that God really has
made blue sky, green grass, and flowers that are pretty fantastic. No
color enhancement required.

Effective communication with God allows more effective communication with those who need to access His status updates. We
can share them face to face and from His book.

DELIVER US FROM SEEKING RICHES

The disciples were astounded. "Then who in the world can be saved?"
they asked. Jesus looked at them intently and said, "Humanly speak-
ing, it is impossible. But not with God. Everything is possible with God."
MARK 10:26–27 NLT

What is it about money that obstructs the way into God's kingdom?

Perhaps for you, money may be a source of security, while others may see their wealth and status as personal validation. But the pursuit of wealth itself can take up your time, pulling you away from family, worship, and service to others. The accumulation of wealth can prompt you to buy things that require more time spent earning money so that you can afford them.

The more you're loaded down with the pursuit and management of money, the harder it becomes to free yourself to be present for God. Wealth can gradually take you captive, and the more you're surrounded by people who pursue it, the easier it becomes to justify the pursuit of "just a little more."

Jesus assures you that while wealth can wreck your soul, God can save you. Your only recourse is to fall on God's mercy and to trust Him fully for the salvation of your soul. Tempting as it is to say that wealth is a blessing from God, it may just as easily become your downfall if you aren't living by faith.

A CLEAR LINE

As the time approached for him to be taken up to heaven,
Jesus resolutely set out for Jerusalem.
LUKE 9:51 NIV

Jesus knew false arrest, torture, crucifixion, and death waited for Him in Jerusalem. But He was determined. The word *sterizo* in this verse means "to make firm, to strengthen, or to confirm."

It's an amazing statement that clearly illustrates the great challenge that confronts all who pursue spiritual vitality and growth. There comes a moment when to go forward, to enjoy the life in God we hunger for, we must face a painful challenge, leave something behind, and that something in us must die.

Abraham left family behind in Harran. Moses faced murder charges in Egypt. Paul's self-righteousness died on the road to Damascus. David had his giant, Joseph had a prison, and Peter had his shame. All of them passed through their ordeal and found God waiting on the other side.

It's different for every man. Some face the painful challenge of confessing sin and making amends to those they've harmed. Some have to leave behind a career, friends, or family. Ambition, pride, selfishness, or lust must die in others. It may cost cherished relationships, pleasures we enjoy, or the future we want. It will cost. . .everything. And we know it.

But we must follow Christ, face the challenge, live through the pain, and kill what must die. Like Christ, we must be firm, strong, and resolute! If we aren't, we will fail.

But we don't have it in us. We aren't that strong. Remember. . . "I can do all this through him who gives me strength" (Philippians 4:13).

SUSTAINING GRACE

*Let us then approach God's throne of grace with confidence,
so that we may receive mercy and find grace to
help us in our time of need.*
HEBREWS 4:16 NIV

Many of us live our entire lives in search of our father's approval. Inherent in his perceived approval is a list of accomplishments he expects us to complete. For some, it's a six-figure income, a seven-figure house, and a beautiful wife. For the more spiritually minded, it could be an expectation to become a pastor, a full-time missionary, or *at least* an elder or deacon.

The problem with all of these expectations is twofold. First, God may not be in any of them. He may have something completely different in mind for us. Second, once we get caught up in seeking our father's approval at the expense of point number one, we end up playing a game of merit. As long as we do what our earthly father wants us to do, we are on track to gain his approval. But the moment we stumble, his approval is withdrawn, and often we become a shell of what we could have been.

God, on the other hand, tells us to approach His throne of grace with confidence. Notice that it is called a "throne of grace," not a throne of rules we have to follow to earn His love or approval. As we approach Him with confidence, we receive even more grace (rather than judgment), and that grace sustains us in time of need.

CAST YOUR CARES ON GOD

*Cast your cares on the LORD and he will sustain you;
he will never let the righteous be shaken.*
PSALM 55:22 NIV

This passage of scripture has been a source of great comfort to millions of believers, yet some people protest, "I wish it *were* that simple! When huge problems come, you simply calmly hand them to God and He takes care of everything?" This is a valid question, so let's look at this verse in context.

Earlier in the psalm, David spoke of serious threats, of conspiracies, of battles raging against him, and of the stinging betrayal of friends. (This likely happened during the civil war when Absalom revolted.) David confessed his fear, saying, "My heart is in anguish within me; the terrors of death have fallen on me. Fear and trembling have beset me" (vv. 4–5).

David was eventually able to cast his cares on God and experience peace, but it wasn't a quick or easy process. He also had to plan, strategize, and lead his forces against his enemies' attacks. And he had to pray desperately day after day, several times a day. He said, "Evening, morning and noon I cry out in distress" (v. 17). David *continually* cast his cares and fears upon God, until he finally received assurance that God had heard him and would answer.

Yes, you *can* simply calmly hand small problems over to God, but when huge problems assail you, you may have to desperately and repeatedly cast your cares on Him. And He will answer.

RENEWED DAILY

Therefore we do not lose heart. Though outwardly we are wasting away, yet inwardly we are being renewed day by day.
2 CORINTHIANS 4:16 NIV

It's easy to become discouraged as the years go by and you start to age, wrinkles begin to mark your face, and your strength eventually fails. You look at your reflection and wonder who hung a photo of your grandfather where the mirror used to be. You feel like—in the words of the Bible—you're "wasting away."

An unknown psalmist lamented, "My days are like a shadow that declineth; and I am withered like grass. But thou, O LORD, shall endure for ever; and thy remembrance unto all generations" (Psalm 102:11–12 KJV). It seems unfair. Mortals are like flowers of the field: they live a few decades, rapidly bloom, then quickly reach old age and wither, while the immortal God remains eternal and awesome throughout all generations.

But take heart! Even though you're fading outwardly, within you're growing in increasing glory. David prayed, "Let the beauty of the LORD our God be upon us" (Psalm 90:17 KJV). And it will be. "My flesh and my heart faileth: but God is the strength of my heart, and my portion for ever" (Psalm 73:26 KJV).

God will keep your heart and your faith strong, and He is already renewing your spirit. One day He will renew your physical body too and give you an immortal, powerful, eternally young body.

FLATTERY WILL GET YOU NOWHERE

Now I urge you, brethren, keep your eye on those who cause dissensions and hindrances contrary to the teaching which you learned, and turn away from them. For such men are slaves, not of our Lord Christ but of their own appetites; and by their smooth and flattering speech they deceive the hearts of the unsuspecting.

ROMANS 16:17–18 NASB

Paul was always watchful of his flock. He poured out his life to build the church of Christ on a solid foundation. But he knew others would come who worked only for their own interests and who were slaves "of their own appetites." You can tell who they are, he warns, because they create arguments where there shouldn't be any. They stand out because they teach what is contrary to the truth found in Christ. Jesus described these same people: "Beware of the false prophets, who come to you in sheep's clothing, but inwardly are ravenous wolves. You will know them by their fruits" (Matthew 7:15–16 NASB). What kinds of "fruits"? For one, their "smooth and flattering speech," which never has a place in the body of Christ. Flattery always comes from an ulterior motive: to manipulate the listener. It always serves the flesh.

To heed Paul's warning about such people, we need to be sure we are not one of the "unsuspecting." The *unsuspecting* are those who have never made the effort to mature in Christ. "For everyone who partakes only of milk is not accustomed to the word of righteousness, for he is an infant" (Hebrews 5:13 NASB). Growing in our understanding of Christ is the only way to guard against deception.

A MOST IMPORTANT COMMAND

*Whoever claims to love God yet hates a brother or sister is a liar.
For whoever does not love their brother and sister, whom they have
seen, cannot love God, whom they have not seen. And he has
given us this command: Anyone who loves God
must also love their brother and sister.*

1 John 4:20–21 NIV

Let's face it: some people are very difficult to love. They're too loud,
too opinionated, too overbearing, too unlearned, too. . .you get the
point. But the apostle John has some very strong words as to how
we as followers of Christ are to relate to even the most unlovable
among us.

If you can't love someone who's right in front of you, John taught,
then how can you say you love a God you can't even see? That's putting
John's message rhetorically, for of course the answer is that saying
we love God but not the people He's placed in our lives makes us. . .
well, liars.

Ouch!

So when you encounter one of the "unlovable"—and there are
plenty of them out there!—love them the way Jesus loved, unconditionally and sacrificially. And when your words and acts of love
don't change them in the least, love them all the more. It's God's
job to change people. . . . It's your job to love them the same way
He loves you.

RECOVERING THE LOST

*If you know people who have wandered off from God's truth,
don't write them off. Go after them. Get them back and
you will have rescued precious lives from destruction.*

JAMES 5:20 MSG

It's easy to write off people who have backslidden from the faith. You tell yourself that it's a free country, and it's their decision, after all. And these things are true. Plus, you tell yourself, they knew full well what they were doing when they went back to their worldly ways. And that too is true. But the question is: Are you *concerned* about them? Do you pray for them and reach out to them?

Jesus said:

> *"What man of you, having a hundred sheep, if he loses one
> of them, does not leave the ninety-nine in the wilderness, and
> go after the one which is lost until he finds it? And when he
> has found it, he lays it on his shoulders, rejoicing. And when
> he comes home, he calls together his friends and neighbors,
> saying to them, 'Rejoice with me, for I have found my sheep
> which was lost!' "*
> (Luke 15:4–6 NKJV)

Jesus took it for granted that *every* person listening would be motivated to scour the desert for a lost sheep, asking, "What man does *not* go after it until he finds it?" And how much more valuable is a person than a sheep?

In the end, the person must decide whether he'll return to the Lord or not, but you can be a big part of helping restore him.

FINDING JOY IN THE LORD

*Even though the fig trees have no blossoms, and there are no grapes
on the vines; even though the olive crop fails, and the fields lie empty
and barren; even though the flocks die in the fields, and the
cattle barns are empty, yet I will rejoice in the LORD!*
HABAKKUK 3:17–18 NLT

The prophet Habakkuk foresaw a day of trouble coming, and he took to prayer. How much better is it to be in prayer before trouble begins so your heart can be prepared and resolved to endure it joyfully than to be surprised by it and grumble?

Habakkuk saw a time of drought in which the trees, vines, and crops would fail and most of the livestock would be dead. (This was likely the drought described in Jeremiah 14:1–6.) Yet, Habakkuk said he would rejoice in the Lord. In a preemptive strike against his own soul, he was filling himself up with faith and trust in God so bitterness couldn't creep into his heart when everything went astray.

Have you ever prayed a prayer like this? You probably aren't directly reliant on trees, vines, crops, and livestock, but you are reliant on your employer. If the economy takes a downturn and you're laid off, are you prepared to find joy in the Lord anyway? He is well able to place you in a new position. But will you praise Him during the interim time of uncertainty?

SUPERHERO SUBSTITUTE

*We have seen and testify that the Father
has seen and testify that the Father
has sent the Son as Savior of the world.*
1 JOHN 4:14 NKJV

More than 125,000 people attend Comic Con each year. This annual convention is dedicated to comic books and everything developed from those stories. Each month, more than $250,000,000 is spent on the most popular comic books. Worldwide ticket sales for movies that are based on comic books are in the billions. At least three collectible comic books have sold for more than a million dollars each. Comic book heroes are big business.

People love superheroes because they're passionate about identifying with someone with the power to rescue people from bad situations.

First Timothy 1:15 (MSG) says, "Here's a word you can take to heart and depend on: Jesus Christ came into the world to save sinners."

We're born. We sin. We need rescue.

Jesus isn't make-believe. He is more than a compelling story. He's God's champion. He faced the toughest enemy mankind has ever known—and won.

We read comic books because we want a hero. We want to be rescued. We want everything to be all right in the world.

Comic books are a fun substitute, but that's all they are. Spend all the money you want on comic books, but colorful pages can never replace God's living rescue plan.

We need a hero. God gave us Jesus—no charge.

SEEING GOD BY LOOKING BACK

The godly will see these things and be glad, while the wicked are struck silent. Those who are wise will take all this to heart; they will see in our history the faithful love of the LORD.
PSALM 107:42–43 NLT

What is filling your mind today? What have you pondered so far?

You're probably surrounded by entertainment, news reports, and commercials that can easily fill your thoughts. Your work and family surely occupy important spots in your mind as well. But how often do you pause to remember the ways that God has been at work in the past week, month, or even year? It's possible that His love may appear far off simply because you need to spend a little time today considering His faithful love.

Whether you're entertaining doubts or uncertain about the future, your faith can be bolstered by taking a moment to notice the ways that God has offered comfort, reassurance, guidance, or the peace of His presence. Just as God's people are expected to learn from their mistakes, there's also great benefit in remembering His provision.

As you consider your next steps, whether at home, work, or in your church community, you can take comfort in remembering God's past actions on your behalf. Sometimes you don't need Him to perform another miracle. You just need to notice what He has already done for you.

WELL-SEASONED SPEECH

Conduct yourselves with wisdom toward outsiders, making the
most of the opportunity. Let your speech always be with grace,
as though seasoned with salt, so that you will know
how you should respond to each person.
COLOSSIANS 4:5–6 NASB

Biblical wisdom is less about fortune cookie clichés than about instruction for right living. The prophets and disciples of the scriptures spoke wisdom that could change lives and were not concerned with answering every philosophical question people raised. They knew that right living makes a person wise by biblical standards and spoke truth to help people understand their choices in all manner of circumstances.

Like the prophets of the Bible, we are surrounded by people who do not see the kingdom of God and need spiritual truths explained. Thus we will always be surrounded by opportunities to share our hope and our faith if we are prepared—not with clever sayings, or a rehearsed speech, or even theological arguments, but with words that are gracious and practical.

"Let no unwholesome word proceed from your mouth, but only such a word as is good for edification according to the need of the moment, so that it will give grace to those who hear" (Ephesians 4:29 NASB).

It's true some people will only be interested in engaging us to debate our faith, but any opportunity to speak of Christ is a good one. Let us just remember to speak as He would, graciously treating each person as an individual created in the image of God.

CHASING FANTASIES

Those who work their land will have abundant food,
but those who chase fantasies have no sense.
PROVERBS 12:11 NIV

All of us have land to till each workday. It is our lot, and it has been assigned to us to provide for our families. For some, it is physical land; for others, it is a real estate office, a teller window, a delivery truck, a taxicab, or an office. While our tasks may feel like drudgery at times, an attitude of diligence and gratitude can, and should, spur us on.

Just as farmers work in different stages—from cultivation, to preparing for the crop to come, to harvest, our jobs require constant preparation. Even established real estate agents have to stay informed of current property laws while also meeting with new clients on a regular basis and maintaining relationships with current clients. It's a never-ending, time-consuming cycle. It doesn't have to come at the expense of hobbies or even starting a new small business though.

When Solomon condemns fantasy chasing in the verse above, he's referring to sloth and inactivity—not hardworking entrepreneurs who are busy tilling new ground. In Adam Clarke's *Commentary on the Bible*, he says it this way, "He who, while he should be cultivating his ground, preparing for a future crop, or reaping his harvest, associates with fowlers, coursers of hares, hunters of foxes, or those engaged in any champaign amusements, is void of understanding."

THE JOY OF SUFFERING

Dear friends, do not be surprised at the fiery ordeal that has come on you to test you, as though something strange were happening to you. But rejoice inasmuch as you participate in the sufferings of Christ, so that you may be overjoyed when his glory is revealed.
1 PETER 4:12–13 NIV

Suffering and opposition for the sake of Christ isn't just a sign that we have cast our lot with Jesus. Suffering is a way to meet with Christ on a deeper level. As we face opposition, slander, or worse, we create a space in our lives to more fully experience Christ. By choosing to suffer for Christ, we are denying our own desires and our sinful natures—the very things that come between ourselves and Him. In fact, suffering is guaranteed for us as we take up the cause of Christ. If you are suffering for a season, God can and will meet you and even use that suffering to bring more of His presence and peace into your life.

Most importantly, by choosing to suffer, we are taking a step of faith to believe that God has something better for us. We have the hope of His glory one day as we leave our own wills behind. While our desires promise us joy and fulfillment in the short term, these are fleeting and cannot compare to the joy we can experience today in the presence of the Lord, let alone when we are united with Him one day.

SHARE YOUR GIFT

Each of you should use whatever gift you have received to serve others, as faithful stewards of God's grace in its various forms.
1 PETER 4:10 NIV

Today, most board meetings follow *Robert's Rules of Order*. There may be no law that makes it mandatory, but these rules bring order to "meeting chaos."

In 1876, U.S. Army Colonel Henry Martyn Robert created the rules based on similar laws used by America's House of Representatives in bringing stability to their sessions. There are a few things Robert changed, but the reason behind his writing the "rules" was personal.

Thirteen years earlier, Robert had been asked to lead a business meeting at his church. By his own admission, he couldn't effectively lead that meeting. The issue of slavery caused the meeting to fall into chaos, and Robert lost control. Robert determined to reform the rules for meetings because there was a need in his own church.

We might think someone else is taking care of all the needs within our church. We can believe we have no responsibility. We just stand by and allow other capable hands to do the work. God might just be asking someone that looks a lot like you to step up and help by using the skills He's given you.

Ephesians 2:10 (MSG) says, "[God] creates each of us by Christ Jesus to join him in the work he does, the good work he has gotten ready for us to do, work we had better be doing."

Whatever gift God has given you, He gave because He wants you to share it.

A COACH'S WORLD

You have heard me teach things that have been confirmed by many reliable witnesses. Now teach these truths to other trustworthy people who will be able to pass them on to others.

2 TIMOTHY 2:2 NLT

This is the age of executive coaching. Corporations have discovered that coaching or mentoring shouldn't end after a new employee has been on the job for a few months. Employers don't want you to stop learning new skills.

You may be getting some of your own executive coaching today in church. You may not think of church as coaching, but it can be. It should be. As Christian men we start with learning biblical basics, but we never learn it all. Our entire lives can be spent being coached and coaching others.

Barnabas coached Paul. Paul coached Timothy. Timothy coached his own congregation. Great coaching makes great teams.

Because we don't know everything, we need a coach and we need to be a coach. Jesus never had much good to say about spiritual pretenders. Matthew 23:27 (MSG) says, "You're hopeless, you religion scholars and Pharisees! Frauds! You're like manicured grave plots, grass clipped and the flowers bright, but six feet down it's all rotting bones and worm-eaten flesh."

Intense? Yeah!

When we think we've learned all there is to learn, we need to think again. God never wants us to stop learning, stop sharing, or stop growing. Be a coach. Find a coach. Encourage a coach. There's a lot of growing just waiting on your response.

THE NATURE OF LOVE

*If I have a faith that can move mountains, but do not have love,
I am nothing. If I give all I possess to the poor. . .that I may
boast, but do not have love, I gain nothing.*
1 CORINTHIANS 13:2–3 NIV

You may wonder, "How could I give all that I possess to alleviate the suffering of the poor and *not* have love? Isn't such giving a clear proof of love?" Besides, Jesus told the rich young ruler, "Sell your possessions and give to the poor and you will have treasure in heaven" (Matthew 19:21 NIV). But Paul clarifies that even if you give all that you have to the poor but have selfish motives for doing so ("that I may boast"), you'll gain nothing and receive no reward.

Paul goes on in verses 4–7 to give the definition of love. Love is *not* boastful or easily angered; love is patient, kind, humble, honors others, seeks others' benefit, and keeps no record of wrongs. So even if you go through an outward show of charity but are boastful, easily angered, impatient, envious, proud, self-seeking, or unforgiving, you aren't motivated by God's love.

Jesus also promised that if you have great faith, you can say to a mountain, " 'Be removed and be cast into the sea,' " and it will be done (Matthew 21:21 NKJV), but as Paul pointed out, "If I have a faith that can move mountains, but do not have love, I am nothing." So *love*—love God and others—first and foremost, and you'll be greatly rewarded in all you do.

KNOWING JESUS

Whatever were gains to me I now consider loss for the sake of Christ. What is more, I consider everything a loss because of the surpassing worth of knowing Christ Jesus my Lord.

PHILIPPIANS 3:7–8 NIV

Paul had an exceptional education in two worlds. He was born a Roman citizen, and from reading his epistles, it's clear that he had a wide knowledge of Greek literature. He quoted Greek writers such as the Cretan poet Epimenides in Titus 1:12 and both Epimenides and the Cilician poet Aratus in Acts 17:28. And in 1 Corinthians 15:33, he quoted from *Thais*, a popular comedy written by the Greek playwright Menander.

On the other hand, Paul "conformed to the strictest sect of [his] religion, living as a Pharisee" (Acts 26:5 NIV). He moved to Jerusalem where, as he said, "I studied under Gamaliel and was thoroughly trained in the law of our ancestors" (Acts 22:3 NIV). Even the Roman governor Festus recognized Paul's great learning (Acts 26:24).

Paul had once been self-assured and cocky because of his vast studies, but when he became a Christian, he "resolved to know nothing. . .except Jesus Christ" (1 Corinthians 2:2 NIV). He pared his focus way back and concentrated wholly on knowing the Son of God and "the depth of the riches both of the wisdom and knowledge of God" (Romans 11:33 KJV).

Knowledge is good, but don't forget life's main focus.

NO ONE SAID IT WOULD BE EASY

As for you, you were dead in your transgressions and sins.
EPHESIANS 2:1 NIV

No one said getting from where we are to where we want to be in God is easy. Anyone who says it's easy is a liar. Anyone who believes it's easy is a fool.

James said we should rejoice in trials because of what they produce in us (James 1:2–4).

Paul compared this life to the harsh discipline of an athlete in training (1 Corinthians 9:24–27).

Jesus warned us that we would have trouble in this world (John 16:33).

The Bible compares our spiritual journey to gold in the refiner's fire or clay on the potter's wheel (Proverbs 17:3; Jeremiah 18:1–5).

In his great work *Summa Theologica*, Thomas Aquinas seems to echo Ephesians 2:1–2 when he warned against "the world, the flesh and the Devil."

When we pursue Christ with all our hearts, we live a life that challenges the world around us and may prompt an angry, hostile response. They hate Him and all who follow Him.

That pursuit draws us into spiritual warfare. Our enemy uses all his power and influence to deceive us, block our way, and make sure we pay a high price for following God.

But we are our own worst and greatest enemy. We run from, resist, and resent the struggles we inevitably face. We want glory without the cross. It never, ever happens that way.

No one said it would be easy. . .just worth it!

THE KINGDOM OF GOD

*For the Kingdom of God is not a matter of what we eat or drink,
but of living a life of goodness and peace and joy in the Holy Spirit.*
ROMANS 14:17 NLT

If you've been part of a church for any length of time, then you know that strong differences of opinion sometimes arise over whether Christians should listen to certain styles of music, attend movies, eat or drink certain things, and any number of other issues. Paul wrote Romans 14 to keep believers from judging one another over such matters. The specific issues were different in his day, but the same sentiment continues to modern times.

But the kingdom of God is not a matter of what you eat or drink. It's about living a life of goodness and peace and joy in the Holy Spirit. Some Christians can enjoy the blessings of wealth without sinning, while others cannot. Some can listen to mainstream music without sinning, while others cannot. The same could be said for watching movies. However, flaunting such freedom is not in the spirit of today's verse.

In Romans 14:23 (NLT), Paul said each Christian is bound by his own conscience: "But if you have doubts about whether or not you should eat something, you are sinning if you go ahead and do it. For you are not following your convictions. If you do anything you believe is not right, you are sinning."

GOD AND FAMILY

*But if a widow has children or grandchildren, these should learn
first of all to put their religion into practice by caring for
their own family and so repaying their parents and
grandparents, for this is pleasing to God.*

1 TIMOTHY 5:4 NIV

Next to a man's commitment to God, there is no commitment more
important than his commitment to be a godly son, brother, husband,
and father. Nothing will leave a more lasting impact on the generations
to come, and nothing will matter more to him in the end.

Sadly, it seems that many men have abandoned their critical role
in the family to pursue their own wants, needs, and desires. They seem
to care little for the impact of their choices on their wives, children,
and future generations. Being a godly husband and father just doesn't
seem important. Nothing could be further from the truth!

We are called to lead our families in faithfully following God, to
willingly sacrifice, to love our spouses like Christ loved the church,
and to guide our children to a life devoted to God and His service. We
are called to be protectors, providers, and examples of godly living.

It's true: there is no such thing as a perfect man, husband, or
father. We all make mistakes, have regrets, and wish we had done
some things differently. But perfection isn't required. A commitment
to live for God and lead and love our family is.

LISTEN!

"Now then, my children, listen to me; blessed are those who keep my ways. Listen to my instruction and be wise; do not disregard it."
PROVERBS 8:32–33 NIV

Listening is always harder than talking. We all want others to know how we feel, to understand why we act and see things as we do. When people don't listen to us, we feel insignificant and disrespected.

It's easy to forget other people need the same thing from us. When we don't listen to our wives, children, friends, and coworkers, they feel ignored, uncared for, and mistreated. But when we listen well, we open the door to greater intimacy and understanding; we build trust and strengthen the bonds of our relationships. That's why listening is so important.

Before anyone else, we need to listen to God and His Spirit in our lives. All too often when we pray, we talk too much and listen too little. Our family comes next. We need to listen to our wives. How else can we know their hopes, dreams, and fears? We need to listen to our children. It's the best way to earn our place in their lives for the rest of our lives. Our wives don't always need to know what we think. Our children don't always need correction or a lecture. Sometimes they just need us to love them enough to let them talk, listen carefully, empathize with their feelings, and show them the dignity and respect every person longs for.

Isn't that what God does for us when we pray?

DON'T STOP NOW

*Fight the good fight of faith; take hold of the eternal life to which
you were called, and you made the good confession
in the presence of many witnesses.*

1 TIMOTHY 6:12 NASB

Timothy, who was called to minister, was to put off the cares of this world—namely the love of money that leads so many astray (1 Timothy 6:10). Instead, he was to fight the good fight of faith to advance the Gospel.

Timothy's vocational calling might have been different from yours, but his spiritual calling was quite similar. You're to be in the world, but not of it (John 17:15–17). You're to set your mind on things above, not on the things of this earth (Colossians 3:2). You're not to be conformed to this world, but be transformed by the renewing of your mind (Romans 12:2). As such, you're called to fight the good fight as well.

How is your fight going? If you don't sense a battle, then you probably aren't engaged in one. If, however, you feel the tension between this world and the next and are actively engaged in overcoming your sinful habits and tendencies, then you're right where God wants you. Don't stop now. The world needs to see your witness. Wrestle, fight, and pray because eternity is at stake for all of humanity.

THE ULTIMATE PAYBACK

Don't repay evil for evil. Don't retaliate with insults when people insult you. Instead, pay them back with a blessing. That is what God has called you to do, and he will grant you his blessing.

1 PETER 3:9 NLT

In the heat of an argument or as you encounter a frustrating situation, it's hard to resist trading insults or giving someone a piece of your mind. As social media and e-mail make it possible to argue without seeing someone face to face, you often experience the worst parts of your anger and discord without the filter of empathy or understanding.

Peter challenges you to bless those who insult you and to avoid any kind of retaliation. While he was writing to Christians who were being actively marginalized and persecuted for their faith, his message remains powerful as you seek to infuse your world with God's hope.

You gain very little from insulting others, and even the act of receiving an insult can be good for you. Perhaps you need reminders that you define yourself as part of God's people and His beloved child. Although an insult may tend to undermine your fragile ego, as you release hurt or anger and hand over a blessing, you bring the other person one step closer to God while reminding yourself of where you find your identity.

FIGHT FOR FREEDOM

*Stand fast therefore in the liberty by which Christ has made us free,
and do not be entangled again with a yoke of bondage.*

GALATIANS 5:1 NKJV

The Slavery Abolition Act officially eliminated slavery throughout the British Empire in August of 1834. Many of the men and women in England's Anti-Slavery Society were spurred to action by their Christian beliefs, notably William Wilberforce—who spent the last twenty years of his life fighting for abolition.

Slavery in the biblical world was a different matter than the kidnapping variety that conscripted free labor for growing empires in the second half of the past millennium. The Bible, however, specifically condemned kidnapping another person (see Exodus 21:16).

Now, the New Testament refers to believers as "slaves" to Christ several times (Romans 1:1; Ephesians 6:6; 1 Peter 2:16), but the imagery the Bible often uses, such as in today's verse, is of Christ setting believers *free* from bondage. Paul addressed this paradox when he wrote, "The one who was a slave when called to faith in the Lord is the Lord's freed person; similarly, the one who was free when called is Christ's slave" (1 Corinthians 7:22 NIV).

Jesus came to set you free from the "yoke of bondage," but then urges you to voluntarily join Him in serving others, saying, "Take my yoke upon you and learn from me. . . . For my yoke is easy and my burden is light" (Matthew 11:29–30 NIV).

FEELING SMALL?

*When I consider your heavens, the work of your fingers, the moon and
the stars, which you have set in place, what is mankind that you
are mindful of them, human beings that you care for them?*

PSALM 8:3–4 NIV

The story is told of a naturalist named William Beebe, who was a good
friend of President Theodore Roosevelt. After dinner one night, the
two men went for a walk. Roosevelt pointed skyward and observed,
"That is the Spiral Galaxy in Andromeda. It is as large as our Milky
Way. It is one of a hundred billion galaxies. It consists of one hundred billion stars, each larger than our sun. Now I think we are small
enough. Let's go to bed."

King David lived thousands of years before Roosevelt, so he had
no real clue as to the vastness of the created universe. Still, what he
could observe with his naked eye in the skies over Israel way back
then still astonished him. But even more amazing to him was the
fact that the God who had created it all could look down from His
throne in heaven and not just take notice of him, but love him and
think about him.

That's a wonderful thought, isn't it? We should never lose our
sense of awe and wonder that the all-powerful God who created
such a vast cosmos is the same all-loving God who cares so deeply
for us as individuals.

ALWAYS THE BEST POLICY

Truthful lips will be established forever,
but a lying tongue is only for a moment.
PROVERBS 12:19 NASB

If you've ever looked someone in the eye and wondered if they were telling you the truth, then you understand the uneasy feeling it creates. Sometimes, of course, it's easy to tell when a person is lying, like when a child blurts out, "It wasn't me!" Even if people don't outright lie to you, but just "shade the truth," is that any less deceptive? Maybe the consequences are less severe for a child with cookie crumbs on his mouth than a man with blood on his hands, but neither is without deceit. The acorn of deception may not always grow into an oak, but it still has all the same DNA—whether we plan the lie or whether it just pops out when we're caught off guard.

The value God places on truthfulness has always been made plain in the Bible. The power of truth is that it lasts. It's eternal because it comes from the very nature of God. Jesus claimed to be "the truth" itself (John 14:6 NASB) and promised that "the truth will make you free" (John 8:32 NASB). God wants us to live in truth and the Truth to live in us. "Behold, You desire truth in the innermost being" (Psalm 51:6 NASB), and so God sends the Helper who is "the Spirit of Truth" (John 15:26 NASB) to indwell believers. We keep pace with the Holy Spirit by living honestly and affirm our connection to God as His children. Truth is our heritage and our birthright as members of God's family.

LOVING THE SINNER. . .

*Be merciful to those who doubt; save others by snatching
them from the fire; to others show mercy, mixed with fear—
hating even the clothing stained by corrupted flesh.*

JUDE 22–23 NIV

"Love the sinner, hate the sin."

This is one of those "Christian clichés" that don't appear any-where in the Bible—at least not verbatim—but are solidly grounded in biblical truth.

Think about it: the Bible teaches that God hates sin and that we likewise are to hate sin. For example, Psalm 97:10 (NIV) tells us, "Let those who love the LORD hate evil, for he guards the lives of his faithful ones and delivers them from the hand of the wicked."

On the other hand, the Bible enjoins believers to " 'love your neighbor as yourself,' " and to treat others with respect and love (Mark 12:31 NIV). Furthermore, we are called to love sinners by pray-ing for them and by witnessing to them about the gift of salvation through Christ.

Just as it would not be loving for a doctor to refuse to tell a patient he is sick and will die unless he receives treatment, it is not loving for Christians to neglect to tell sinners that they need the Savior to save them from eternal death.

So hate sin. Hate it so much that you will go to whatever lengths are necessary to see that people are saved from its terrible conse-quences. At the same time, love the sinner so much that you'll pray for him and witness to him for as long as it takes.

COMMITMENTS THAT MATTER

Now all has been heard; here is the conclusion of the
matter: Fear God and keep his commandments,
for this is the duty of all mankind.
ECCLESIASTES 12:13 NIV

We all make commitments. And, we all know some commitments matter more than others. If we can't keep our commitment to have coffee with a friend, it's not a big deal. If we don't keep our commitments to our wives and children, it's a very big deal!

What we are committed to shapes and makes up much of our lives. There are some things to which we must make unwavering, permanent commitments if we expect to leave a legacy that matters.

The first and most fundamental commitment any Christian man must make is his commitment to God and the Christian life. It has to be nonnegotiable. No matter what comes, no matter what challenges we face, no matter how great our successes or failures, our commitment to God is the anchor that holds in the storm and the compass that guides our days.

There are plenty of examples of men who have given up on their commitment to God and following Him. All of them have some things in common. First, in a moment of trial and temptation, they wavered and broke their commitment. Second, their grip on God gradually loosened. In the end, they and those they loved suffered, and they left a woeful legacy.

How committed to God are you today? Are you wavering? Are you losing your grip?

LEARNING AND GROWING

*For this reason, since the day we heard about you, we have not
stopped praying for you. We continually ask God to fill you with the
knowledge of his will through all the wisdom and understanding that
the Spirit gives, so that you may live a life worthy of the Lord and
please him in every way: bearing fruit in every good work,
growing in the knowledge of God.*

COLOSSIANS 1:9–10 NIV

Great men know there is always more to learn and they are ready to
learn it. In fact, all of us want the people we deal with—our physicians,
attorneys, financial advisors, and others—to be learners. We want
the best they can give us now, not what they learned years ago. We
expect them to keep up!

But we all know men who aren't learners. Sometimes it's pride.
They don't believe others have anything to teach them. Sometimes it's
insecurity. They don't believe they can master new things. But most
of the time, it's just neglect and laziness. We're comfortable without
the hard work of learning so why put out the effort?

People can get away with that in some things but never in their
spiritual lives. Today's verses make it clear that "a life worthy of the
Lord" is a life that is growing in the knowledge of God through the
wisdom and understanding of the Spirit. The truth is that no matter how
much we know of God and His wisdom, there is always more to know.

Have you learned something new about God this week, this
month, or this year?

MIND YOUR OWN BUSINESS

*Make it your goal to live a quiet life, minding your
own business and working with your hands.*
1 THESSALONIANS 4:11 NLT

When Paul said, "Make it your goal," he meant that *this* is what you as a Christian are to focus on, *this* is what you are to strive for: to live an uneventful life, to keep busy with gainful employment, and stay out of trouble.

This sounds a lot like what many Christians are *already* doing—working unobtrusively at a nine-to-five job. It might not seem like a goal worth striving for. Wouldn't it be much more exciting to travel from city to city like Paul, preaching the Gospel full-time, stirring up the crowds, causing citywide riots in the amphitheater, getting beaten up, and so on?

Exciting? Yes. But remember, Paul never went *looking* for such thrills and spills. He was happier to quietly stick to a schedule, teaching disciples day after day at Tyrannus's school in Ephesus, faithfully instructing church leaders, and working in silence for long hours, sewing tents.

There is much to be said in favor of holding down a steady job, year after year, humdrum and unexciting as it might seem. God is in just such faithful obscurity.

This is an ideal state for Christians to live in: "Then the church throughout Judea, Galilee and Samaria enjoyed a time of peace and was strengthened. . . . Encouraged by the Holy Spirit, it increased in numbers" (Acts 9:31 NIV).

SECOND THOUGHTS

"We can't attack those people; they are stronger than we are."
NUMBERS 13:31 NIV

Moses sent twelve spies into Canaan in preparation for the coming invasion. All of them had waited a lifetime for the fulfillment of God's promise and the conquest of the land. All of them were delivered from Egypt, crossed the Red Sea, and saw the presence of God at Mt. Sinai and the miracles in the desert. But ten of the spies had second thoughts (Numbers 13:31–33).

On the threshold of their greatest adventure, these ten took a long, hard look at the challenges and decided it wasn't worth it. They preferred the world they knew, even if it was in the wilderness, to the battles before them. It was the defining moment for all twelve spies. Ten died in the wilderness they preferred. Two reached the Promised Land and lived their most cherished dreams.

Every man faces moments when the likelihood of success seems small, the obstacles insurmountable, and the costs immeasurable. Those who turn back never fulfill their wild, wonderful dreams. Those who press on may fail, but they fail daring greatly.

On the threshold of a great spiritual adventure, of leaving behind the wilderness of this world and pursuing a great and glorious life in God, some turn back and refuse to step into that new life. They are afraid. It costs too much. Victory seems impossible.

But those who refuse to retreat press on to live an incredible adventure of faith and follow God into the promised land of a rich, full life.

No one can make that choice for us. Will we live by fear or faith?

WHAT MOTIVATES YOU TO PRAY?

Enter his gates with thanksgiving; go into his courts with praise.
Give thanks to him and praise his name. For the LORD is
good. His unfailing love continues forever, and his
faithfulness continues to each generation.
PSALM 100:4–5 NLT

You may be most likely to pray in a time of need, but your own cir-cumstances shouldn't be the first thing on your mind when you enter a time of worship or prayer. In fact, you may struggle to pray if you don't approach God with thanksgiving and praise. Thanksgiving and praise keep your circumstances in proper perspective.

Why do you turn to God in prayer? Is it because of something you want? Or are you moved toward God because of His goodness, unfailing love, and faithfulness throughout the generations? Without a reality check into the love, goodness, and faithfulness of God, who knows which direction your prayers will go?

You come to God because you're His beloved child. You come to God in prayer because He could never forget His own or leave His children behind. You come to God in prayer because you can trust His goodness even if you can't understand His place in your circumstances.

You have every reason to praise God as you enter into prayer. Skip-ping the praise that He is due could result in some very self-centered prayers that miss an understanding of how deeply God cares for you.

ENCOURAGE ONE ANOTHER DAILY

But encourage one another daily, as long as it is called "Today,"
so that none of you may be hardened by sin's deceitfulness.
HEBREWS 3:13 NIV

Motivational speaker Jim Rohn once said, "You are the average of the five people you spend the most time with." You can find a variation of that sentiment in 1 Corinthians 15:33 (NIV) when the apostle Paul quoted Greek poet, Menander: "Do not be misled: 'Bad company corrupts good character.' " In a passive sense, we become the type of people we hang out with.

As Christians, we are called to be active in our pursuit of godliness. One of the ways we are to be active is to encourage one another each day. If we don't, sin will fool us, making us easy prey for Satan— much like the lone sheep is easy prey for the hungry wolf. Receiving such encouragement presupposes that we are active members in a congregation and that people there know us well enough to offer and receive encouragement from us.

If that's not the case for you, then find a good, Bible-believing church. Once you have found a place of worship, seek a kindred spirit or two and figure out the best way to encourage one another on a continual basis. Some Christian men exchange Bible verses via text message every day. Others meet for coffee a couple of times each week. And others sneak away during the lunch hour to pray for one another. Find what works for you, and devise a plan.

SPIRITUAL VITALITY

He answered, " 'Love the Lord your God with all your heart and with all your soul and with all your strength and with all your mind'; and, 'Love your neighbor as yourself.' "
LUKE 10:27 NIV

There is no relationship more important to any man than his relationship with God because every other relationship depends on it. When a man loses his connection to God, his relationship with his wife, his children, his friends, and everyone else in his life suffers.

We are called to love God with all our heart, soul, mind, and strength. The question is how? Maintaining and developing a deeper, more vital relationship with God requires what every other successful relationship demands—time, intention, practice, and service.

Great relationships take time. The problem isn't God. He'll give us all the time we want. The problem is we don't take time to pray, worship, study His Word, and listen to His voice.

Great relationships aren't accidental. They are intentional. We have to want spiritual vitality and intentionally do what must be done to experience a greater degree of God's presence.

Great relationships require practice. We have to actively and consistently do what builds up our relationship with God.

Finally, great relationships mean we serve. We invest our time, creativity, and energy into those things that benefit the other person. Serving brings us close to the heart of God.

If we stop working at any relationship, it grows cold. We must intentionally and habitually invest time and energy into those practices that bring us close to God.

GOSSIP—STOP IT!

A gossip betrays a confidence,
but a trustworthy person keeps a secret.
PROVERBS 11:13 NIV

Gossip is one of those all-too-common sins that we might think of as a "little" one. . . certainly not on par with the "biggies" like adultery, murder, or theft. But when you look at what the Bible has to say about gossip, you'll find that God takes it very, very seriously.

In the first chapter of Paul's letter to the Romans, he writes about God's punishment on sinful humans for their lawlessness. He goes on to provide a list of sinful individuals whose behavior makes them deserving of God's judgment. Right there in verse 29 is the word *gossips*.

Let's get real with ourselves here. God hates gossip, and He hates it because it destroys what He has created and has worked so hard to restore and protect—the name of another person. So let's be very careful not just what we say *to* another person, but also what we say *about* him or her. Let's think before we speak about another. Let's ask ourselves first if what we are about to say is true. Then let's ask ourselves if our words are loving and helpful. . .or if they just damage another's reputation.

And if the words we are about to speak don't pass muster, let's keep them to ourselves.

LIFE PRIORITIES

Therefore, since we are surrounded by such a great cloud of witnesses,
let us throw off everything that hinders and the sin that so easily
entangles. And let us run with perseverance the race marked out for
us, fixing our eyes on Jesus, the pioneer and perfecter of faith.
HEBREWS 12:1–2 NIV

Living out our values means establishing priorities. Some things are important and worthy of our time, investment, and energy. Other things are great if we get to them. But there are things that we shouldn't do, not because they are sinful but because they distract us from what is more important.

These verses give us a way to think about our priorities. First, we should eliminate sin and everything that hinders a godly life. Things that interfere with our life in Christ or distract us from our calling should never end up on our "to do" lists. Second, we should live the life God has called us to with perseverance. Staying spiritually, emotionally, relationally, and physically healthy and happy is a priority. Fulfilling our responsibility as God's ambassadors, sons, husbands, and fathers in ways that honor God and further His kingdom isn't optional. Those responsibilities must be our priority. Finally, we should do all that while staying focused on Jesus and delighting in the joy of a life well lived.

No one disputes the wisdom found in these verses. It's just hard to understand and harder to live by. That should not keep us from trying. Achieving what's most important in life is always challenging and always worth it!

FREEDOM'S PURPOSE

All things are lawful for me, but not all things are profitable.
All things are lawful for me, but I will not be mastered by anything.
1 Corinthians 6:12 nasb

Grace wouldn't be grace if it didn't allow us room to make mistakes without fear of losing our relationship with God. Grace is God's determination that our sin will not stand between Him and us. As believers, we have come to accept Christ's work alone for our reconciliation to God. In Christ, God fulfills the demands that the Old Testament Law made upon man and eliminates our need to rely on any set of laws to make us acceptable to Him.

But there is always the chance that such a wonderful freedom can be misused. As writer Philip Yancey says, "Grace implies a risk, the risk that we might abuse it." Some Corinthian believers, freed from the arduous burden of legalism, were using their new "freedom" as an excuse to indulge in unprofitable things—a spiritual waste of time. Some had gone further, becoming addicted to activities that, although technically allowable, had replaced God as the focus of their lives. How absurd to think that God's gift of grace would push aside the One who gave it! The whole point of grace was to free us to move *toward* our Father not *away* from Him.

No amount of rationalizing should overrule godly common sense (Hebrews 5:14). God wants preeminence in our lives, and even death will be overcome to achieve this end. So for today, let us use our freedom to become like Him, not to test the limits of His patience.

WHERE TO TURN WHEN YOU'RE AFRAID

When I am afraid, I put my trust in you. In God, whose word I praise—
in God I trust and am not afraid. What can mere mortals do to me?
PSALM 56:3–4 NIV

You don't need to be an expert in child behavior to know what a small child does when he's afraid, worried, in pain, or just needs comfort. Of course, he runs straight to the arms of his loving parents (more often than not to Mom).

It seems instinctive, doesn't it?

Life is filled with opportunities for us to be overcome by fear and anxiety. And when we enter times in our lives when we feel afraid, worried, and overwhelmed, it can be tempting just to curl up somewhere and try to wait it out alone.

Jesus once told His followers that if they wanted to enter the kingdom of heaven, they needed to do so with the heart attitude like that of a little child (see Matthew 18:2–4). Those moments of fear and worry are good examples of those many times when we need to be like little children.

When life is throwing so much at you that you feel like your fear will overcome you, do the same thing a small child does when he's afraid: run straight to the arms of your heavenly Father, who is more than able to calm your heart. . .and calm the storm that is going on around you.

A LIFE OF GENEROSITY

Remember this: Whoever sows sparingly will also reap sparingly,
and whoever sows generously will also reap generously.
2 CORINTHIANS 9:6 NIV

Generosity is long remembered. So is stingy selfishness!

Scrooge, the main character in Dickens' *A Christmas Carol*, has become the epitome of stingy selfishness, of a man so concerned with himself he ignored the needs of all those around him, including his family, his employees, and his neighbors. But after his dramatic encounter with the ghosts of Christmas past, present, and future, he becomes so generous that "it was always said of him, that he knew how to keep Christmas well, if any man alive possessed the knowledge."

Like Scrooge, we would do well to consider generosity in light of our past, present, and future. God is generous with His children in giving us far more than we need and treating us far better than we deserve. His generosity is best expressed in His most generous gift, His own Son, Jesus. It's impossible to imagine a more generous gift to any less deserving.

Today's verse reminds us that both stingy selfishness and joyous generosity have consequences in the future. A large measure of our future joy, in this world and the next, depends on generosity today. True generosity isn't about how much; it's possible to give a great deal and not be truly generous. Generosity is a matter of the heart attuned to a generous God. It is the result of gratitude for what He has done and trusting in what He will do.

PASSIONATE LIVING

Whatever you do, work at it with all your heart, as working for the Lord, not for human masters, since you know that you will receive an inheritance from the Lord as a reward.
It is the Lord Christ you are serving.
COLOSSIANS 3:23–24 NIV

We all pursue our passions and our passions inevitably drive our lives in their direction. That's not the question. The real question is—what are those passions?

Sadly many men settle "for grime when [they] could reach for glory" (Carl F.H. Henry). Their passions burn for power, possessions, pleasures, and pride. They settle for paths that give temporary pleasure but are ultimately unfulfilling and destructive.

Paul made it clear that the only passion worth living and dying for is an all-consuming passion for God and His work in the world. Nothing can take its place. Nothing is as satisfying or rewarding. Most Christian men wouldn't disagree. But most of us don't pursue that passion. We are distracted by the shiny baubles of the world, dig for fool's gold, and end up empty and exhausted.

William Borden, heir to the great Borden Dairy fortune, was a student at Yale when he found his passion for Christ. He followed that passion and led the great Christian student movement of the early twentieth century. He turned his back on his family's business and fortune and pursued his call to serve God in China. He died on the way and is buried in Cairo, Egypt.

In his journal Borden wrote, "No reserves. No retreats. No regrets." Passion!

LETTING GO OF GRUDGES

"So if you are presenting a sacrifice at the altar in the Temple and you suddenly remember that someone has something against you, leave your sacrifice there at the altar. Go and be reconciled to that person. Then come and offer your sacrifice to God."
MATTHEW 5:23–24 NLT

Your worship and your treatment of others are linked. Broken fellowship with a neighbor or colleague can get in the way of your worship of God, and your only path to freedom is through confession and forgiveness.

Perhaps your own pride has offended someone or a grudge has poisoned your relationship. If you give in to anger, you then demand your rights and this can cause divisions or alienate you from others. Whatever you are holding on to, your ability to pray and to worship freely will be damaged by the same things that damage your relationships.

Pride is always destructive, whether before God or before others. A grudge could point to a self-righteousness that keeps you from receiving God's mercy, let alone showing mercy to others. Anger counteracts the humility that keeps you in your place before God.

If you want to know where you stand before God, one of the first places to look should be in your relationships with others. Do your interactions or relationships indicate that you think too highly of yourself? What steps can you take to remedy that?

TROUBLE LETTING GO

"Let me kiss my father and mother goodbye,"
he said, "and then I will come with you."
1 KINGS 19:20 NIV

Elisha had trouble letting go (1 Kings 19:19–21). When the prophet Elijah threw his mantle over Elisha's shoulders, he made Elisha his successor. But Elisha's first reaction was to go home and say goodbye to his parents. He had trouble letting go.

His reaction reminds us of those who made excuses for not following Christ. In His parable of the great banquet (Luke 14:15–23), Jesus recounted three kinds of things people have trouble releasing.

The first man bought land and needed to see it. He couldn't let go of his *place*. The second man bought oxen and had to see them. He couldn't let go of his *possessions*. The third man wanted to be with his new wife. He couldn't let go of *people*.

Both Elisha and the characters in Christ's parable had the opportunity for a new life and a tremendous adventure. But the stories end very differently.

Elisha goes back, slaughters his oxen, burns the plow, and (we assume) bids farewell to his parents. He severed the ties to his past and went after his future (1 Kings 19:21).

The characters in Christ's parable cling to their place, possessions, and people. They wouldn't let go. They lost the opportunity, missed the feast, and watched others enjoy what could have been theirs.

It's a simple truth. We need empty hands to take up our cross and follow Him (Mark 8:34–38).

A GOOD FOUNDATION

See to it that no one takes you captive through philosophy and empty deception, according to the tradition of men, according to the elementary principles of the world, rather than according to Christ.
COLOSSIANS 2:8 NASB

The test of every building is in its foundation. No matter how fine in appearance it is, if the foundation is faulty, the whole structure is at risk. Sadly, this is also the way our lives can be if we build our thinking on faulty reasoning and shifting philosophies. The world offers its perspective and solutions to our problems twenty-four hours a day, over television, radio, in bookstores, newspapers, and around the lunch table. The voice of this world rarely lacks confidence and the advice often seems wise and time tested. The proponents of worldly philosophies may even mean well, but they don't perceive the empty nature of their own beliefs. Why would they? *If it was good enough for Dad*, it's reasoned, *it's good enough for me.* Traditions passed down from one generation to the next carry weight whether they're right or wrong.

Then there are those current worldviews specifically designed for the marketplace—money-making offerings pushed in books, DVDs, and infomercials. They are easily identified because they are built on the simplest principles of this world: promotion of self, pursuit of pleasure, get-rich-quick schemes, emphasis on appearance, promises of simple solutions to complex problems.

But Christ offers truth, reality, and a future that is eternal rather than fleeting. If we build upon His work and His words, we will avoid the captivity of a dying world and the loss of our opportunity for a solid foundation.

STRENGTH THROUGH TRIBULATIONS

Not only so, but we also glory in our sufferings,
because we know that suffering produces perseverance.
Romans 5:3 niv

If we had to guess what words flowed through the pen of the apostle Paul following today's verse, we might try this: "What doesn't kill you makes you stronger."

Of course that's not what Paul wrote, but it might make for a good summary for what he actually jotted down. He actually wrote that perseverance produces "character; and character, hope. And hope does not put us to shame, because God's love has been poured out into our hearts through the Holy Spirit, who has been given to us" (Romans 5:4–5).

Right! We might think after reading those words. *What doesn't kill me truly can make me stronger.*

Paul knew as well as anyone that God could and did use his suffering and tribulation (and he endured more than his share of both during his ministry) to strengthen him and to give him the character and drive it took to endure whatever a hostile world threw at him.

Just as an athlete's training regimen (the weight-lifting and the cardio work alike) tears his body down but later makes it stronger and more fit for competition, tribulation can make us stronger, more Christlike, and better fit for the work God has given us to do.

JUMPSTART YOUR PRAYER LIFE

In the same way, the Spirit helps us in our weakness. We do not know what we ought to pray for, but the Spirit himself intercedes for us through wordless groans.

ROMANS 8:26 NIV

As men, we often have a more difficult time expressing ourselves verbally than women do about things that matter. That doesn't mean we aren't emotional or passionate, and it certainly doesn't mean we don't need to feel a connection with other people, but when it comes to finding the right words to build relationships, they are hard to find.

In 2007, researchers from the University of Arizona conducted an eight-year study and determined that, contrary to popular opinion, men and women speak approximately the same amount of words each day: 16,000. It also found that men tended to talk more about technology and sports, while women talked more about relationships. In other words, men talk about things and what other people are doing, while women speak about how they connect with people.

Maybe this explains why so many Christian women are prayer warriors while Christian men are busy talking about theology. Since we struggle to express ourselves in relationship, we struggle to talk to God. We talk about Him instead. But the Spirit is here to help us in our weakness, even going so far as to pray for us when we don't know what to say. That implies we are actually talking to God on some level. Where we fall short, the Spirit takes over. Find both comfort and motivation in that truth to jumpstart your prayer life.

WHO JESUS CHRIST IS IN US

For it pleased the Father that in Him all the fullness should dwell,
and by Him to reconcile all things to Himself, by Him,
whether things on earth or things in heaven,
having made peace through the blood of His cross.
COLOSSIANS 1:19–20 NKJV

In a classic *Peanuts* cartoon, Charlie Brown hears that Snoopy is writing a book of theology and tells him, "I hope you have a good title." Snoopy lifts his hands off the typewriter, closes his eyes, and thinks to himself, *I have the perfect title.* He then types "Has It Ever Occurred to You That You Might Be Wrong?"

True, we probably haven't thought of even 10 percent of the questions we should be asking, let alone answering, biblically, intellectually, and experientially. Still, we have learned and experienced so much that is true. Truths we can't review too often!

Truly transforming? Reviewing the dozens of "who I am in Christ" statements compiled and popularized by Neil T. Anderson, and more than doubled in size by others. Untold millions have experienced spiritual healing, health, and hope by reading them.

What would happen, however, if we turned the equation around? Specifically, what would happen in our heart and life if we began affirming what's true about "who Jesus Christ is in me"?

When we ponder "who Jesus Christ is in me," what immediately comes to mind? We can thank the Lord daily for His sovereignty (greatness), providence (goodness), holiness (glory), love (graciousness), and mystery (God alone knows). Let's continue to consider these majestic truths about our Lord and Savior.

AT THE CORE: VALUES

What is more, I consider everything a loss because of the surpassing worth of knowing Christ Jesus my Lord, for whose sake I have lost all things. I consider them garbage, that I may gain Christ.

PHILIPPIANS 3:8 NIV

A man's values are those things most important to him.

Every day we are confronted with choices that rest on and often reveal what we truly value. Often the greatest challenge is sorting out competing values and choosing between good things. Is advancing our career more valuable than time with our children? Is work more important than worship? Are our hobbies more valuable than our wives' happiness? Do we value that purchase more than staying out of debt and the financial well-being of our family? Do we value momentary pleasure more than our purpose?

In this verse, Paul expresses his greatest value. Nothing, absolutely nothing was more valuable to him than knowing Jesus. He willingly let go of everything else and considered it little more than garbage compared to the insurmountable value of Christ in his life. Paul's core value echoed Christ's statement that loving God is the greatest commandment.

Are we like Paul, ready to value our relationship with God more than our ambition, pride, pleasure, and our desire for success, money, and status? Can we give them up? The answer to that question has a profound impact on each man, his family, and his future.

CHARACTER THAT MATTERS: COURAGE

*"Have I not commanded you? Be strong and courageous.
Do not be afraid; do not be discouraged, for the LORD
your God will be with you wherever you go."*

JOSHUA 1:9 NIV

Winston Churchill, lion of the British Empire, once famously remarked, "Courage is rightly esteemed the first of human qualities. . .because it is the quality that guarantees all the others." Our values don't matter if we don't have the courage to act on them when faced with a great challenge.

After years in Robbins Prison, Nelson Mandela said, "I learned that courage was not the absence of fear, but the triumph over it. The brave man is not he who does not feel afraid, but he who conquers that fear."

Standing on the edge of the Promised Land and years of war, God encouraged Joshua to "be strong and courageous" and banish fear and discouragement. But it wasn't up to Joshua to triumph over his fear. His courage rested on a solid foundation and so does ours.

We can have courage when we follow God's command. If we do what He calls us to, obey His Word and honor Him, God fights for us. He will be our ally in the battle.

We can have courage because God is with us wherever our obedience takes us and in whatever battles we face. God is with us! So be strong and courageous. We have no reason to be afraid or discouraged when we are on God's side.

THE TANGLED WEB OF DECEPTION

Do not lie to each other, since you have taken
off your old self with its practices.
COLOSSIANS 3:9 NIV

The goal of any fly fisherman is to catch fish by using hooks adorned with fur, feathers, hair, and other materials in such a way that they imitate an insect or other living creature fish like to eat. A good fisherman uses flies he knows can *deceive* a hungry fish into biting.

While no one would criticize or condemn a fly fisherman for practicing this form of deception, the Bible tells you repeatedly that as followers of Christ, you are to be completely honest with others in how you speak to them and how you treat them—no "white lies," twisted truths, or spin.

You live in a world in which politicians, marketers, and many others regularly practice all sorts of deception in an effort to get people to cast their votes or spend their money in a way they want them to. But it should never be that way for believers.

As a Christian man, you damage your relationship with God—and your witness for Christ—when you speak untruthfully or when you behave in such a way as to deceive others. On the other hand, when you make honesty a big part of who you are, you please your heavenly Father and glorify Him in front of those around you.

THE FLIP SIDE OF FAITH

But My righteous one shall live by faith; and if he
shrinks back, My soul has no pleasure in him.
HEBREWS 10:38 NASB

People usually assume that *doubt* is the opposite of faith. But in the New Testament (NASB) the words *doubt* or *doubting* appear only a handful of times, while *fear* or *afraid* show up over one hundred times. While we can't build theology over a single observation, it's clear that a life of faith is often a battle against fear.

Fear certainly was the synagogue official's test when, in faith, he had begged for Jesus to heal his sick daughter. Then his little girl died. Jesus, knowing the man's heart, comforted him with these words, "Do not be afraid any longer, only believe" (Mark 5:36 NASB).

Later, Jesus, knowing the fear Peter would face after He was arrested, said, "Simon, Simon, behold, Satan has demanded permission to sift you like wheat; but I have prayed for you, that your faith may not fail" (Luke 22:31–32 NASB).

Of course God is not pleased when His people give in to fear because it means we are shrinking back from *Him*. But the good news is that we have a Father and a Savior who knows our weakness and "has not given us a spirit of timidity, but of power and love and discipline" (2 Timothy 1:7 NASB). We move forward in faith as we keep in step with the Spirit who is our Helper (John 14:16). We may well wrestle with fear, but we are never alone in the struggle.

BEING PATIENT WITH GOD

*Wait for the L*ORD*; be strong and take
heart and wait for the L*ORD*.*
PSALM 27:14 NIV

It's so commonly spoken that it's become something of a Christian cliché, but in light of today's scripture verse, it bears repeating here: "God answers prayers in one of three ways—yes, no, and not yet."

Of course we're happy to receive that "Yes" from God, and sometimes we can understand why He says "No." But that "Not yet"—that one can really mess with us. When we pray for something we know is God's will (say, the salvation of a loved one or personal spiritual revival), we're often flummoxed when it doesn't happen right away. So we keep praying—sometimes over a period of years—and waiting.

The scriptural truth of the matter is that God often makes His people wait before He answers their requests. We may not understand why we have to wait, so we must cling to the truth that God's ways and thoughts are different from ours (see Isaiah 55:8).

So be patient and keep seeking God. He has made literally hundreds of promises in scripture, and His track record of keeping them still stands at one hundred percent.

Our part of this grand bargain is to wait patiently, knowing that God's very nature keeps Him from letting us down.

THE MIRACLE OF PSALM TWENTY-TWO

"My God, my God, why have you forsaken me?"
MARK 15:34 NIV

With these words, Jesus quoted the opening phrase of Psalm 22.

Yes, He was expressing His despair. The presence of sin will do that. But when a Jew of that time heard a portion of a psalm quoted, he would remember the whole psalm. Psalms were sung every Sabbath at the synagogue, so it's like any song you've heard since you were a kid: you remember the whole thing.

Psalm 22 was a psalm of shame for those who were crucifying Jesus. It predicted exactly what they were doing ("They hurl insults. . . 'Let the LORD rescue him.'" Psalm 22:7–8 NIV). After they heard Jesus say this, and were thus reminded of the whole psalm, they were gone!

It also predicts the result of this martyrdom: "All the families of the nations will bow down before him" (v. 27).

Not only did Jesus' Jewish hearers remember the whole psalm, but when Jesus quoted the first line, He remembered it too. So when He expresses the first lines, He also expresses the beautiful hope of the whole psalm: "He has. . .listened to his cry for help" (v. 24).

This is not just despair; this is not just torture predicted; it is despair leading to faith in a glorious future. Jesus was in such control that He could use this psalm to declare all of this to those around Him. . .and to Himself.

God, help us to do the same in our times of despair.

JESUS CHRIST OFFERS FORETASTES OF HEAVEN

"Go back and report to John what you have seen and heard: The blind receive sight, the lame walk, those who have leprosy are cleansed, the deaf hear, the dead are raised, and the good news is proclaimed to the poor."

LUKE 7:22 NIV

Two thousand years ago, Jesus Christ's earthly ministry gave the men, women, youth, and children around Him amazing foretastes of what is eternal for each of His followers. Those foretastes cover a wide horizon. To name but a few: seeing individuals raised from the dead, seeing other individuals healed spiritually, seeing others healed physically, seeing yet other persons healed psychologically.

Let's not make the mistake, however, of thinking that wonderful foretastes of heaven aren't *ours* to experience *today*. As followers of Jesus Christ, our sins past, present, and future are already all forgiven, yet we experience it anew each time we confess our sins. Immediately afterward, we want to slow down and savor that specific experience of being forgiven. If we do, we enjoy a delicious foretaste of heaven.

Even though our salvation is all-encompassing, it doesn't mean we don't sin—any more than it means we never get sick, never suffer trials, never wrestle with temptation, never fail, never fall, never fear cancer, and never end up dying. Aren't these means, while on this planet, helping us to continue longing for heaven?

What we don't want to miss is the critical need to slow down and savor each specific foretaste experience this side of eternity. In a real sense, these are Jesus Christ's rich and valuable gifts to us.

HE KNOWS WHAT WE'RE THINKING

*Finally, brothers and sisters, whatever is true, whatever is noble,
whatever is right, whatever is pure, whatever is lovely,
whatever is admirable—if anything is excellent
or praiseworthy—think about such things.*

PHILIPPIANS 4:8 NIV

We've all known those married couples who know each other so well
that they seem to know what the other is thinking. In truth, however,
no one—not even the ones with whom we share our most intimate
relationships—can possibly know everything we think.

However, there is one who knows our every thought—our Father
in heaven. King David knew this, which is why he wrote, "You have
searched me, LORD, and you know me. . . . You perceive my thoughts
from afar" (Psalm 139:1–2 NIV).

God knows our thoughts—all of them. He knows the things that cross
our minds that we'd never share with anyone, even our closest friends.

That's the proverbial two-edged sword, isn't it? On one hand,
we're like David, who seemed to welcome his heavenly Father's
loving intrusion into his thoughts when he prayed, "Search me, God,
and know my heart; test me and know my anxious thoughts" (Psalm
139:23 NIV). On the other hand, we may think, "Oh no! I don't want
Him to know I'm thinking about *that.*"

This is one of those situations when it's good to speak honestly
to our heavenly Father. Since He knows our thoughts anyway, we
can bring them all to Him and, like David, pray, "Search my heart
and my thoughts, and help me to think on the things You want me
to be thinking."

GOD'S MIGHTY PROTECTION

*The Lord is faithful, and he will strengthen
you and protect you from the evil one.*
2 THESSALONIANS 3:3 NIV

This verse can be a tremendous source of comfort to you in times when the devil, the enemy of your soul, is attacking you. The Lord wants you to know in no uncertain terms that He won't leave you to face the enemy on your own but is *certain* to be with you and empower you so that you'll have the strength to resist the devil. And God will protect you from him.

Elsewhere in the Bible, God promises, "Resist the devil, and he will flee from you" (James 4:7 KJV). He won't always flee the instant you first stand up to him. You may have to steadfastly resist the enemy for some time, but eventually he will buckle under the pressure of the unrelenting power of God, turn, and flee.

The Bible assures you: "God is faithful, who will not allow you to be tempted beyond what you are able, but with the temptation will provide the way of escape also, so that you will be able to endure it" (1 Corinthians 10:13 NASB). The enemy is always seeking to tempt you to do evil, to choose the selfish path, but God has promised to be faithful to strengthen you to help you resist him. And He is more than able to help you emerge victorious.

KEEP YOUR WORD!

Above all, my brothers and sisters, do not swear—not by heaven or by earth or by anything else. All you need to say is a simple "Yes" or "No." Otherwise you will be condemned.
JAMES 5:12 NIV

Have you ever known someone you knew you could depend on? The kind of guy who always showed up for coffee when he said he would? The kind who you knew would keep his word when he tells you he will help you with those not-too-enjoyable tasks such as moving or painting your house?

That's the kind of friend we'd all like to have, isn't it? But, going a step further, it's the kind of friend we should strive to be.

Some Christians take the words of today's Bible verse quite literally, avoiding making any kinds of promises, taking any kinds of oaths, or entering into contracts with others. But even for someone who doesn't follow this verse by the letter (there are situations in today's world where it's impossible not to take oaths or enter into contractual agreements), there's something about James's words that strongly implies a simple but important principle: *be a man who can be taken at his word.*

In other words, be the kind of man who is so dependable, so true to his word, that no one ever has to ask, "Do you promise?" Be the man whose "yes" can always be taken as "yes" and whose "no" can always be taken as "no."

YOU SHARE FROM GOD'S GENEROSITY

*"But when you give to someone in need, don't let your left hand
know what your right hand is doing. Give your gifts in private,
and your Father, who sees everything, will reward you."*

MATTHEW 6:3–4 NLT

Everything you have is a gift from God, and so Jesus challenges your desire to gain the praise of fellow men and church leaders when you give generously from your possessions. Giving as freely as you have received without the hope of recognition saves you from the illusion of self-sufficiency and pride in your own abilities. If you're depending on God for your provision, then your generosity to others is between you and God as you give as freely as you have received.

Think about it: the more attached you become to your money and possessions, the less likely you are to see God as your provider and sustainer. Most importantly, the less you live by faith, the more dependent you will become on the opinions of others. Without seeking God's praise first and foremost, you run the risk of building your life on the unstable foundations of what others think and say.

Giving from your possessions also ensures that you won't become dependent on them for your security. Privately giving to others may be one of the purest acts of faith possible.

ATTRACTING SINNERS

When the Pharisee who had invited him saw this, he said to himself,
"If this man were a prophet, he would know who is touching
him and what kind of woman she is—that she is a sinner."
LUKE 7:39 NIV

Simon, a Pharisee, invited Jesus to dine with him and some of his friends. But a sinful woman crashed the party after learning Jesus would be there. She broke down in tears when she saw Him and began washing His feet with her tears, kissing them, and pouring perfume over them, causing Simon to question whether Jesus was a prophet, as many believed Him to be.

Simon expected Jesus to view the woman the way he did. The religious rules he embraced as a Pharisee didn't allow him to interact with notorious sinners, so surely Jesus wouldn't interact with her either. But the woman wasn't bound by any such rules. She simply saw Jesus for who He was, and she was drawn to Him, knowing Him to be full of mercy. She approached Him from behind, perhaps feeling unworthy to be in His presence, and then lovingly displayed her love for Him. To Simon's amazement, Jesus praised this woman's actions.

Holding to a certain theological bent and then drawing inferences from that theology, as men are wont to do, is of little value if we forget mercy. You will know you have forgotten mercy if the unregenerate are repelled by you and your religious rules rather than attracted to Christ, who lives in you.

THE IMPORTANCE OF PLANNING

*The plans of the diligent lead to profit
as surely as haste leads to poverty.*
PROVERBS 21:5 NIV

The word *planning* sometimes gets a bad rap among certain segments of the Christian world. Some of us don't think it's important to make a plan; instead, they would rather keep their options open and let the Holy Spirit guide their every step on the fly.

Other believers, when God gives them a vision for something, want to plan everything out to the smallest detail so that they don't head out in the wrong direction.

Is either approach necessarily wrong? Like many things in the Word of God, there is usually a point of balance between moving out when God calls you to move and making sure you have a plan of action.

There may be times when God directs you to move out immediately (see Abram in Genesis 12:1–4), but in most instances, when He gives you a vision for something He wants to accomplish through you, it's wise to avoid rushing into it before you carefully plan and weigh your options.

So by all means, have a plan. But just make sure that you prayerfully and humbly submit your planning process to God so that He can guide you in every step you take.

GOD'S LITTLE HELPERS

Now Sarai, Abram's wife, had borne him no children. But she had an Egyptian slave named Hagar; so she said to Abram, "The LORD has kept me from having children. Go, sleep with my slave; perhaps I can build a family through her."

GENESIS 16:1–2 NIV

God promises Abram (Abraham) a son, who will be the beginning of a great nation. This promise of descendents is repeated and repeated. Eventually Sarai (Sarah), who is old and barren, gets the bright idea of giving her servant, Hagar, to Abraham to bear this child of promise. This is not an unusual arrangement for that time. They would of course prefer to have children together, but Sarai thinks she is too old.

So Sarai, God's little helper, decides to give Yahweh's promise a little boost with her own little plan. The first result of this plan is hatred between the mothers and their children. The end result of this plan is the deathly, scorpions-in-a-bottle hatred between Arabs/Muslims and Jews that continues unabated to this day. This hatred continues because, while only the Jews' claim is legitimate, both are true.

Why doesn't God reveal to us the whole timeline of His plans for our lives? Why does He force us to live with day-to-day, one-step-at-a-time trust in His long-range plans?

He remembers Sarai and Abram and the cost of humans playing God's little helper.

Let's let God be God. Let's do what's at hand with all our heart (Colossians 3:23–24) while we listen for God's leading; then let's trust the God who knows the end from the beginning.

WATCH YOUR LANGUAGE!

*But now you must also rid yourselves of all such things as these: anger,
rage, malice, slander, and filthy language from your lips.*

COLOSSIANS 3:8 NIV

At a men's Bible study, a middle-aged man who had come to Jesus
after decades of hard living—drinking, fighting, carousing, and cussing—
shared with his brothers in Christ what God had been doing in his life.

"God has taken away the drinking, the chasing women, and the
fighting," he said. "I don't want any part of those things anymore."

"Amen!"

"Praise God!"

After the impromptu moment of praise and worship had finished,
the man went on: "It seems like there's one area where I just haven't
changed, and that's in the way I talk sometimes. Sometimes when
I get angry or frustrated, I still have a tendency to let fly with the
cussing now and again, even though I know it doesn't please Him."

This sounds like he's headed in the right direction, doesn't it?
Whether because of his past or perhaps a wife who constantly "reminded" him about his frequent use of profanities, he knew God isn't
pleased when His people cuss and swear like longshoremen.

The apostle James wrote that "no human being can tame the tongue"
(James 3:8 NIV), and many of us have found that to be especially true
when it comes to foul language. While it's an oversimplification to say
"Just stop it," we can have victory in the way we talk when we commit
our speech to God and ask Him, through His Holy Spirit, to help us to
speak only words that glorify and please Him.

TOO FAR GONE?

*"So I will restore to you the years that the swarming locust has eaten,
the crawling locust, the consuming locust, and the chewing locust."*
JOEL 2:25 NKJV

Have you ever looked at someone you know or some famous person and thought, *That person is just too far gone to ever turn to God*? If you have, then consider the story of Michael Franzese, a former New York mobster who ranked high in the notorious Colombo crime family.

In the 1980s, Franzese earned millions of dollars weekly for the Colombo family. At one point, his criminal activities made him a billionaire, but that all ended after he was indicted on fourteen criminal counts and later imprisoned for ten years. Now a free man, Franzese no longer serves the Colombo crime family. Now he serves Jesus Christ as a public speaker and author. (To hear his testimony, just search for his name on YouTube.)

Your job as Christian is not to judge people or their sinful actions. Your job is to love them and pray for them, asking God to do in their lives what only He can do.

If you were to tell Michael Franzese that someone is so far gone that they can never turn to Jesus for forgiveness, he'd likely tell you that believing that is to deny everything Jesus Christ did when He died for the sins of all humankind.

Wise words from a man who knows well about such things.

BEING "REAL" WITH GOD

*Immediately the boy's father exclaimed,
"I do believe; help me overcome my unbelief!"*
MARK 9:24 NIV

It's amazing how desperation can often bring out the best in people. When the chips are down and when our backs are against the wall (pick your own cliché here), we're often forced to get real with one another. . .and with God.

The man who spoke the words in today's scripture verse was at a point where he had no choice but to turn to Jesus for help. He apparently knew enough about Jesus to know that He had miraculously healed many people. But it is equally apparent that he had his doubts as to whether Jesus could help *him*.

Jesus responded to this man's kernel of faith. . .and to his honesty. He healed the man's son and then used the incident to teach His followers some things about real, mountain-moving, demon-repelling faith.

Jesus repeatedly and consistently taught His followers that they could do anything if they had faith. Those same promises hold true for us today. But in those times when we wonder if we have "enough" faith, when we wonder if God can reach down and make a difference in our lives, our best first step might be to confess honestly, "I do believe, Lord. Help me overcome my unbelief."

WISDOM PUTS YOU IN YOUR PLACE

Fear of the LORD is the foundation of true wisdom. All who obey his commandments will grow in wisdom. Praise him forever!
PSALM 111:10 NLT

Everyone wants to be wise, but fear is rarely valued as a positive virtue. Fear is typically associated with running away, living in paranoia, or lacking any kind of stability. Jesus repeatedly told His disciples to *not* be afraid, so why would the writer of this psalm note that "fear of the Lord" is the foundation of wisdom? Isn't fear the opposite of faith?

What if this "fear" isn't quaking at the thought of God but is a humbling, unsettling grasp of God's holiness and power? The accounts of God showing up among the people in the Old Testament are truly fear-inspiring, but God was also very careful to avoid terrifying people. Even when Moses reflected the glory of God, he veiled his face. God doesn't use His glory and power in order to terrify you into submission. Jesus reaches out to you in love, saying, "Do not fear" (Luke 12:32 NKJV).

However, if you begin to imagine that you're wiser than God, capable of controlling your life, or free to do as you please, the fear of God's power and holiness can offer a helpful correction. Should God choose to show up, you'll have a fearful reminder of how unwise your life choices have been.

PUT YOUR TRUST IN GOD

*Trust in the LORD with all your heart and lean not on your
own understanding; in all your ways submit to
him, and he will make your paths straight.*

PROVERBS 3:5–6 NIV

No matter your level of education, you don't have all the answers
to whatever life throws at you. Whether it's a difficult predicament,
unexpected turn of events, or a tragic loss, you may find yourself
struggling to solve a problem and unable to explain why something
negative has happened. Friend, God has all the answers. You don't
need to look any further or seek comfort from anyone else. He has
your best interest at heart. He knows what you need. All you have
to do is submit to Him, praise Him for the successes in your life, and
turn to Him at times of hardship. The Lord will guide you through
every situation no matter the circumstances. But, you must ask Him
to direct you, and you must seek God's will in everything you do. Turn
every area of your life over to Him. There's no halfway with God. You
can't choose to follow Him some of the time and ignore Him other
times. If you make Him a vital part of everything you do, He will lead
you because you will be working to accomplish His will. God knows
what is best for you. He is a better judge of what you need than you
are, so you must trust Him completely in every choice you make.

THE SLOW CREEP OF COMPROMISE

King Solomon, however, loved many foreign women besides Pharaoh's
daughter—Moabites, Ammonites, Edomites, Sidonians and Hittites.
They were from nations about which the LORD had told the Israelites,
"You must not intermarry with them, because they will surely
turn your hearts after their gods." Nevertheless,
Solomon held fast to them in love.

1 KINGS 11:1–2 NIV

After King Solomon's wealth and wisdom are presented in striking detail, the author of Kings offers a sobering note that all is not well in the king's heart: he had married many foreign women who turned him away from the Lord. It's likely that Solomon didn't think a few foreign wives could be that much of a threat to his devotion to God. After all, he lived in the epicenter of worship for Yahweh. What harm could a few foreign alliances through marriage do to his heart?

Sure enough, his heart gradually drifted further from God, and he became more tolerant of foreign gods. As he added new wives and allegiances with neighboring kingdoms, Solomon lost sight of Yahweh as he filled his time joining his wives in their idol worship. Even the wisest king was no match for the slow creep of compromise in his devotion to the true God.

As you examine your heart today, ask whether there are places or issues where you're compromising—even if it's just a little. Sin's most powerful trick is convincing us that it's not a big deal and that we can handle ourselves. It's a slow drift away from God, and we'll spare ourselves and our families pain if we recognize it sooner than later.

HEAVENLY CORRECTION

*Moreover, we have all had human fathers who disciplined us
and we respected them for it. How much more should
we submit to the Father of spirits and live!*

HEBREWS 12:9 NIV

We tend to run at the first hint of correction. Correction is humiliating and pride-crushing, even when it's justified. When you were growing up and faced the possibility of corporal punishment, or you expected the loss of certain privileges because you did something that was worthy of correction, you probably not only hid, but you also fretted, begged, and pleaded before finally submitting to your punishment.

But, assuming you weren't physically abused, when you were older you were thankful that your earthly father cared enough to correct you, because it made you the man you are today. You probably even respect your father for stepping in when the situation warranted it because now you can see the fruit.

The writer of Hebrews indicates that something much larger is at stake than simply becoming a better person. When we go astray spiritually, our heavenly Father has to step in because *true life* is at stake, meaning eternity in heaven.

Putting the theological debate about eternal security aside and just examining this verse for what it says, God loves us enough to correct us in such a fashion that will keep us from experiencing true death as the result of our wayward actions. If you are experiencing His correction or have done so recently, rejoice! You are being prepared for heaven by our Creator.

LONGSUFFERING LOVE

Love. . .is not irritable, and it keeps no record of being wronged.
1 CORINTHIANS 13:4–5 NLT

Some men are just plain grouchy. They're easily irritated and quick to respond negatively. Far from "keeping no record of being wronged," they keep detailed mental tabs of the times people step on their toes. They may overlook an offense once or twice but keep repeating it, and they write you off.

If *you* do this to others, you may feel justified in having such an attitude, arguing that you can't go through life being a doormat. Or you may reason, "This is just the way I am, rough and unvarnished—like it or leave it." What then did God *intend* when He inspired the apostle Paul to pen the above verse?

Paul was no pushover. When he needed to speak out for what was right, he stood up boldly and refused to back down. He opposed the Judaizers in Antioch and engaged in a heated argument with them. He even publicly rebuked Peter, leader of the Jerusalem church (Acts 15:1–2; Galatians 2:11–14). But Paul wasn't defending his personal rights in such cases, much less a wounded ego. When it came to offenses against himself, Paul was longsuffering.

Longsuffering love means precisely that: love that suffers (puts up with someone) for a long time. May God give you such love.

LEAVING HOME

When Jacob learned that there was grain in Egypt, he said to his
sons, "Why do you just keep looking at each other?"
GENESIS 42:1 NIV

It's easy to identify with Jacob's frustration. Caught in a great famine, the specter of starvation loomed over his family. But his sons denied the coming crisis and procrastinated. They sat around looking at each other as if they didn't know what to do!

Many of us are more like Jacob's boys than Jacob. We are comfortable where we are, and when faced with a long and difficult journey, we'd rather stay home. We don't move until we have to. But by then it can be too late.

This story sheds light on our spiritual lives. Like Jacob's family, we can't find what we need most where we are now. Our relationship with Christ once nourished our souls but has become as dry as a famine-plagued desert. Second, we are reluctant to move. The status quo is just easier. Third, a crisis is looming. Ultimately we will starve and die if we don't do what must be done. Our wives and families will suffer along with us. Finally, we know where to go to find what we need.

Embarking on a life-giving spiritual journey means leaving comfortable but sinful habits behind, enduring the rigors of a new and different life, overcoming barriers, and dealing with our past failures. But the riches of the kingdom of God wait at the end of the journey.

KNOWING WHEN TO HIDE

A prudent man foresees evil and hides himself,
but the simple pass on and are punished.
PROVERBS 22:3 NKJV

Sometimes situations call for us to stand boldly against injustice or in favor of the oppressed. The prophet Nathan stood against King David and his sin of adultery (2 Samuel 12). Peter and John stood against Annas, Caiaphas, and other members of the high priest's family when they were told never to teach anything about the name of Jesus again (Acts 4).

Other times we are called to run and hide, as mentioned in the verse above. The New International Version, New Living Translation, New American Standard Bible, the New King James Version, and The Message describe the person in this verse as "prudent." In other words, they are wise—immersed in the scriptures, able to know the difference about when to stand and when to run. And when trouble is on the way—the type of trouble that doesn't need to be confronted, they run. Noah heard God's voice, saw impending trouble, and he hid in the ark. Joseph was tempted by Potiphar's wife, and he ran in the opposite direction.

Do you see trouble coming in your own life? What is your first instinct? Whatever it is, how does it compare or contrast with the wisdom of the verse above? If you haven't fully developed your sense of discernment, consider enlisting the help of a godly friend who can help you navigate the situation and maybe avoid one of the biggest mistakes of your life.

HOW WE GROW

So get rid of all evil behavior. Be done with all deceit, hypocrisy, jealousy, and all unkind speech. Like newborn babies, you must crave pure spiritual milk so that you will grow into a full experience of salvation. Cry out for this nourishment, now that you have had a taste of the Lord's kindness.

1 PETER 2:1–3 NLT

Jesus told His followers to become like children in order to enter the kingdom of God (Matthew 18:3), but Peter seems to take things a step further, telling his readers to become like infants.

Imagining infants who have a simple, single-minded dependence on their mothers for milk, you can catch a glimpse of what Peter has in mind. Perhaps his readers struggled with many serious sins such as envy, hypocrisy, criticism, and deceit because they had turned their faith into something complex. They wondered if they could work harder in order to overcome these many spiritual struggles.

Peter assured them that trying harder wouldn't cut it. They had to become all the *more* dependent on God's nurturing care for them. There's no hope outside of God's spiritual provision for His children.

You may long to stop envying or to become more spiritual, but these are merely dead ends. Your longing should be for the presence of the Lord instead. When you have tasted the goodness of the Lord, you'll find deliverance from your greatest struggles.

THE DIVINE PROMISE

Through these he has given us his very great and precious promises,
so that through them you may participate in the divine nature,
having escaped the corruption in the world caused by evil desires.

2 PETER 1:4 NIV

Simply avoiding hell isn't the point of salvation. Arguably that might be enough from a human perspective, but God has something more in mind for us, something far more interesting and exciting.

God's plan, as incredible as it may sound, is that we should partake in and reflect His own divine nature. He wants children that look and sound and act like their Father, free from corruption inside and out. "Therefore, having these promises, beloved, let us cleanse ourselves from all defilement of flesh and spirit, perfecting holiness in the fear of God" (2 Corinthians 7:1 NASB).

What were God's promises? That He would live among His people and be their God, that they would be set apart from the world, even counted as His sons and daughters (2 Corinthians 6). How are those promises fulfilled? Through His Holy Spirit living in us:

"I will give them an undivided heart and put a new spirit in them" (Ezekiel 11:19 NIV).

"When you believed, you were marked in him with a seal, the promised Holy Spirit" (Ephesians 1:13 NIV).

The role of the Holy Spirit is to create a people who could freely and honestly interact with God. Without His working in us, nothing in our experience will ever change, and He won't get the children He wants. Only through the Holy Spirit indwelling and empowering us can we live out the full plan of our salvation.

PRESERVED FOR THE KINGDOM

Love the LORD, all his faithful people! The LORD preserves those who are true to him, but the proud he pays back in full.

PSALM 31:23 NIV

In today's verse, the psalmist, King David, explains the benefit of faithfulness to the Lord: He preserves you.

But in what sense? Don't bad things happen to faithful believers? Certainly you know believers who have died in car accidents, suffered from cancer, or been victims of violence. While God does sometimes intervene in certain cases but not in others, the psalmist isn't referring to the here and now as much as he is speaking of the eternal.

Bible commentator John Gill makes this observation in his *Exposition of the Entire Bible*: "These he not only preserves in a providential way, but he preserves them in a way of special grace; he keeps them. . . from the evil of sin; from a total and final falling away by it; from the evil of the world, so as not to be drawn off from Christ and his ways, either by its frowns or flatteries; and from the evil one, Satan, from being destroyed by him and his temptations; and these are preserved safe to the kingdom and glory of Christ."

Spend some time this morning thanking God for preserving you in spite of your unworthiness. And then set your mind and will on being faithful to Him.

SPEAKING JOYFULLY

He put a new song in my mouth, a hymn of praise to our God.
Many will see and fear the LORD and put their trust in him.
PSALM 40:3 NIV

Those who follow Jesus Christ have more reason than anyone to think thoughts and speak words that reflect the joy God's Word says us we are to have. Jesus has promised us abundant life here on earth, as well as an eternity in paradise. What's not to love about that?

Sadly, too many Christians play the part of Gloomy Gus (for the brothers in the faith) or Debbie Downer (for the sisters) as though they were born for it.

Have you ever known a professing believer who always seems to be complaining and grumbling about what's been going on in his life, a believer who, on the outside anyway, seems completely devoid of the joy of the Lord? That person isn't a lot of fun to be around, is he? Which brings us to another question: Are *you* that kind of Christian?

The Bible is filled with examples of men whose life situations weren't exactly reasons in and of themselves for happy or joyful attitudes. But instead of spending their time moaning and groaning, they focused on what God was doing in and through them. The result? The joy of the Lord so filled them that everyone they spoke to or wrote to could see it.

Never let it escape you that even when life throws difficulty and suffering your way, you can have the joy of the Lord so fill you that you can't help but let it affect the way you speak.

SPIRITUAL PROSPERITY

*Better is the poor who walks in his integrity than
one who is perverse in his lips, and is a fool.*
PROVERBS 19:1 NKJV

The man who walks in his integrity is satisfied at the end of the day. He's done an honest day's worth of work, treated people well, and comes home to a meal that no king would necessarily desire, but it fills his stomach and he's thankful for it. He has nothing to be ashamed about. He's put forth his best effort, and tomorrow is another day.

The man who is crooked, however, is foolish. He speaks lies and cuts corners to get ahead. He mistreats people for his own gain. He dines extravagantly and drives fancy vehicles. His conscience bothers him from time to time, but he rationalizes his actions, telling himself that everybody does wrong things. He covers up his sins and falls asleep scheming about the next day.

Not surprisingly, the Hebrew word for *integrity* in today's verse can be translated as "prosperity." So, better is the poor who walks in his spiritual prosperity than the one who is perverse in his lips. That would seem to indicate a spiritual divide between the person who spends time tending to spiritual matters versus the person who spends time scheming to get ahead.

Proverbs 19:1 doesn't really speak about middle ground or about the middle class and its values. So ask yourself which side of the spectrum you're currently on and which values you're cultivating.

COMFORT IN TIMES OF STRESS

Trouble and distress have come upon me,
but your commands give me delight.
PSALM 119:143 NIV

New Christians, or those still working to become more mature in their faith, are sometimes shocked that the Christian life isn't free of trouble and stress. Some of them can even become disillusioned when they realize that many facets of their new life are like their old one in that they face a lot of the same problems they did before they were saved.

The plain biblical truth is that God never promised you an easy or trouble-free life. In fact, many scriptures promise you exactly the opposite. Take these words straight from the mouth of Jesus: "In this world you will have trouble" (John 16:33 NIV).

If life here on earth hasn't already affirmed that truth for you, take a closer look at today's verse. Notice that the psalmist doesn't thank God for keeping his life free of trouble and stress. Instead, he freely acknowledges that he's going through a rough time and that the troubles he's enduring are affecting him internally.

But this same psalmist ends his declaration that he's going through some difficulties with these words of hope: "Your commands give me delight." He had learned an important life lesson, namely that God didn't always keep his life free of problems but was always there for him, even in the most difficult of times.

REST IN THE LORD

The Lord replied, "My Presence will go
with you, and I will give you rest."
Exodus 33:14 NIV

This is a tremendously encouraging promise. Moses apparently had a pretty clear idea of the hardships that awaited them in the barren Sinai Desert and of the enemies that they'd face in Canaan, which is why he pleaded with the Lord, "If your Presence does not go with us, do not send us up from here" (v. 15). Moses knew that they didn't dare face such challenges unless God was with them.

However, as it turned out, even though God upheld His end of the bargain and did mighty miracles to bless them and protect them, the Israelites constantly doubted and disobeyed Him. The result? God vowed, "So I swore in My wrath, 'They shall not enter My rest' " (Psalm 95:11 NKJV).

God still promises to give His people perfect peace and rest, and this can only be found by dwelling in His presence. The Bible promises that "he who dwells in the secret place of the Most High shall abide under the shadow of the Almighty," and "under His wings you shall take refuge" (Psalm 91:1, 4 NKJV). That's where you want to be—under His wings and close to His heart.

Have you found rest by spending time in the presence of God? Spend some time in prayer today, meditating on Him and His Word.

THE BIBLICAL WORK ETHIC

*The stingy are eager to get rich and are
unaware that poverty awaits them.*
PROVERBS 28:22 NIV

You don't have to look far to find get-rich-quick schemes. They are never presented as such, but if you listen to the pitch for any length of time, it's hard to conclude otherwise. Often, those who are at the lower levels of these schemes have the best of intentions. They are just trying to make a little money on the side, but when they hear the promises of greater riches if they can sign up more people, they start to see real dollar signs.

The Bible warns against such selfishness, saying you will end up worse off than you can imagine. Commentators say that such a heart leads to envy, dishonesty, and covetousness—grieving over those who have more. Such wealth is gone as quickly as it comes. In the most extreme cases, freedom is lost as well. To make matters worse, when these schemes topple, those who are involved lose their reputation and even friendships among those they take down with them.

The biblical work ethic has always been about slow and steady growth (Proverbs 6:6, Matthew 20:1–16), accomplished with hard work that is performed with the utmost of integrity, as unto the Lord (Colossians 3:23). If you are weighing a business opportunity that isn't in line with either of those principles, run from it. It isn't from God.

RAISED FOR OUR FORGIVENESS

He was delivered over to death for our sins and
was raised to life for our justification.
ROMANS 4:25 NIV

Peter and John stayed close to Jesus after He was arrested, and John—being "known to the high priest"—was allowed into the high priest's confines, where Jesus was first interrogated. John went back to bring Peter in (John 18:15–16). It was shortly after this that Peter denied, with curses, that he even knew Jesus.

It is a measure of Peter's later honesty and humility that he let the account of his denial be put into writing. But perhaps this helps explain his extraordinary relief at seeing his Lord alive again.

Peter was the first disciple to enter Jesus' tomb. And in Luke 24:34, reference is made to Jesus appearing to Simon Peter alone, before the famous "closed doors" appearances to the eleven disciples. Why this concentration on Peter?

The denial.

Here's Luke again: When Peter disowned Jesus for the third time, "the Lord turned and looked straight at Peter. . .and [Peter] went outside and wept bitterly" (Luke 22:61–62 NIV).

What an incredible moment. Peter had heaped on Jesus His own personal crucifixion. So when Peter met Jesus alive again and found that He would absolve him from his guilt in person *because He had risen*, the relief—mixed with shame at having denied his Lord—must have hit Peter like a tidal wave.

Crucified to forgive our sins, risen to deliver that forgiveness. What a delivery that was for Peter! And for us.

THE HIGH ROAD OF FORGIVENESS

*Make allowance for each other's faults, and forgive anyone
who offends you. Remember, the Lord forgave
you, so you must forgive others.*

COLOSSIANS 3:13 NLT

We live in a time when it seems that even the slightest verbal barb or insult can start a war of words—on social media or through other forms of modern technology. The exchanges can be ugly too; just think of the last time you read or heard of a "Twitter war" between two celebrities. One insult can start a seemingly endless string of messages, sometimes turning into a highly personal electronic game of "Can you top this?"

That's just fallen human nature, isn't it? In and of themselves, people aren't prone to just "take the high road" and let insults and "cuts" go without responding in kind. But God tells His people that it should never be that way with you. He challenges you in His Word to choose forgiveness, even when someone has intentionally or maliciously caused you pain.

So the next time someone cuts you off in traffic, the next time someone carelessly speaks hurtful words, or the next time you've been offended because of something someone did, take the high road and forgive that person.

That's the road God took when He extended forgiveness to you through His Son, Jesus Christ, and it's the same high road He wants you to take with those who have insulted or hurt you.

WANTING GOD'S BEST FOR YOU

I, Paul, am on special assignment for Christ, carrying out God's plan laid out in the Message of Life by Jesus. I write this to you, Timothy, the son I love so much. All the best from our God and Christ be yours!
2 TIMOTHY 1:1–2 MSG

What does it mean to want and receive God's best for you? First, it means discarding inadequate, insufficient, ignoble thoughts of God. Herman Melville said, "The reason the mass of men fear God, and at bottom dislike Him, is because they rather distrust His heart, and fancy Him all brain like a watch." Second, wanting God's best means seeing Him as He really is. David Needham writes, "I am convinced that the answers to every problem and issue of life for both time and eternity are resolved through a correct understanding of God." Third, receiving God's best means shedding your intense desire for temporal pursuits and possessions. George MacDonald observed, "Man finds it hard to get what he wants, because he does not want the best; God finds it hard to give, because He would give the best, and man will not take it." Fourth, wanting and receiving God's best means desiring His will over and against your own will. C. S. Lewis put it this way: "There are two kinds of people: those who say to God, 'Thy will be done,' and those to whom God says, 'All right, then, have it your way.' " What did you hope to gain this year? Have you gained it yet? If yes, is it God's best? If no, again, is it God's best?

GOD IS YOUR STRENGTH

Though we are overwhelmed by our sins, you forgive them all.
PSALM 65:3 NLT

How often do you mistake being strong in the Lord with simply being strong on your own?

There are no caveats in this psalm about being stronger than your sins. There are no special exceptions for people who are especially determined when it comes to their weaknesses and imperfections. Sin may overpower you, no matter how much you may want to choose obedience. This is not to excuse sinning. The Bible says, after all, that one of the fruits of the Spirit is self-control (Galatians 5:22–23). So God does expect you to resist sin.

But you can't make yourself more determined or more focused on your own. Your one and only recourse is the mercy and grace of a loving God. If you want to find your strength each day, you must find God, even if that requires beginning with a confession of your failures and weaknesses.

Whether you feel overwhelmed and powerless or you're gritting your teeth in determination, you'll never advance to a point that you'll be able to blot out your own sins. If you rely on your strength and willpower, you'll most assuredly lose eventually. But God's mercy and strength will be there to meet you and deliver you. So cry out to God for His strength.

Once you rest in God, your strength will be endless.

MODELING CONSISTENT SELF-CONTROL

Teach the older men to be temperate, worthy of respect, self-controlled, and sound in faith, in love and in endurance.
TITUS 2:2 NIV

The apostle Paul left Titus, one of his charges, behind in Crete to do the difficult work of appointing leaders for the churches in each town (Titus 1:5). Paul gave him instructions about which type of men to choose as leaders, as well as instructing him about the type of people they would be ministering to.

Paul quoted and confirmed what one of the Cretan prophets said, "The people of Crete always tell lies. They are greedy and lazy like wild animals" (Titus 1:12 CEV). He wanted Titus to be hard on such people so they could grow strong in their faith (v. 13). This brings us to the verse above regarding older men in Crete. Ordinarily, older men don't need to be told to have self-control and to be serious and sensible, but apparently the older men in Crete were among those who were greedy and lazy and therefore needed to hear this message.

When young Christian men are unable to look up to older men in the faith in matters of appetite control, a sense of hopelessness can set in. If older Christian men cannot temper the flesh, what hope does a young man have? Regardless of where you find yourself on the age spectrum, self-control is not only possible, but followers of Christ are called to exhibit it.

MORE THAN AN "ATTA BOY!"

*Praise the LORD, all you nations. Praise him, all you people
of the earth. For his unfailing love for us is powerful;
the LORD's faithfulness endures forever. Praise the LORD!*
PSALM 117:1–2 NLT

Christian men demonstrate wisdom every time they praise God. Nations who honor God make the right choices. Every bit of praise and every word of honor should be a response to the God who never fails to love and who demonstrates His faithfulness every moment of each new day.

Some translations say God's love is *steadfast*. This word suggests something unmovable—like a mountain or a house-sized boulder in the middle of a stream. God's love is unfailing, powerful, and guaranteed to last forever. It's not going anywhere.

You can't earn it, make Him love you more, or make Him love you less. You're one of His creations, and His love extends to every human ever born—even the ones you don't like.

This is where the praise should be lavished on a magnificent God. He's good. He's mighty. He loves you. Praise and honor isn't simply an "Atta boy!" shouted out to God. Your praise should take the time to think of the many blessings you've discovered in your walk with God that brought you to this moment. By remembering the past, you're able to see more clearly that God's unfailing love has always been enough to get you to, through, and beyond life's toughest moments.

THE ODDS ARE IN YOUR FAVOR

*The Spirit of the Lord GOD is upon me, because the LORD has
anointed me to bring good news to the afflicted; He has sent me
to bind up the brokenhearted, to proclaim liberty to captives,
and freedom to prisoners; to proclaim the favorable year
of the LORD, and the day of vengeance of our God.*

ISAIAH 61:1–2 NASB

Our God is an amazingly giving Person. He sent His Son to bring the
good news of a truly amazing opportunity. Christ was sent to proclaim
"the favorable *year* of the Lord" and "the *day*" of judgment by God.
That's a 365 to 1 ratio in our favor! This propitious arrangement is
symbolic of God's great mercy and patience, "not wishing for any
to perish but for all to come to repentance" (2 Peter 3:9 NASB). He
is interested in us in a way that does not always make sense. Even
Jesus' disciples didn't quickly grasp this divine patience, eager to
"command fire to come down from heaven and consume" those
who rejected Christ (Luke 9:54 NASB). The Lord's response was firm:
"But He turned and rebuked them, and said, 'You do not know what
kind of spirit you are of; for the Son of Man did not come to destroy
men's lives, but to save them' " (Luke 9:55–56 NASB).

God wants *all* to repent. To confuse this time of favor and opportunity is to be of a *different spirit* than the Lord; not "regard[ing]
the patience of our Lord as salvation" (2 Peter 3:15 NASB) is to miss
God's heart and the chance to be part of it.

LIVING WITH INTEGRITY

At this, the administrators and the satraps tried to find grounds
for charges against Daniel in his conduct of government affairs,
but they were unable to do so. They could find no corruption in him,
because he was trustworthy and neither corrupt nor negligent.

DANIEL 6:4 NIV

The famous Christian motivational speaker Zig Ziglar once said, "With integrity, you have nothing to fear, since you have nothing to hide. With integrity, you will do the right thing, so you will have no guilt." The Old Testament prophet Daniel demonstrated integrity in every part of his life. He honored God—and God honored the prophet in return. . .and also saved him from becoming some hungry lion's lunch (see Daniel 6:10–23).

Daniel had his enemies, but it turns out he had nothing to fear, simply because he had conducted all his affairs in a way that honored and pleased his God.

Bottom line: a real man of God will conduct every part of his life the way the Bible says a man of God should. That's just what integrity looks like.

You honor and please God and establish a good reputation with others when you make sure you live every part of your life—your family life, your work life, and every other aspect—with integrity.

When you do just that, God will honor you in return.

HOME SWEET HOME?

As long as we are at home in the body we are away from the Lord.
2 Corinthians 5:6 niv

In 2 Corinthians 5:1–10, Paul was speaking about his struggle between life and death. He realized that this physical life in some ways kept him from being "at home" with the Lord.

There is no doubt about it. We are "at home" in this physical world. Our planet is the one place in the universe where life flourishes. We were made for this place. More precisely, this world was created to be our home. Humankind, created in the image of God, was the ultimate purpose of all creation (Genesis 1:26–27).

But this world as it now exists is not our true home. We were never meant for this sin-ravaged and broken planet. We were never meant to experience the suffering and sadness of a cursed world. We were meant to enjoy intimacy with God without any barrier (Genesis 3).

Being "at home" also means being in a place where we feel comfortable, at rest, and at ease. Another way to think about Paul's insight is that the more comfortable we are, the more at home we feel in our sinful culture and society, the further we are from being at home with Christ and enjoying our walk with Him.

We should not be "at home" with this world's values, lifestyles, and priorities. We should be restless in this world. If we aren't uncomfortable here, we will never be truly "at home" with Christ.

THE PRIVILEGE OF PAIN

*For you have been given not only the privilege of trusting
in Christ but also the privilege of suffering for him.*
PHILIPPIANS 1:29 NLT

When the apostle Paul wrote of suffering, he did so with authority. He had suffered threats of death and more severe beatings than he could count. He had suffered through sleeplessness, hunger, thirst, and cold. His life as a servant of Jesus Christ was one of constant danger and great personal suffering (see 2 Corinthians 11:23–28).

But this same man not only wrote of suffering for Christ as a privilege, he also wrote of suffering as a means to grow in his faith: "We also glory in our sufferings, because we know that suffering produces perseverance; perseverance, character; and character, hope. And hope does not put us to shame, because God's love has been poured out into our hearts through the Holy Spirit, who has been given to us" (Romans 5:3–5 NIV).

In America these days, Christians don't suffer the way Paul did. This is a time and a place of peace and prosperity. But when you suffer—be it from a personal loss, an illness, a disability, or other difficulties—you can look at it as a privilege and a blessing. And you can live in the assurance that your joy is not based on your suffering or on your *lack* of suffering, but in knowing God intimately and walking with Him every day.

CURB APPEAL

The LORD says, "I will guide you along the best pathway for your life. I will advise you and watch over you."
PSALM 32:8 NLT

Curbs are a very useful, if not underappreciated, invention. They guide water to drains, provide a place for small boys to sit and dream on a warm summer day, provide a shape to streets, and act as a boundary for those who need to park.

Curbs are intended to keep us from going where we shouldn't go while framing the route we should take.

We need curbs. We make better decisions with curbs. We find safety because of curbs. When everyone acknowledges these boundary markers, traffic flows smoothly. Imagine the chaos if people decided it was better to drive across lawns or parks.

We have our own set of internal curbs. These are the boundaries we learned as we grew up. This might include something simple like not touching a hot stove or something more complex like not taking something that doesn't belong to you.

God has given us curbs in the Bible, His good commands that direct us how to live wisely and lovingly as His children. When we refuse to live within these curbs, we find ourselves in trouble while we ruin things that belong to other people.

Cars are perfectly equipped to ride between the curbs on the street—so are we when it comes to God's commands in scripture.

HOW LONG?

*"As in the days when you came out of Egypt,
I will show them my wonders."*
MICAH 7:15 NIV

The women have to avert their eyes, cover them, or the pain snaps through their eyes straight into the front of their heads. They know it's the right tomb. It has the same stone, though it's been moved. And that's the cloth that Jesus' body was rolled in, blood and all.

But suddenly two men are there in lightning-bright garments. Such brilliance replacing such gloom throws them to the ground. They're stunned and amazed. Something unimaginable is happening. But the instruction is simple: "Get up, and go tell his disciples."

Later, they follow Jesus north to Galilee. Jesus is speaking, and a low cloud rolls down the slope—they'd seen it happen on these mountains a thousand times—but then this cloud is blowing back up to the sky with Jesus on it, hands outstretched.

Then, suddenly that headache again: the same two men (*men?*) blazingly dressed, and they barely hear what these men say because of the wonder of how they look and their amazement at what just happened. They can't stop staring. But then the two men say, "What are you doing standing here? He told you what to do!"

How long has it been since God's wonders have left us speechless? Have we seen grace in the trust of a child, grandeur in a sunset, a forest, or a tall ship? How long has it been since an angel has had to bring us back down to earth while we were standing open-mouthed with wonder?

THE SHIELD OF FAITH

In addition to all, taking up the shield of faith with which you will
be able to extinguish all the flaming arrows of the evil one.
EPHESIANS 6:16 NASB

The shield of faith is a very important part of your spiritual battle gear. It's primarily a defensive piece of weaponry. The KJV mentions "fiery darts," what we now refer to as flaming arrows. In ancient days, archers would unleash a vast barrage of arrows at one time against an enemy army. The best thing that the attackers could do was to hold up their shields to protect themselves from the deadly hail.

At times, the archers would cover their arrowheads in pitch and set them aflame to start fires in the opposition's camp. But if the arrows were stopped by shields, they went out harmlessly, without causing damage.

These flaming arrows are the lies of the devil, and in this passage God is promising that if you have faith in His Word, it will render Satan's onslaught of lies harmless. This is very important, because the devil continually seeks to wound you or take you out of commission with his discouragement, condemnation, and lies.

Don't become a casualty. Keep your shield of faith up to prevent his mental and spiritual attacks from taking you out. Your faith in God's love and mercy will "extinguish *all* the flaming arrows of the evil one."

FORSAKING WRONG DESIRES AND FEARS

*I eagerly expect and hope that I will in no way be ashamed, but will
have sufficient courage so that now as always Christ will be
exalted in my body, whether by life or by death.*

PHILIPPIANS 1:20 NIV

When are you most at risk of losing courage and feeling ashamed?
First, when you pursue wrong desires. Second, when you give in
to fear. Wrong desires often revolve around making more money,
amassing power, pursuing illicit sexuality, and pouring endless hours
into online multi-user games. All four are terribly damaging. Wrong
fears are just as bad. Imminent danger—real or perceived—triggers
the strongest of human emotions. Fear is hardwired into your brain.
It causes you to shut up, freeze up, give up. The good news: you can
rewire your thoughts, beliefs, and automatic responses. If anyone
proved that, it was Mother Teresa. One of her most haunting prayers:

> *Deliver me, O Jesus, / From the desire of being loved, / From
> the desire of being extolled, / From the desire of being honored,
> / From the desire of being praised, / From the desire of being
> preferred, / From the desire of being consulted, / From the
> desire of being approved, / From the desire of being popular,*
>
> *Deliver me, O Jesus, / From the fear of being humiliated, / From
> the fear of being despised, / From the fear of suffering rebukes,
> / From the fear of being slandered, / From the fear of being
> forgotten, / From the fear of being wronged, / From the fear of
> being ridiculed, / From the fear of being suspected. / Amen.*

ONLY THE UNQUALIFIED NEED APPLY

But the Lord said to Samuel, "Do not consider his appearance or his height, for I have rejected him. The Lord does not look at the things people look at. People look at the outward appearance, but the Lord looks at the heart."

1 Samuel 16:7 niv

What does a king look like? If you had asked that question in the days of Saul and David, you would have heard a lot about personal appearance: height, muscular build, and even tone of voice. Of course, people longed for kings who could lead competently, but the prophet Samuel made the common mistake of confusing a kingly bearing with kingly competence. Don't we all make the same mistake of assuming that the person who looks the part is the best qualified for ministry or leadership?

The Lord turns such thinking over, declaring that He looks on the heart. The heart trumps any other measure of competence or qualification. Perhaps this means that we should change the criteria we have for our leaders, but don't overlook the possibility that this passage applies to you as well. If you sense a potential call to serve in a place or capacity that feels beyond your skill set or abilities, there's a chance that God is still calling you forward in faith. The heart that is oriented toward God can accomplish far more than accumulated wisdom and experience. If you feel woefully unqualified for God's call, you're in very good company. In fact, God takes particular delight in using the supposedly "unqualified" to bless others.

THE LIVING AND WORKING WORD

We also constantly thank God that when you received the word
of God which you heard from us, you accepted it not as the
word of men, but for what it really is, the word of God,
which also performs its work in you who believe.
1 THESSALONIANS 2:13 NASB

In the first chapter of the Bible, we see that God's spoken Word was powerful enough to bring all of creation into being. John 1 further explains that the "Word of God" is the person of Jesus Christ Himself, through whom all things were created and find their purpose. Throughout the Bible, we see that God's Word continues to work since the beginning—giving life, protecting, enlightening, redeeming, effecting change according to God's will.

"So will My word be which goes forth from My mouth; it will not return to Me empty, without accomplishing what I desire, and without succeeding in the matter for which I sent it" (Isaiah 55:11 NASB).

God's Word works because it is *alive*. Jesus declares that "the words that I have spoken to you are spirit and are life" (John 6:63 NASB). The writer of Hebrews similarly asserts that "the word of God is living and active" (Hebrews 4:12 NASB). It works because it simply can't sit still!

Paul was delighted with the Thessalonians because they accepted his message as the authoritative, purposeful, and *living* thing that it was, and by doing so, opened up its divine power to work in their lives.

SPIRITUAL INVESTMENTS

*Godliness actually is a means of great gain
when accompanied by contentment.*
1 TIMOTHY 6:6 NASB

Godliness always begins with identifying yourself as a man willing to follow God. This decision can include a profound sense of gratitude to the One you're certain holds the answers to living life well, has a plan for your life, and customized it specifically for you. Godliness seeks to line up personal decision-making within the framework of God's Word.

Instead of being fixated on what you don't own, godly living suggests that being content with what you have is a better option. The reason is simple. This current life is extremely short when compared with the eternal life God has prepared for His children, and some things people invest in have extremely short shelf lives.

Matthew 6:19–20 (NASB) says, "Do not store up for yourselves treasures on earth, where moth and rust destroy, and where thieves break in and steal. But store up for yourselves treasures in heaven, where neither moth nor rust destroys, and where thieves do not break in or steal."

Spending time chasing things you can never take to heaven is a poor use of time and resources. The three greatest investments you'll ever make in life are relationships with God, family, and friends. People are the only investments you have any chance of seeing again in heaven.

Godliness + contentment = God's approved life investment strategy.

BECOME A GOD PLEASER

*Am I now trying to win the approval of human beings, or of God?
Or am I trying to please people? If I were still trying to
please people, I would not be a servant of Christ.*
GALATIANS 1:10 NIV

The apostle Paul was indeed a people pleaser at one point in his life. As a Pharisee, he studied to show himself approved by men. As a persecutor of those who followed Jesus, he pleased men by holding the coats of the men who stoned Stephen to death (Acts 7:58). He even approached the high priest at one point for permission to persecute Christians (Acts 9:1–2).

Post conversion, Paul became a God pleaser, contending for the Gospel at all cost, no matter what man thought. His letter to the Galatian church was a warning. He heard that they were straying from God and ultimately the Gospel as it had been taught to them by the apostles. His language was sharp, saying, "I pray that God will punish anyone who preaches anything different from our message to you! It doesn't matter if that person is one of us or an angel from heaven" (Galatians 1:8 CEV).

As believers, we are called to love one another and our neighbors as ourselves. And we are called to be humble. But when a false gospel is presented, we must speak the truth as lovingly as possible. We cannot afford to be people pleasers when it comes to the Gospel. Souls are at stake. We are not servants of Christ if we compromise in this area.

SIN?

*Dear friends, if our hearts do not condemn us, we have
confidence before God and receive from him anything we ask,
because we keep his commands and do what pleases him.*

1 JOHN 3:21–22 NIV

Overcoming sin: it's the challenge of every Christian's life. We struggle, we strain, we "put things before the Lord" that we don't like in
our lives, we attack one area at a time, and we do a lot of good. We
trust God, we ask for the Holy Spirit to help us in practical ways, and
He does it. This is all great, but there is a side of this that gets little
notice. Most of us overcome sin daily in ways we don't even recognize,
ways we can easily build on.

Church. Worshiping God. That's not sin. Shut-in visitation, prison
visitation, prayer or devotions with the family, devotional books. No
sin there. Relaxation. Recreation. Exercise. Working on the "honey-
do" list. Yes, it can be overdone. But when we ride, are we sinning?
Not likely. We're staying healthy; we can maybe live and serve the
Lord longer. No sin there.

Family barbecues? Sitting on the porch with my wife? Any sin
there? No!

When we spend our energy for God's kingdom, when we spend
our energy on the good, we don't leave energy or time for sin. That
is, indeed, overcoming sin; and we barely even realize it. Then, when
we look at all the sins that don't happen in our lives, it gives us mo-
mentum to build on, to keep sin out of our lives.

KIND WORDS SPOKEN

*Kind words are like honey—sweet to the
soul and healthy for the body.*
PROVERBS 16:24 NLT

In recent years, leaders in the modern corporate or business world have made an interesting discovery: many, if not most, workers tend to perform better when the boss or supervisor gives them verbal pats on the back for their good work. This may be old news to you, but it was apparently a revelation to many hard-boiled business leaders.

This challenges you as a Christian to consider something: Would the same principle work on your wife and children, your friends, and your coworkers, or the people you lead in the workplace? Well, if you take today's verse to its logical conclusion. . .yes, it would!

People are just naturally *wired*—or should we say *created*—to need affirming, kind words. And while there is certainly a place for correction and discipline, never forget that everyone needs to hear some kind words coming from those they love and those whom God has placed in authority over them.

Do you want to see the best in your wife and children, in your friends, and in those you work with? Try speaking kind words to them. Verbalize your observations of something they're doing well. Let them know you appreciate them for the things they do and for who they are. Let them know they're valued. The results just might pleasantly surprise you.

OVERFLOWING

*For we wanted to come to you—I, Paul, more than once—and yet
Satan hindered us. For who is our hope or joy or crown of exultation?
Is it not even you, in the presence of our Lord Jesus at
His coming? For you are our glory and joy.*
1 Thessalonians 2:18–20 NASB

Paul's enthusiasm for the Thessalonian believers bursts forth in these words, using language usually reserved for God Himself. Imagine! Paul's "hope" and "joy" and "glory" are tied to this small group of people into whom he has poured his life. When Jesus returns, Paul plans on showing them off.

When we come to Christ, we begin our experience as a child of God. We are adopted (Romans 8:15) and begin rethinking our lives as one of His offspring. Then as we share our faith and help people grow in Christ, we begin to see the *other* side of the relationship— the parental side. God's side. This is what Paul is expressing and why he speaks so joyfully. He's displaying the same excited attitude toward the Thessalonians that God has about all of us—pride and joy!

Paul reflects God's joy toward his own "children" in the faith because God's parental joy is contagious. Like Paul did with the Thessalonians, God rejoices over us, brags about us, dotes on us, and takes pride in us—and the things He's preparing in heaven for those who love Him are beyond imagination (1 Corinthians 2:9). When we see Him face to face, we will truly understand what an extravagant parent God is. We will rejoice in Him, and He will rejoice in us.

PLEASING THE WEAKER BROTHER

We who are strong ought to bear with the failings
of the weak and not to please ourselves.

ROMANS 15:1 NIV

If you've ever wondered whether you fall into the "stronger" or "weaker" brother camp as expressed in the scriptures, the truth in Romans 15:1 might help you answer that question.

Generally speaking, stronger brothers have been and continue to be immersed in the Word. They have clarity regarding the precepts of God. They are under authority and accountable. And they treat those who are just starting out in their faith journey with the utmost respect and patience—so much so that they try to please their brother rather than themselves.

When it comes to matters of food and drink and various other issues that fall under the banner of Christian liberty, stronger Christians should never attempt to flaunt such liberties, but rather be sensitive toward the weaker believer who is still formulating his personal theological understanding of such things.

If that means not ordering a glass of wine at dinner with a weaker brother who might object, then the stronger believer gladly does so out of love and concern for how his actions might be perceived by the weaker brother.

As the weaker brother grows, he will find himself in the presence of newer, weaker brothers, and your witness of loving him right where he was will help him to do the same for others.

NERVOUS, NERVOUS, NERVOUS

For what I received I passed on to you as of first importance:
that Christ died for our sins according to the Scriptures, that he
was buried, that he was raised on the third day according to
the Scriptures. . . . But by the grace of God I am what I am.
1 CORINTHIANS 15:3–4, 10 NIV

We are God's ambassadors. This means that people will hold God to whatever we say about Him. On top of that, if what we tell people about God is wrong, He isn't going to back it up.

Yet He will hold us accountable for it.

Quite a spot to be on. We'd better explain Him correctly, or God will hold us accountable. As will the world.

We catch it coming, and we catch it going. Who on earth can handle that kind of responsibility? The answer is. . .nobody can.

That's why the stories He asks us to tell are so breathtakingly simple. Whether it's the story of Jesus or our own story that we tell the world, they're both almost impossible to get wrong!

Plus, we have the Holy Spirit to back us up, to give our words power, and to prod us if we go off on some tangent.

And He has left us His Word, which tells the life of Jesus and what He did to save us four times—in black and white, unmistakable. And surely we know our own testimony! This isn't metaphysics. It isn't some convoluted quest for enlightenment. There is little to be nervous about.

ASKING GOD FOR EVEN MORE COURAGE

"The thief comes only to steal and kill and destroy;
I came that they may have life, and have it abundantly."
JOHN 10:10 NASB

Life is full of circumstances that test our courage. Winston Churchill once said, "Without courage, all other virtues lose their meaning." It doesn't matter that you're honest, for instance, if you're afraid to tell the truth. Or that you're responsible if you're afraid to try anything new. It's ironic that our society is bent on the idea of trying to become more rebellious, more risk-taking, less inhibited, more outrageous, less self-controlled. Many blame these trends on the 1960s, but the reality is—people have always been bent away from self-control. This bent against self-control, however, inevitably hurts our community, our family, and our friends. Ultimately, it hurts us. If you and I lack self-control, who's in control of our thoughts, speech, and actions? One option is we're giving in to the desires of the nature we were born with. That nature's passions and desires are anything but positive, healthy, or life-giving. Another option is we may be manipulated or controlled by the Devil. If we let Satan control us, he will rob us of everything that's good in our lives. He will tempt us to take risky, dangerous, physically destructive, or suicidal actions that could kill us. So what other option is there? It's the option Jesus calls having "life. . . abundantly." Whatever you do today, choose that option! Specifically, ask God to strengthen you in your inner man, to cleanse and fill you, to cause you to be more self-controlled and courageous than ever.

FIRST IMPRESSIONS

Just then Boaz arrived from Bethlehem and greeted the harvesters,
"The LORD be with you!" "The LORD bless you!" they answered.

RUTH 2:4 NIV

When you're first introduced to Boaz, a key character in the beautiful story of redemption that is the book of Ruth, you get a pretty good idea of what kind of man he is. After he greets his workers with a hearty "The LORD be with you!" they respond with an equally enthusiastic "The LORD bless you!"

These words give you a great first impression of Boaz, don't they? Right away, you know that Boaz is a godly man who apparently treats his servants with kindness and compassion, and you know they know him as a man who loves God and others.

As you make your way through Ruth's story, you find that your first impressions of Boaz are well-founded. He indeed is a man who loves God and cares for the well-being of those who enter his sphere of influence.

Someone has rightly observed that you have only one chance to make a first impression. What kind of first impression do your words and actions make on those you meet? Do you think people who encounter you know right away that you're a man who loves God and loves other people—no matter their position in life—and wants to bless them?

That's a first impression any follower of Jesus should want to make on everyone he meets.

OPENING YOUR EYES

For since the creation of the world His invisible attributes, His eternal power and divine nature, have been clearly seen, being understood through what has been made, so that they are without excuse.

ROMANS 1:20 NASB

Invisibility doesn't mean inaccessibility. Just because a thing cannot be seen doesn't mean it can't be known or understood in some meaningful way. The air we breathe is an example. So are the inner qualities of people: diligence, intelligence, impatience. When we see a beautiful painting, we see clearly the invisible quality called *talent*. In the same way, God declares that at least two of His invisible qualities have been "clearly *seen*" from the creation itself. First, His eternal power, that He is outside of time, without beginning and without end. We don't have to wonder who came before Him or who will come after Him. What He promises to mankind will endure since there are no circumstances that can surprise Him. The second invisible quality is His divine nature. He is above the created order and not one of us. He was not born and will not die. He is the first and final authority of all things.

The irony of *seeing* the invisible is resolved in creation itself. The fullest revelation of God in Christ is not required for God to hold mankind accountable for at least the two qualities He has *published* across time and space. As the psalmist writes: "The heavens are telling of the glory of God; and their expanse is declaring the work of His hands. Day to day pours forth speech, and night to night reveals knowledge" (Psalm 19:1–2 NASB).

INSPIRED PEOPLE INSPIRE PEOPLE

[Hezekiah] encouraged them with these words: "Be strong and courageous. Do not be afraid or discouraged because of the king of Assyria and the vast army with him, for there is a greater power with us than with him. With him is only the arm of flesh, but with us is the LORD our God to help us and to fight our battles." And the people gained confidence from what Hezekiah the king of Judah said.
2 CHRONICLES 32:6–8 NIV

King Hezekiah stands in front of the people of Judah as they stare down an imminent siege from the terrifying Assyrian army, a force known for their murderous, grisly, and shocking terror tactics. Assyria's King Sennacherib does his best to terrorize Hezekiah; temporarily, the plan works. Read what happens next:

> *King Hezekiah and the prophet Isaiah son of Amoz cried out in prayer to heaven about this. And the LORD sent an angel, who annihilated all the fighting men and the commanders and officers in the camp of the Assyrian king. So he withdrew to his own land in disgrace. . . . So the LORD saved Hezekiah and the people of Jerusalem from the hand of Sennacherib. . . He took care of them on every side.*
> (2 Chronicles 32:20–22 NIV)

Hezekiah, trusting only in God's deliverance, was able to inspire an entire city despite a seemingly hopeless situation. As we've seen throughout this month, God heard and answered in an overwhelming way.

It's another story of God's action to encourage us today in our own lives.

A FOOL'S GAME

"The king reflected and said, 'Is this not Babylon the great, which I myself have built as a royal residence by the might of my power and for the glory of my majesty?' While the word was in the king's mouth, a voice came from heaven, saying, 'King Nebuchadnezzar, to you it is declared: sovereignty has been removed from you, and you will be driven away from mankind, and your dwelling place will be with the beasts of the field. . .until you recognize that the Most High is ruler over the realm of mankind, and bestows it on whomever He wishes.' "

DANIEL 4:30–32 NASB

Success and achievement are great—unless they lead you to forget basic spiritual truths. Truths like "You cannot really accomplish anything apart from God." He is the *Most High* and no matter how much we may achieve on earth, our "success" is ultimately His gift, for His purposes.

Another spiritual truth that's easily forgotten in the midst of success is that arrogance always invites correction. As the apostle Peter says, "God is opposed to the proud, but gives grace to the humble" (1 Peter 5:5 NASB). He doesn't *ignore* the proud, or *work around* them—He actively *opposes* them. When we are tempted to slap ourselves on the back, we should take note, as Nebuchadnezzar eventually did, that we are playing a fool's game. And you don't have to be some prideful "overachiever" to get God's attention. Anyone who takes credit for what God has done can enjoy His harsh mercy. God rebukes the foolishness of high and low alike because He is merciful to all.

KNOWING YOUR SOURCE

*Every good and perfect gift is from above,
coming down from the Father of the heavenly lights.*
JAMES 1:17 NIV

In a 2016 interview featured on the ESPN feature show *E:60*, interviewer Jeremy Schaap asked retiring sports broadcasting legend Vin Scully, "What are the moments that give you the most pride?"

Scully, a man of faith who began his broadcasting career in 1949, replied, "I don't know about pride. I try to keep that word out of my life. I really mean that when I say it. I'm not prideful. Because what has happened to me, I believe in all honesty, it was a gift that was given to me. I can lose that gift as soon as I get out of this chair. . .so there's really no pride."

The Bible has a lot to say about pride, and none of it's good. God tells us in His Word that He hates human pride and that He will actively oppose those with pride-filled hearts and minds (James 4:6).

But today's verse gives believers a great antidote for human pride, and it's this: keep in mind that every good thing we have and every good thing we accomplish in this life is a gift from God. So when the devil whispers in your ear that you should feel pride over something you've done, you do well to simply answer, "It's all a gift from my Father in heaven."

WHITEWASHED REBELLION

*"I want to see a mighty flood of justice,
an endless river of righteous living."*
AMOS 5:24 NLT

The people of Israel said the right things, sang great songs, and got together to celebrate their national religion. The prophet Amos wasn't impressed. God showed him where the people were at. He told them in verse 12, "I know the vast number of your sins and the depth of your rebellions." So God invited the people to come back to Him and seek His heart once more. He told them to hate evil and love what was good, stop the show and pretense, and cease the meaningless offerings (Amos 5:14–15, 22–23).

Hadn't they done the right things publicly, attended the expected religious services, and sought to show evidence of faithfulness? Yes, but God also saw every moment *out* of the public eye. He saw their divided heart. He was aware that they were engaged in whitewashed living, and it was time to confront their rebellion.

He wasn't interested in their diligent spiritual *to-do* list. God wanted the hearts of His people to line up with the desires of His heart. Righteous living and compassion were rarely practiced.

Today, God continues to look for righteous living among His people. He desires to see compassion poured out on behalf of those who need love more than a hearty "Serves you right." God still desires a people whose outer life lines up with His truth.

WHEN THINGS MAKES NO EARTHLY SENSE

*By faith Noah, when warned about things not yet seen,
in holy fear built an ark to save his family.*
HEBREWS 11:7 NIV

The unknown writer of Hebrews opens the eleventh chapter of his epistle by defining faith as "confidence in what we hope for and assurance about what we do not see" (Hebrews 11:1 NIV). He then goes on to show what that means through several Old Testament examples.

One of those examples is Noah, who, in obedience to God's command, built a giant ship called an ark to preserve him, his family, and representatives of every living creature from perishing during the Flood.

Noah's story is one of amazing faith on the part of one man. When you read God's instructions to him (see Genesis 6:12–22), you notice that not once did Noah question or test God. The end of this passage simply tells us that, "Noah did everything just as God commanded him" (Genesis 6:22 NIV). And because of his faith and obedience in the face of something he couldn't yet see, his family and all the animals were saved.

The apostle James tells us that even evil spirits believe in God—and tremble in fear (James 2:19). Faith, therefore, means not just believing in God, but believing God when He speaks and then acting on His promises and commands even when they don't make any earthly sense.

STRIVING VERSUS CONTENTMENT

I saw that all toil and all achievement spring from one person's envy of another. This too is meaningless, a chasing after the wind.

ECCLESIASTES 4:4 NIV

People were trying to keep up with the Joneses and Jonahs even back in Bible times. Solomon took a long, hard look at the agrarian society of his own Middle Eastern kingdom and realized that all toil and all achievement sprang from one person's envy of another. Most Israelites weren't wealthy and usually had just enough to make ends meet. Yet even they prided themselves in what few comforts, objects of beauty, and amenities they could afford.

People are always comparing themselves to those around them, even though the Bible says that they, "measuring themselves by themselves, and comparing themselves among themselves, are not wise" (2 Corinthians 10:12 KJV). This was such a persistent problem that right from the beginning God commanded, "You shall not covet. . . anything that is your neighbor's" (Exodus 20:17 NKJV). When you covet their belongings, you're likely to scheme to *take* those things.

In fact, even trying to accumulate material possessions through your own hard work can be misguided. The Bible says that any "pursuit of happiness" that expresses itself in the accumulation of things is bound to fail. It's "meaningless, a chasing after the wind." Jesus emphasized that "one's life does not consist in the abundance of the things he possesses" (Luke 12:15 NKJV). So, learn to be content.

WORKING WITH ALL YOUR HEART

*Whatever you do, work at it with all your heart, as working for
the Lord, not for human masters, since you know that you
will receive an inheritance from the Lord as a reward.
It is the Lord Christ you are serving.*
COLOSSIANS 3:23–24 NIV

How strange that the all-powerful, omniscient Lord God, Creator
of heaven and earth, allows human hands and hearts to do His will.
The man of noble character trusts God to work in and through him.
Such a man doesn't waste his time longing for a life without God's
calling and purpose. He certainly doesn't waste it longing for a life
of excitement, dissipation, pleasure, and ease. A noble man is a
God-filled, purpose-driven, and busy man. His hours and minutes are
measured and meaningful. "Being busy is not a sin," Max Lucado wisely
observes. "Jesus was busy. Paul was busy. Peter was busy. Nothing of
significance is achieved without effort and hard work and weariness.
That, in and of itself, is not a sin. But being busy in an endless pursuit
of things that leave us empty and hollow and broken inside—that
cannot be pleasing to God."

Looking back on the past month, what is your experience? To what
degree were you a noble man? Granted, God designed us to exercise,
sleep, eat. He designed us to shave, shower, dress. He designed us to
rest, relax, and recreate with family and friends. But that's not all—as
we will continue to consider in coming days.

OUT OF YOUR MIND

At this point Festus interrupted Paul's defense.
"You are out of your mind!"
Acts 26:24 NIV

When they heard Paul's story, King Agrippa and the Roman proconsul, Festus, thought he was insane. From their perspective, the evidence was overwhelming. Saul of Tarsus, the brilliant Jewish rabbi and trusted member of the Sanhedrin, abandoned a promising career to join and promote the outlawed sect he once wanted to destroy. He literally went from persecutor to persecuted preacher!

Paul stood before men who held his life in their hands and babbled on about dead men coming back to life and a heavenly vision, and then he tried to persuade them to join his movement (Acts 26)! No wonder Festus thought he was crazy and Agrippa was insulted!

Others may think great adventurers are out of their minds. Adventurers want to do what others think can't be done, take journeys others think are impossible, follow a vision others can't see, and take risks others fear. But that's what makes them heroes!

Deep in the heart of every man is an adventurer, a dreamer, and a hero. Like Paul, we long to follow the wild paths of a great vision. And, like Paul, that journey—the hero's journey—begins with an encounter with the living Christ.

The journey to spiritual transformation and a radical faith in God, participating in His work in the world, and finding our place in His kingdom is life's greatest adventure.

But we shouldn't be surprised if those around us say, "You are out of your mind!"

GOD REMEMBERS YOU

*God. . .will not forget your work and the love you have
shown him as you have helped his people.*
HEBREWS 6:10 NIV

Sometimes, despite God's promise to never leave or forsake you (Hebrews 13:5), you may feel like He has forgotten you. Isaiah urged, "The LORD has comforted His people and will have compassion on His afflicted. But Zion said, 'The LORD has forsaken me, and the Lord has forgotten me.' " To which God responded, "Can a woman forget her nursing child and have no compassion on the son of her womb? Even these *may* forget, but I will *not* forget you" (Isaiah 49:13–15 NASB, emphasis added).

It's difficult to imagine a nursing mother—the very epitome of tender love—having no compassion on her newborn child, but God assures you that His love for you is even deeper and stronger.

Perhaps you sometimes feel like God doesn't notice your faithful service for Him. One time, Isaiah—echoing the Jews' cry—lamented, "I have toiled in vain, I have spent My strength for nothing and vanity." Then, refusing to remain discouraged, he declared, "Yet surely the justice due to Me is with the LORD, and My reward with My God" (Isaiah 49:4 NASB).

God's love for you is eternal, and He notices every tiny thing you do. One day soon He will proclaim His love for you before all heaven and lavishly reward you.

ALLOWING GOD TO WRITE THE STORY

[David] said to Saul. . ."This day you have seen with your own eyes how the LORD delivered you into my hands in the cave. Some urged me to kill you, but I spared you; I said, 'I will not lay my hand on my lord, because he is the LORD's anointed.' See, my father. . . I cut off the corner of your robe but did not kill you."
1 SAMUEL 24:9–11 NIV

Despite having to constantly run from Saul, David's faith remained strong. His commitment to God's will and God's timing was absolute. Finding himself in the back of a cave while Saul sat tantalizingly within his grasp, David exercised almost unbelievable self-control. Even David's troops encouraged him to kill Saul, yet David resisted. He was content to let God be the one writing his story, refusing to take matters into his own hands.

How many men would have acted differently in this situation? How many men act in haste and trust in their own wits and instincts, hastily moving forward into business or personal situations that are fraught with potential consequences?

David wasn't going to usurp the throne of Israel. God had anointed him, and he trusted in God to make him the leader of His people whenever God wanted.

Are you facing a big decision? A major life change? Commit yourself to a time of prayer, of seeking God's face. Search the scriptures for God's leading, and discuss your situation with trusted and godly advisors. Time spent this way is never wasted.

IS TRUSTING GOD A "RISK"?

Those who live in the shelter of the Most High will find rest in the shadow of the Almighty. This I declare about the LORD: He alone is my refuge, my place of safety; he is my God, and I trust him.
PSALM 91:1–2 NLT

What would make you feel secure? For some it's a particular place. For others it may mean a certain amount of money in the bank or a particular position at work. Everyone craves security and assurances that they'll be safe from the storms of life that are sure to come.

What does it look like to dwell in God's shelter today and to have God's shadow over you? Perhaps it means releasing control over a specific life circumstance. For others, it may be a step of faith that feels more like a risk than a place of safety or security under God. The irony of living by faith and trusting God as your sole refuge and stronghold can feel risky and even a little chaotic as you perfect your faith in God.

As you grapple with your desires for security and safety, the words of this psalm challenge you to rethink your place under the protection of God. How does it feel to have God as your refuge and stronghold? Does it feel like a risk right now? Are there ways you can learn to grow deeper in your trust in God today?

THINK BEFORE YOU SPEAK

Out of the same mouth come praise and cursing.
My brothers and sisters, this should not be.
JAMES 3:10 NIV

Ever had someone ask you if your ears had been burning? That's a humorous way of saying that they'd been involved in a recent conversation with someone else, and *you* were the subject.

Human beings seem to love talking about other people, don't they? And sometimes those conversations aren't what the Bible would call "edifying." It's probably safe to say that every man, if he really thought about it, can recall moments in the recent past when he spoke unkind or damaging words about another person—more often than not, out of that person's earshot.

God takes the words His people speak very seriously, and He isn't pleased when you speak negatively of another person—even when what you say is factually true. That's why the apostle Paul wrote, "Do not let any unwholesome talk come out of your mouths, but only what is helpful for building others up according to their needs" (Ephesians 4:29 NIV).

So think before you speak. If the words you're thinking build up another person and enhance his or her reputation, then by all means feel free to speak them. But if they tear another down and hurt that person's good name, keep them to yourself. . .and then see if you can't think of something good to say instead.

CONTRIBUTORS

Mark Ammerman is a freelance writer and illustrator. He lives in central Pennsylvania.

Rev. Robin Burkhart, PhD, has served for more than thirty years as a pastor, author, educator, and denominational leader. His varied background includes ministry in Latin and South America, the Caribbean, Europe, Africa, and the People's Republic of China. He is the father of three adult children and five grandchildren.

Ed Cyzewski is the author of *A Christian Survival Guide: A Lifeline to Faith and Growth* and *Coffeehouse Theology: Reflecting on God in Everyday Life* and is the coauthor of *The Good News of Revelation* and *Unfollowers: Unlikely Lessons on Faith from Those Who Doubted Jesus.* He writes about prayer and imperfectly following Jesus at www.edcyzewski.com.

Quentin Guy writes from the high desert of New Mexico to encourage and equip people to know and serve God. He currently works in publishing for Calvary Albuquerque and has cowritten such books as *Weird and Gross Bible Stuff* and *The 2:52 Boys Bible*, both of which are stuck in future classic status. A former middle school teacher, he serves with his wife as marriage prep mentors and trusts God that his children will survive their teenage years.

Glenn A. Hascall is an accomplished writer with credits in more than a hundred books. He is a broadcast veteran and voice actor and is actively involved in writing and producing audio drama.

Rob Maaddi has been a Philadelphia sports writer for the Associated Press since 2000. He's covered the Super Bowl, World Series, NBA

Finals, Stanley Cup Finals, and numerous major sporting events throughout his career. Rob; his wife, Remy; and their twin girls, Alexia and Melina, reside in South Jersey.

Jess MacCallum is president of Professional Printers, Inc., in Columbia, South Carolina. Author of two previous books, he is father of two daughters and a son.

Chuck Miller lives in Sylvania Township, Ohio. He worked for fourteen years as a high school English, journalism, and Bible teacher in the public schools of Lexington, Kentucky, and then at Toledo Christian Schools. He worked as a hospital chaplain—nights and weekends, the "disaster shift"—for seven years and currently works in the surgical instrument department of that hospital and as a freelance writer of devotions and poetry. Some of his devotional work and poetry can be found on his website, BardofChrist.net. He's been married for forty-two years; his four-year-old grandson Preston (aka "Pres-Tron"!) is the joy of his life.

David Sanford serves on the leadership team at Corban University, which is consistently ranked by *US News Best Colleges* as one of the Top 10 colleges in the West. Among his many credits, David has served as executive editor of *Holy Bible: Mosaic*, general editor of the popular *Handbook on Thriving as an Adoptive Family*, coauthor of the bestselling *God Is Relevant*, and author of *If God Disappears*. Better yet? David is husband to Renée, dad to five, and grandpa to nine (and one in heaven).

Ed Strauss was a freelance writer living in British Columbia, Canada, who passed into heaven in 2018. He authored or coauthored more than fifty books for children, tweens, and adults. Ed had a passion for biblical apologetics and besides writing for Barbour, was published by Zondervan, Tyndale, Moody, and Focus on the Family. Ed has three children: Sharon, Daniel, and Michelle Strauss.

Tracy M. Sumner is a freelance author, writer, and editor in Beaverton, Oregon. An avid outdoorsman, he enjoys fly-fishing on world-class Oregon waters.

Mike Vander Klipp is a professional editor and writer who works in the Zondervan Bible Division of HarperCollins Christian Publishing. He and his writer/editor wife live with their teenagers, the cats, and the dog in Grand Rapids, Michigan.

Lee Warren is published in such varied venues as *Discipleship Journal*, Sports Spectrum, Yahoo! Sports, ChristianityToday.com, and Crosswalk.com. He is also the author of the book *Finishing Well: Living with the End in Mind* (a devotional), and he writes regular features for *The Pathway* newspaper and Living Light News. Lee makes his home in Omaha, Nebraska.

SCRIPTURE INDEX

DEVOTIONAL INSPIRATION FOR EVERY MAN!

Wise in the Word

Created just for men, here are devotional readings based on one hundred key Bible words and concepts—including Authority, Calm, Focus, Perseverance, and Victory. You'll be inspired to think deeply on God and His Word, "which is able to make you wise for salvation through faith which is in Christ Jesus" (2 Timothy 3:15 NKJV).

Hardback / 978-1-64352-219-7 / $12.99

Prayers for Difficult Times Men's Edition

Here's a practical guide of short prayer starters that will help you pray confidently during difficult times. From illness and relationship issues to struggles with self-worth and daily life stresses, dozens of topics are covered. Each section opens with a short devotional thought and applicable scripture.

DiCarta / 978-1-68322-615-4 / $12.99